WE LIVE HERE

Detroit Eviction Defense
and the battle for housing justice

Jeffrey WILSON **Bambi KRAMER**

SEVEN STORIES PRESS

new york • oakland • london

A Seven Stories Press First Edition

The people quoted in this book have given the authors permission to use their names.

Seven Stories Press
140 Watts Street
New York, NY 10013
www.sevenstories.com

College professors and high school and middle school teachers may order free examination copies of Seven Stories Press titles. Visit https://www.sevenstories.com/pg/resources-academics or email academic@sevenstories.com.

Graphic design by Bambi Kramer
Fonts in use are released under SIL license:
Archivo | Omnibus-Type
Oswald | Vernon Adams, Kalapi Gajjar, Cyreal
Roboto Serif | Commercial Type, Greg Gazdowicz

Library of Congress Cataloging-in-Publication data is on file

ISBN: 978-1-64421-242-4 (paperback)
ISBN: 978-1-64421-243-1 (ebook)

Printed in the USA

9 8 7 6 5 4 3 2 1

CONTENTS

SOLIDARITY AND HOME DEFENSE: THE CASE OF DETROIT

JEFFREY WILSON

This comic centers on the fourth anniversary celebration of Detroit Eviction Defense (DED). During the festivities, members recounted their stories fighting housing dispossession. In doing so, they offer a model of place-based struggle that has won some eighty homes back from the brink of eviction. Emerging out of the Occupy Movement of 2011, DED is a grassroots coalition of homeowners, anarchists, faith-based activists, union members, and community advocates. To understand DED's strategies, it is helpful to have a clear picture of the city's housing history and modes of eviction.

DISPOSSESSION BY THE NUMBERS

Housing displacement in Detroit typically takes two forms: mortgage and/or tax foreclosure. A mortgage foreclosure happens when a financial institution takes possession of a property for nonpayment and is the central focus of this book. Tax foreclosure, detailed in the appendix, is when the local municipality takes possession of a property for three consecutive years of nonpayment and subsequently auctions the house, more often than not to real estate speculators.

Between 2005–2013 Detroit recorded nearly 70,000 mortgage foreclosures impacting approximately 30 percent of residential properties (Akers & Seymour, 2019). One activist describes these mortgage foreclosures and the subsequent fallout as a "hurricane without water" (Interview, 2016). The sentiment seems correct and the problem grows significantly when taking mortgage and tax foreclosures together. Between 2005 and 2015, 1 in 3 properties in the city faced either a mortgage or tax foreclosure (Kurth, 2015). Approximately 160,000 foreclosures were executed, impacting 120,000 homes or 48 percent of all residential properties. Of these homes, 27,000 experienced a kind of double dispossession of a mortgage foreclosure and then a tax foreclosure (Akers & Seymour, 2019).

While mortgage foreclosures have devastated individual families, some of these properties also cost the city millions. As the *Detroit News* reported, nearly 56 percent of these mortgage-foreclosed homes were in some state of disrepair as of 2015, with nearly 13,000 slated for demolition, costing Detroit $200 million (Kurth, 2015).

Mortgage foreclosures in Detroit are not isolated, but are built upon a frenzy of subprime lending. In the four years leading up to the housing market crash of 2008, nearly $4 billion in predatory loans was injected into the city's housing market. Such lending practices are a contemporary iteration of what Keeanga-Yamahtta Taylor has termed "predatory inclusion." The fair housing era facilitated more robust access to the housing market for many African Americans. Yet this was not the end of discrimination or segregation. Black people continued to pay exorbitant rates and face unequal terms for housing that was often of substandard quality, as Taylor comments. This inclusion was another way that "Black bodies become vessels through which racial capital extracts value" (Denvir, 2020). Detroit before the 2008 market crash is a reminder of the impacts of predatory inclusion. While subprime lending averaged 24 percent of the national market, a kind of predatory inclusion drove rates in Detroit to an average 68 percent in 2005. In some targeted neighborhoods this number rose to 80 percent of all mortgages (Kurth & MacDonald, 2015).

While the pre-2008 mortgage regime produced inclusionary practices, the post housing market crash strengthened exclusionary practices. A Bridge Michigan analysis of mortgages found that in 2007 African Americans received 75 percent of mortgage loans in Detroit but by 2017 this decreased to 48 percent, despite the fact that Black people make up nearly 80 percent of the city's population. White people comprised only 10 percent of Detroit's population but received 17 percent of loans in 2007 and 58 percent in 2017. Several Detroit neighborhoods, which had once generated 600 mortgages in 2007, produced zero in 2017 (Wilkinson, 2019). Homes are still being purchased in Detroit, but for many residents nontraditional and much riskier arrangements such as land contracts or rent-to-own are the only avenues for homeownership. Housing advocates estimate that 1 in 10 evictions result from land contracts, yet these numbers might be much higher as such agreements are not required to be registered by the city (Einhorn & Mondry, 2021).

The waning of mortgage foreclosures by the mid-2010s was followed by a series of catastrophic tax foreclosures. Approximately 100,000 tax foreclosures were triggered in the city between 2011 and 2015 (Atuahene, 2020). The peak was 24,793 foreclosures occurring in 2015 (Aguilar, 2020). In tax foreclosure, homes that are behind three years are then sent to tax auction. These auctions have moved online since 2015, facilitating speculators from around the world in buying properties in Detroit, as the appendix of this book outlines.

Tax foreclosure as dispossession is only part of the story. Wayne County now leverages Detroit's tax debt to make a profit. The City of Detroit is paid annually for an individual's delinquent taxes by Wayne County. Essentially this makes it so that Detroit does not have unpaid taxes on the ledger. In order to lend Detroit this money, the county borrows annually from individual investors or banks. To pay off these loans Wayne County then collects unpaid property taxes from delinquent Detroit homeowners, charging them an additional 4 percent interest rate or higher. As Bridge Magazine notes, "profit [for the county] comes from borrowing at 5 percent or less and getting up to 22-percent return on delinquent taxes, creating the surplus controlled by the county treasurer." Key to this is that the largely white suburbs get to control the surplus generated from Black residents of Detroit. The article continues by noting, "in 2004, Wayne County began to collect Detroit's delinquent taxes, doubling the county's surplus of fees and interest from delinquent taxes to an average of $33 million from $15 million per year" (Kurth et al., 2017).

As a consequence, Detroit, once a city known as a center of Black homeownership, has shifted from a city in which homeowners were the majority to a city in which renters are the majority. The housing stock now has 124,000 owned units and 140,000 rentals (Ruggiero et al., 2020). Coupled with the pandemic, this shift has placed struggles against housing dispossession on different footing. At the forefront now are tenant rights.

WE LIVE HERE: DETROIT EVICTION DEFENSE

This book is a celebration of place-based struggle against the forces of dispossession outlined above. Recounted are stories by Detroiters, primarily Black women, who fought and organized to save their homes from a mortgage foreclosure. Together with local activist group DED, these women answer the question "what will Detroit look like in the future?" by asserting that "there is no Detroit without us!" Told in eight chapters, families who have lived in the city for generations detail their deeply personal stories of falling behind on mortgage payments, going through the eviction process, and fighting to keep their homes. In doing so, these stories work against the unexamined assumption that foreclosures are caused by individual irresponsibility. As each family discusses their particular situation, this idea is upended and we can discern that it is not individual fault but rather the contours of racial capitalism that usurp Black and Latinx wealth. While each story has its own particular points of emphasis, the heart of this book is about transformation, resistance, and solidarity in the face of housing loss.

These stories contradict a popular image of the city as a kind of blank canvas. A canvas to be painted as a collection of cheap properties that entice real estate speculators from around the world, as a creative playground for artists or a landscape for billionaires to resculpt downtown, and as a spot for suburban tourists. Tying these activities together is a view of the city as a functionally empty frontier in need of resettlement. Yet beyond these conventional players in urban growth and development are groups like DED that expand our ability to imagine possible resistances to the future of housing implicit in these exploitative visions.

Central to DED's work are direct action tactics to keep Detroiters in their homes. This ranges from physically stopping bailiffs from entering and evicting families to strategies such as packing the courtroom with DED members during eviction hearings. These tactics emerge from DED's broader organizing, in which homeowners build support in their neighborhoods to mount a defense against eviction. Those facing an impending eviction are urged by DED to go to family, friends, and neighbors to let them know their situation in order to build support for a home defense.

These acts are not insignificant. People facing eviction often feel ashamed and these moments of community building around dinner tables or in church halls creates the solidarity that is necessary to save a home.

WE LIVE HERE

FROM RENT-TO-OWN SCHEMES TO THE REAPPEARANCE OF
LICS IN LIEU OF CONVENTIONAL MORTGAGES, REAL ESTATE
CONTINUES TO SWINDLE AFRICAN AMERICANS IN SEARCH OF
THEIR AMERICAN DREAM IN THE HOUSING MARKET. IT IS NOT
HISTORY REPEATING ITSELF. IT IS THE PREDICTABLE OUTCOME
WHEN THE HOME IS COMMODITY AND IT CONTINUES TO BE
PROMOTED AS THE FULFILMENT AND MEANING OF CITIZENSHIP.

KEEANGA-YAMAHTTA TAYLOR

WHAT KEEPS US GOING, ULTIMATELY, IS OUR LOVE FOR EACH OTHER,
AND OUR REFUSAL TO BOW OUR HEADS, TO ACCEPT THE VERDICT,
HOWEVER ALL-POWERFUL IT SEEMS. IT'S WHAT ORDINARY PEOPLE
HAVE TO DO.
YOU HAVE TO LOVE EACH OTHER.
YOU HAVE TO DEFEND EACH OTHER.
YOU HAVE TO FIGHT.

MIKE DAVIS

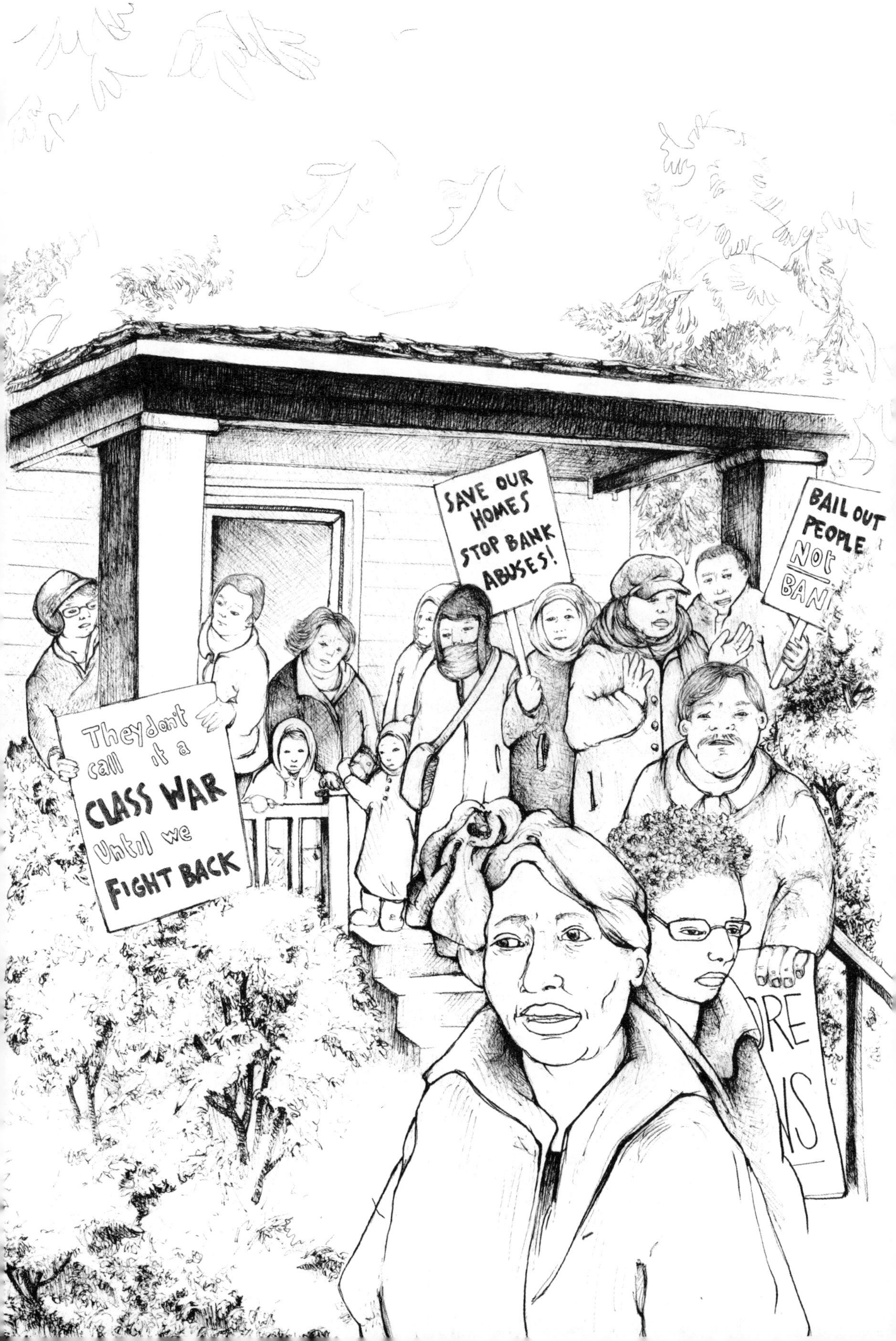
SAVE OUR HOMES STOP BANK ABUSES!
BAIL OUT PEOPLE NOT BAN
They don't call it a CLASS WAR until we FIGHT BACK

DETROIT EVICTION DEFENSE CELEBRATION
SAT, APRIL 16, 2016
ST. JOHN'S CHURCH,
DETROIT, MICHIGAN

JUSTICE
NOT
EVICTION

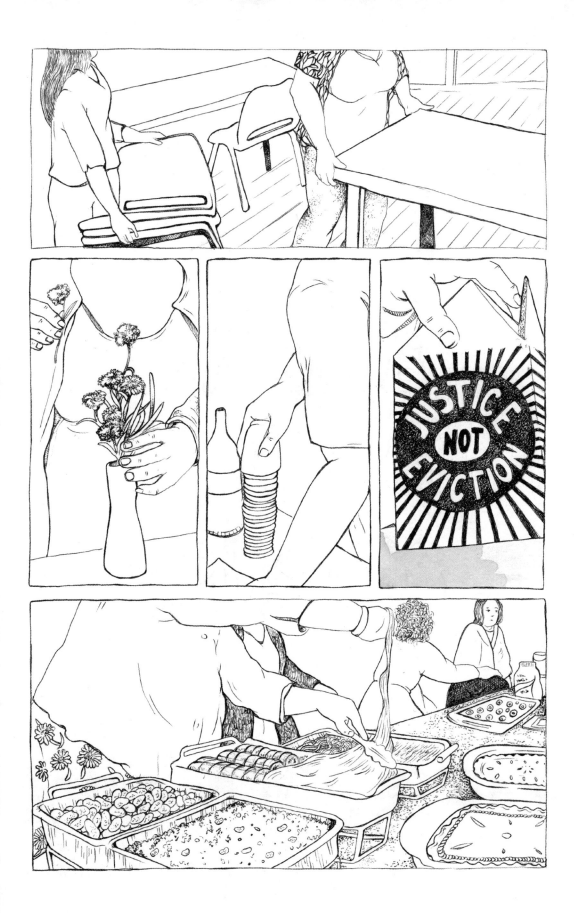

a hoMe
noT Just
a house

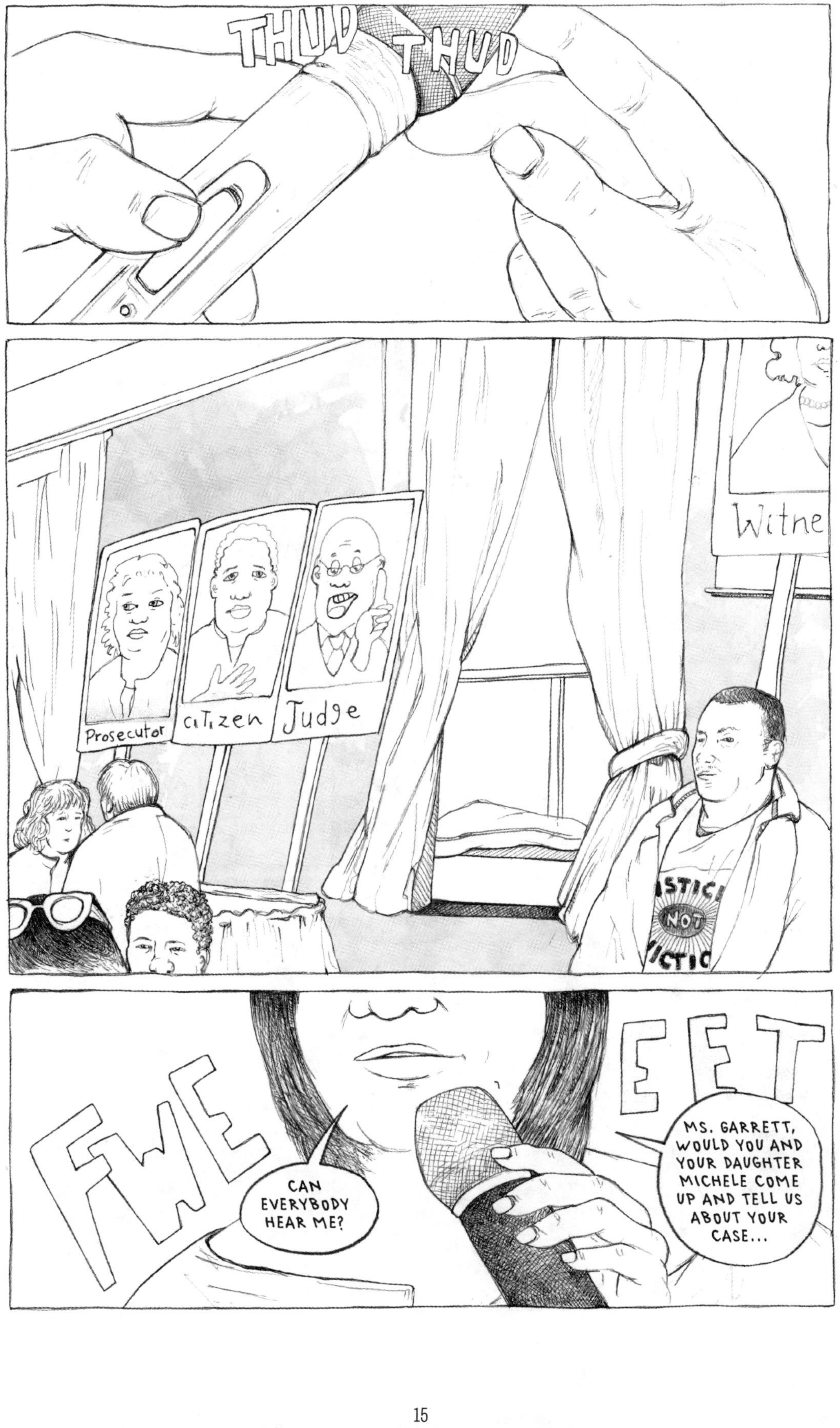
THUD
THUD
Prosecutor
citizen
Judge
Witne
NOT
FWE
EET
CAN EVERYBODY HEAR ME?
MS. GARRETT, WOULD YOU AND YOUR DAUGHTER MICHELE COME UP AND TELL US ABOUT YOUR CASE...

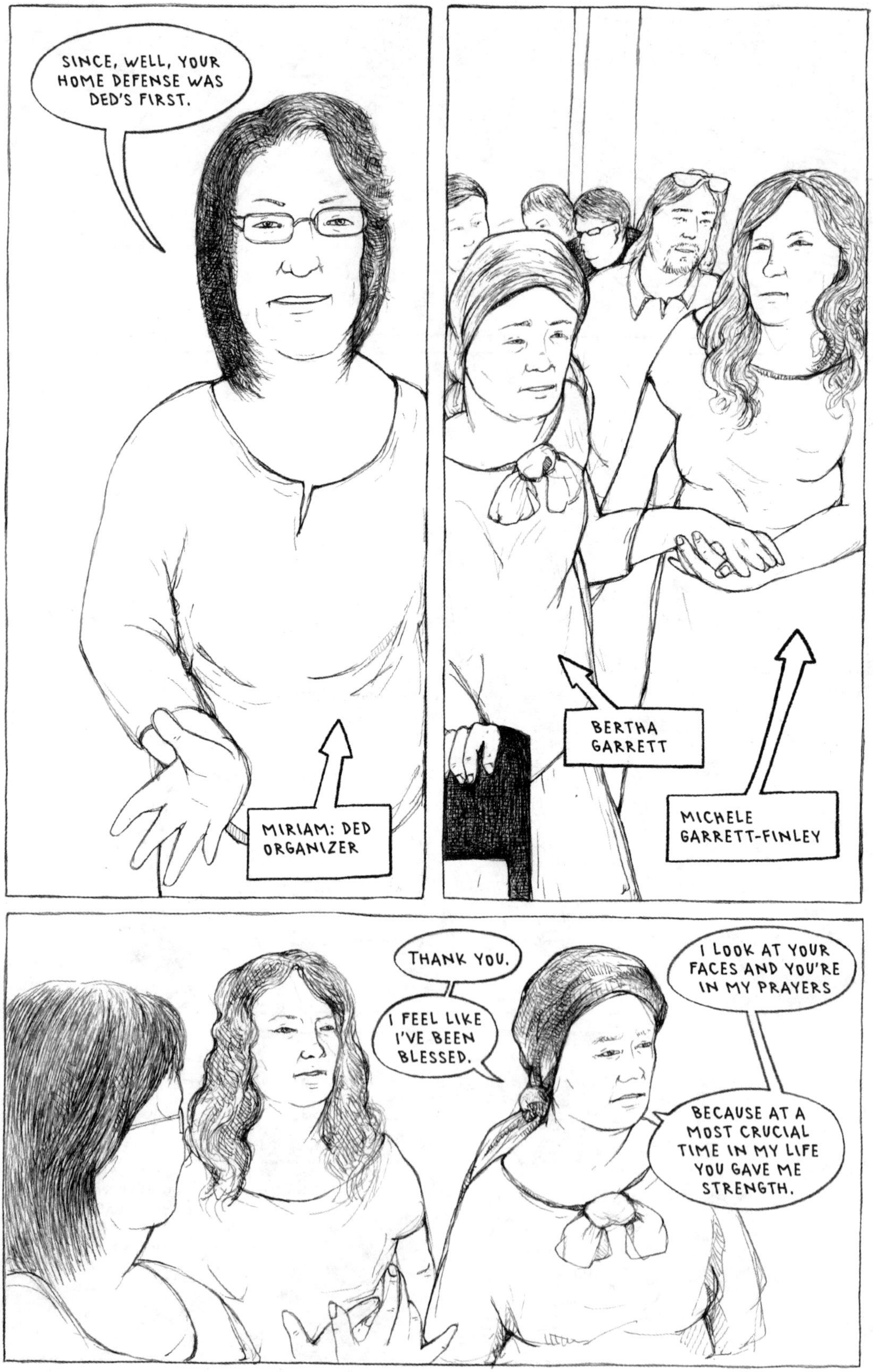
SINCE, WELL, YOUR HOME DEFENSE WAS DED'S FIRST.
MIRIAM: DED ORGANIZER
BERTHA GARRETT
MICHELE GARRETT-FINLEY
THANK YOU.
I FEEL LIKE I'VE BEEN BLESSED.
I LOOK AT YOUR FACES AND YOU'RE IN MY PRAYERS
BECAUSE AT A MOST CRUCIAL TIME IN MY LIFE YOU GAVE ME STRENGTH.

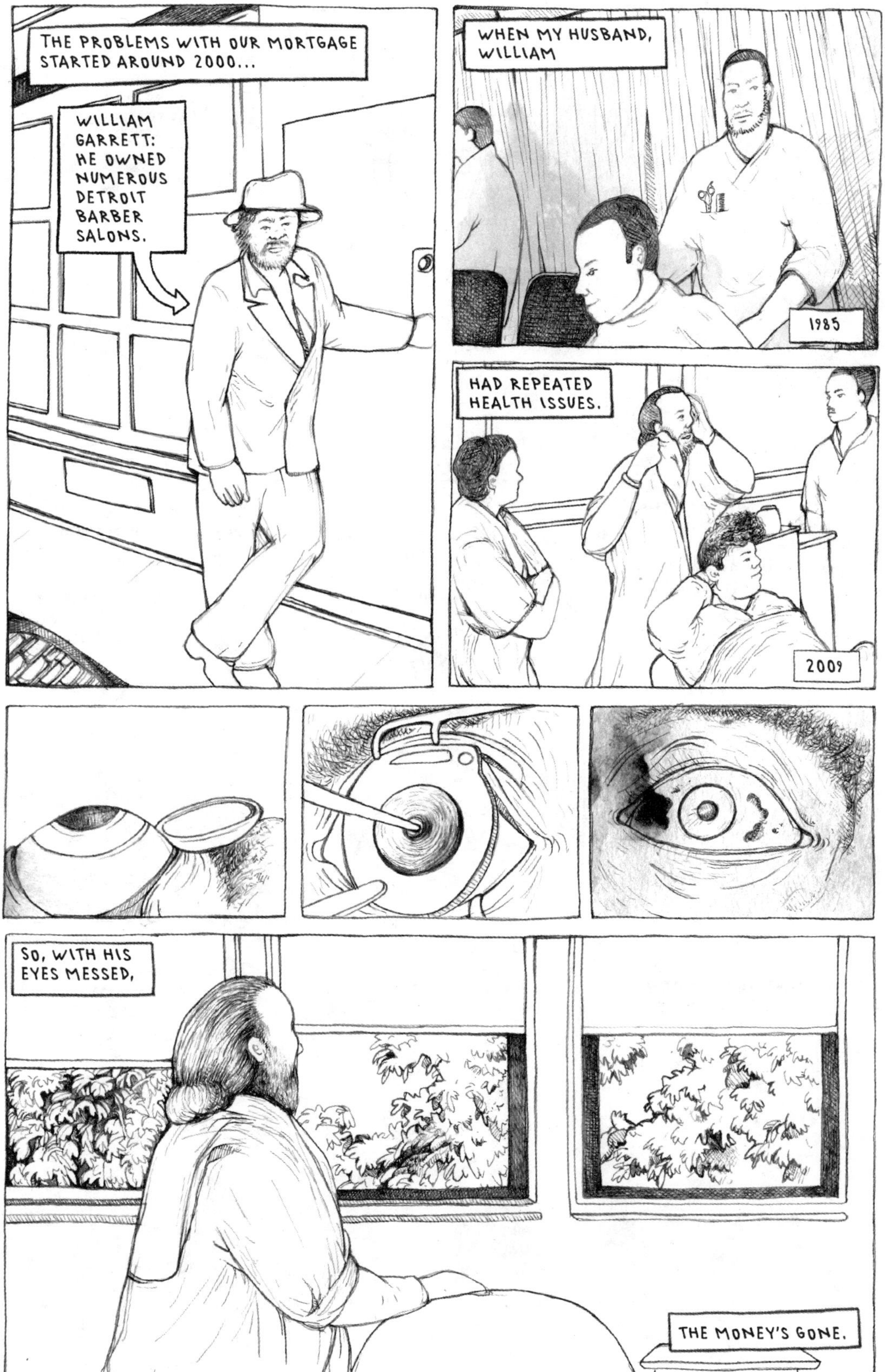
THE PROBLEMS WITH OUR MORTGAGE STARTED AROUND 2000...
WILLIAM GARRETT: HE OWNED NUMEROUS DETROIT BARBER SALONS.
WHEN MY HUSBAND, WILLIAM
1985
HAD REPEATED HEALTH ISSUES.
2009
SO, WITH HIS EYES MESSED,
THE MONEY'S GONE.

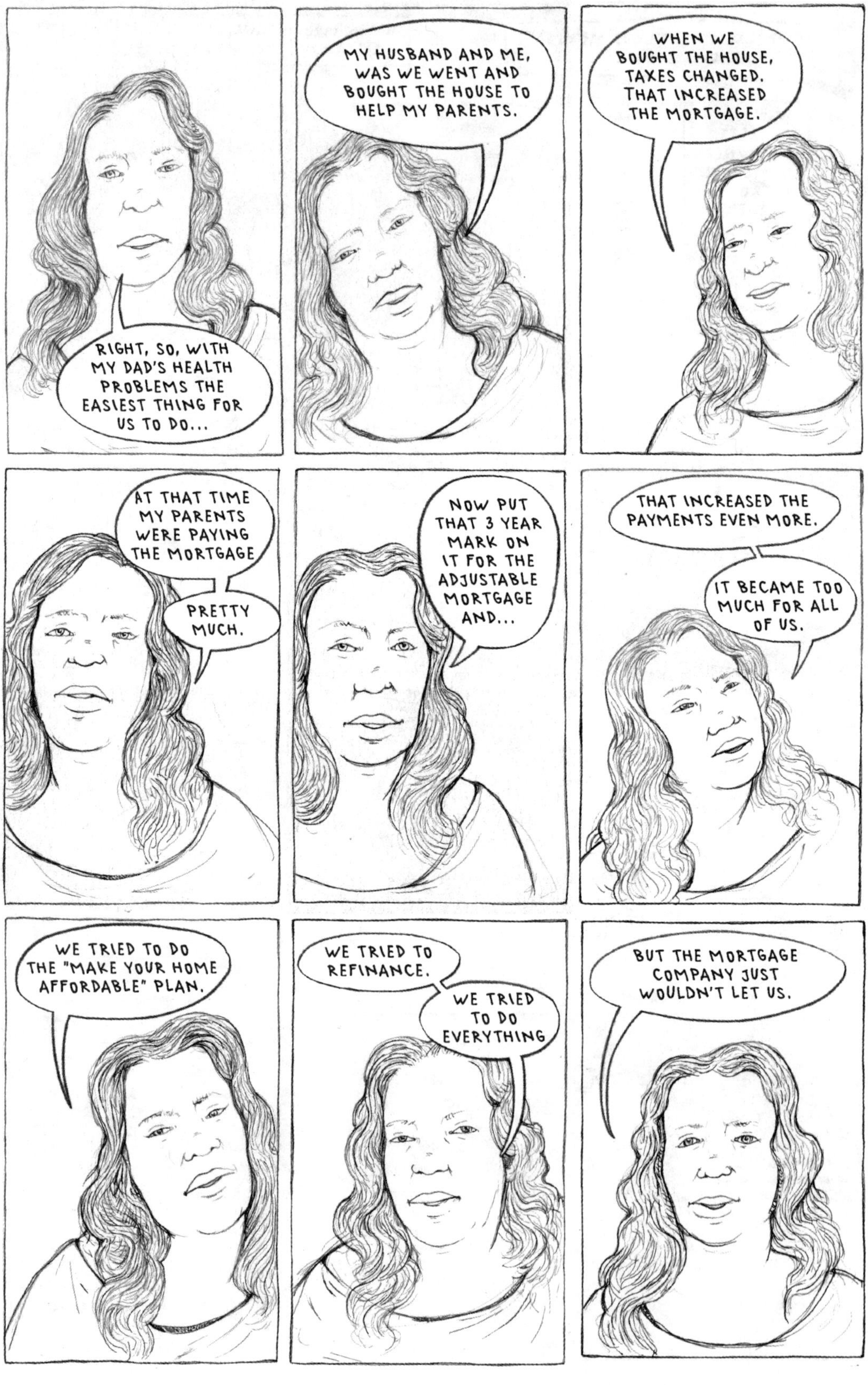
RIGHT, SO, WITH MY DAD'S HEALTH PROBLEMS THE EASIEST THING FOR US TO DO...
MY HUSBAND AND ME, WAS WE WENT AND BOUGHT THE HOUSE TO HELP MY PARENTS.
WHEN WE BOUGHT THE HOUSE, TAXES CHANGED. THAT INCREASED THE MORTGAGE.
AT THAT TIME MY PARENTS WERE PAYING THE MORTGAGE
PRETTY MUCH.
NOW PUT THAT 3 YEAR MARK ON IT FOR THE ADJUSTABLE MORTGAGE AND...
THAT INCREASED THE PAYMENTS EVEN MORE.
IT BECAME TOO MUCH FOR ALL OF US.
WE TRIED TO DO THE "MAKE YOUR HOME AFFORDABLE" PLAN.
WE TRIED TO REFINANCE.
WE TRIED TO DO EVERYTHING
BUT THE MORTGAGE COMPANY JUST WOULDN'T LET US.

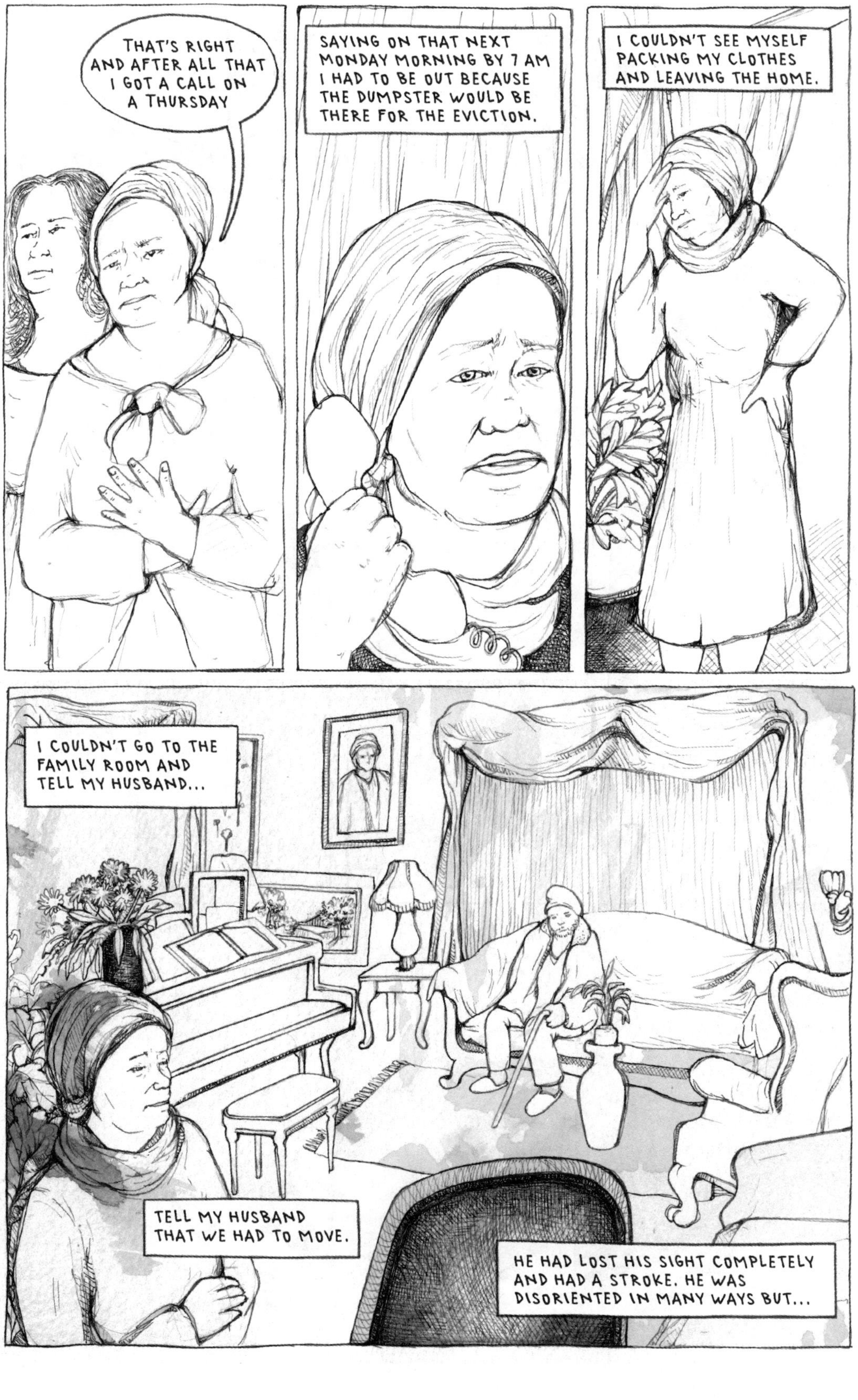
THAT'S RIGHT AND AFTER ALL THAT I GOT A CALL ON A THURSDAY
SAYING ON THAT NEXT MONDAY MORNING BY 7 AM I HAD TO BE OUT BECAUSE THE DUMPSTER WOULD BE THERE FOR THE EVICTION.
I COULDN'T SEE MYSELF PACKING MY CLOTHES AND LEAVING THE HOME.
I COULDN'T GO TO THE FAMILY ROOM AND TELL MY HUSBAND...
TELL MY HUSBAND THAT WE HAD TO MOVE.
HE HAD LOST HIS SIGHT COMPLETELY AND HAD A STROKE. HE WAS DISORIENTED IN MANY WAYS BUT...

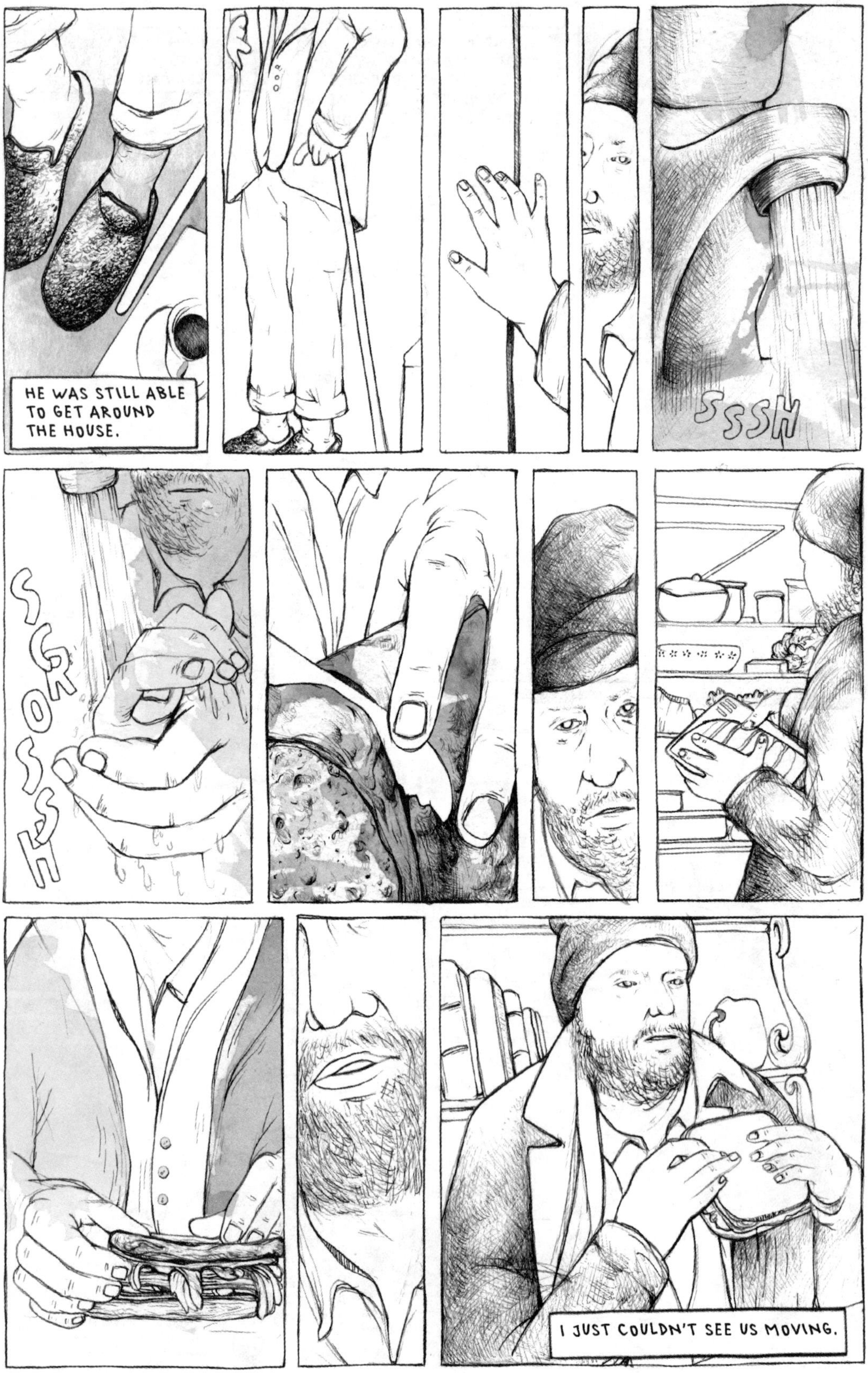
HE WAS STILL ABLE TO GET AROUND THE HOUSE.
SSSH
SCROSSH
I JUST COULDN'T SEE US MOVING.

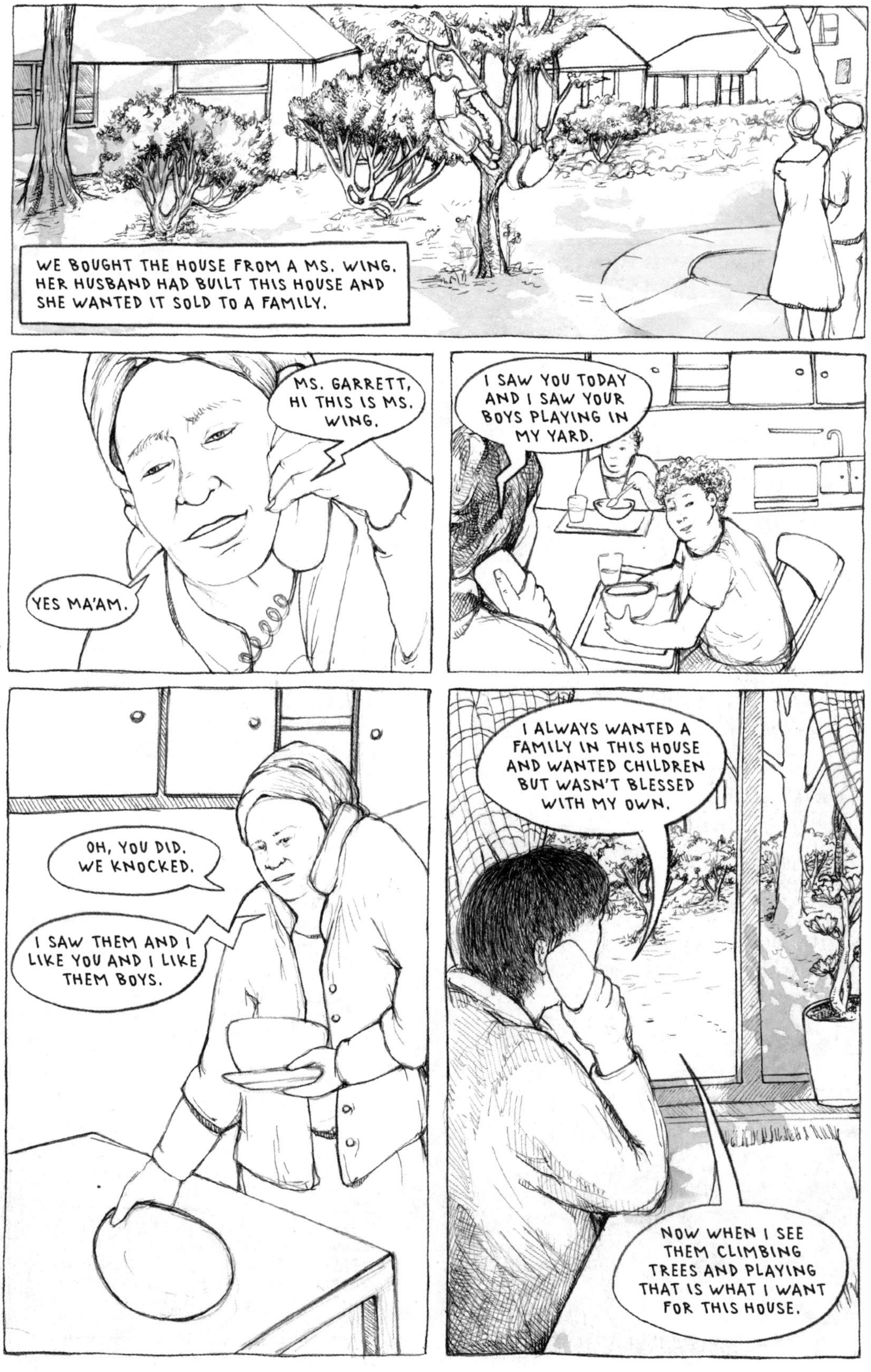

WE BOUGHT THE HOUSE FROM A MS. WING. HER HUSBAND HAD BUILT THIS HOUSE AND SHE WANTED IT SOLD TO A FAMILY.
MS. GARRETT, HI THIS IS MS. WING.
YES MA'AM.
I SAW YOU TODAY AND I SAW YOUR BOYS PLAYING IN MY YARD.
OH, YOU DID. WE KNOCKED.
I SAW THEM AND I LIKE YOU AND I LIKE THEM BOYS.
I ALWAYS WANTED A FAMILY IN THIS HOUSE AND WANTED CHILDREN BUT WASN'T BLESSED WITH MY OWN.
NOW WHEN I SEE THEM CLIMBING TREES AND PLAYING THAT IS WHAT I WANT FOR THIS HOUSE.

SO, SHE INVITED ME OVER THE NEXT DAY. SHE SHOWED ME THE HOUSE AND WE SAT AND TALKED.

AFTER WE BOUGHT THE HOME SHE WOULD OFTEN CALL ME FROM MARYLAND WHERE SHE WENT TO LIVE WITH HER SISTER AND I WOULD TALK TO HER.

SHE WOULD TELL ME WHERE DIFFERENT FLOWERS WERE LOCATED. SHE NEVER REALLY LEFT IN SPRIT UNTIL SHE HAD PASSED AWAY. I FELL IN LOVE WITH THE HOUSE. I CAN UNDERSTAND WHY SHE LOVED IT.

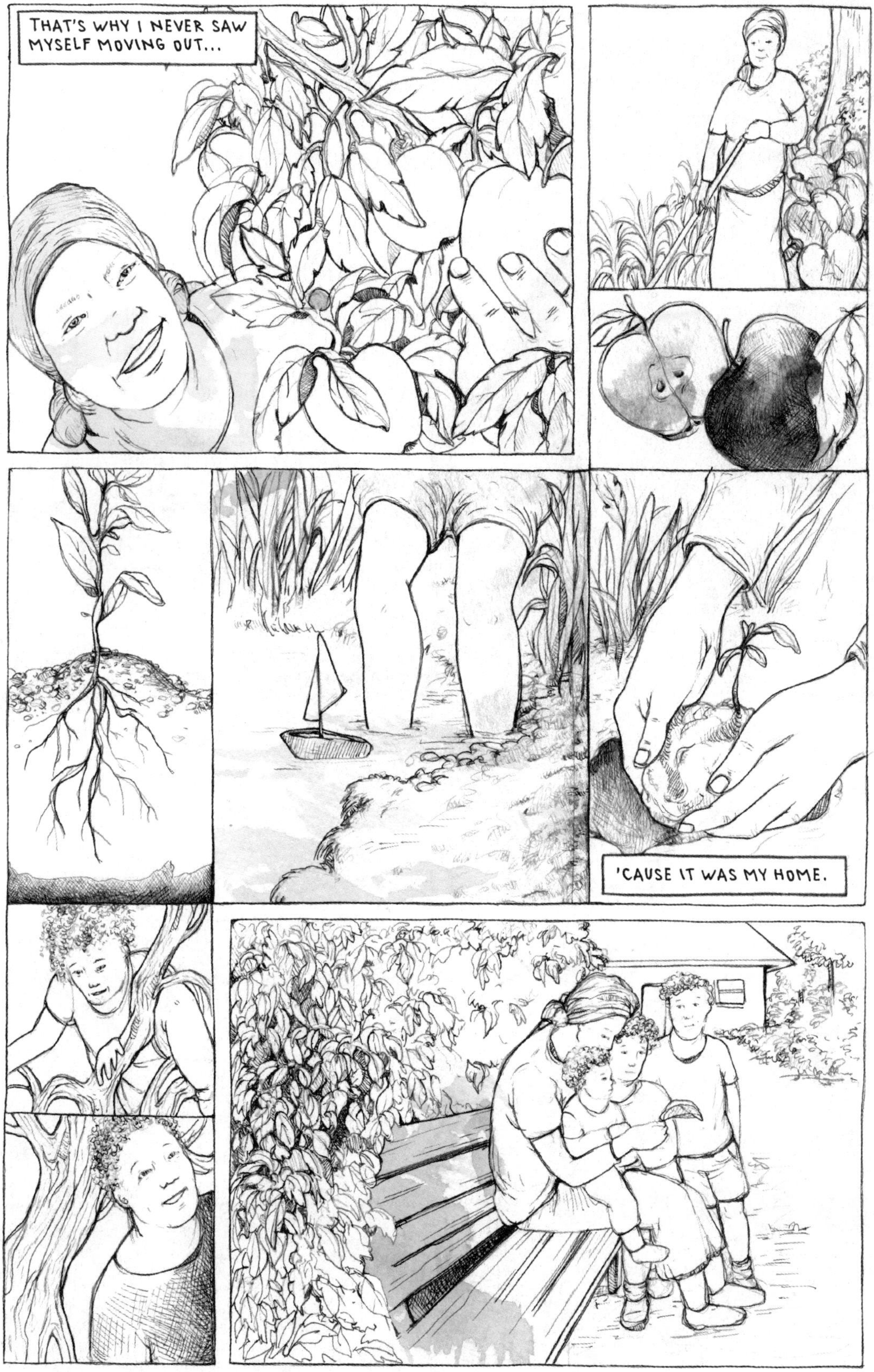
THAT'S WHY I NEVER SAW MYSELF MOVING OUT...
'CAUSE IT WAS MY HOME.

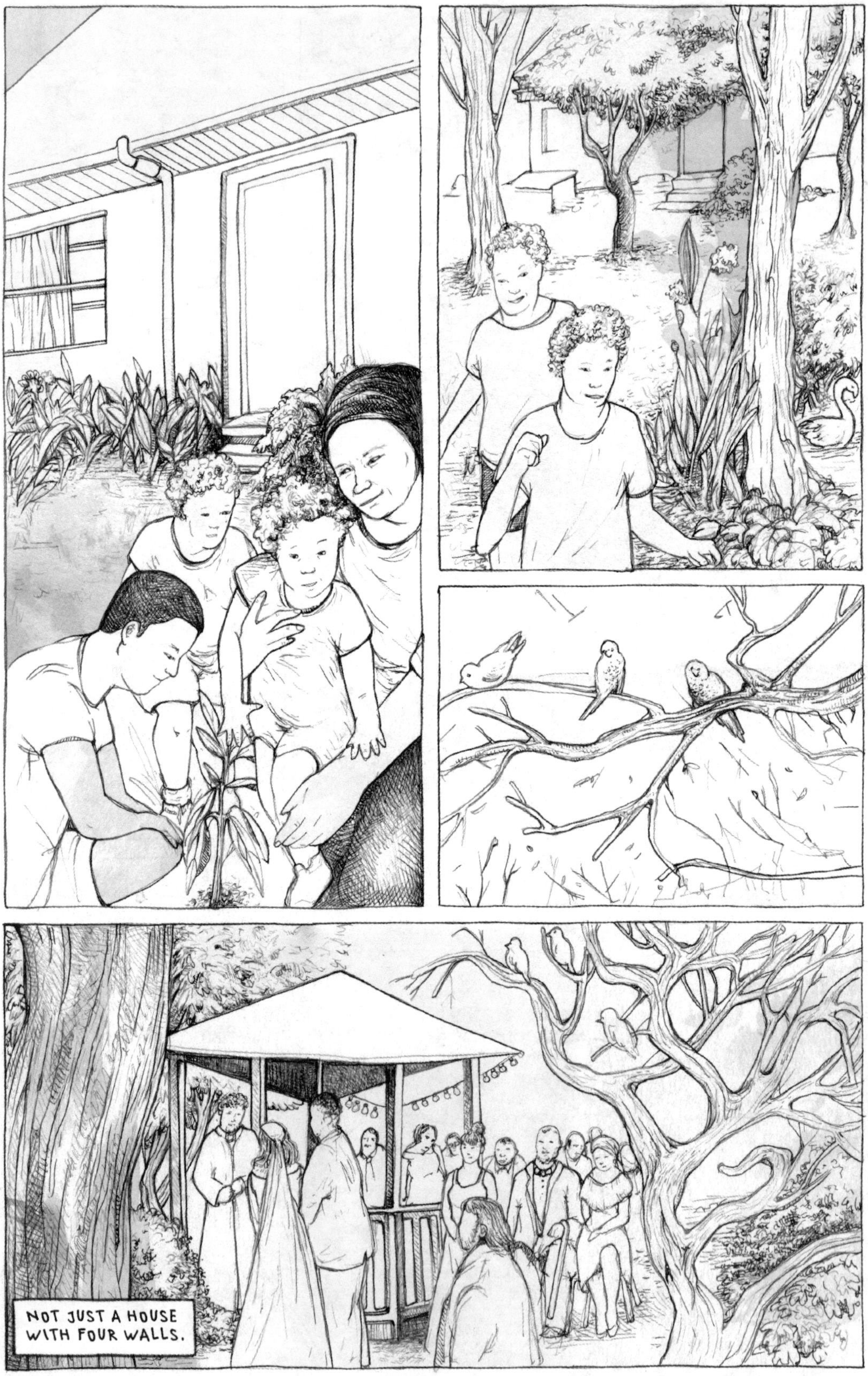
NOT JUST A HOUSE
WITH FOUR WALLS.

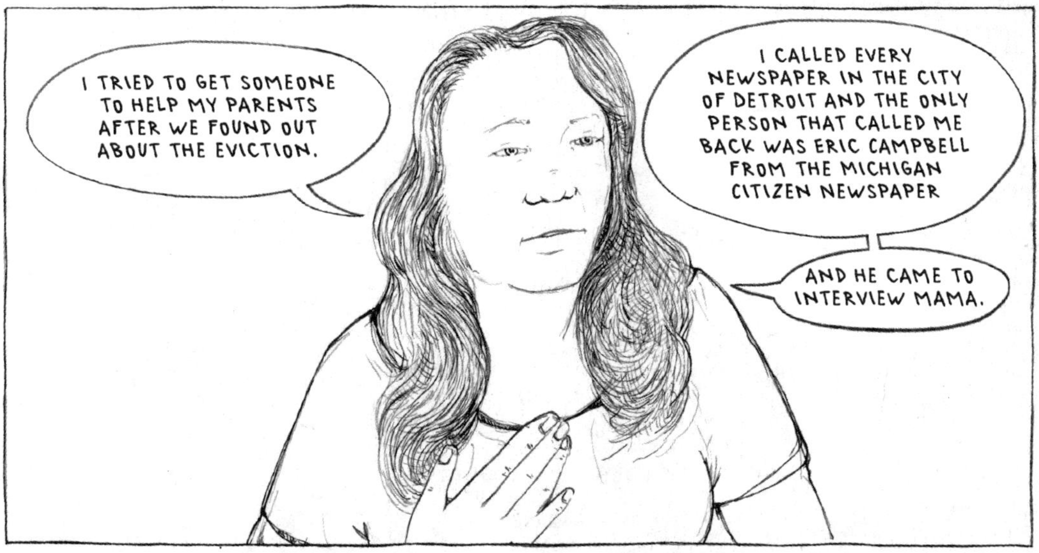
I TRIED TO GET SOMEONE TO HELP MY PARENTS AFTER WE FOUND OUT ABOUT THE EVICTION.
I CALLED EVERY NEWSPAPER IN THE CITY OF DETROIT AND THE ONLY PERSON THAT CALLED ME BACK WAS ERIC CAMPBELL FROM THE MICHIGAN CITIZEN NEWSPAPER
AND HE CAME TO INTERVIEW MAMA.

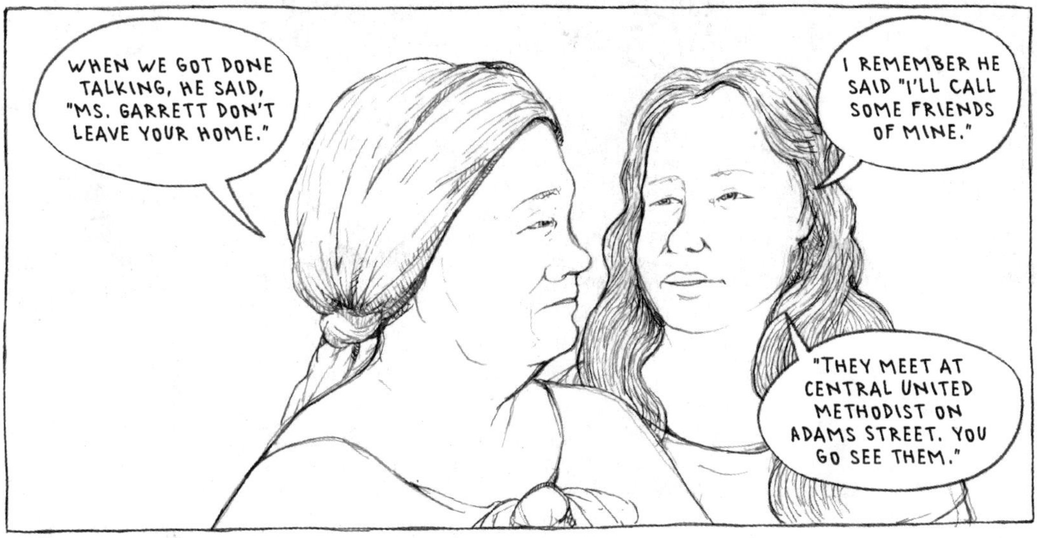
WHEN WE GOT DONE TALKING, HE SAID, "MS. GARRETT DON'T LEAVE YOUR HOME."
I REMEMBER HE SAID "I'LL CALL SOME FRIENDS OF MINE."
"THEY MEET AT CENTRAL UNITED METHODIST ON ADAMS STREET. YOU GO SEE THEM."

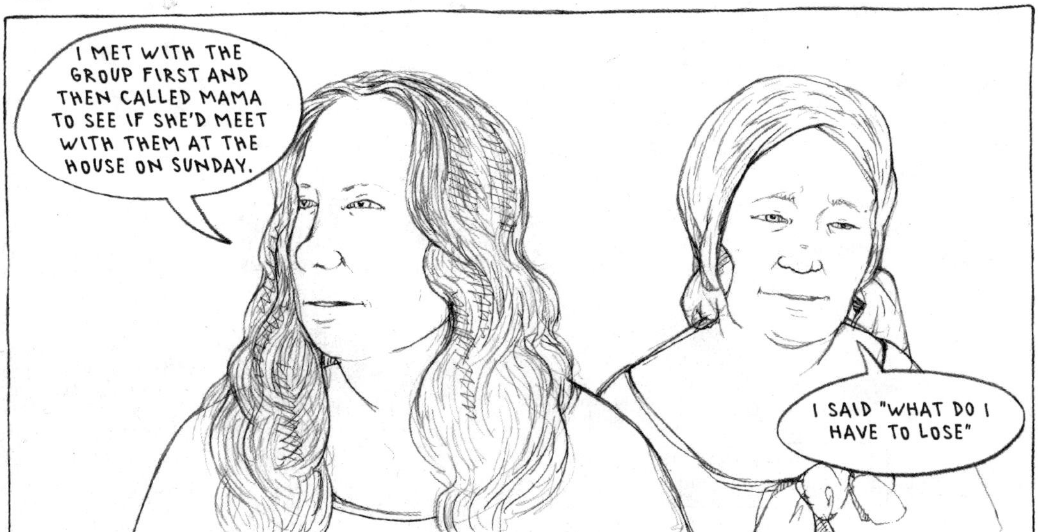
I MET WITH THE GROUP FIRST AND THEN CALLED MAMA TO SEE IF SHE'D MEET WITH THEM AT THE HOUSE ON SUNDAY.
I SAID "WHAT DO I HAVE TO LOSE"

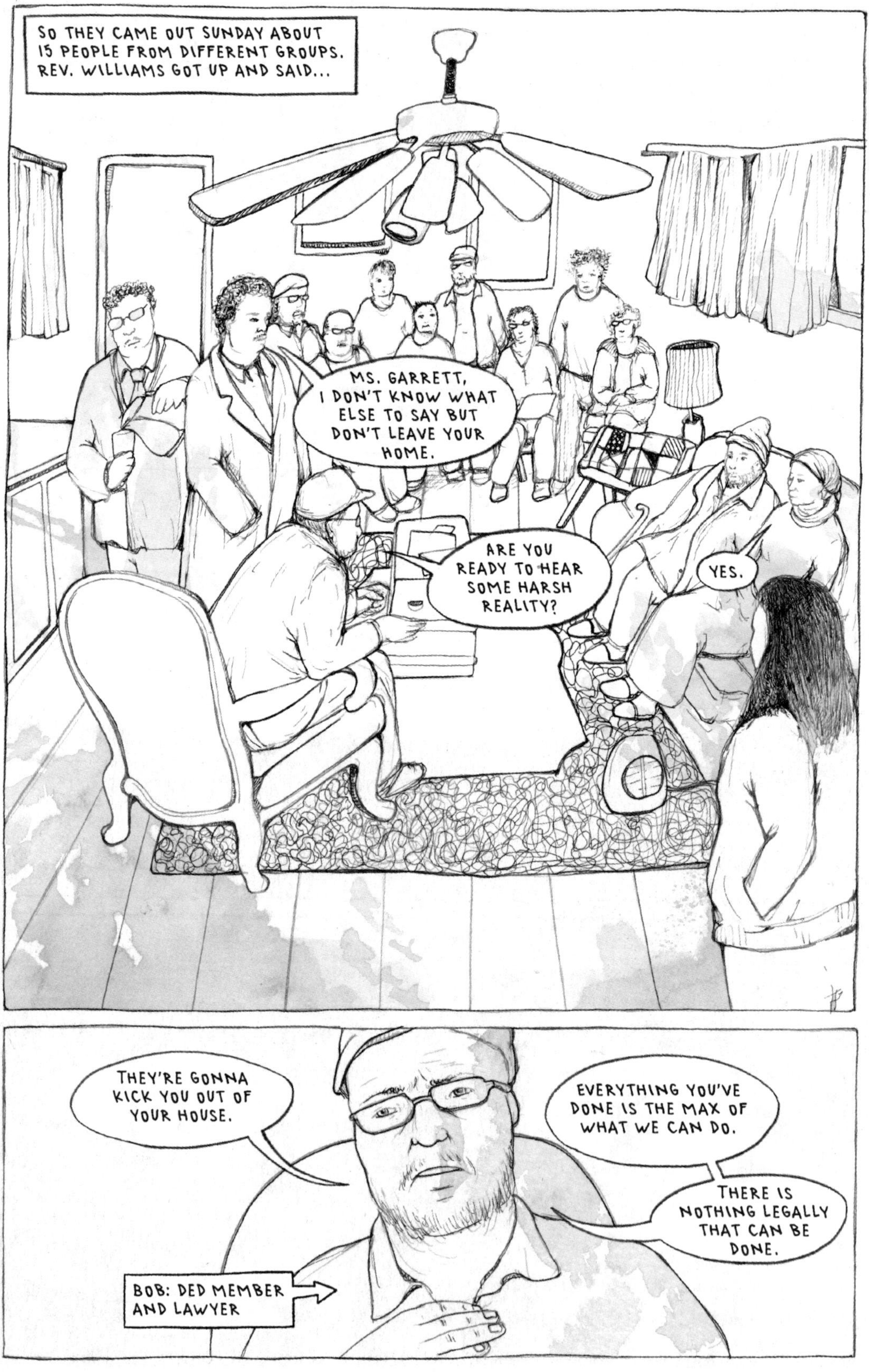
SO THEY CAME OUT SUNDAY ABOUT 15 PEOPLE FROM DIFFERENT GROUPS. REV. WILLIAMS GOT UP AND SAID...
MS. GARRETT, I DON'T KNOW WHAT ELSE TO SAY BUT DON'T LEAVE YOUR HOME.
ARE YOU READY TO HEAR SOME HARSH REALITY?
YES.
THEY'RE GONNA KICK YOU OUT OF YOUR HOUSE.
EVERYTHING YOU'VE DONE IS THE MAX OF WHAT WE CAN DO.
THERE IS NOTHING LEGALLY THAT CAN BE DONE.
BOB: DED MEMBER AND LAWYER

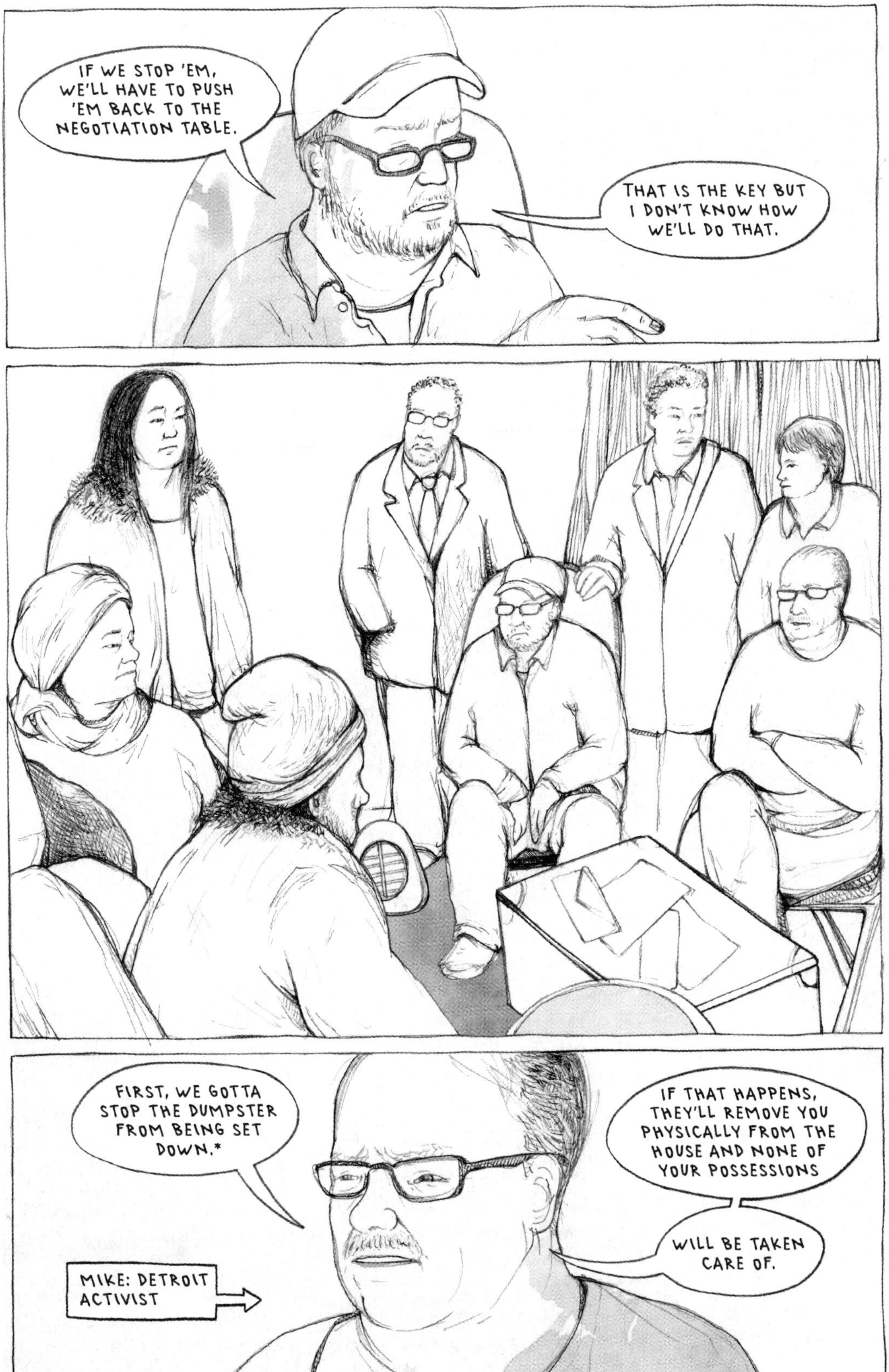
IF WE STOP 'EM, WE'LL HAVE TO PUSH 'EM BACK TO THE NEGOTIATION TABLE.
THAT IS THE KEY BUT I DON'T KNOW HOW WE'LL DO THAT.
FIRST, WE GOTTA STOP THE DUMPSTER FROM BEING SET DOWN.*
MIKE: DETROIT ACTIVIST
IF THAT HAPPENS, THEY'LL REMOVE YOU PHYSICALLY FROM THE HOUSE AND NONE OF YOUR POSSESSIONS
WILL BE TAKEN CARE OF.

*A DUMPSTER BEING PLACED IN SOMEONE'S FRONT YARD IS THE FINAL STEP IN AN EVICTION. TYPICALLY A BAILIFF AND WORK CREW REMOVES ALL THE FORMER OWNER'S POSSESSIONS.

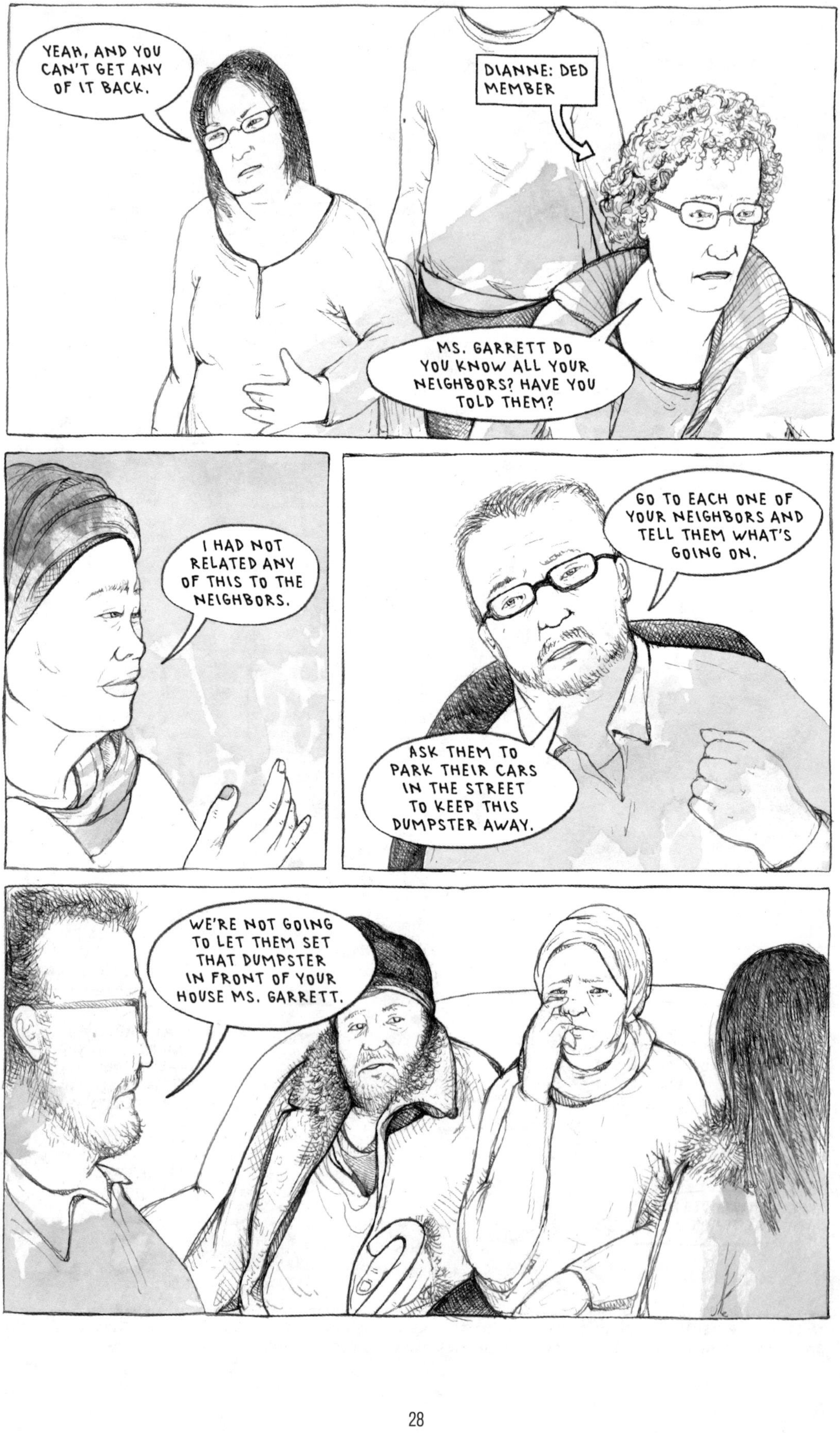
YEAH, AND YOU CAN'T GET ANY OF IT BACK.
DIANNE: DED MEMBER
MS. GARRETT DO YOU KNOW ALL YOUR NEIGHBORS? HAVE YOU TOLD THEM?
I HAD NOT RELATED ANY OF THIS TO THE NEIGHBORS.
GO TO EACH ONE OF YOUR NEIGHBORS AND TELL THEM WHAT'S GOING ON.
ASK THEM TO PARK THEIR CARS IN THE STREET TO KEEP THIS DUMPSTER AWAY.
WE'RE NOT GOING TO LET THEM SET THAT DUMPSTER IN FRONT OF YOUR HOUSE MS. GARRETT.

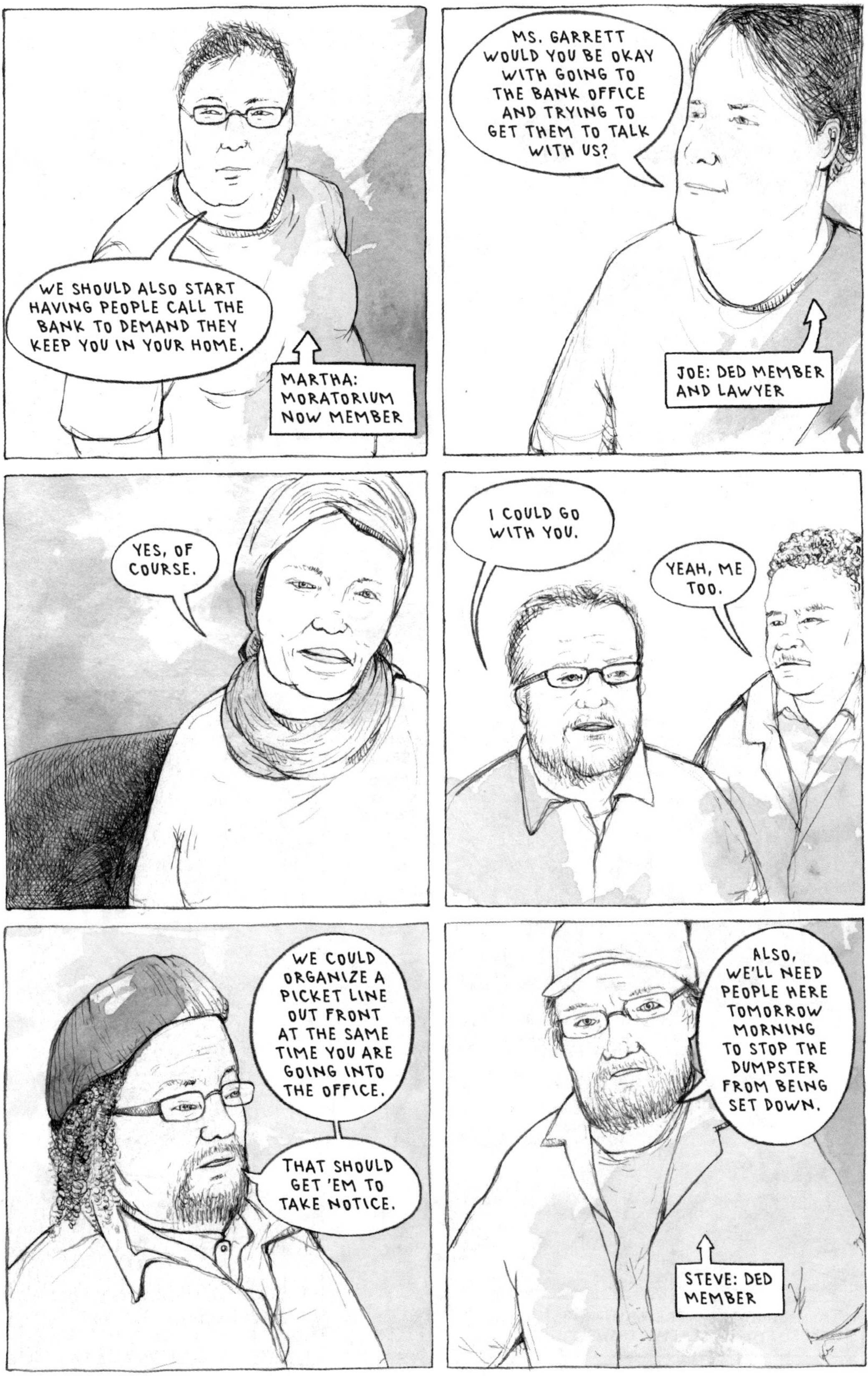
WE SHOULD ALSO START HAVING PEOPLE CALL THE BANK TO DEMAND THEY KEEP YOU IN YOUR HOME.
MARTHA: MORATORIUM NOW MEMBER
MS. GARRETT WOULD YOU BE OKAY WITH GOING TO THE BANK OFFICE AND TRYING TO GET THEM TO TALK WITH US?
JOE: DED MEMBER AND LAWYER
YES, OF COURSE.
I COULD GO WITH YOU.
YEAH, ME TOO.
WE COULD ORGANIZE A PICKET LINE OUT FRONT AT THE SAME TIME YOU ARE GOING INTO THE OFFICE.
THAT SHOULD GET 'EM TO TAKE NOTICE.
ALSO, WE'LL NEED PEOPLE HERE TOMORROW MORNING TO STOP THE DUMPSTER FROM BEING SET DOWN.
STEVE: DED MEMBER

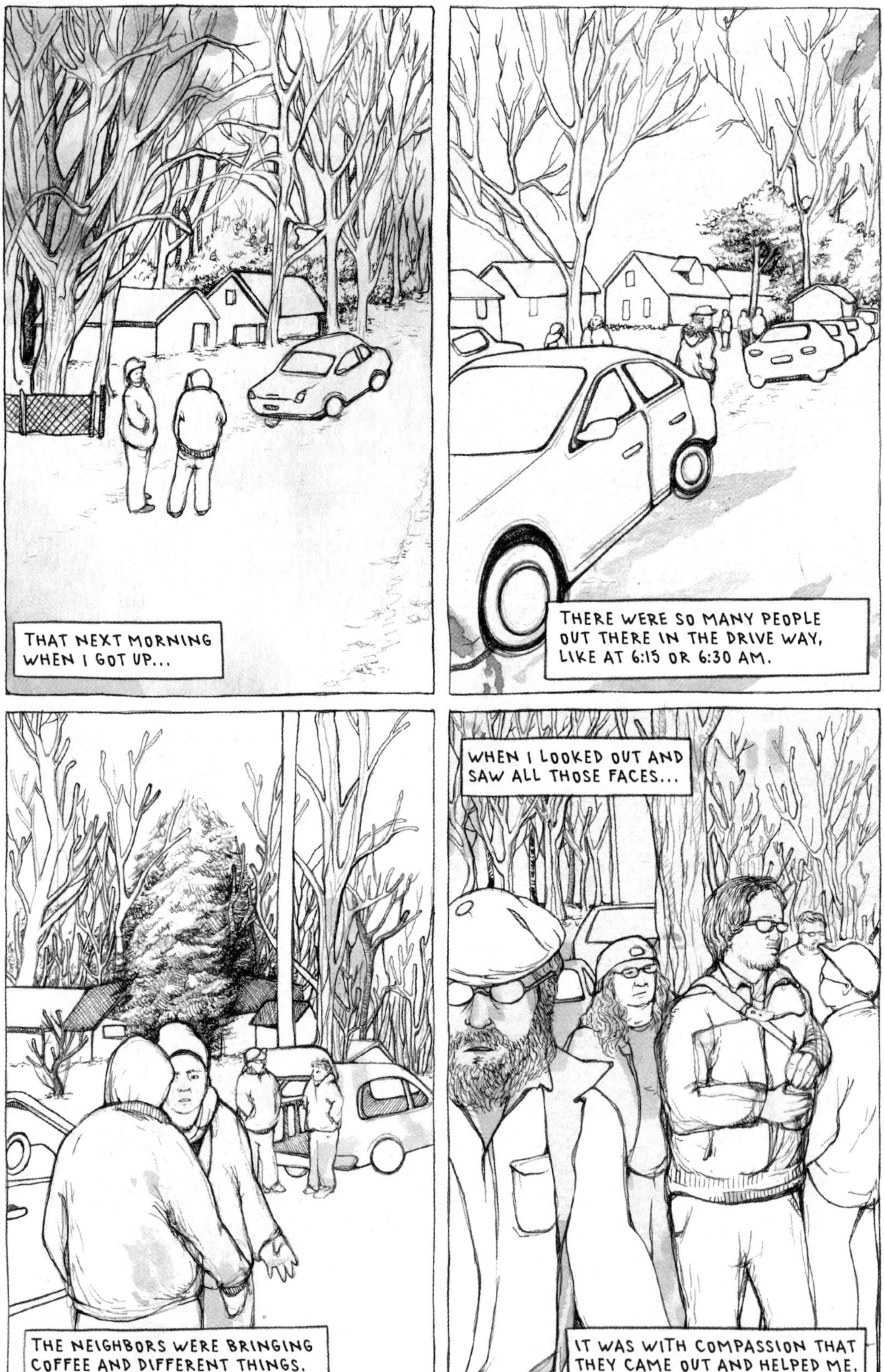
THAT NEXT MORNING WHEN I GOT UP...
THERE WERE SO MANY PEOPLE OUT THERE IN THE DRIVE WAY, LIKE AT 6:15 OR 6:30 AM.
THE NEIGHBORS WERE BRINGING COFFEE AND DIFFERENT THINGS.
WHEN I LOOKED OUT AND SAW ALL THOSE FACES...
IT WAS WITH COMPASSION THAT THEY CAME OUT AND HELPED ME.

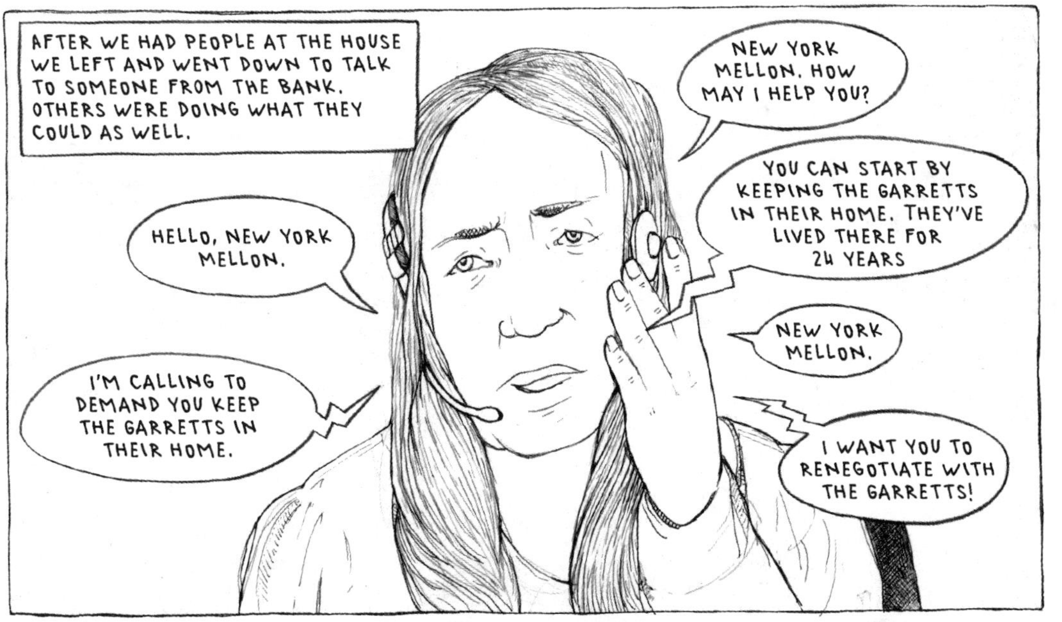
AFTER WE HAD PEOPLE AT THE HOUSE WE LEFT AND WENT DOWN TO TALK TO SOMEONE FROM THE BANK. OTHERS WERE DOING WHAT THEY COULD AS WELL.
NEW YORK MELLON. HOW MAY I HELP YOU?
HELLO, NEW YORK MELLON.
YOU CAN START BY KEEPING THE GARRETTS IN THEIR HOME. THEY'VE LIVED THERE FOR 24 YEARS
NEW YORK MELLON.
I'M CALLING TO DEMAND YOU KEEP THE GARRETTS IN THEIR HOME.
I WANT YOU TO RENEGOTIATE WITH THE GARRETTS!

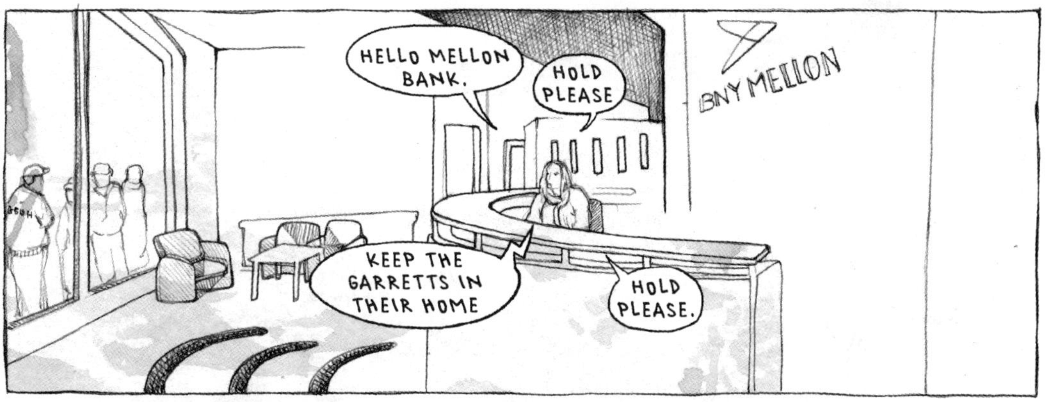
HELLO MELLON BANK.
HOLD PLEASE
BNY MELLON
KEEP THE GARRETTS IN THEIR HOME
HOLD PLEASE.

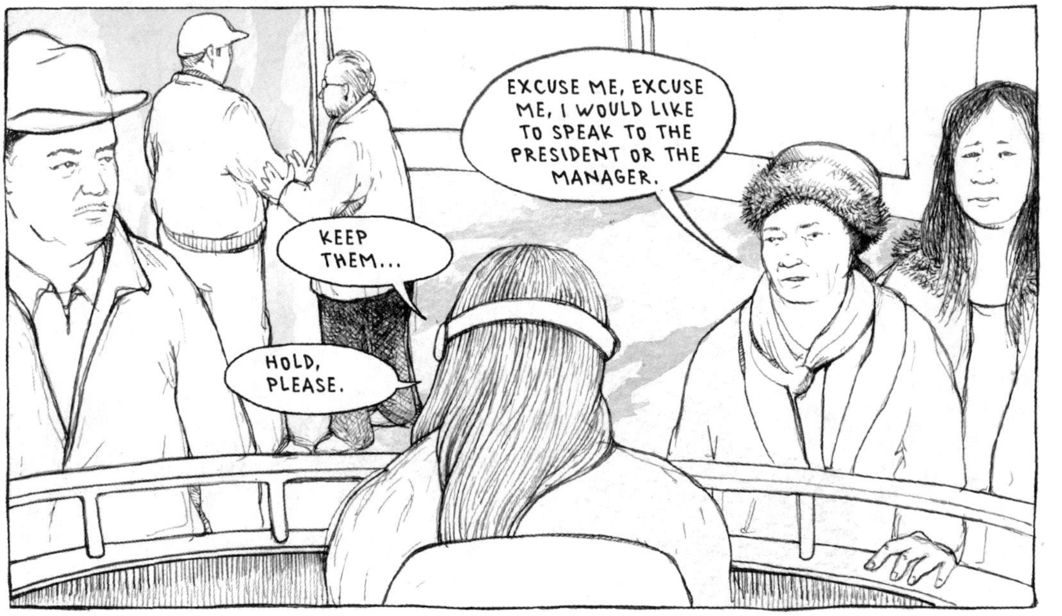
EXCUSE ME, EXCUSE ME, I WOULD LIKE TO SPEAK TO THE PRESIDENT OR THE MANAGER.
KEEP THEM...
HOLD, PLEASE.

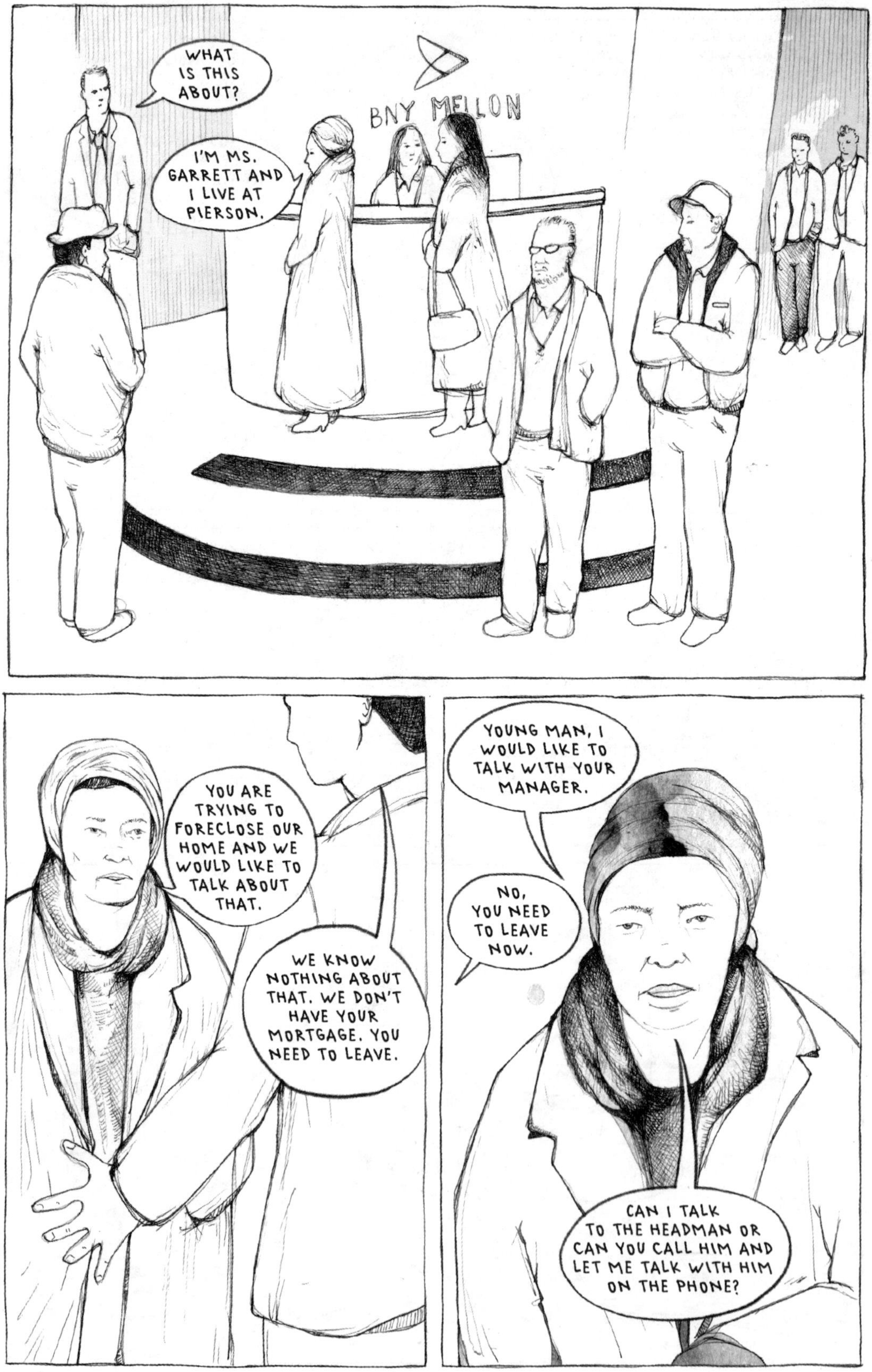
WHAT IS THIS ABOUT?
BNY MELLON
I'M MS. GARRETT AND I LIVE AT PIERSON.
YOU ARE TRYING TO FORECLOSE OUR HOME AND WE WOULD LIKE TO TALK ABOUT THAT.
WE KNOW NOTHING ABOUT THAT. WE DON'T HAVE YOUR MORTGAGE. YOU NEED TO LEAVE.
YOUNG MAN, I WOULD LIKE TO TALK WITH YOUR MANAGER.
NO, YOU NEED TO LEAVE NOW.
CAN I TALK TO THE HEADMAN OR CAN YOU CALL HIM AND LET ME TALK WITH HIM ON THE PHONE?

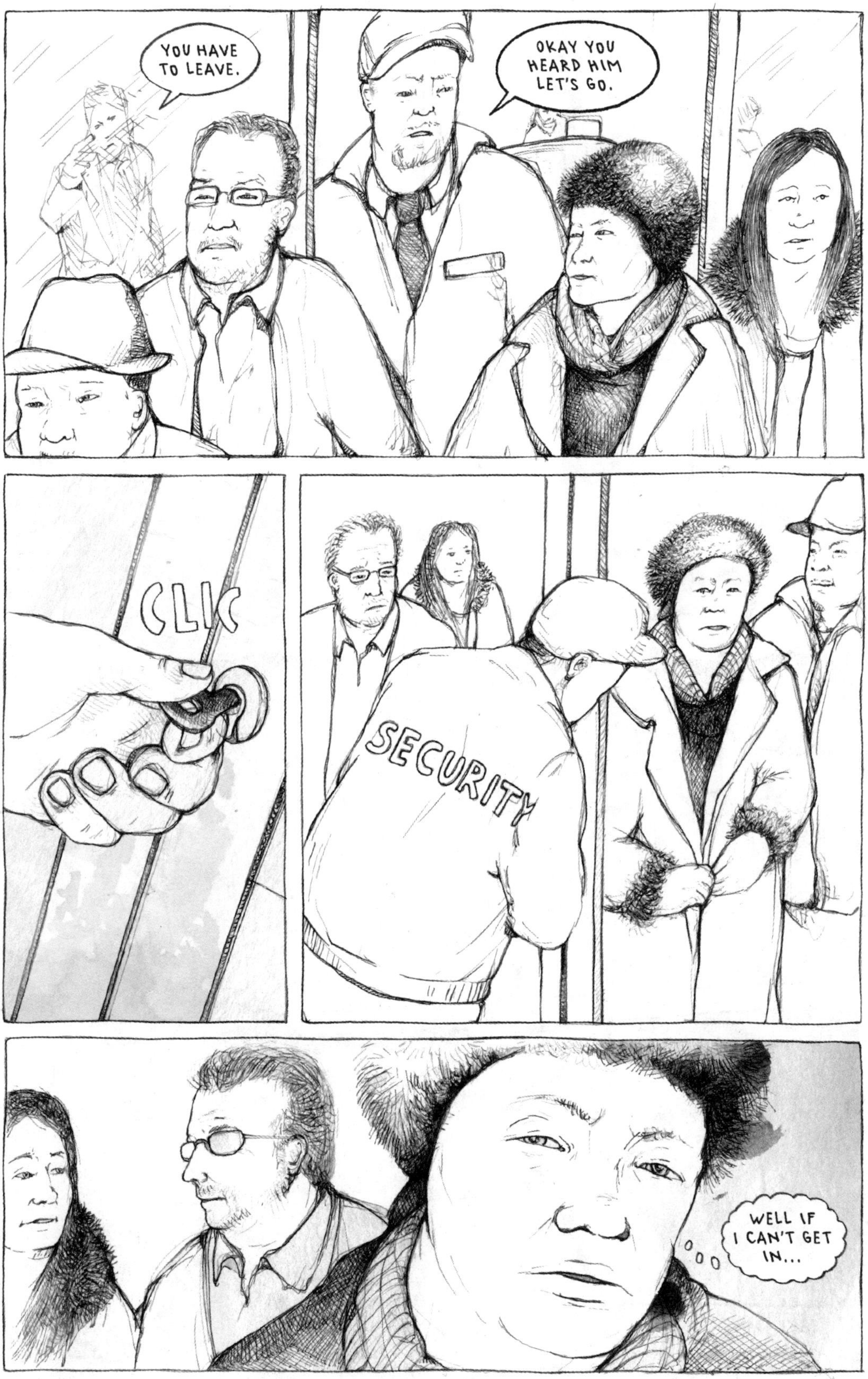
YOU HAVE TO LEAVE.
OKAY YOU HEARD HIM LET'S GO.
CLIC
SECURITY
WELL IF I CAN'T GET IN...

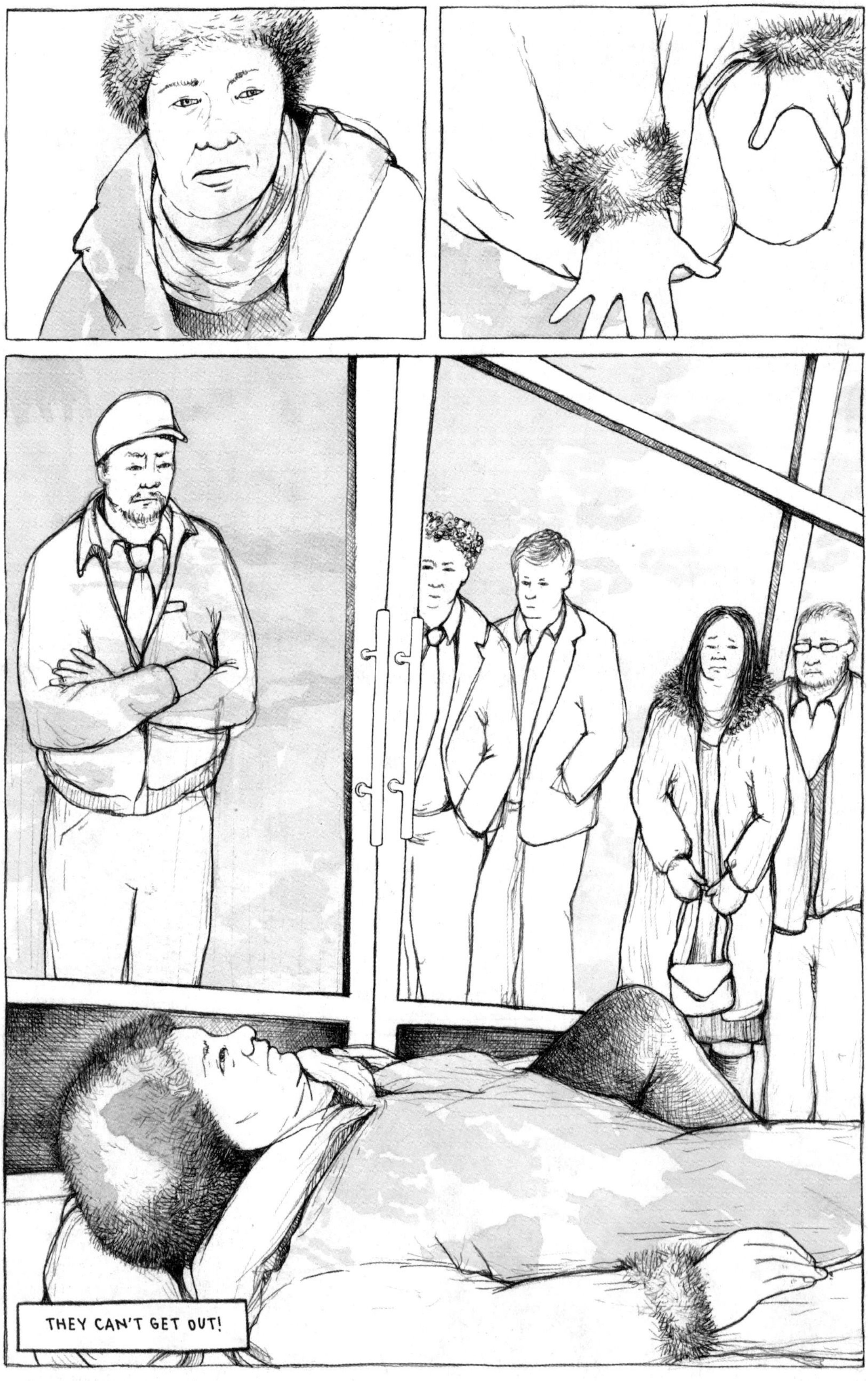
THEY CAN'T GET OUT!

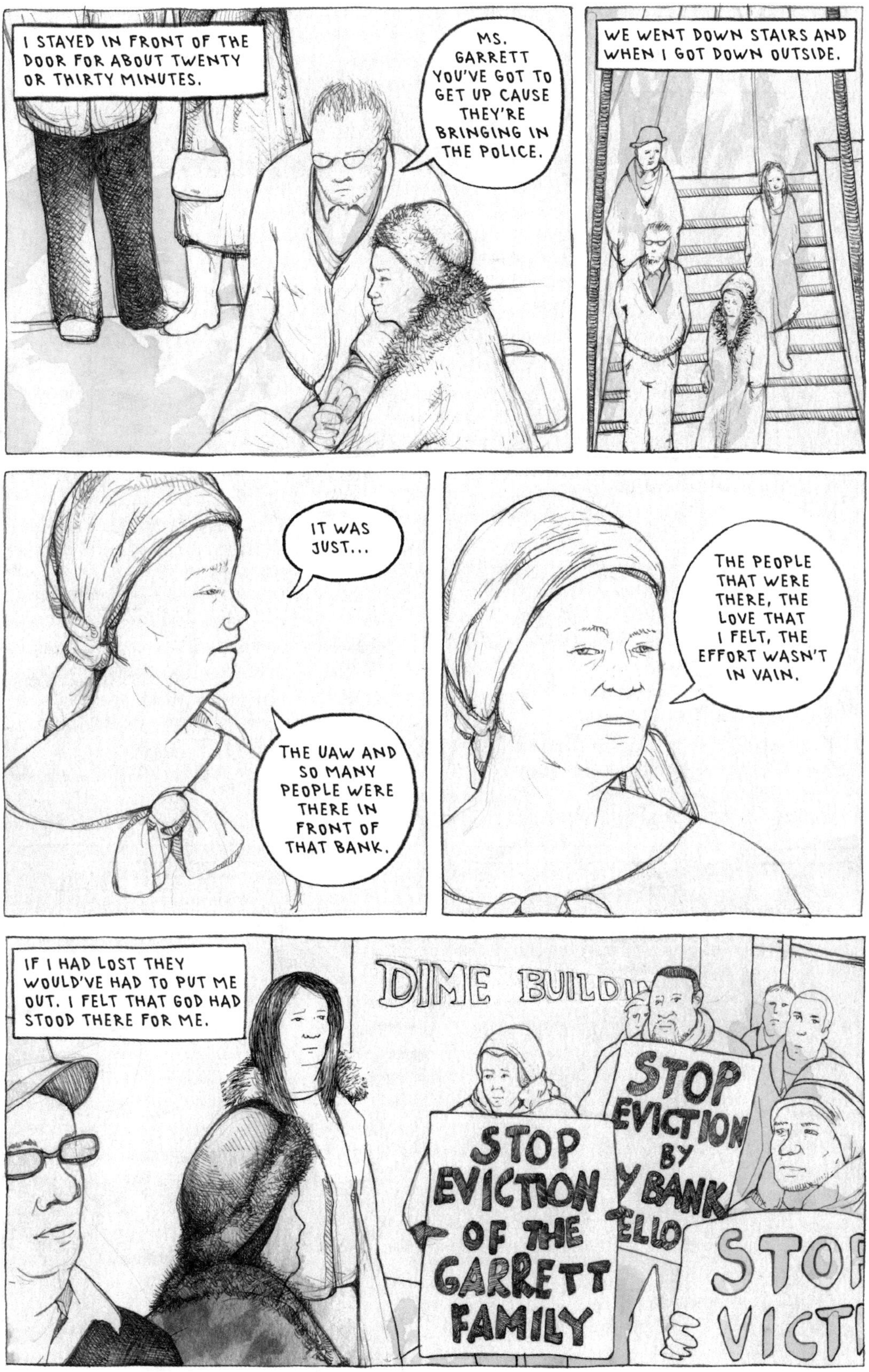
I STAYED IN FRONT OF THE DOOR FOR ABOUT TWENTY OR THIRTY MINUTES.
MS. GARRETT YOU'VE GOT TO GET UP CAUSE THEY'RE BRINGING IN THE POLICE.
WE WENT DOWN STAIRS AND WHEN I GOT DOWN OUTSIDE.
IT WAS JUST...
THE UAW AND SO MANY PEOPLE WERE THERE IN FRONT OF THAT BANK.
THE PEOPLE THAT WERE THERE, THE LOVE THAT I FELT, THE EFFORT WASN'T IN VAIN.
IF I HAD LOST THEY WOULD'VE HAD TO PUT ME OUT. I FELT THAT GOD HAD STOOD THERE FOR ME.
DIME BUILDI
STOP EVICTION OF THE GARRETT FAMILY
STOP EVICTION BY BANK
ELLO
STOP
VICTI

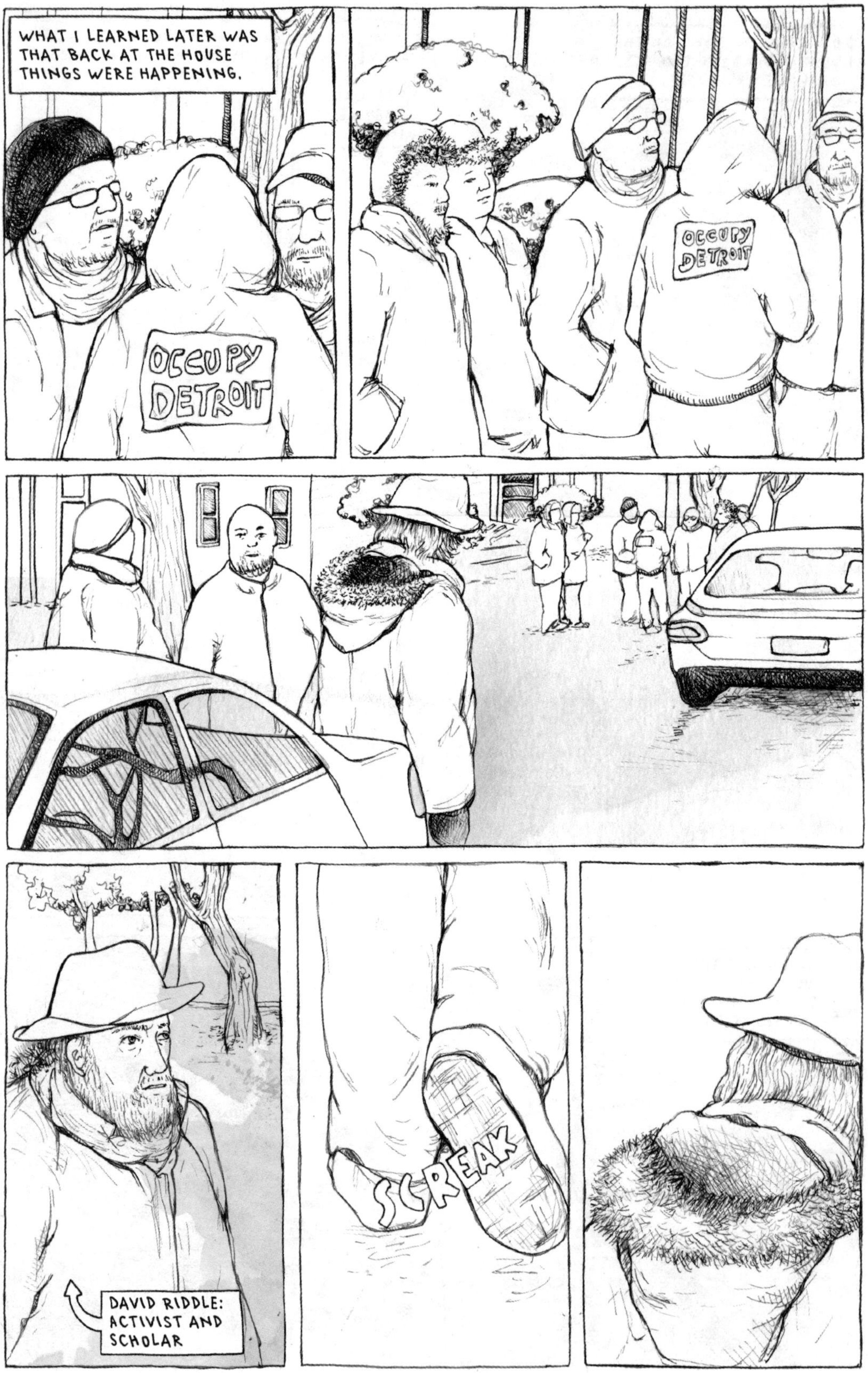
WHAT I LEARNED LATER WAS THAT BACK AT THE HOUSE THINGS WERE HAPPENING.
OCCUPY DETROIT
OCCUPY DETROIT
DAVID RIDDLE: ACTIVIST AND SCHOLAR
SCREAK

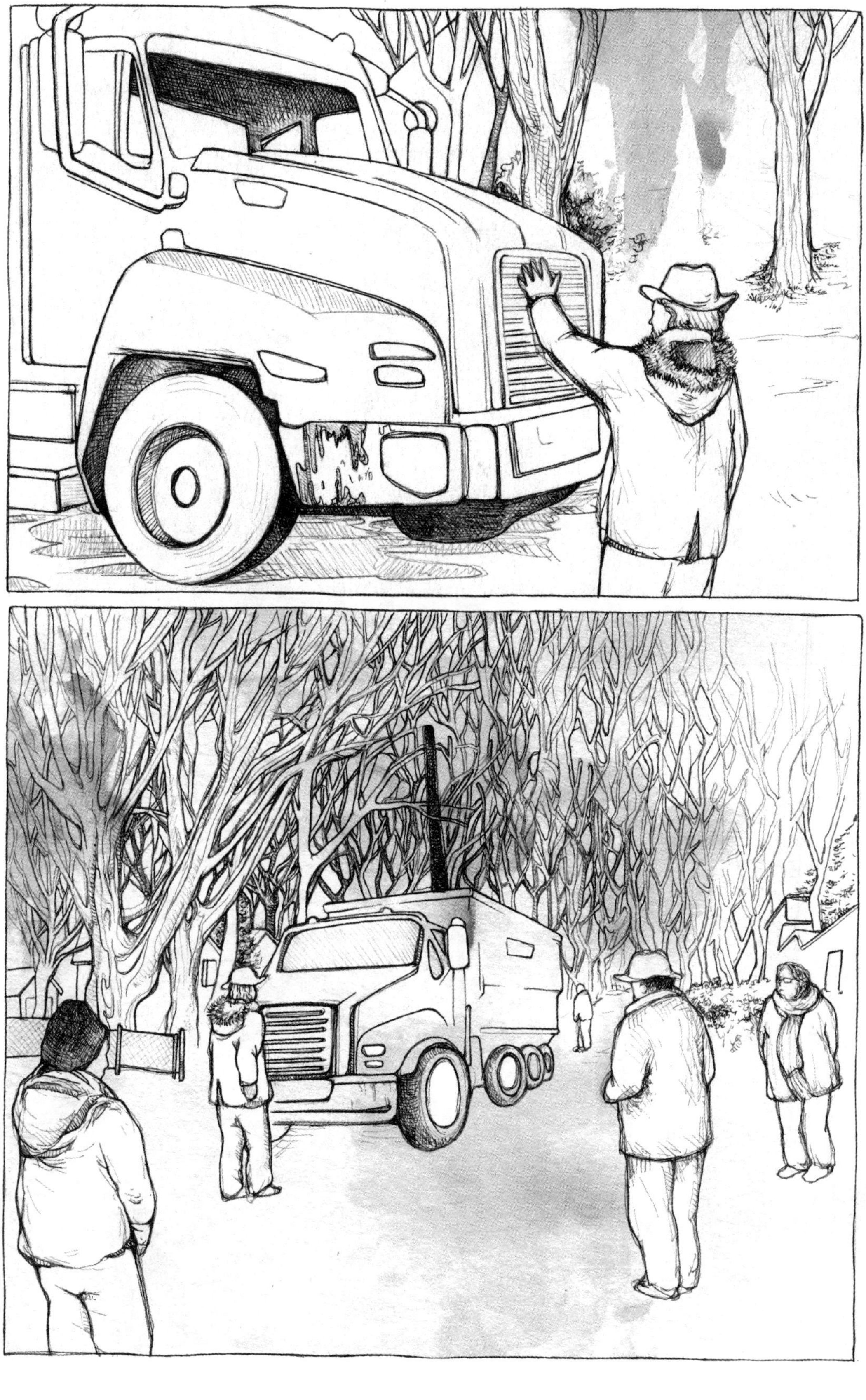

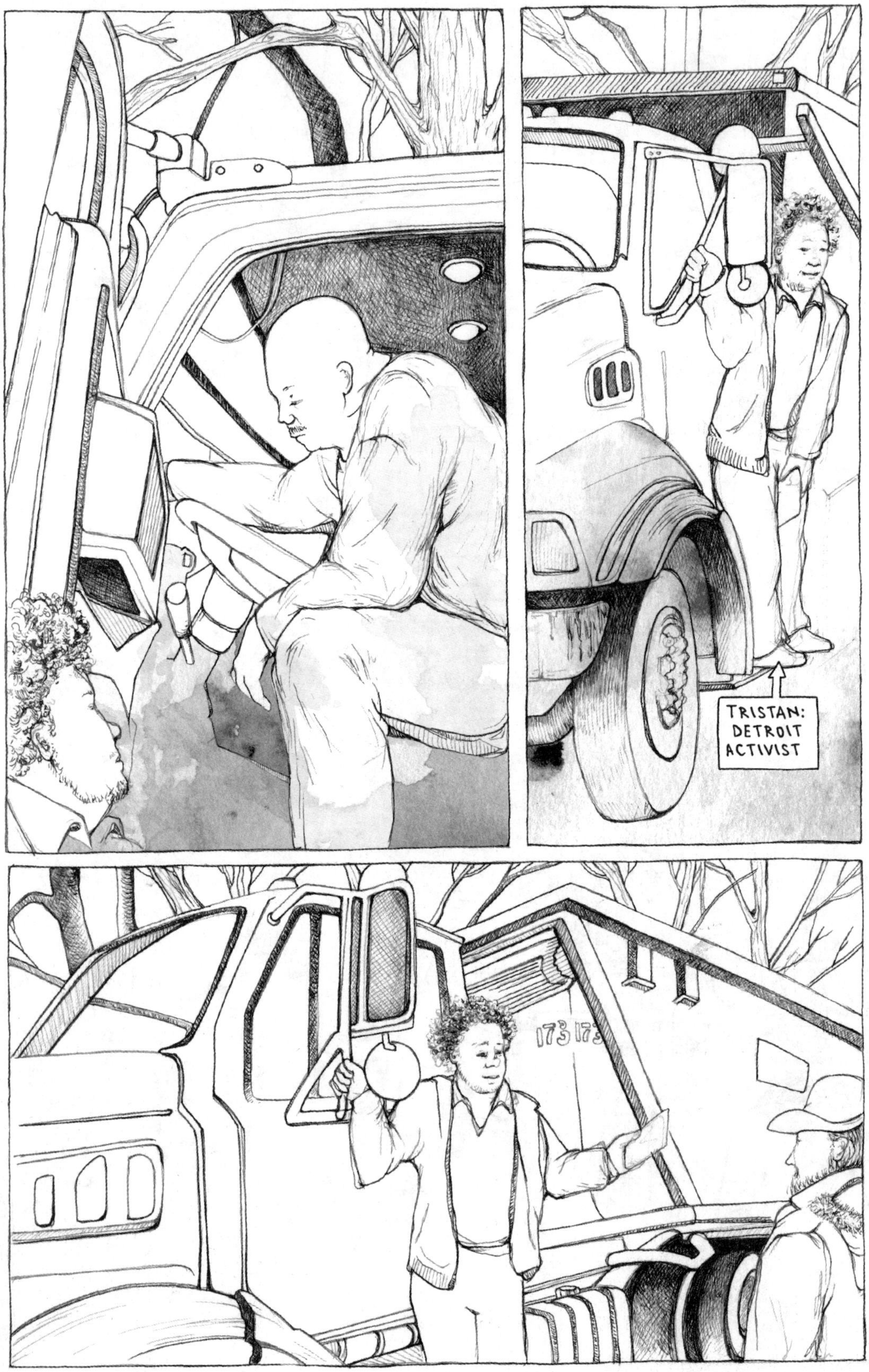
TRISTAN:
DETROIT
ACTIVIST

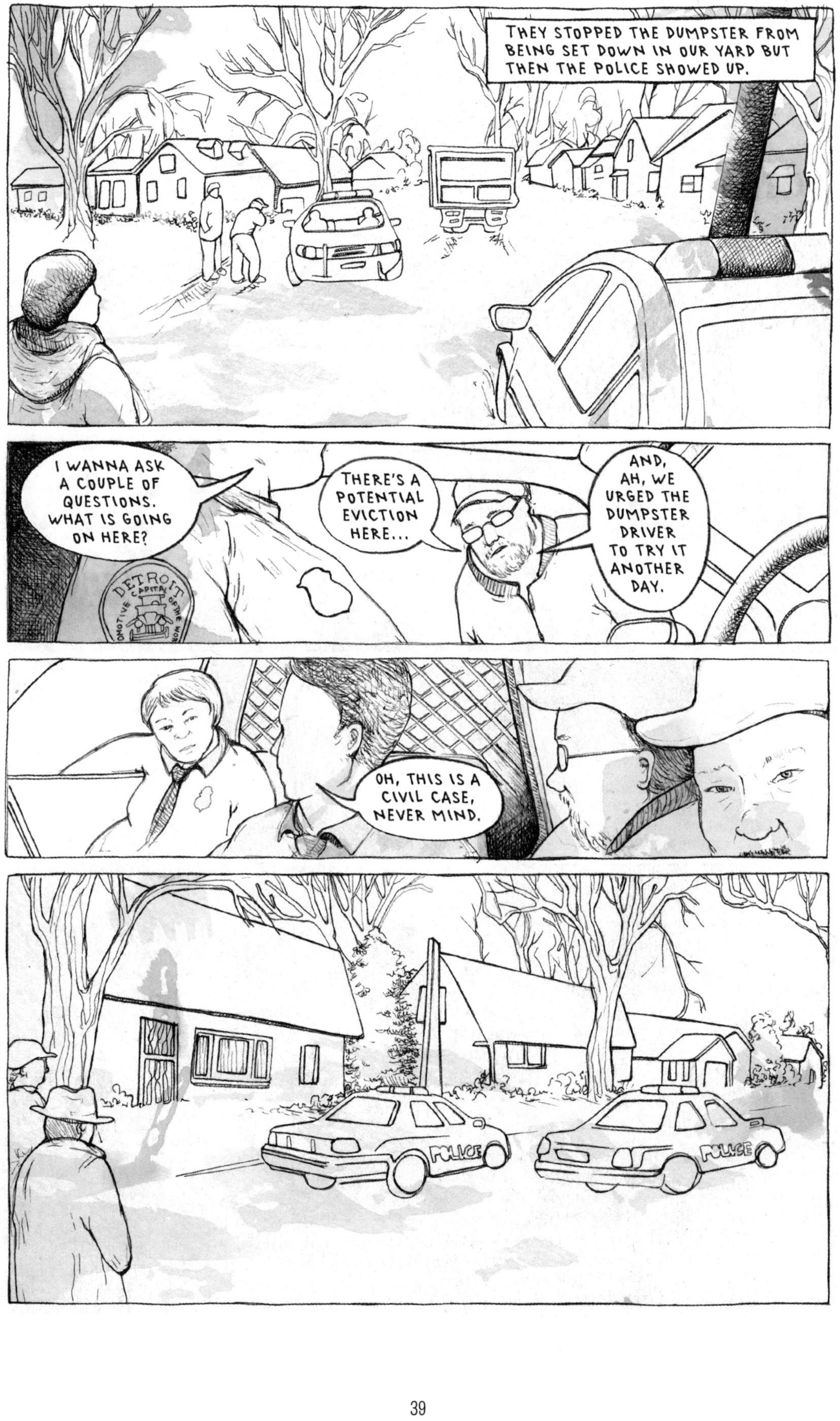
THEY STOPPED THE DUMPSTER FROM BEING SET DOWN IN OUR YARD BUT THEN THE POLICE SHOWED UP.
I WANNA ASK A COUPLE OF QUESTIONS. WHAT IS GOING ON HERE?
THERE'S A POTENTIAL EVICTION HERE...
AND, AH, WE URGED THE DUMPSTER DRIVER TO TRY IT ANOTHER DAY.
DETROIT
OH, THIS IS A CIVIL CASE, NEVER MIND.
POLICE
POLICE

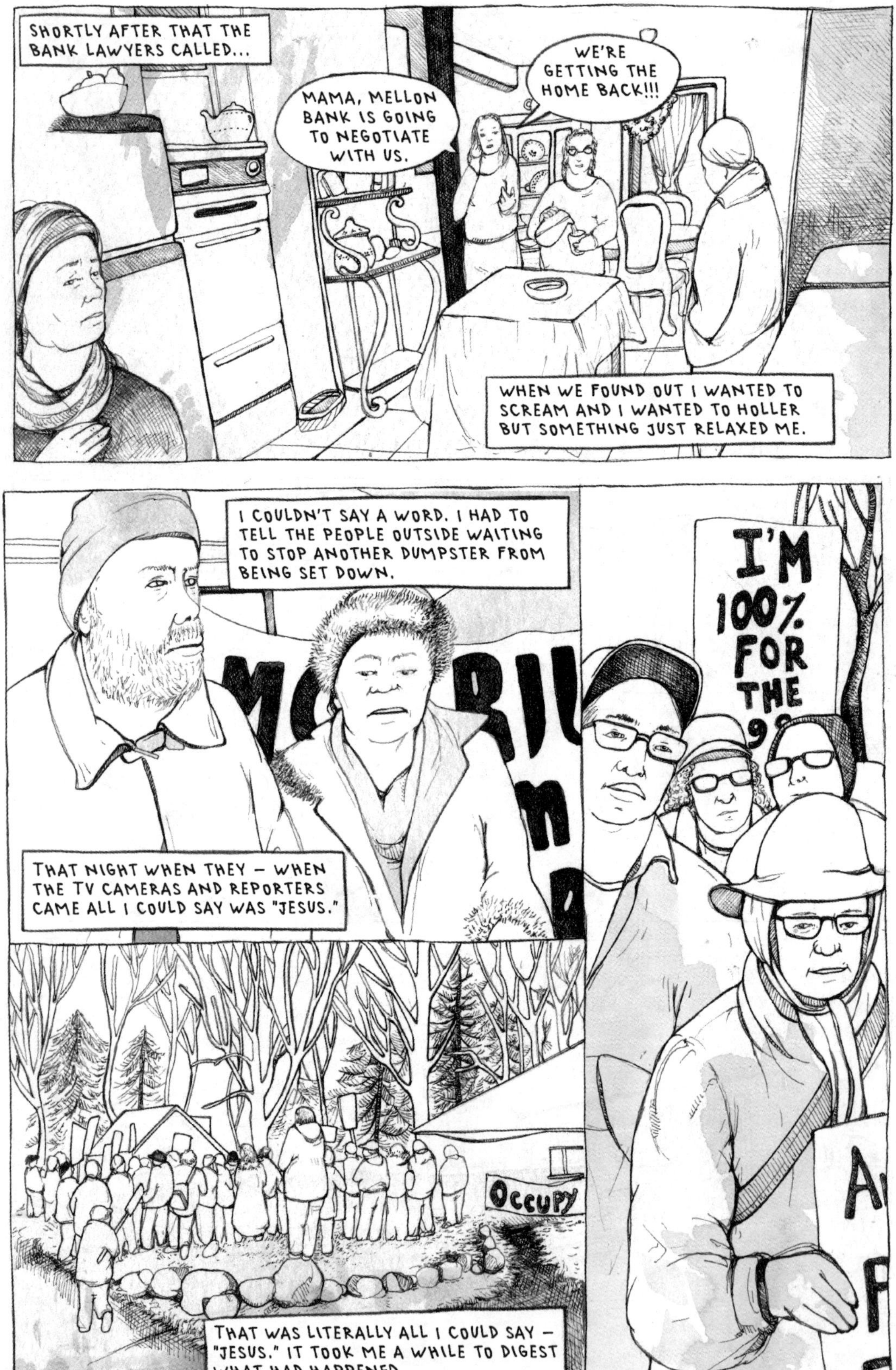
SHORTLY AFTER THAT THE BANK LAWYERS CALLED...
MAMA, MELLON BANK IS GOING TO NEGOTIATE WITH US.
WE'RE GETTING THE HOME BACK!!!
WHEN WE FOUND OUT I WANTED TO SCREAM AND I WANTED TO HOLLER BUT SOMETHING JUST RELAXED ME.
I COULDN'T SAY A WORD. I HAD TO TELL THE PEOPLE OUTSIDE WAITING TO STOP ANOTHER DUMPSTER FROM BEING SET DOWN.
THAT NIGHT WHEN THEY — WHEN THE TV CAMERAS AND REPORTERS CAME ALL I COULD SAY WAS "JESUS."
I'M 100% FOR THE
Occupy
THAT WAS LITERALLY ALL I COULD SAY — "JESUS." IT TOOK ME A WHILE TO DIGEST WHAT HAD HAPPENED.

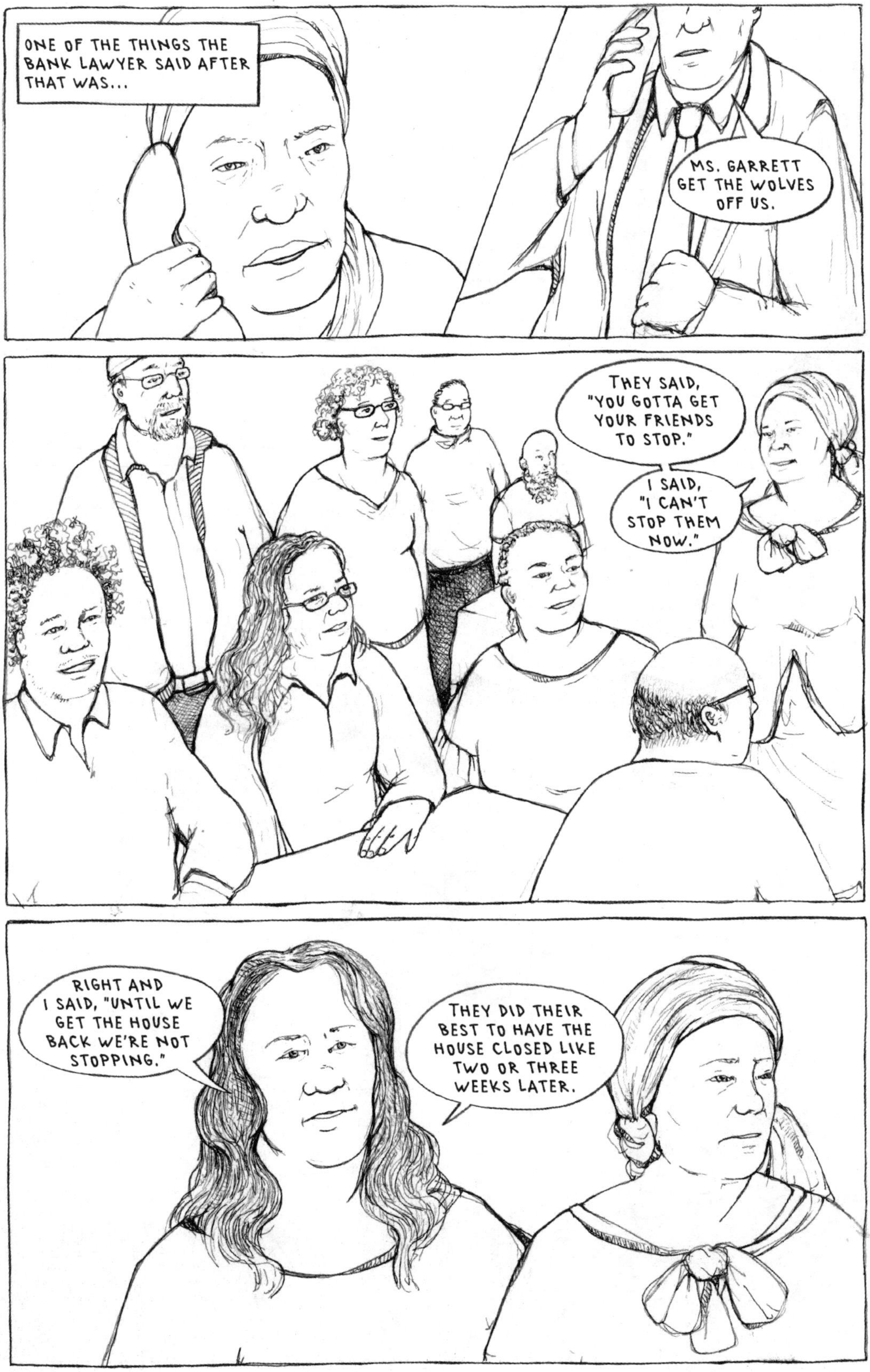
ONE OF THE THINGS THE BANK LAWYER SAID AFTER THAT WAS...
MS. GARRETT GET THE WOLVES OFF US.
THEY SAID, "YOU GOTTA GET YOUR FRIENDS TO STOP."
I SAID, "I CAN'T STOP THEM NOW."
RIGHT AND I SAID, "UNTIL WE GET THE HOUSE BACK WE'RE NOT STOPPING."
THEY DID THEIR BEST TO HAVE THE HOUSE CLOSED LIKE TWO OR THREE WEEKS LATER.

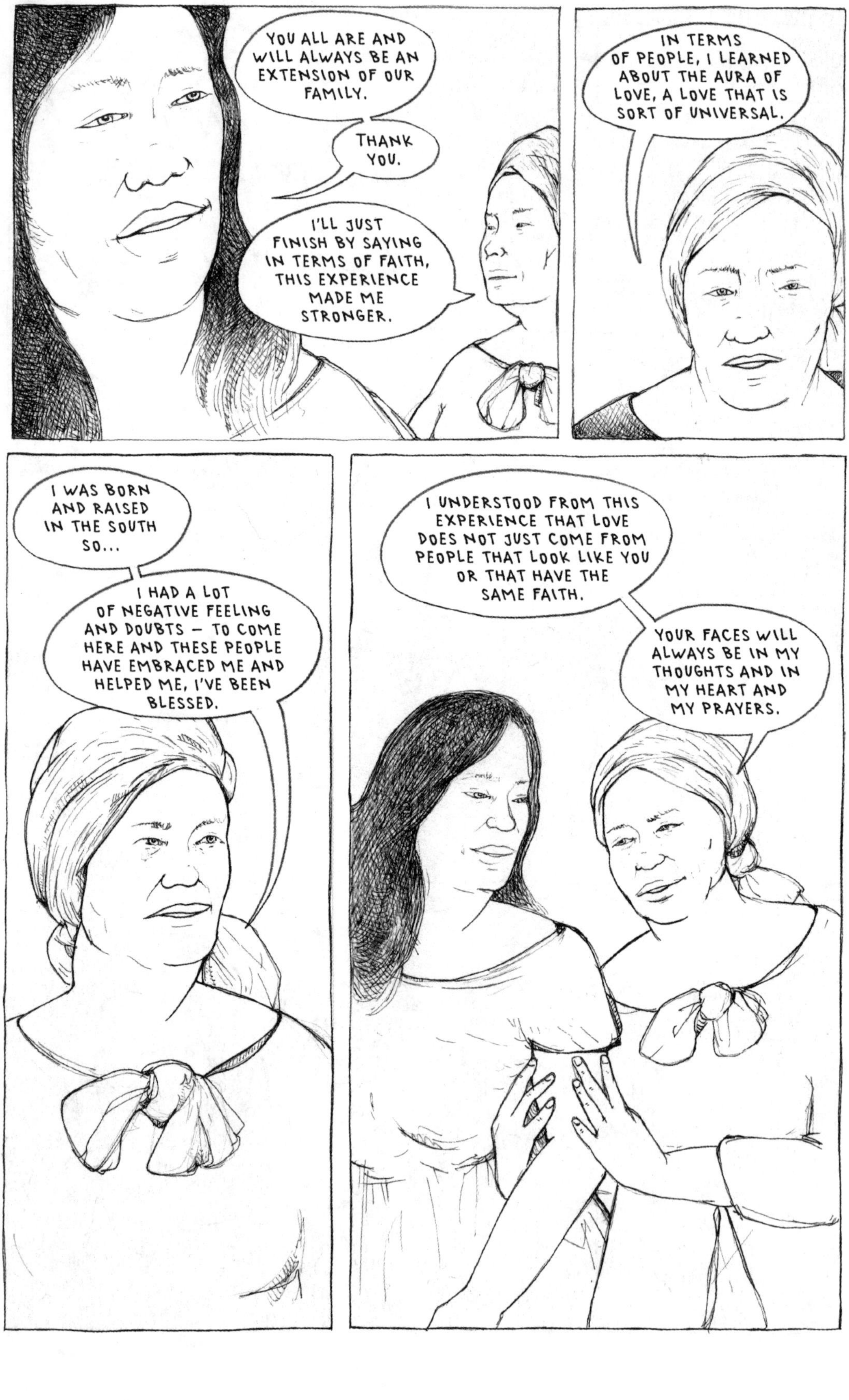
YOU ALL ARE AND WILL ALWAYS BE AN EXTENSION OF OUR FAMILY.
THANK YOU.
I'LL JUST FINISH BY SAYING IN TERMS OF FAITH, THIS EXPERIENCE MADE ME STRONGER.
IN TERMS OF PEOPLE, I LEARNED ABOUT THE AURA OF LOVE, A LOVE THAT IS SORT OF UNIVERSAL.
I WAS BORN AND RAISED IN THE SOUTH SO...
I HAD A LOT OF NEGATIVE FEELING AND DOUBTS — TO COME HERE AND THESE PEOPLE HAVE EMBRACED ME AND HELPED ME, I'VE BEEN BLESSED.
I UNDERSTOOD FROM THIS EXPERIENCE THAT LOVE DOES NOT JUST COME FROM PEOPLE THAT LOOK LIKE YOU OR THAT HAVE THE SAME FAITH.
YOUR FACES WILL ALWAYS BE IN MY THOUGHTS AND IN MY HEART AND MY PRAYERS.

I'm with you 100 percent

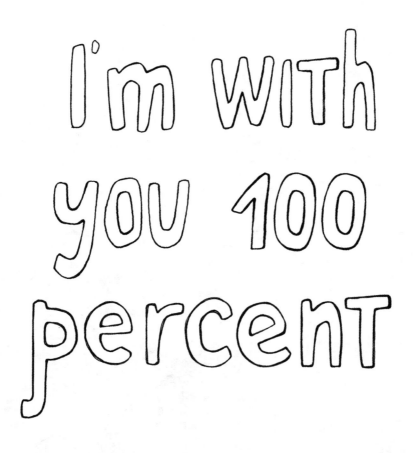

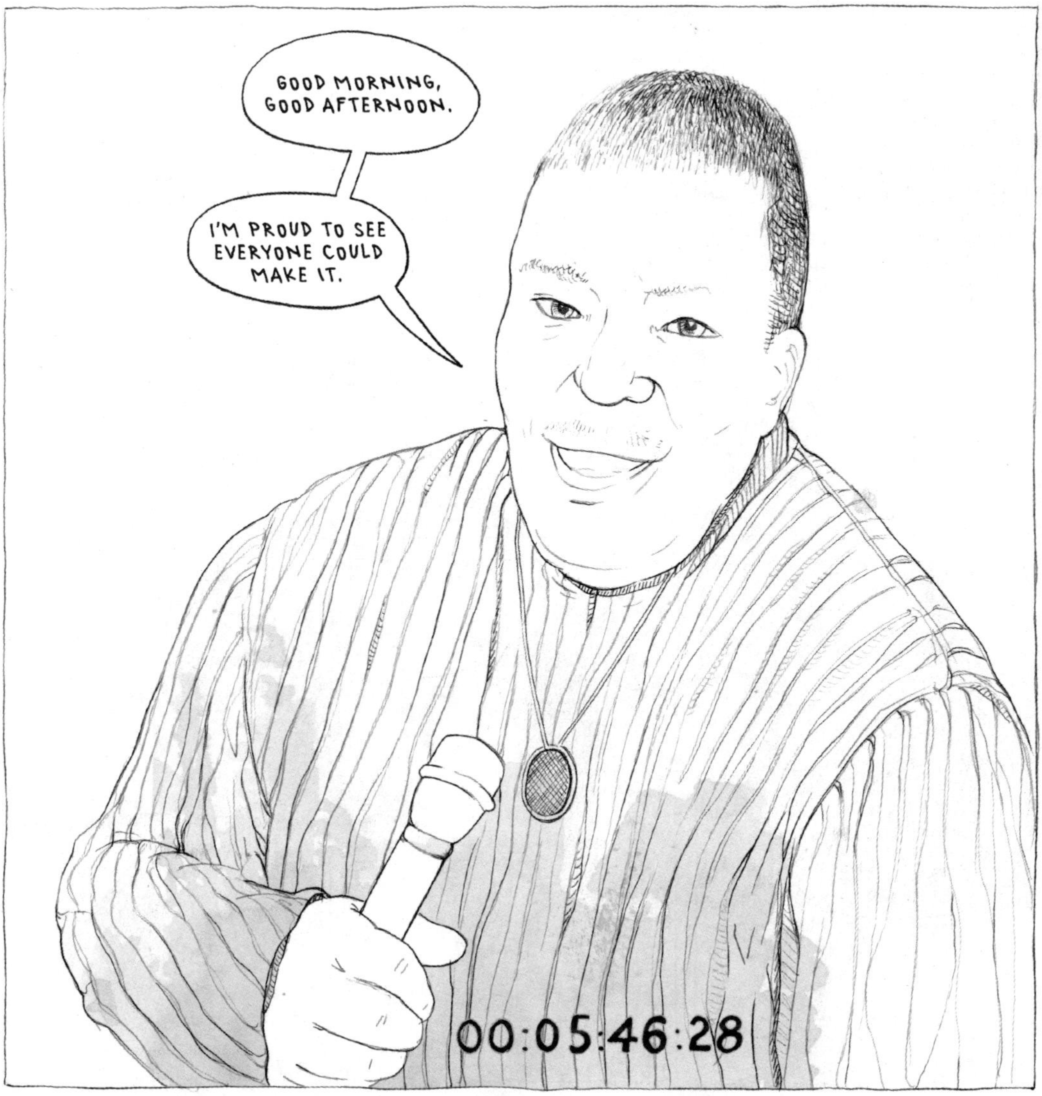
GOOD MORNING, GOOD AFTERNOON.
I'M PROUD TO SEE EVERYONE COULD MAKE IT.
00:05:46:28

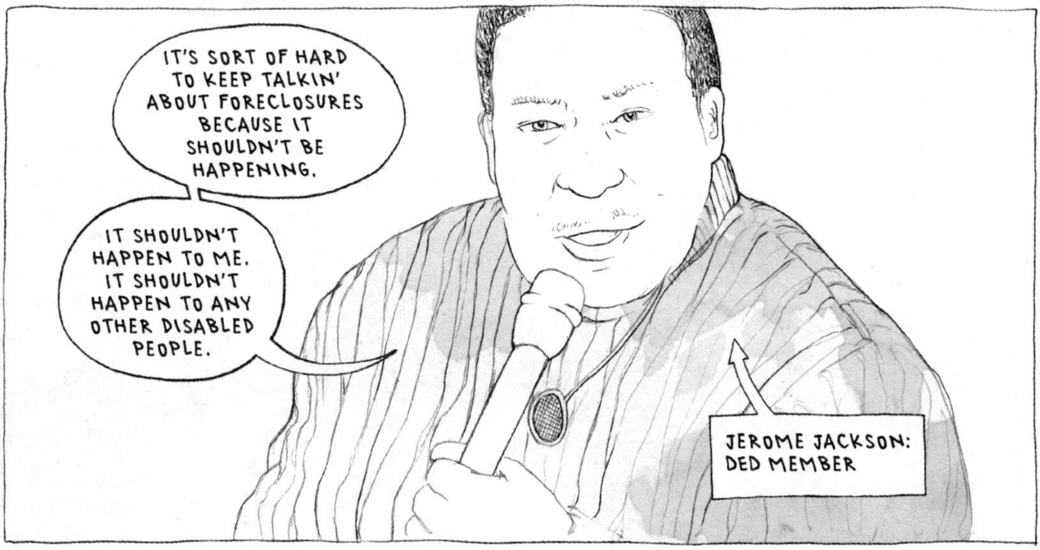
IT'S SORT OF HARD TO KEEP TALKIN' ABOUT FORECLOSURES BECAUSE IT SHOULDN'T BE HAPPENING.
IT SHOULDN'T HAPPEN TO ME. IT SHOULDN'T HAPPEN TO ANY OTHER DISABLED PEOPLE.
JEROME JACKSON: DED MEMBER

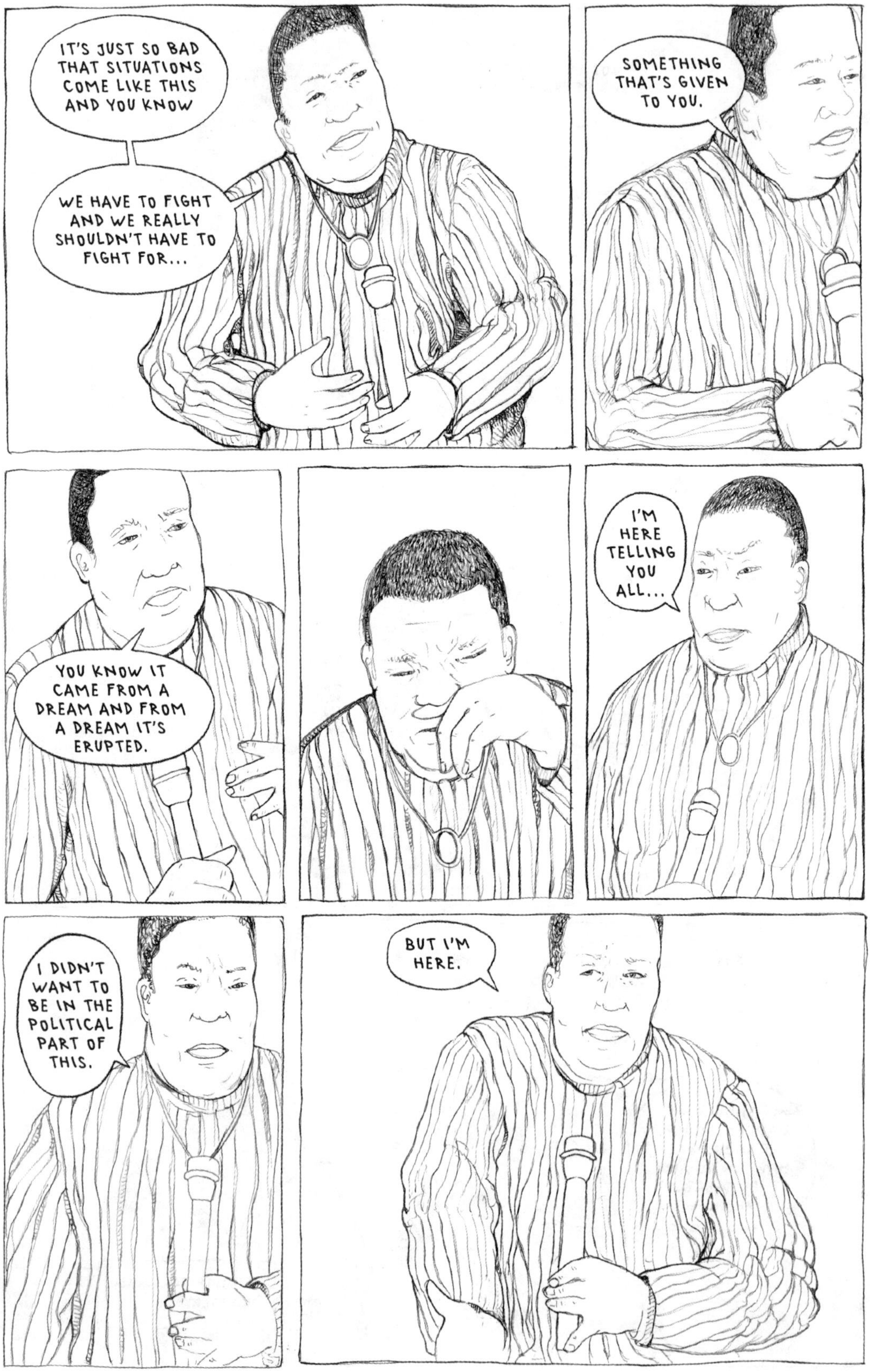
IT'S JUST SO BAD THAT SITUATIONS COME LIKE THIS AND YOU KNOW
WE HAVE TO FIGHT AND WE REALLY SHOULDN'T HAVE TO FIGHT FOR...
SOMETHING THAT'S GIVEN TO YOU.
YOU KNOW IT CAME FROM A DREAM AND FROM A DREAM IT'S ERUPTED.
I'M HERE TELLING YOU ALL...
I DIDN'T WANT TO BE IN THE POLITICAL PART OF THIS.
BUT I'M HERE.

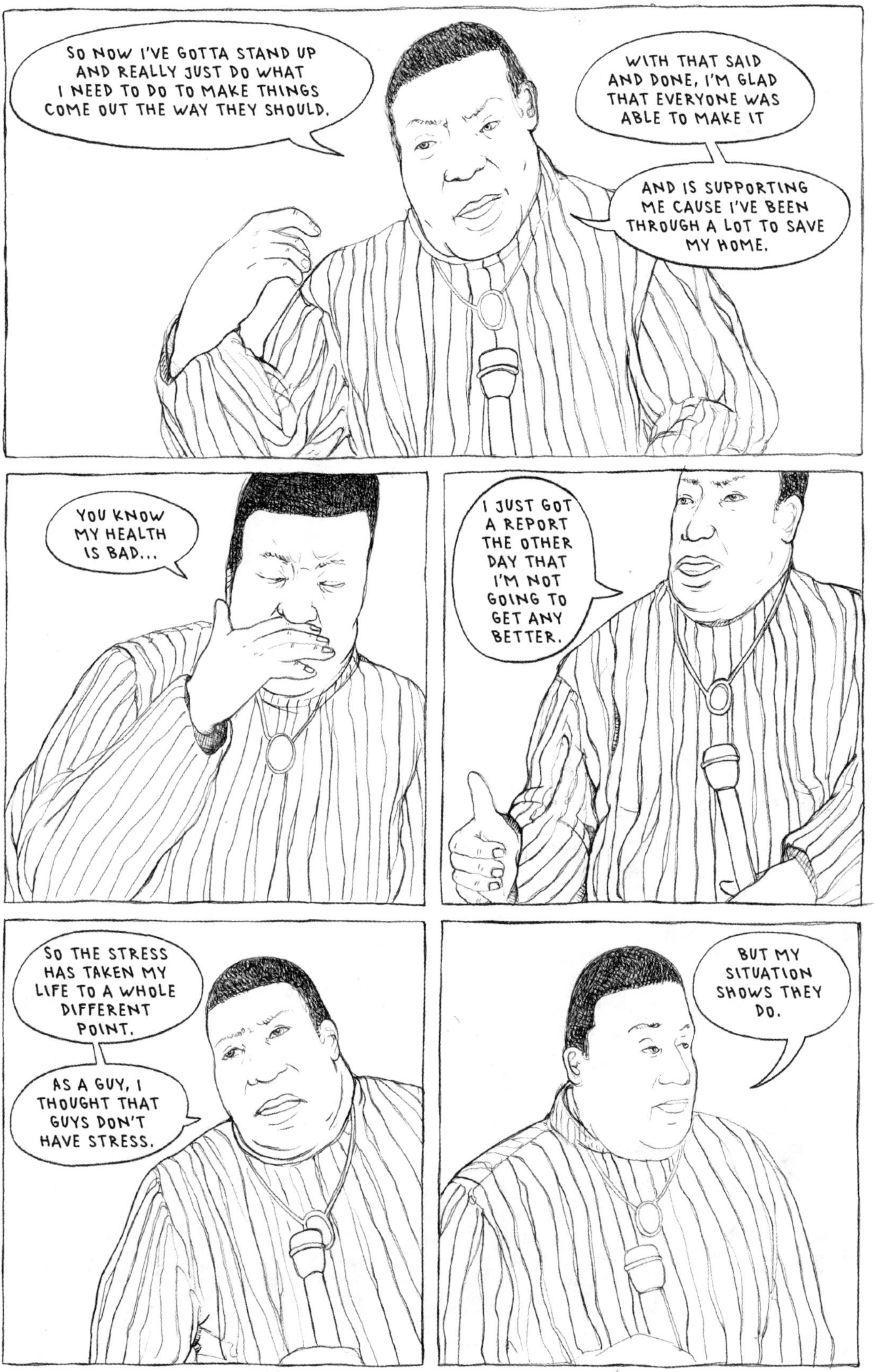
SO NOW I'VE GOTTA STAND UP AND REALLY JUST DO WHAT I NEED TO DO TO MAKE THINGS COME OUT THE WAY THEY SHOULD.
WITH THAT SAID AND DONE, I'M GLAD THAT EVERYONE WAS ABLE TO MAKE IT
AND IS SUPPORTING ME CAUSE I'VE BEEN THROUGH A LOT TO SAVE MY HOME.
YOU KNOW MY HEALTH IS BAD...
I JUST GOT A REPORT THE OTHER DAY THAT I'M NOT GOING TO GET ANY BETTER.
SO THE STRESS HAS TAKEN MY LIFE TO A WHOLE DIFFERENT POINT.
AS A GUY, I THOUGHT THAT GUYS DON'T HAVE STRESS.
BUT MY SITUATION SHOWS THEY DO.

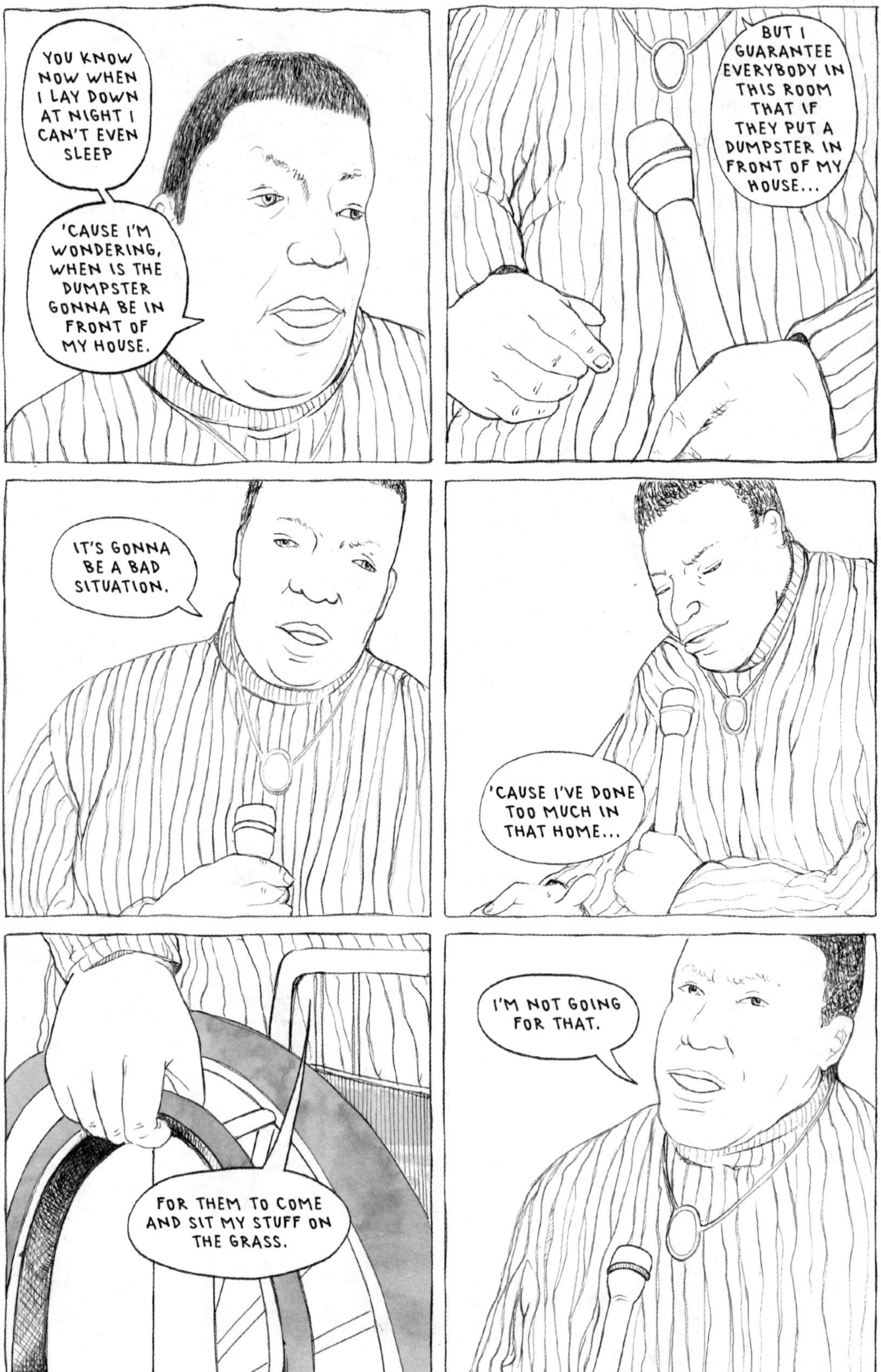
YOU KNOW NOW WHEN I LAY DOWN AT NIGHT I CAN'T EVEN SLEEP
'CAUSE I'M WONDERING, WHEN IS THE DUMPSTER GONNA BE IN FRONT OF MY HOUSE.
BUT I GUARANTEE EVERYBODY IN THIS ROOM THAT IF THEY PUT A DUMPSTER IN FRONT OF MY HOUSE...
IT'S GONNA BE A BAD SITUATION.
'CAUSE I'VE DONE TOO MUCH IN THAT HOME...
FOR THEM TO COME AND SIT MY STUFF ON THE GRASS.
I'M NOT GOING FOR THAT.

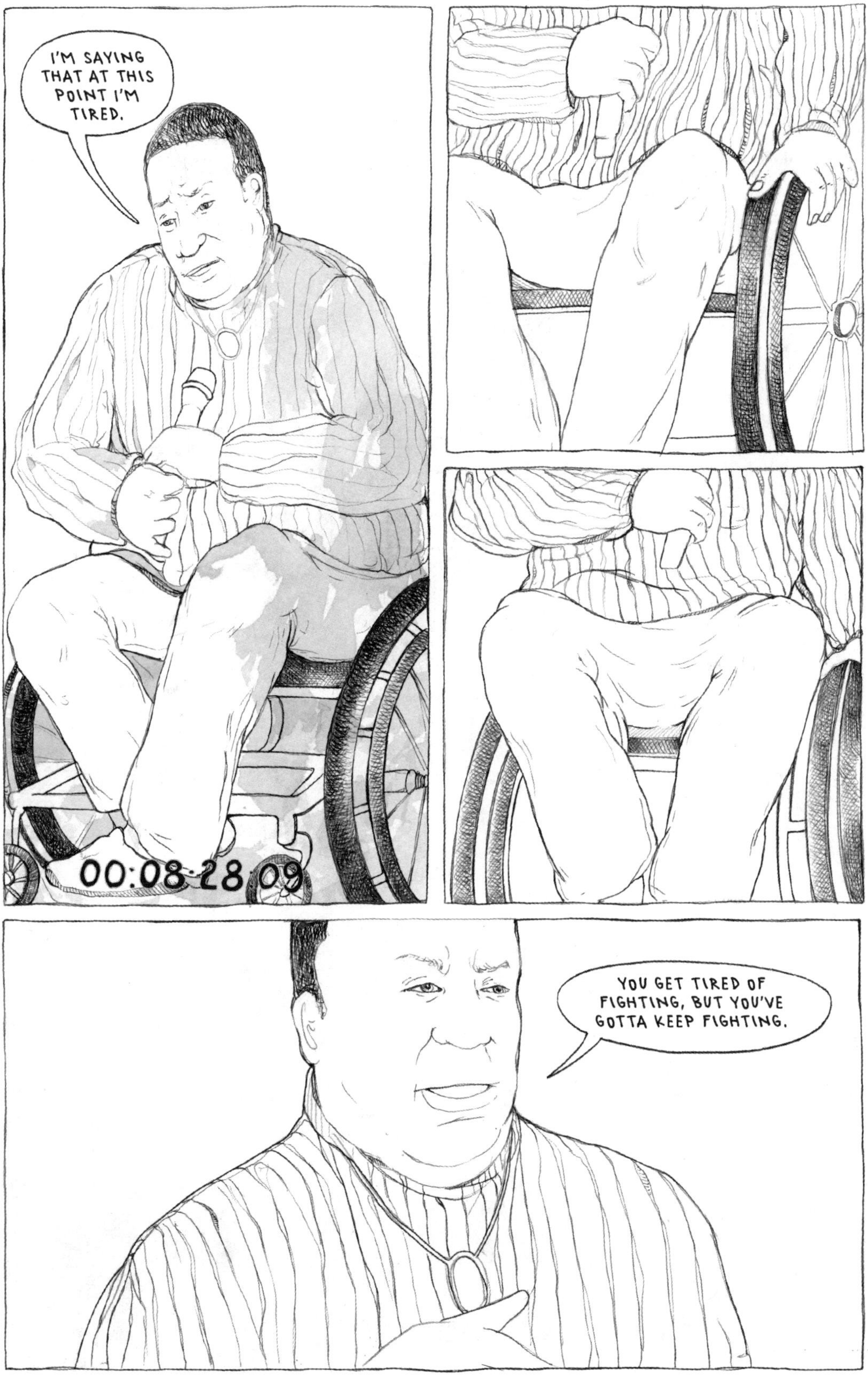
I'M SAYING THAT AT THIS POINT I'M TIRED.
00:08:28:09
YOU GET TIRED OF FIGHTING, BUT YOU'VE GOTTA KEEP FIGHTING.

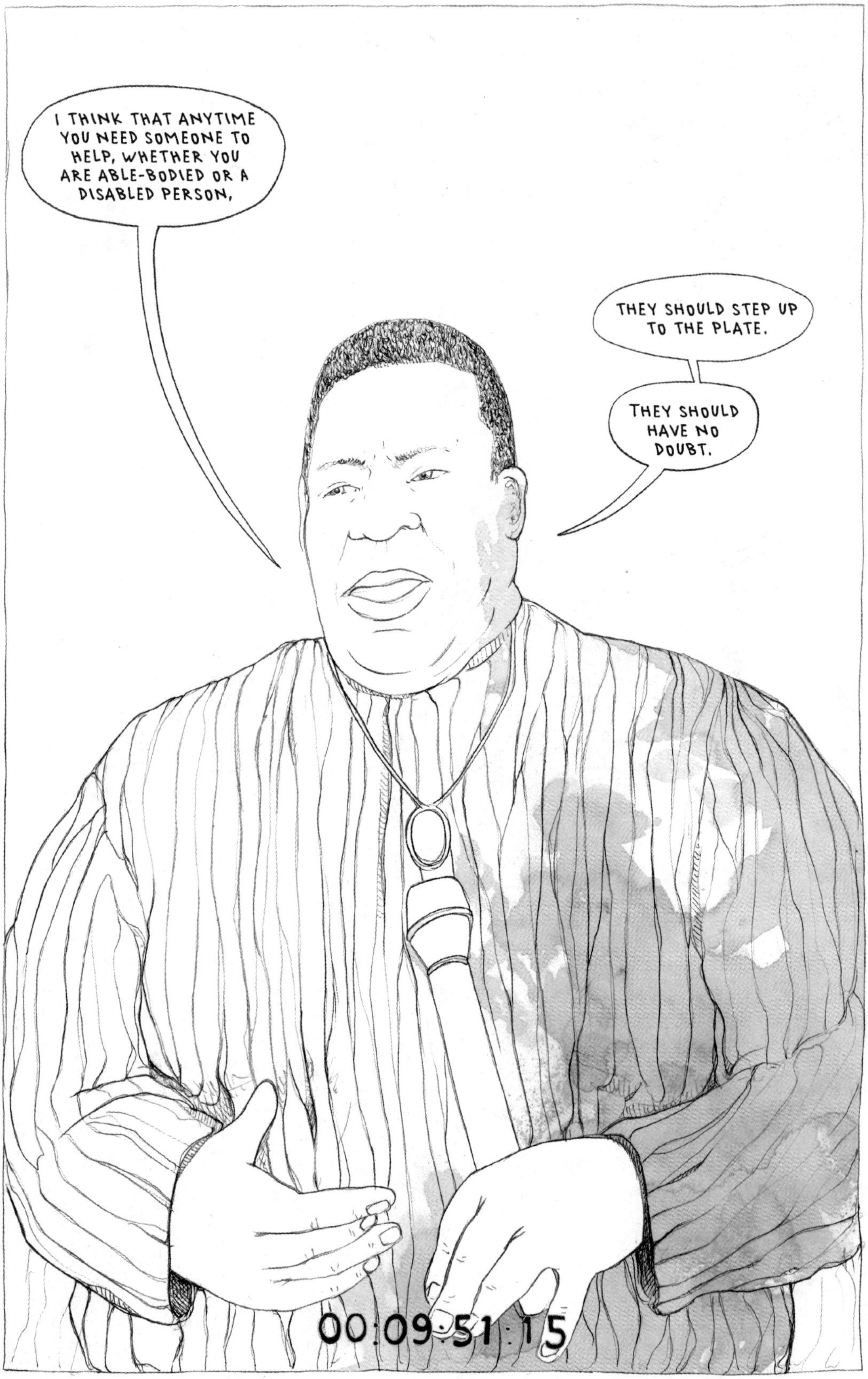
I THINK THAT ANYTIME YOU NEED SOMEONE TO HELP, WHETHER YOU ARE ABLE-BODIED OR A DISABLED PERSON,
THEY SHOULD STEP UP TO THE PLATE.
THEY SHOULD HAVE NO DOUBT.
00:09:51:15

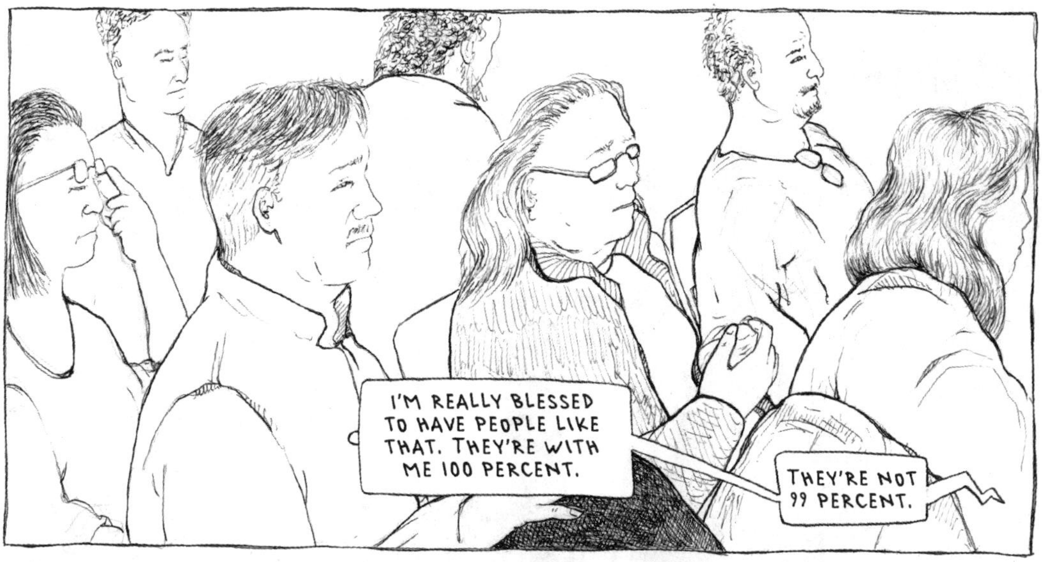
I'M REALLY BLESSED TO HAVE PEOPLE LIKE THAT. THEY'RE WITH ME 100 PERCENT.
THEY'RE NOT 99 PERCENT.

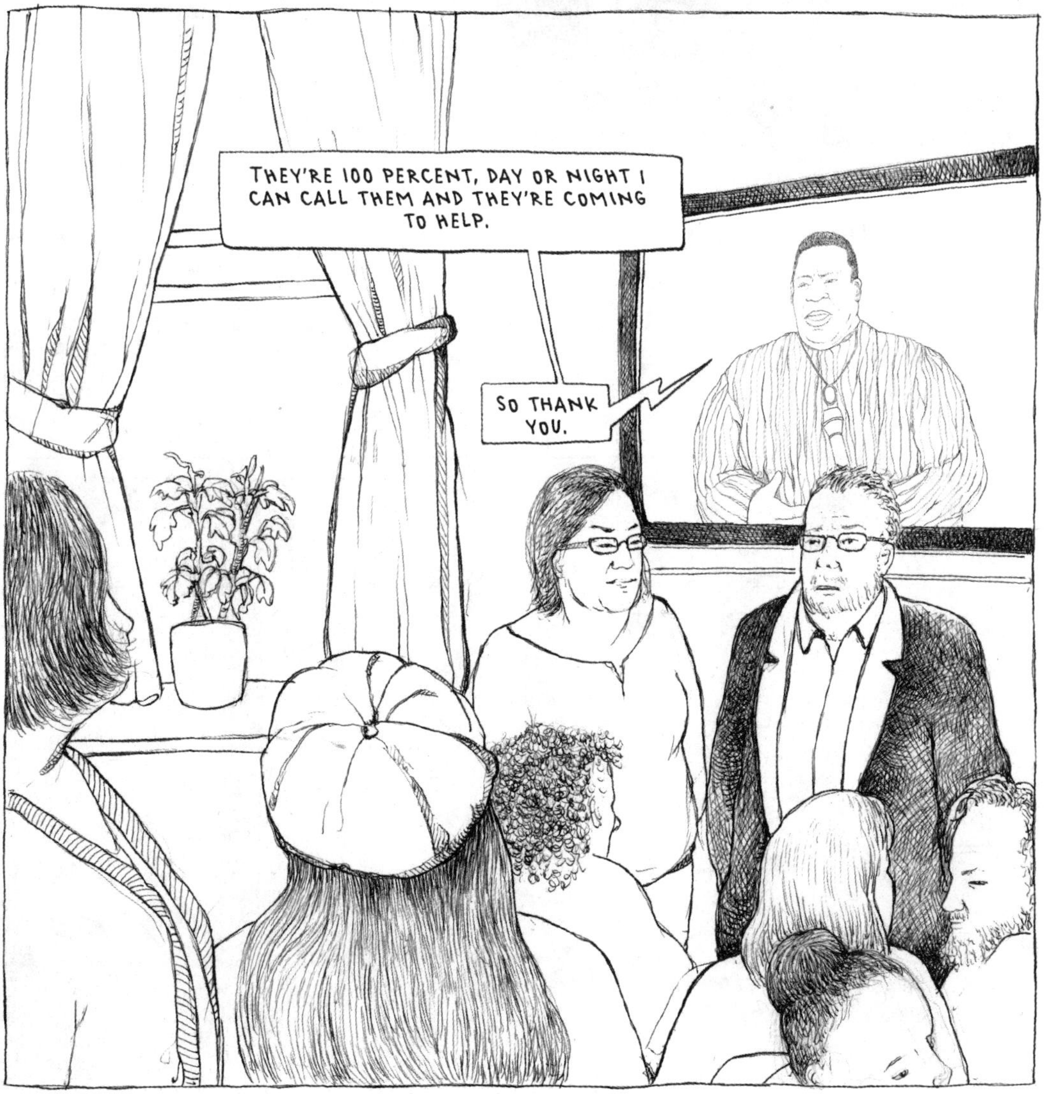
THEY'RE 100 PERCENT, DAY OR NIGHT I CAN CALL THEM AND THEY'RE COMING TO HELP.
SO THANK YOU.

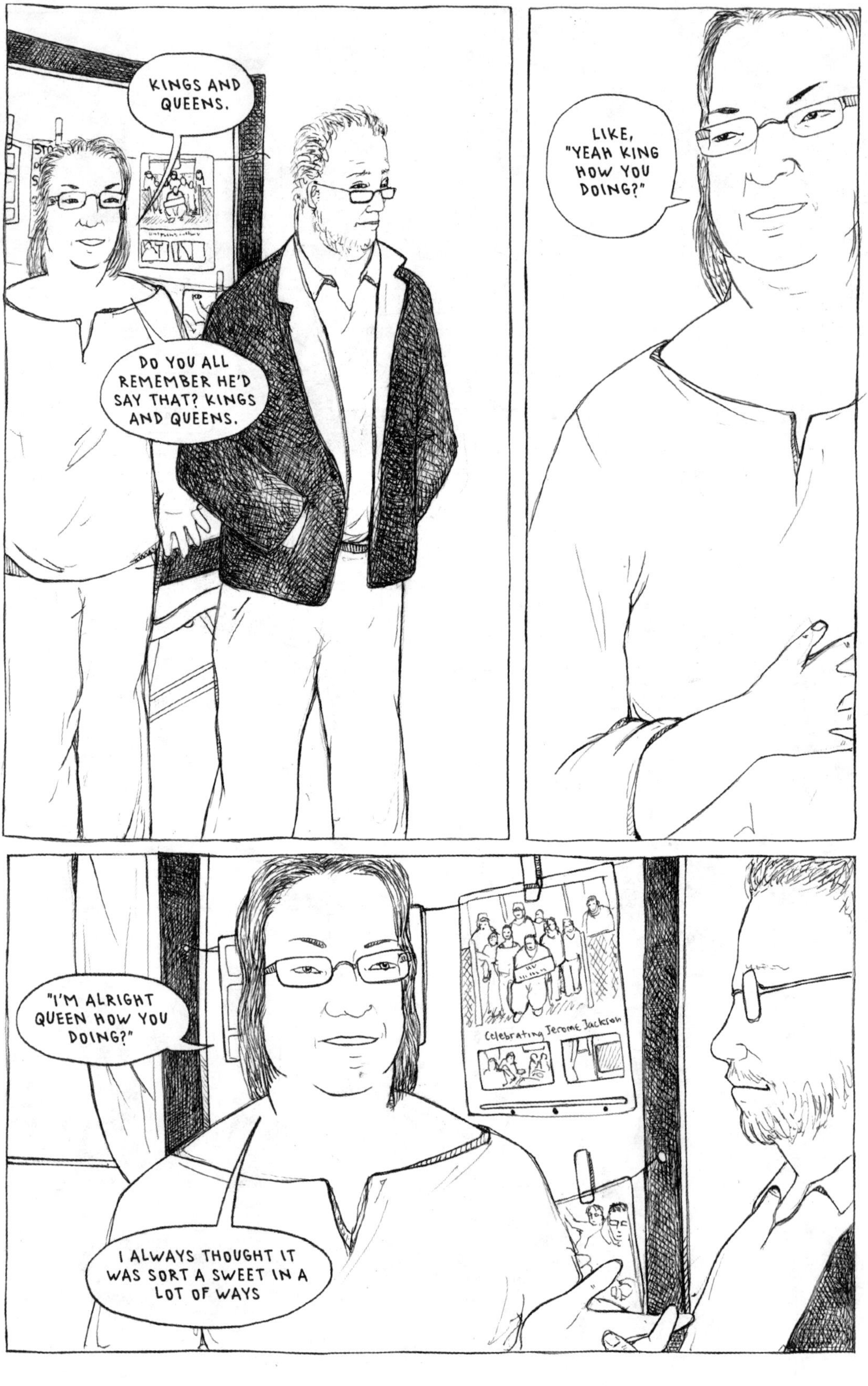
KINGS AND QUEENS.
DO YOU ALL REMEMBER HE'D SAY THAT? KINGS AND QUEENS.
LIKE, "YEAH KING HOW YOU DOING?"
"I'M ALRIGHT QUEEN HOW YOU DOING?"
Celebrating Jerome Jackson
I ALWAYS THOUGHT IT WAS SORT A SWEET IN A LOT OF WAYS

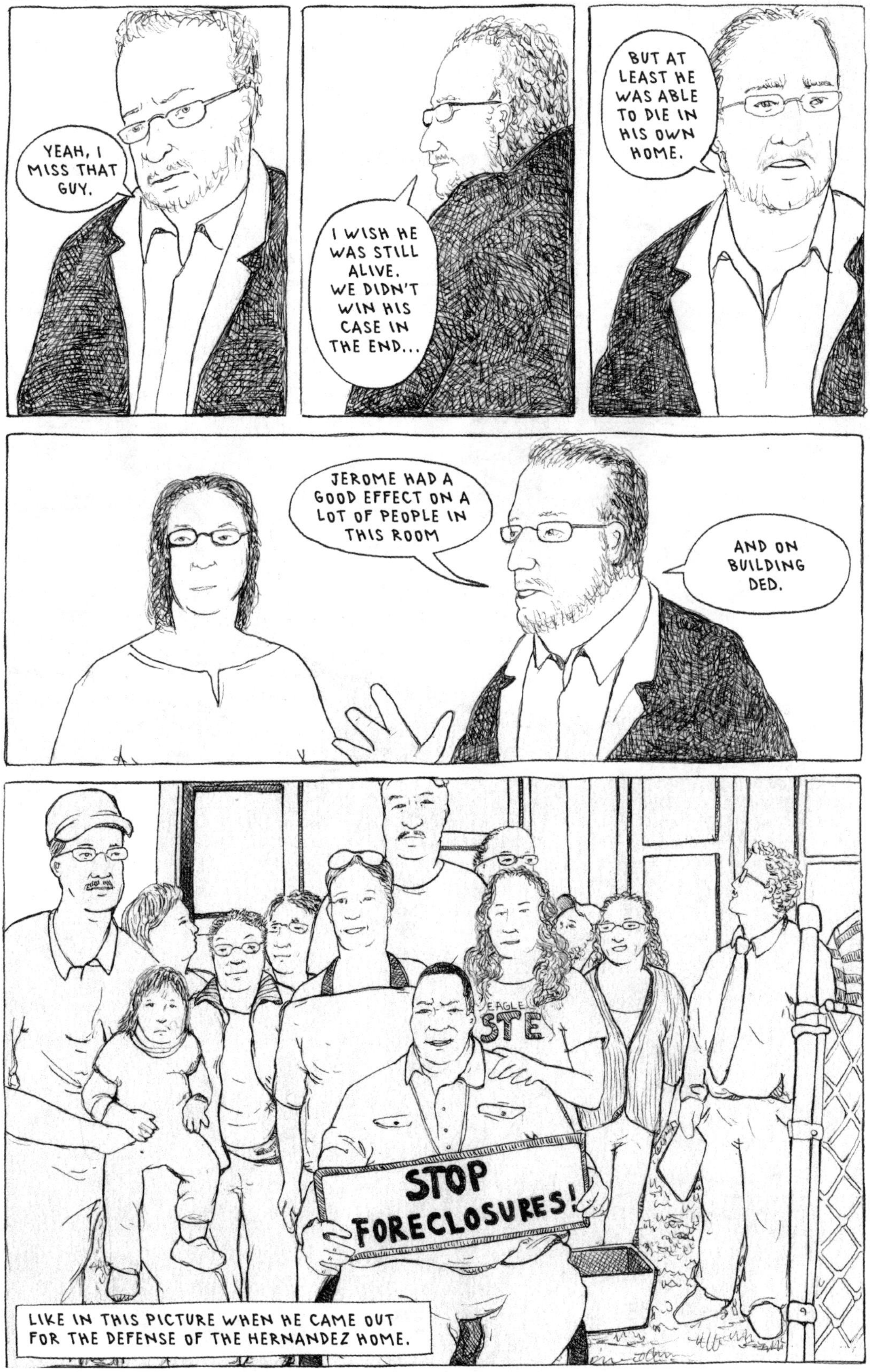
YEAH, I MISS THAT GUY.
I WISH HE WAS STILL ALIVE. WE DIDN'T WIN HIS CASE IN THE END...
BUT AT LEAST HE WAS ABLE TO DIE IN HIS OWN HOME.
JEROME HAD A GOOD EFFECT ON A LOT OF PEOPLE IN THIS ROOM
AND ON BUILDING DED.
STOP FORECLOSURES!
LIKE IN THIS PICTURE WHEN HE CAME OUT FOR THE DEFENSE OF THE HERNANDEZ HOME.

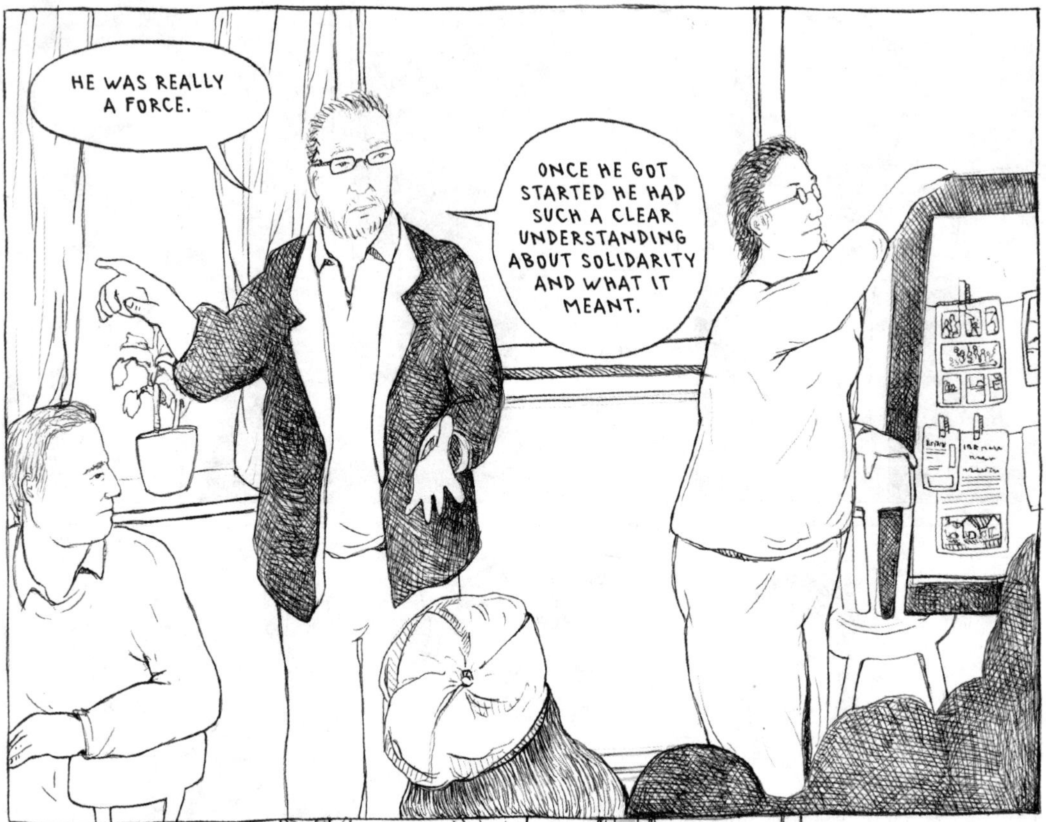
HE WAS REALLY A FORCE.
ONCE HE GOT STARTED HE HAD SUCH A CLEAR UNDERSTANDING ABOUT SOLIDARITY AND WHAT IT MEANT.

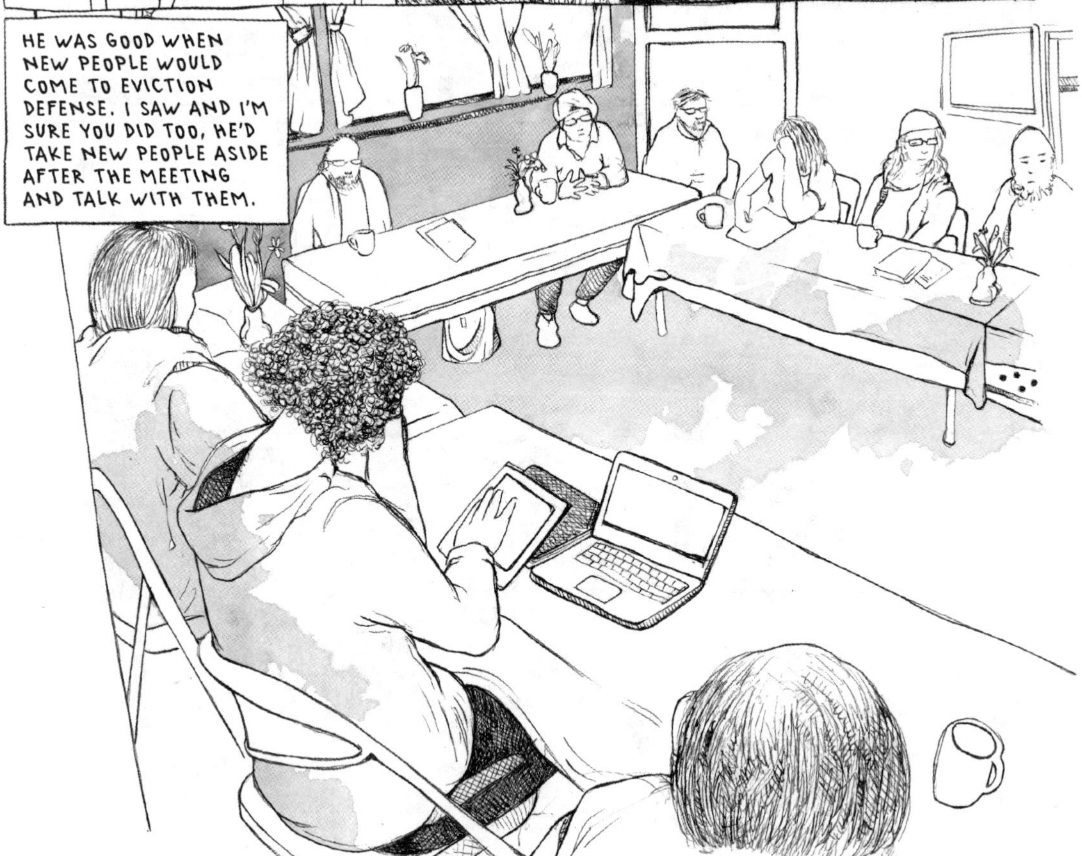
HE WAS GOOD WHEN NEW PEOPLE WOULD COME TO EVICTION DEFENSE. I SAW AND I'M SURE YOU DID TOO, HE'D TAKE NEW PEOPLE ASIDE AFTER THE MEETING AND TALK WITH THEM.

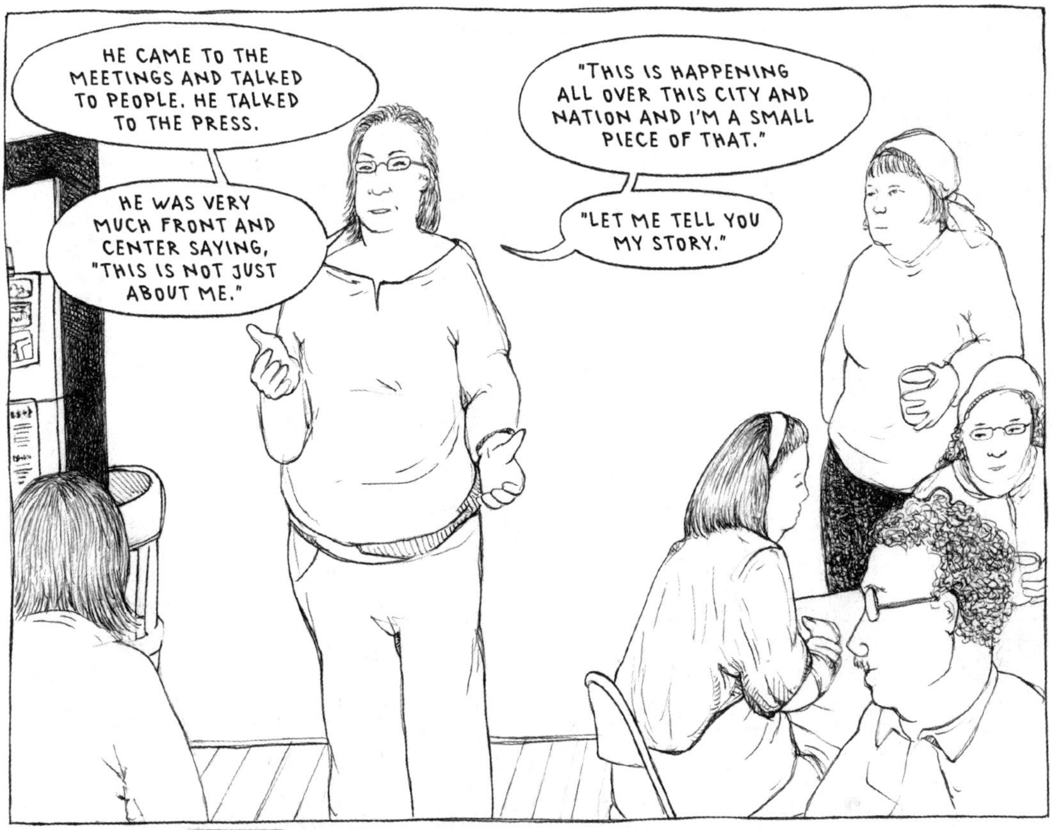
HE CAME TO THE MEETINGS AND TALKED TO PEOPLE. HE TALKED TO THE PRESS.
HE WAS VERY MUCH FRONT AND CENTER SAYING, "THIS IS NOT JUST ABOUT ME."
"THIS IS HAPPENING ALL OVER THIS CITY AND NATION AND I'M A SMALL PIECE OF THAT."
"LET ME TELL YOU MY STORY."

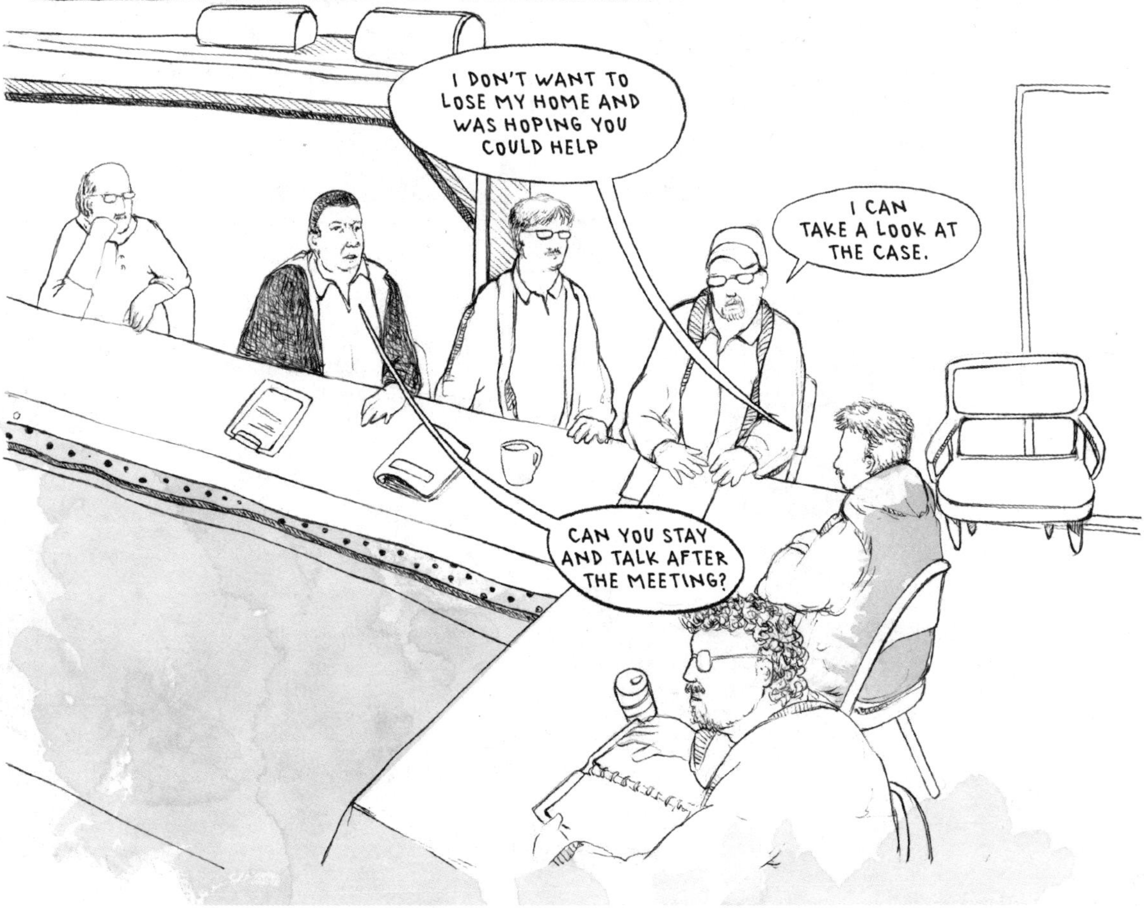
I DON'T WANT TO LOSE MY HOME AND WAS HOPING YOU COULD HELP
I CAN TAKE A LOOK AT THE CASE.
CAN YOU STAY AND TALK AFTER THE MEETING?

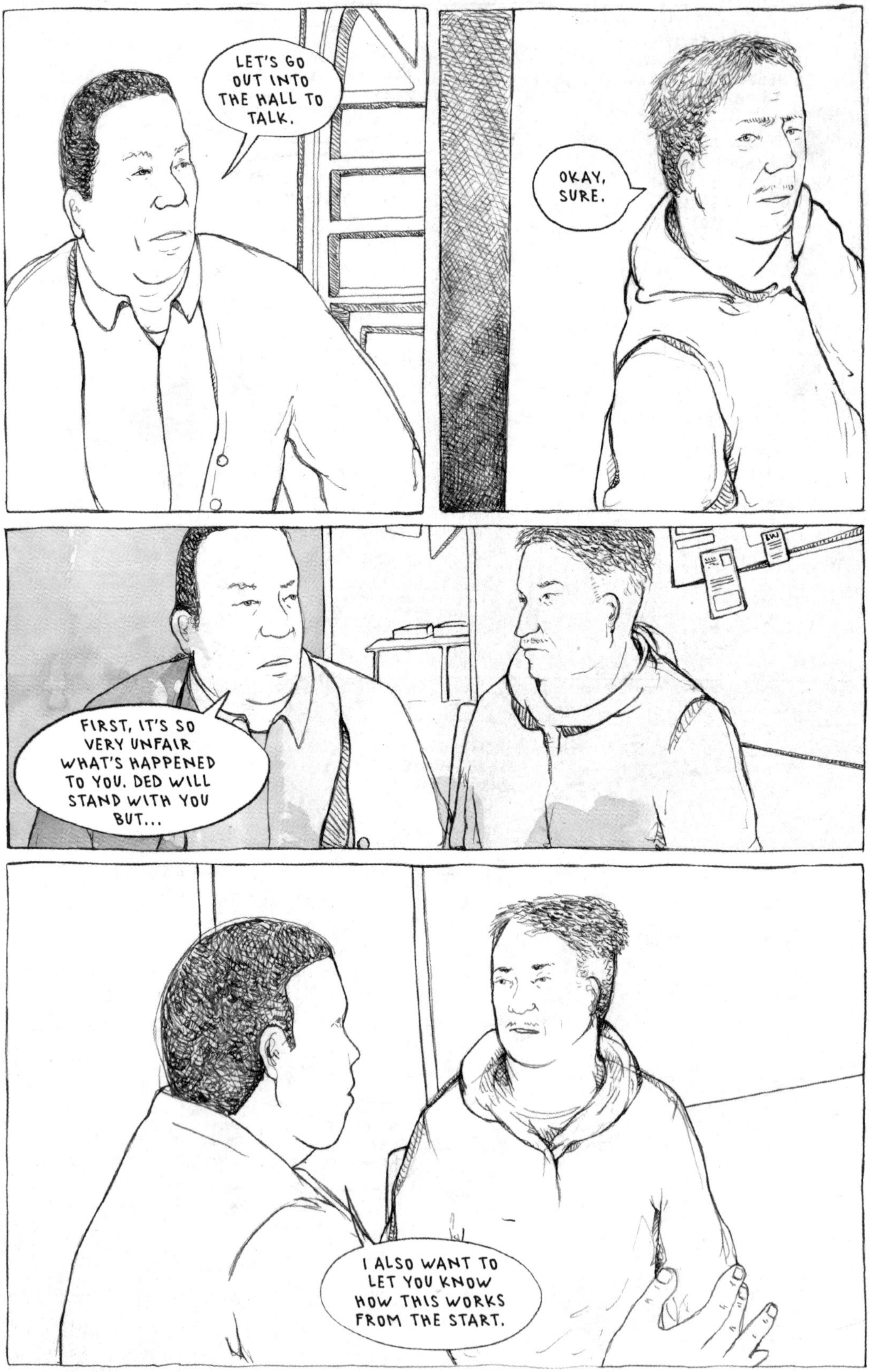
LET'S GO OUT INTO THE HALL TO TALK.
OKAY, SURE.
FIRST, IT'S SO VERY UNFAIR WHAT'S HAPPENED TO YOU. DED WILL STAND WITH YOU BUT...
I ALSO WANT TO LET YOU KNOW HOW THIS WORKS FROM THE START.

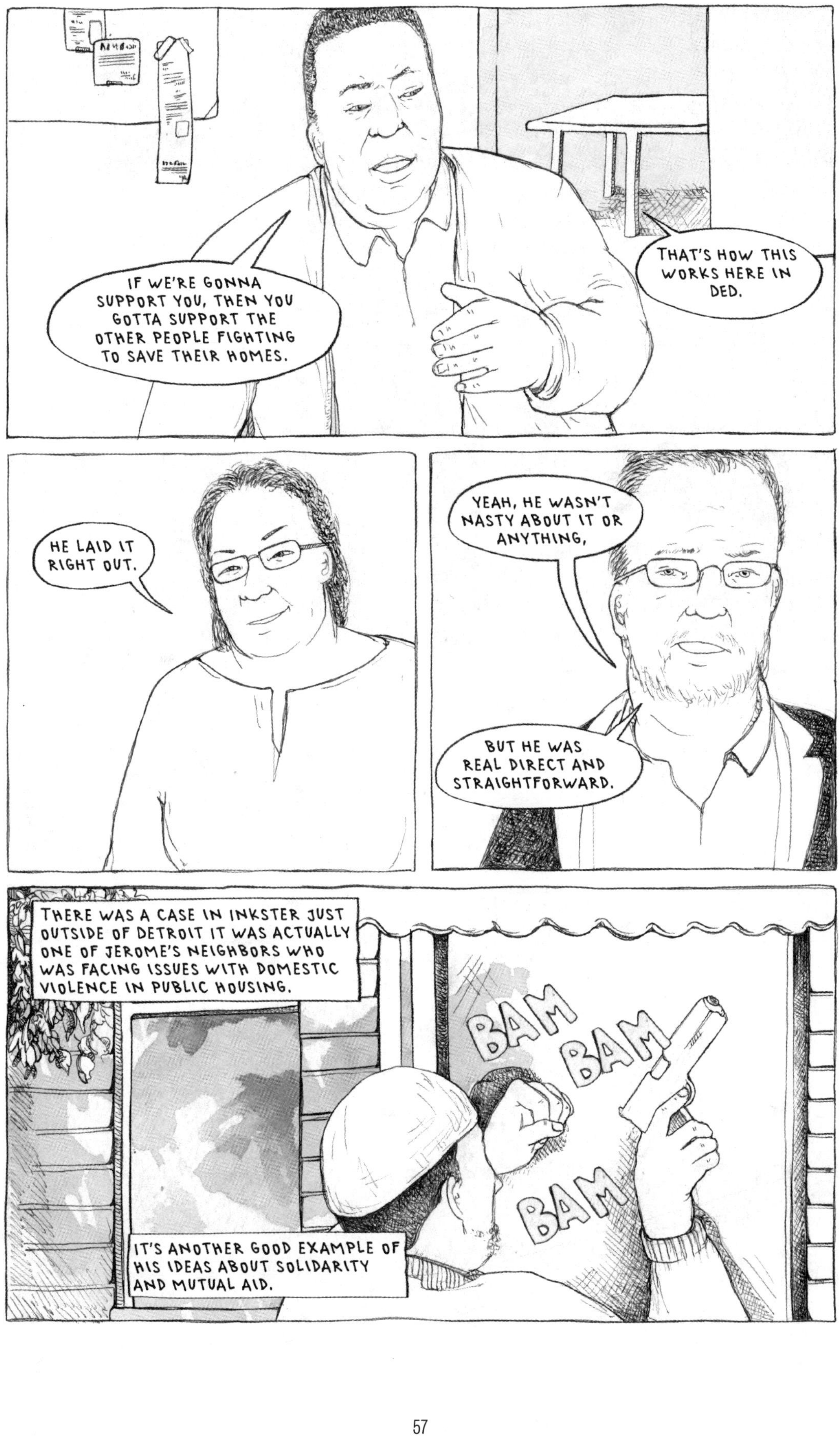
IF WE'RE GONNA SUPPORT YOU, THEN YOU GOTTA SUPPORT THE OTHER PEOPLE FIGHTING TO SAVE THEIR HOMES.
THAT'S HOW THIS WORKS HERE IN DED.
HE LAID IT RIGHT OUT.
YEAH, HE WASN'T NASTY ABOUT IT OR ANYTHING,
BUT HE WAS REAL DIRECT AND STRAIGHTFORWARD.
THERE WAS A CASE IN INKSTER JUST OUTSIDE OF DETROIT IT WAS ACTUALLY ONE OF JEROME'S NEIGHBORS WHO WAS FACING ISSUES WITH DOMESTIC VIOLENCE IN PUBLIC HOUSING.
BAM
BAM
BAM
IT'S ANOTHER GOOD EXAMPLE OF HIS IDEAS ABOUT SOLIDARITY AND MUTUAL AID.

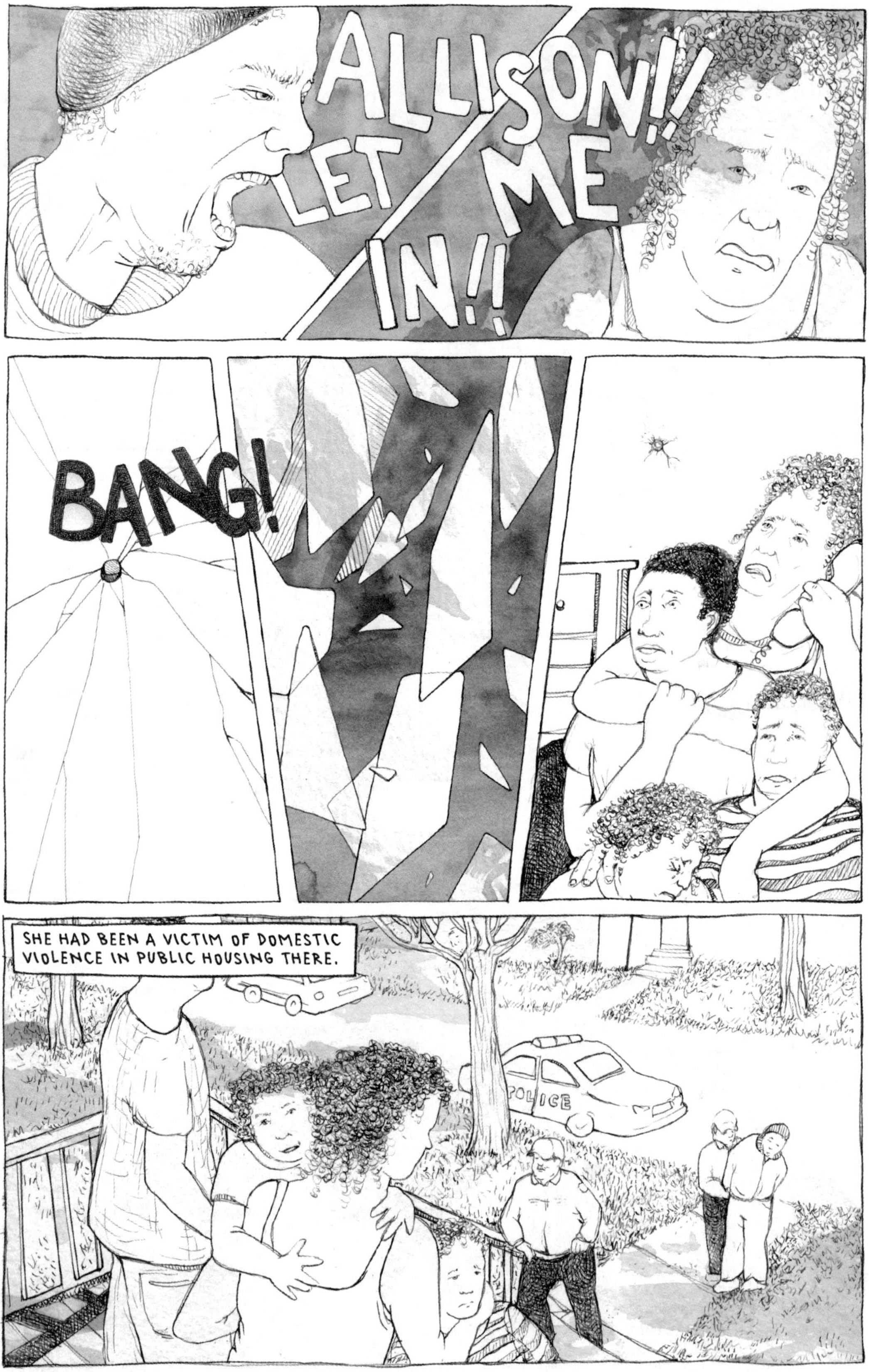
ALLISON!!
LET ME IN!!
BANG!
SHE HAD BEEN A VICTIM OF DOMESTIC VIOLENCE IN PUBLIC HOUSING THERE.
POLICE

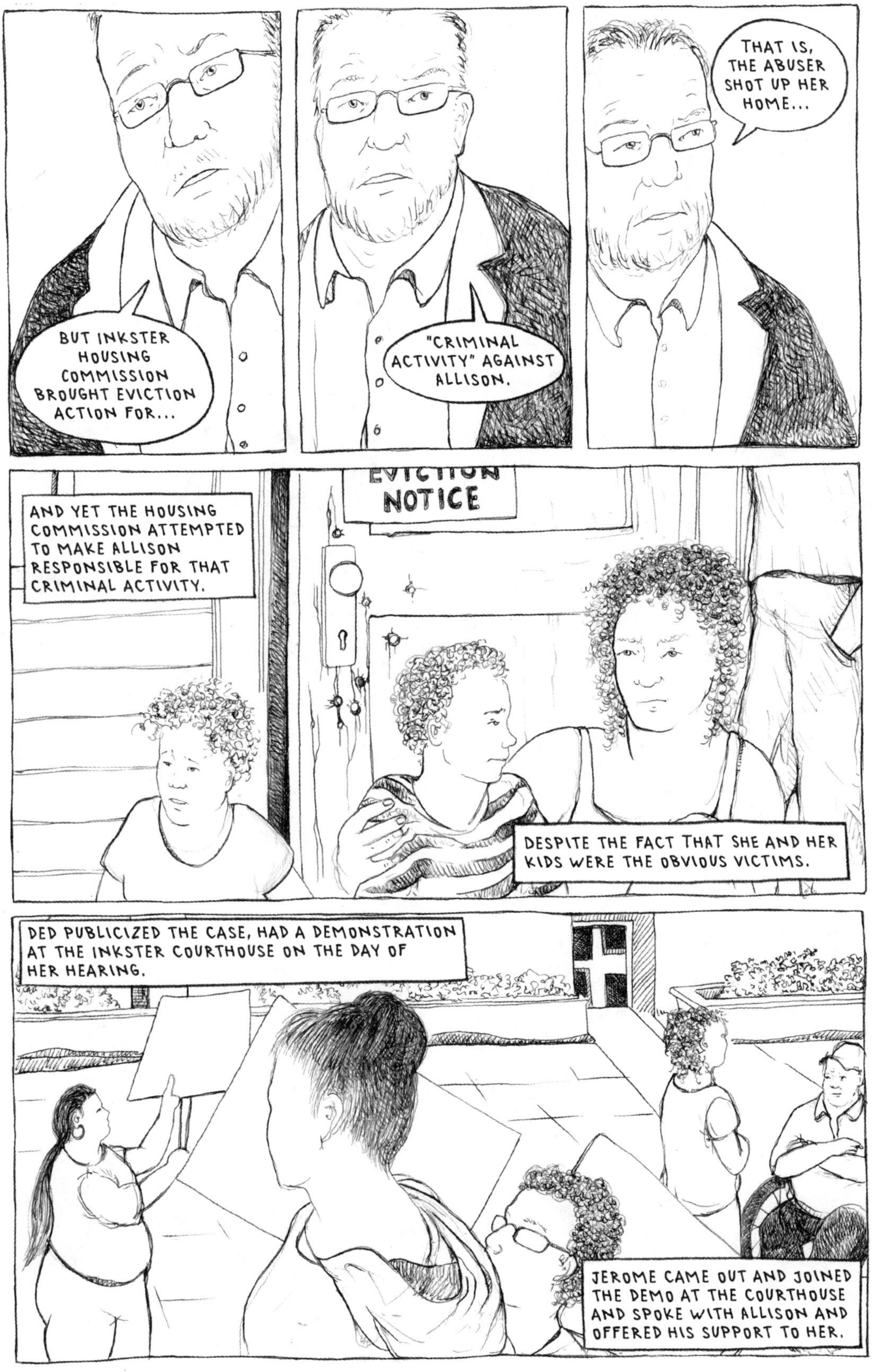
BUT INKSTER HOUSING COMMISSION BROUGHT EVICTION ACTION FOR...
"CRIMINAL ACTIVITY" AGAINST ALLISON.
THAT IS, THE ABUSER SHOT UP HER HOME...
AND YET THE HOUSING COMMISSION ATTEMPTED TO MAKE ALLISON RESPONSIBLE FOR THAT CRIMINAL ACTIVITY.
NOTICE
DESPITE THE FACT THAT SHE AND HER KIDS WERE THE OBVIOUS VICTIMS.
DED PUBLICIZED THE CASE, HAD A DEMONSTRATION AT THE INKSTER COURTHOUSE ON THE DAY OF HER HEARING.
JEROME CAME OUT AND JOINED THE DEMO AT THE COURTHOUSE AND SPOKE WITH ALLISON AND OFFERED HIS SUPPORT TO HER.

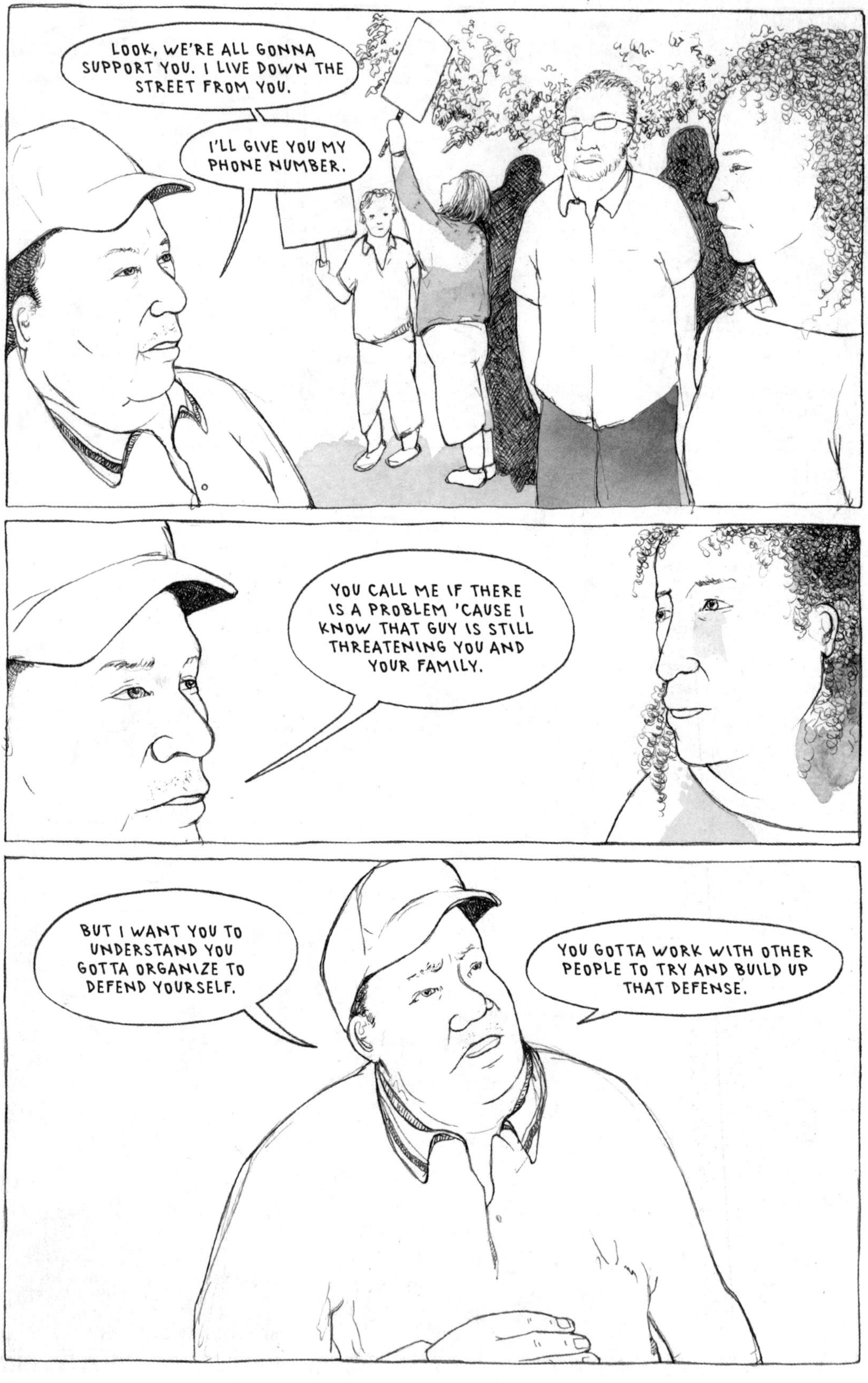
LOOK, WE'RE ALL GONNA SUPPORT YOU. I LIVE DOWN THE STREET FROM YOU.
I'LL GIVE YOU MY PHONE NUMBER.
YOU CALL ME IF THERE IS A PROBLEM 'CAUSE I KNOW THAT GUY IS STILL THREATENING YOU AND YOUR FAMILY.
BUT I WANT YOU TO UNDERSTAND YOU GOTTA ORGANIZE TO DEFEND YOURSELF.
YOU GOTTA WORK WITH OTHER PEOPLE TO TRY AND BUILD UP THAT DEFENSE.

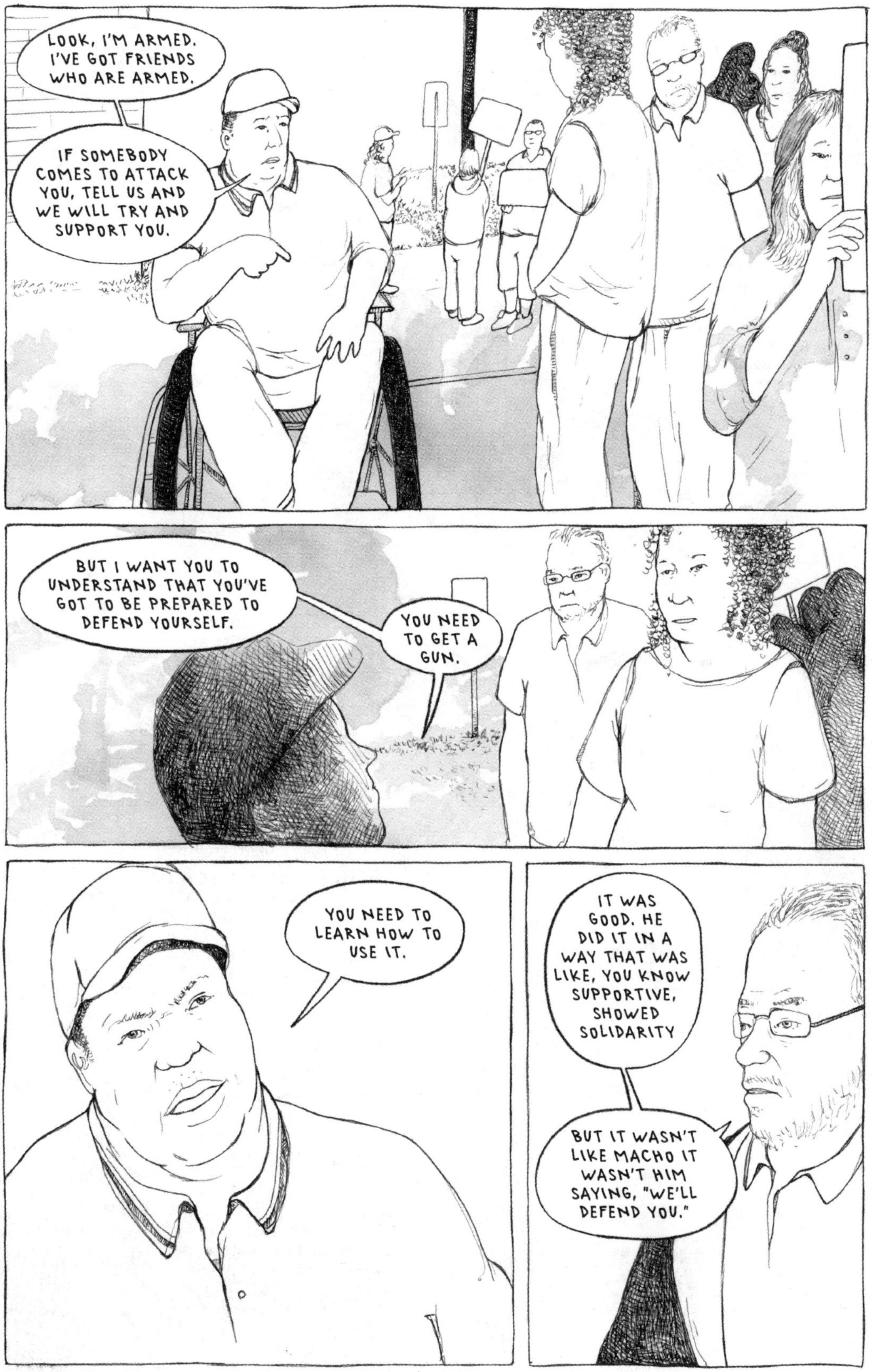
LOOK, I'M ARMED. I'VE GOT FRIENDS WHO ARE ARMED.
IF SOMEBODY COMES TO ATTACK YOU, TELL US AND WE WILL TRY AND SUPPORT YOU.
BUT I WANT YOU TO UNDERSTAND THAT YOU'VE GOT TO BE PREPARED TO DEFEND YOURSELF.
YOU NEED TO GET A GUN.
YOU NEED TO LEARN HOW TO USE IT.
IT WAS GOOD. HE DID IT IN A WAY THAT WAS LIKE, YOU KNOW SUPPORTIVE, SHOWED SOLIDARITY
BUT IT WASN'T LIKE MACHO IT WASN'T HIM SAYING, "WE'LL DEFEND YOU."

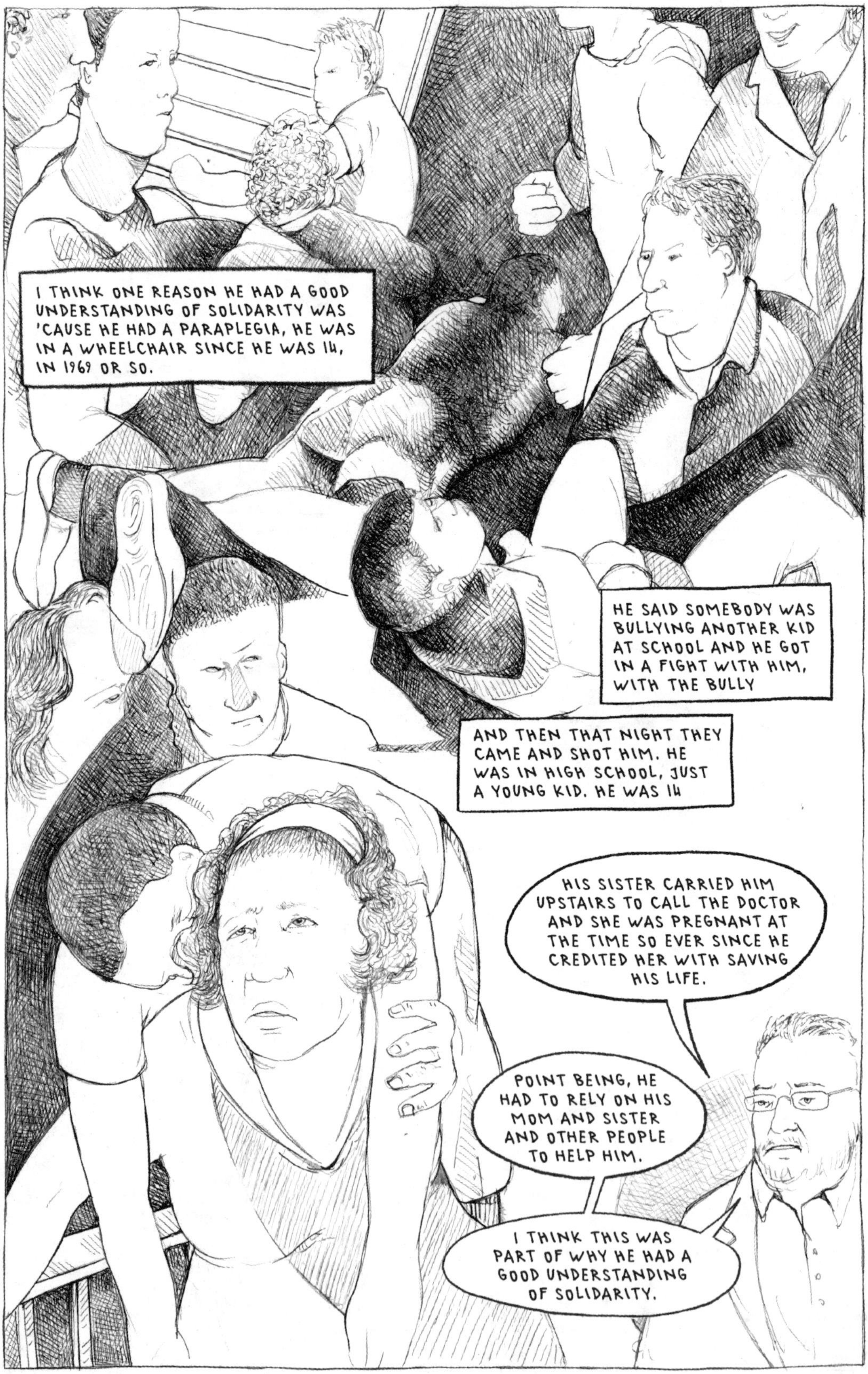
I THINK ONE REASON HE HAD A GOOD UNDERSTANDING OF SOLIDARITY WAS 'CAUSE HE HAD A PARAPLEGIA, HE WAS IN A WHEELCHAIR SINCE HE WAS 14, IN 1969 OR SO.
HE SAID SOMEBODY WAS BULLYING ANOTHER KID AT SCHOOL AND HE GOT IN A FIGHT WITH HIM, WITH THE BULLY
AND THEN THAT NIGHT THEY CAME AND SHOT HIM. HE WAS IN HIGH SCHOOL, JUST A YOUNG KID. HE WAS 14
HIS SISTER CARRIED HIM UPSTAIRS TO CALL THE DOCTOR AND SHE WAS PREGNANT AT THE TIME SO EVER SINCE HE CREDITED HER WITH SAVING HIS LIFE.
POINT BEING, HE HAD TO RELY ON HIS MOM AND SISTER AND OTHER PEOPLE TO HELP HIM.
I THINK THIS WAS PART OF WHY HE HAD A GOOD UNDERSTANDING OF SOLIDARITY.

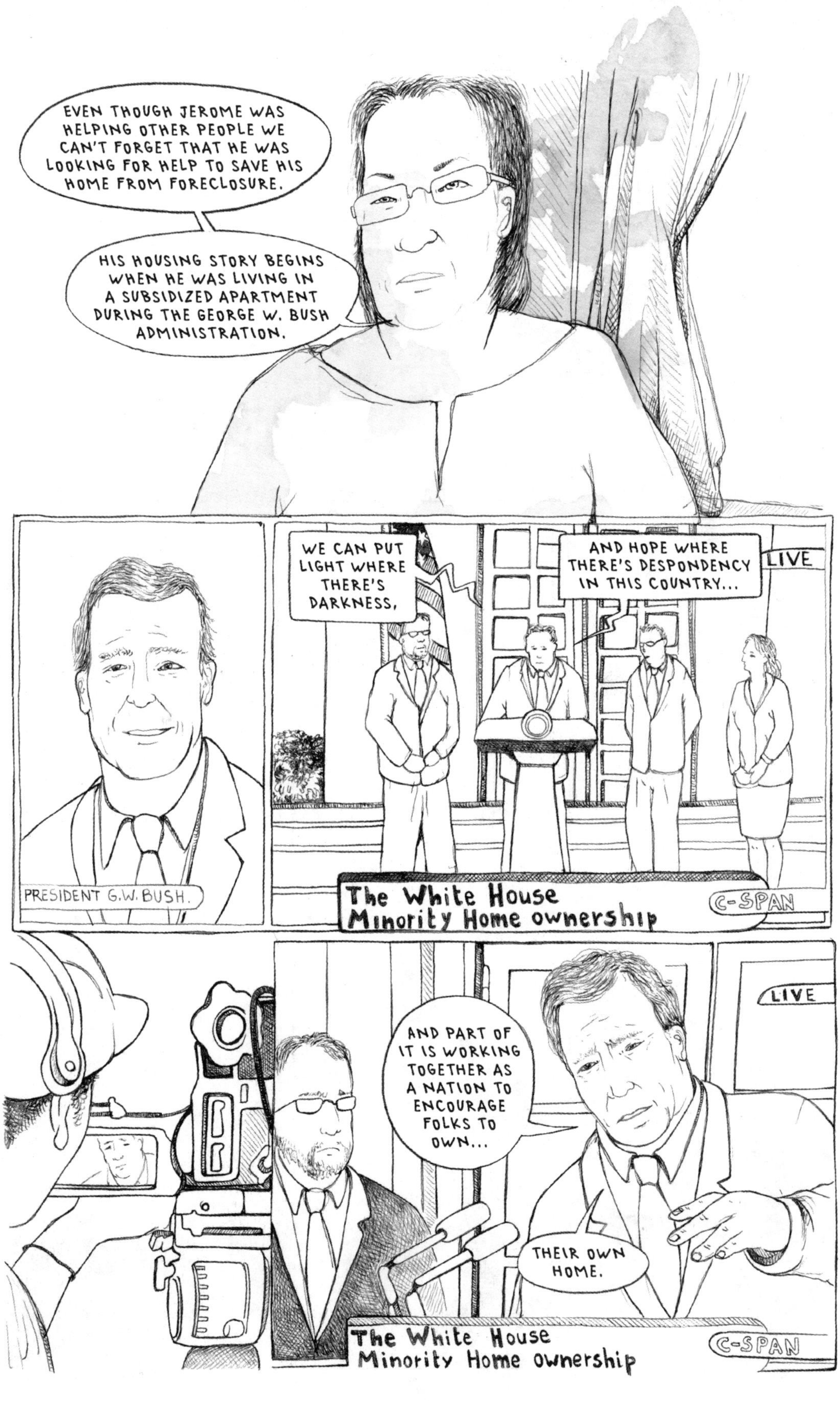
EVEN THOUGH JEROME WAS HELPING OTHER PEOPLE WE CAN'T FORGET THAT HE WAS LOOKING FOR HELP TO SAVE HIS HOME FROM FORECLOSURE.
HIS HOUSING STORY BEGINS WHEN HE WAS LIVING IN A SUBSIDIZED APARTMENT DURING THE GEORGE W. BUSH ADMINISTRATION.
PRESIDENT G.W. BUSH.
WE CAN PUT LIGHT WHERE THERE'S DARKNESS,
AND HOPE WHERE THERE'S DESPONDENCY IN THIS COUNTRY...
LIVE
The White House
Minority Home ownership
C-SPAN
LIVE
AND PART OF IT IS WORKING TOGETHER AS A NATION TO ENCOURAGE FOLKS TO OWN...
THEIR OWN HOME.
The White House
Minority Home ownership
C-SPAN

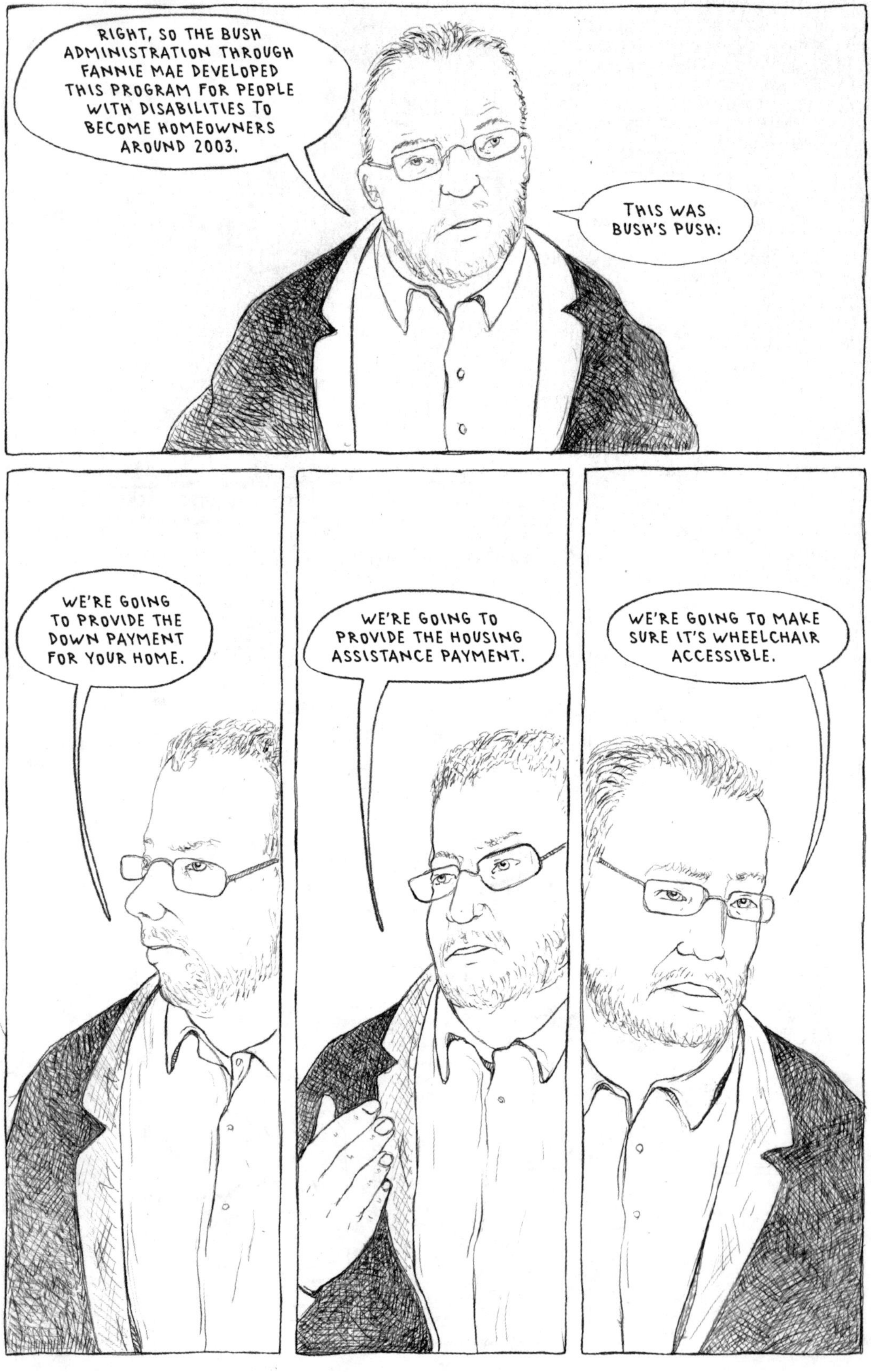
RIGHT, SO THE BUSH ADMINISTRATION THROUGH FANNIE MAE DEVELOPED THIS PROGRAM FOR PEOPLE WITH DISABILITIES TO BECOME HOMEOWNERS AROUND 2003.
THIS WAS BUSH'S PUSH:
WE'RE GOING TO PROVIDE THE DOWN PAYMENT FOR YOUR HOME.
WE'RE GOING TO PROVIDE THE HOUSING ASSISTANCE PAYMENT.
WE'RE GOING TO MAKE SURE IT'S WHEELCHAIR ACCESSIBLE.

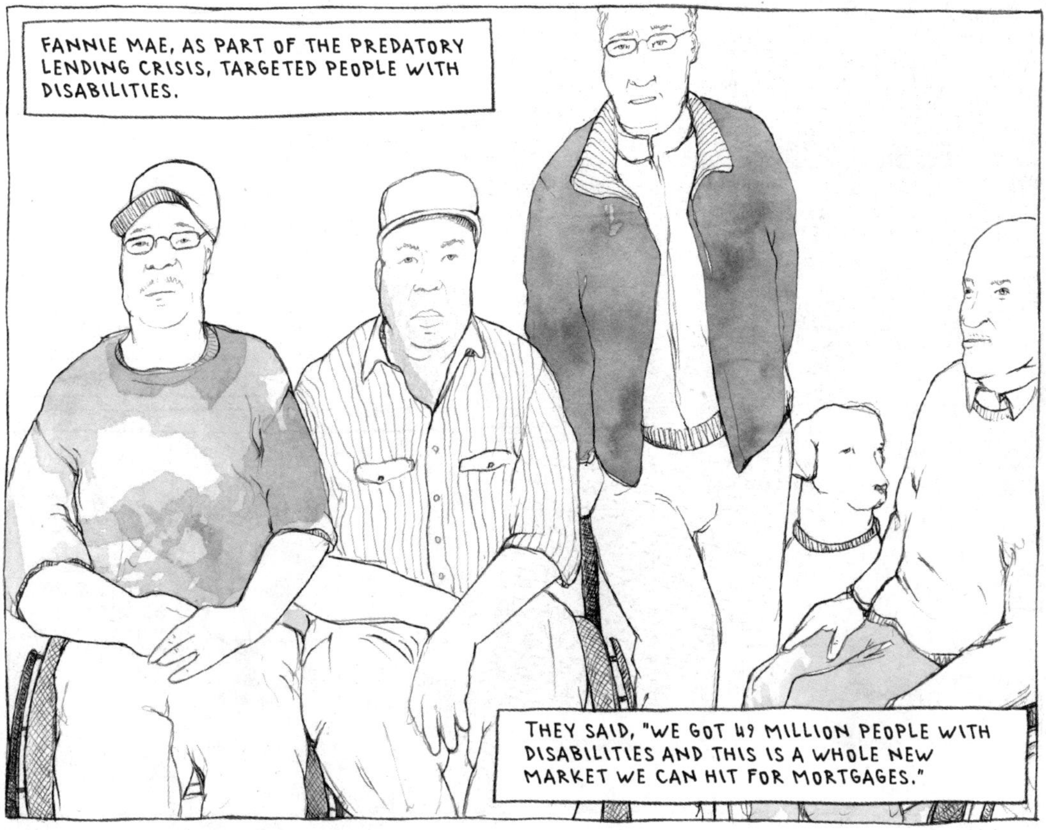
FANNIE MAE, AS PART OF THE PREDATORY LENDING CRISIS, TARGETED PEOPLE WITH DISABILITIES.
THEY SAID, "WE GOT 49 MILLION PEOPLE WITH DISABILITIES AND THIS IS A WHOLE NEW MARKET WE CAN HIT FOR MORTGAGES."

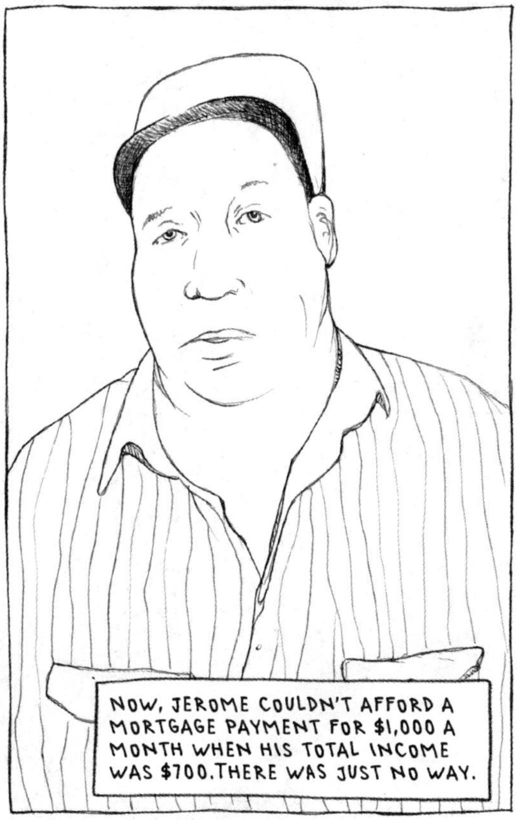
NOW, JEROME COULDN'T AFFORD A MORTGAGE PAYMENT FOR $1,000 A MONTH WHEN HIS TOTAL INCOME WAS $700. THERE WAS JUST NO WAY.

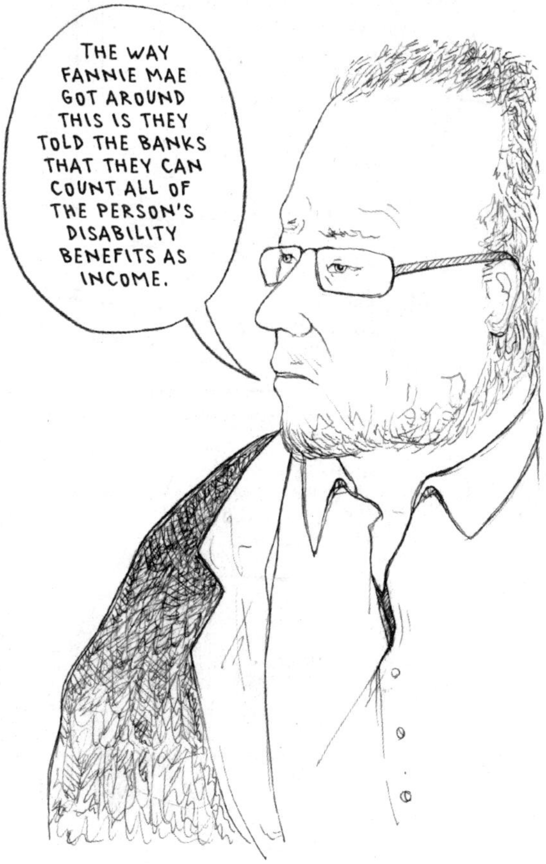
THE WAY FANNIE MAE GOT AROUND THIS IS THEY TOLD THE BANKS THAT THEY CAN COUNT ALL OF THE PERSON'S DISABILITY BENEFITS AS INCOME.

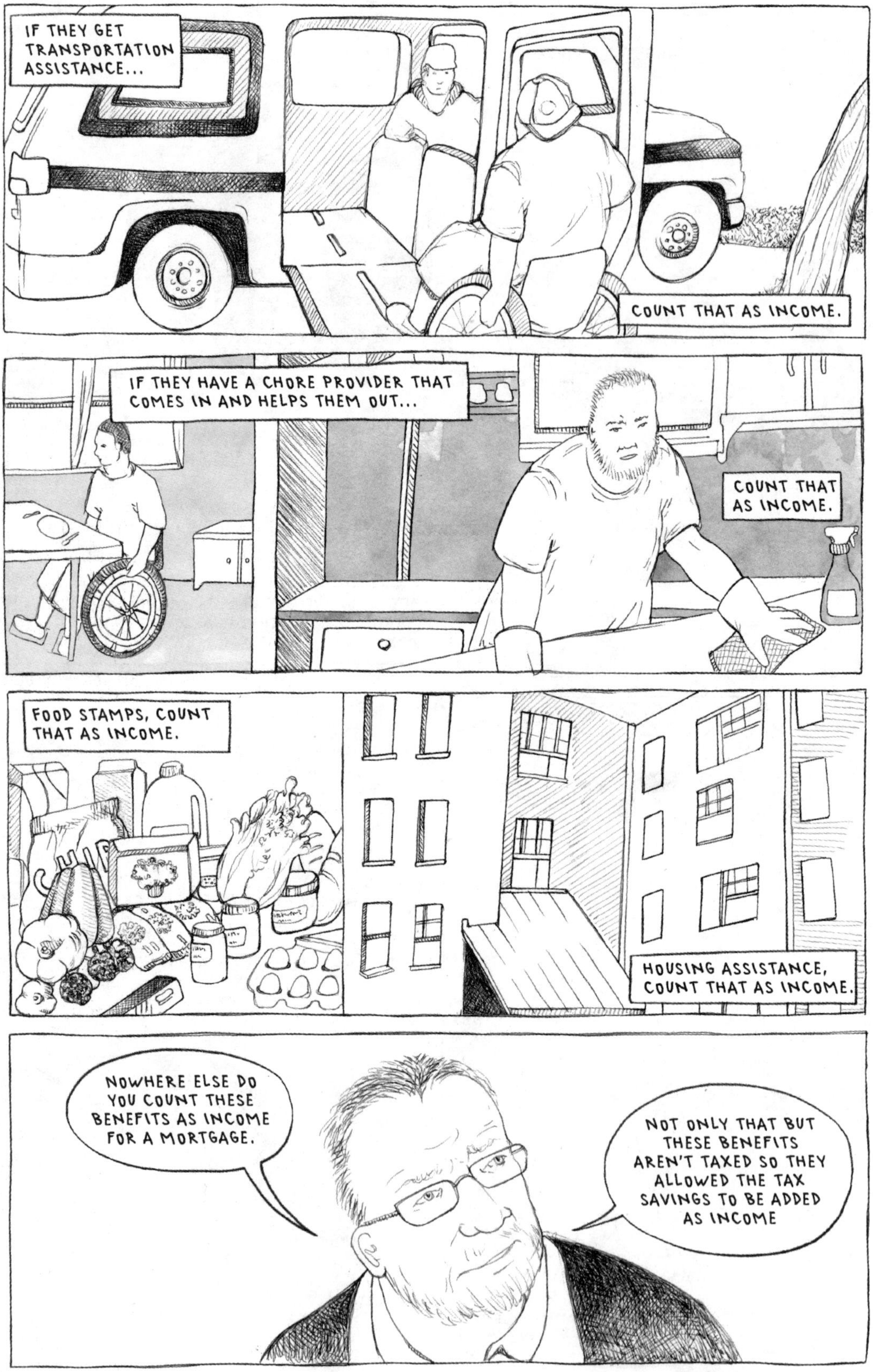
IF THEY GET TRANSPORTATION ASSISTANCE...
COUNT THAT AS INCOME.
IF THEY HAVE A CHORE PROVIDER THAT COMES IN AND HELPS THEM OUT...
COUNT THAT AS INCOME.
FOOD STAMPS, COUNT THAT AS INCOME.
HOUSING ASSISTANCE, COUNT THAT AS INCOME.
NOWHERE ELSE DO YOU COUNT THESE BENEFITS AS INCOME FOR A MORTGAGE.
NOT ONLY THAT BUT THESE BENEFITS AREN'T TAXED SO THEY ALLOWED THE TAX SAVINGS TO BE ADDED AS INCOME

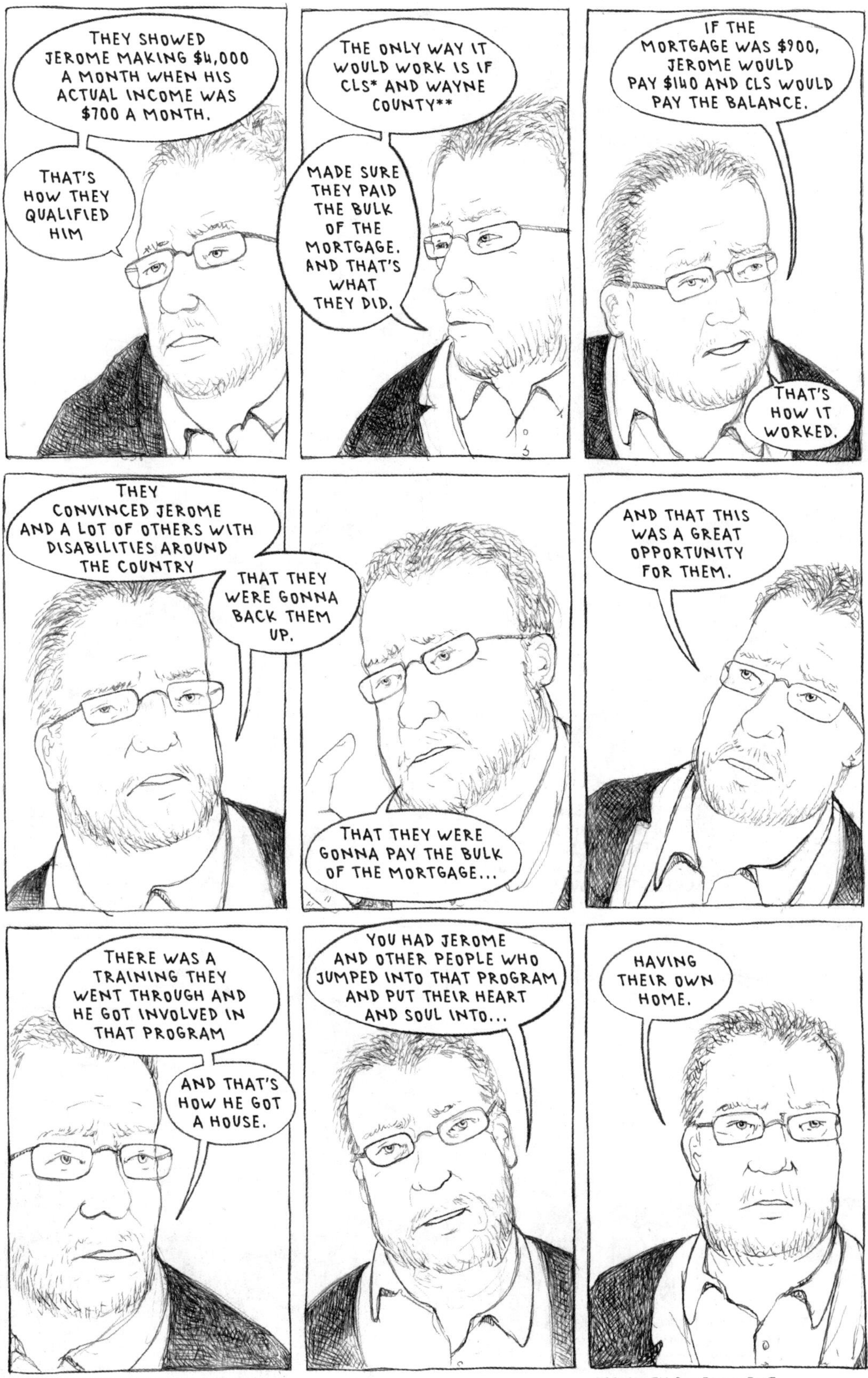
THEY SHOWED JEROME MAKING $4,000 A MONTH WHEN HIS ACTUAL INCOME WAS $700 A MONTH.
THAT'S HOW THEY QUALIFIED HIM
THE ONLY WAY IT WOULD WORK IS IF CLS* AND WAYNE COUNTY**
MADE SURE THEY PAID THE BULK OF THE MORTGAGE. AND THAT'S WHAT THEY DID.
IF THE MORTGAGE WAS $900, JEROME WOULD PAY $140 AND CLS WOULD PAY THE BALANCE.
THAT'S HOW IT WORKED.
THEY CONVINCED JEROME AND A LOT OF OTHERS WITH DISABILITIES AROUND THE COUNTRY
THAT THEY WERE GONNA BACK THEM UP.
THAT THEY WERE GONNA PAY THE BULK OF THE MORTGAGE...
AND THAT THIS WAS A GREAT OPPORTUNITY FOR THEM.
THERE WAS A TRAINING THEY WENT THROUGH AND HE GOT INVOLVED IN THAT PROGRAM
AND THAT'S HOW HE GOT A HOUSE.
YOU HAD JEROME AND OTHER PEOPLE WHO JUMPED INTO THAT PROGRAM AND PUT THEIR HEART AND SOUL INTO...
HAVING THEIR OWN HOME.

* COMMUNITY LIVING SERVICE

**COUNTY GOVERNMENT

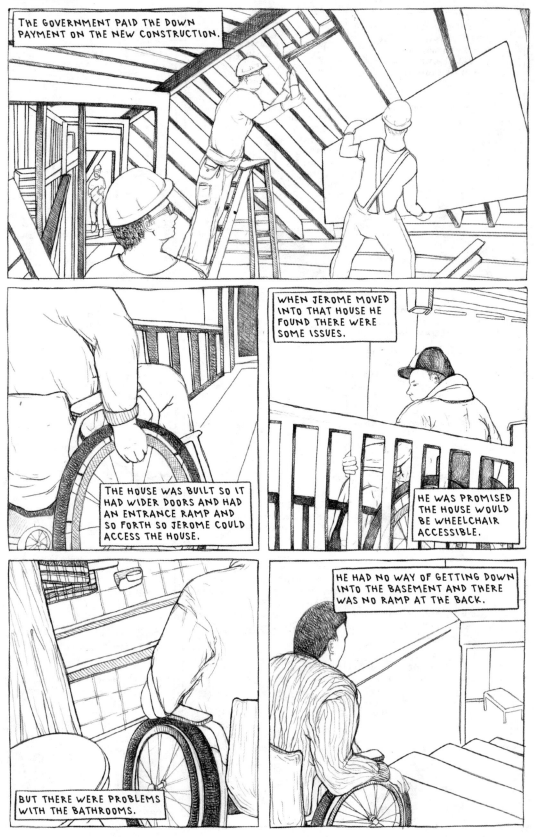

THE GOVERNMENT PAID THE DOWN PAYMENT ON THE NEW CONSTRUCTION.

WHEN JEROME MOVED INTO THAT HOUSE HE FOUND THERE WERE SOME ISSUES.

THE HOUSE WAS BUILT SO IT HAD WIDER DOORS AND HAD AN ENTRANCE RAMP AND SO FORTH SO JEROME COULD ACCESS THE HOUSE.

HE WAS PROMISED THE HOUSE WOULD BE WHEELCHAIR ACCESSIBLE.

HE HAD NO WAY OF GETTING DOWN INTO THE BASEMENT AND THERE WAS NO RAMP AT THE BACK.

BUT THERE WERE PROBLEMS WITH THE BATHROOMS.

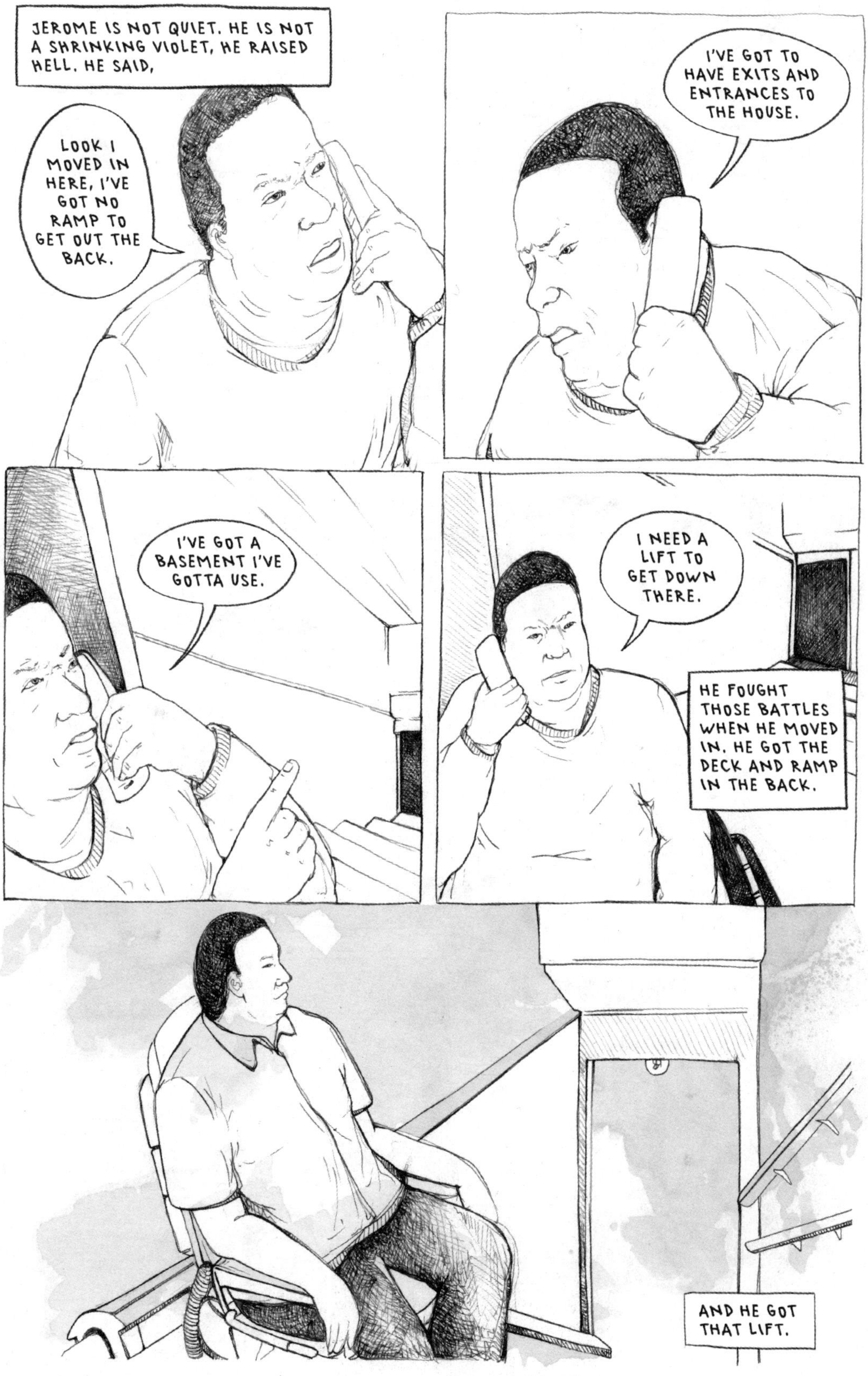
JEROME IS NOT QUIET. HE IS NOT A SHRINKING VIOLET, HE RAISED HELL. HE SAID,
LOOK I MOVED IN HERE, I'VE GOT NO RAMP TO GET OUT THE BACK.
I'VE GOT TO HAVE EXITS AND ENTRANCES TO THE HOUSE.
I'VE GOT A BASEMENT I'VE GOTTA USE.
I NEED A LIFT TO GET DOWN THERE.
HE FOUGHT THOSE BATTLES WHEN HE MOVED IN. HE GOT THE DECK AND RAMP IN THE BACK.
AND HE GOT THAT LIFT.

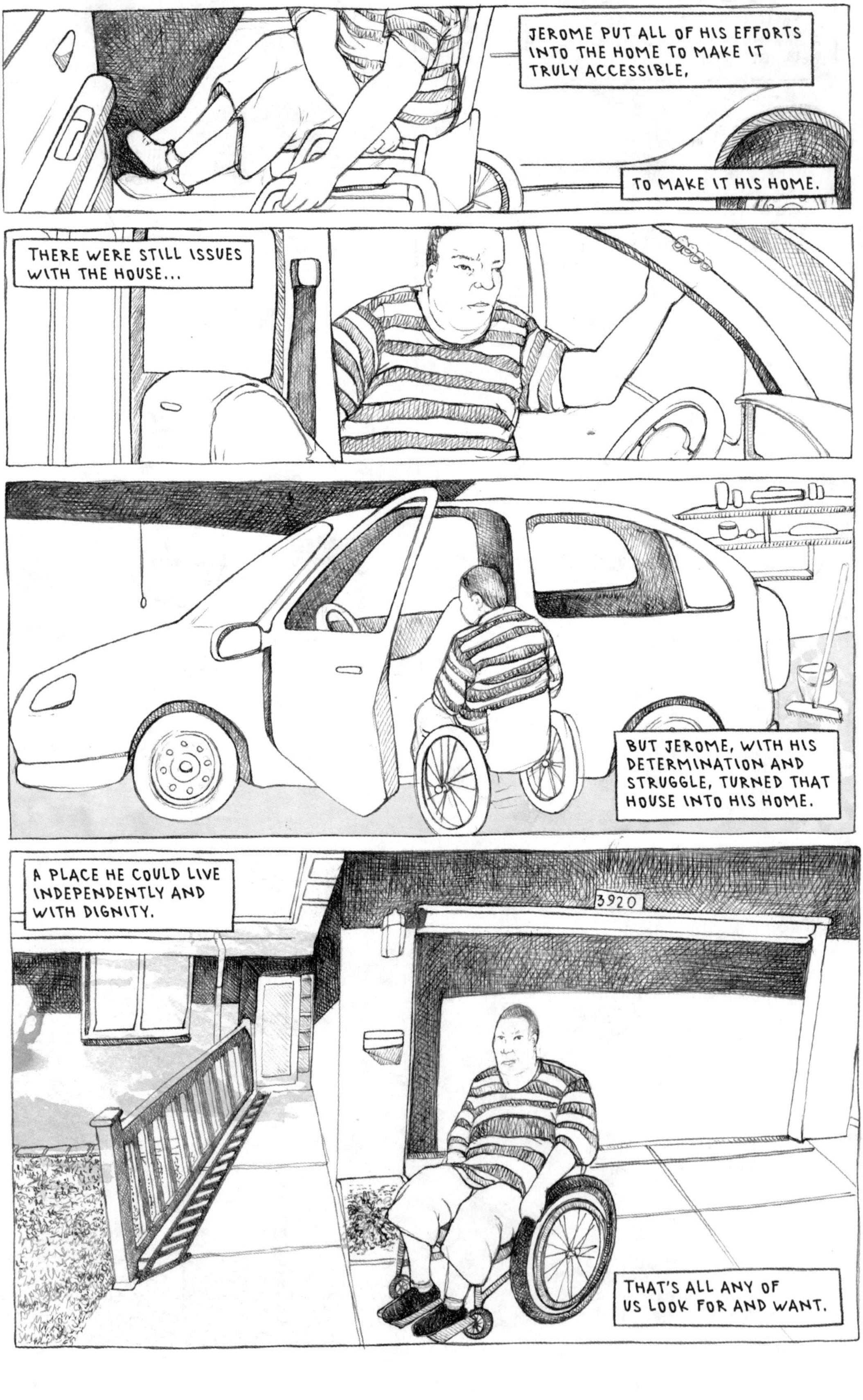
JEROME PUT ALL OF HIS EFFORTS INTO THE HOME TO MAKE IT TRULY ACCESSIBLE,
TO MAKE IT HIS HOME.
THERE WERE STILL ISSUES WITH THE HOUSE...
BUT JEROME, WITH HIS DETERMINATION AND STRUGGLE, TURNED THAT HOUSE INTO HIS HOME.
A PLACE HE COULD LIVE INDEPENDENTLY AND WITH DIGNITY.
3920
THAT'S ALL ANY OF US LOOK FOR AND WANT.

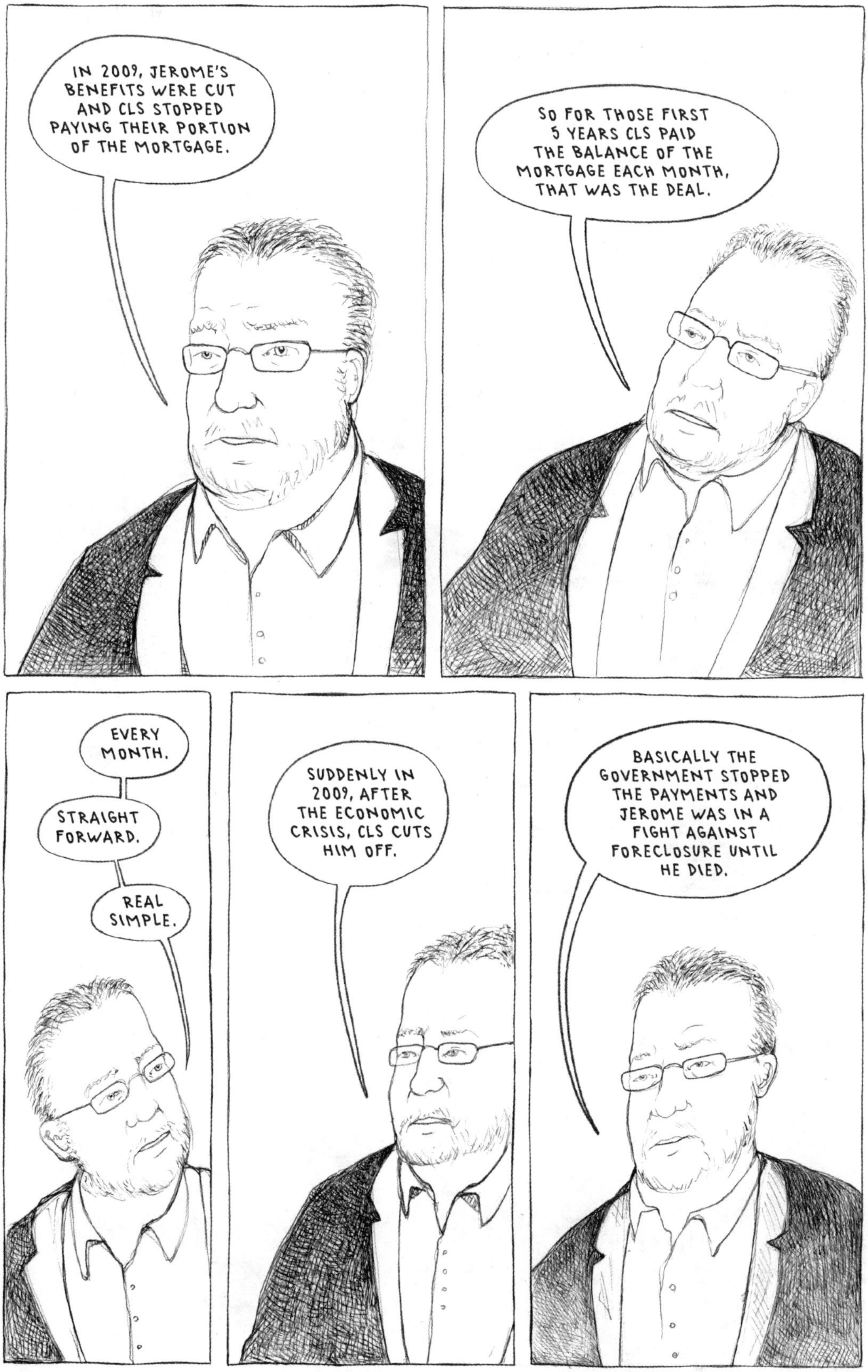
IN 2009, JEROME'S BENEFITS WERE CUT AND CLS STOPPED PAYING THEIR PORTION OF THE MORTGAGE.
SO FOR THOSE FIRST 5 YEARS CLS PAID THE BALANCE OF THE MORTGAGE EACH MONTH, THAT WAS THE DEAL.
EVERY MONTH.
STRAIGHT FORWARD.
REAL SIMPLE.
SUDDENLY IN 2009, AFTER THE ECONOMIC CRISIS, CLS CUTS HIM OFF.
BASICALLY THE GOVERNMENT STOPPED THE PAYMENTS AND JEROME WAS IN A FIGHT AGAINST FORECLOSURE UNTIL HE DIED.

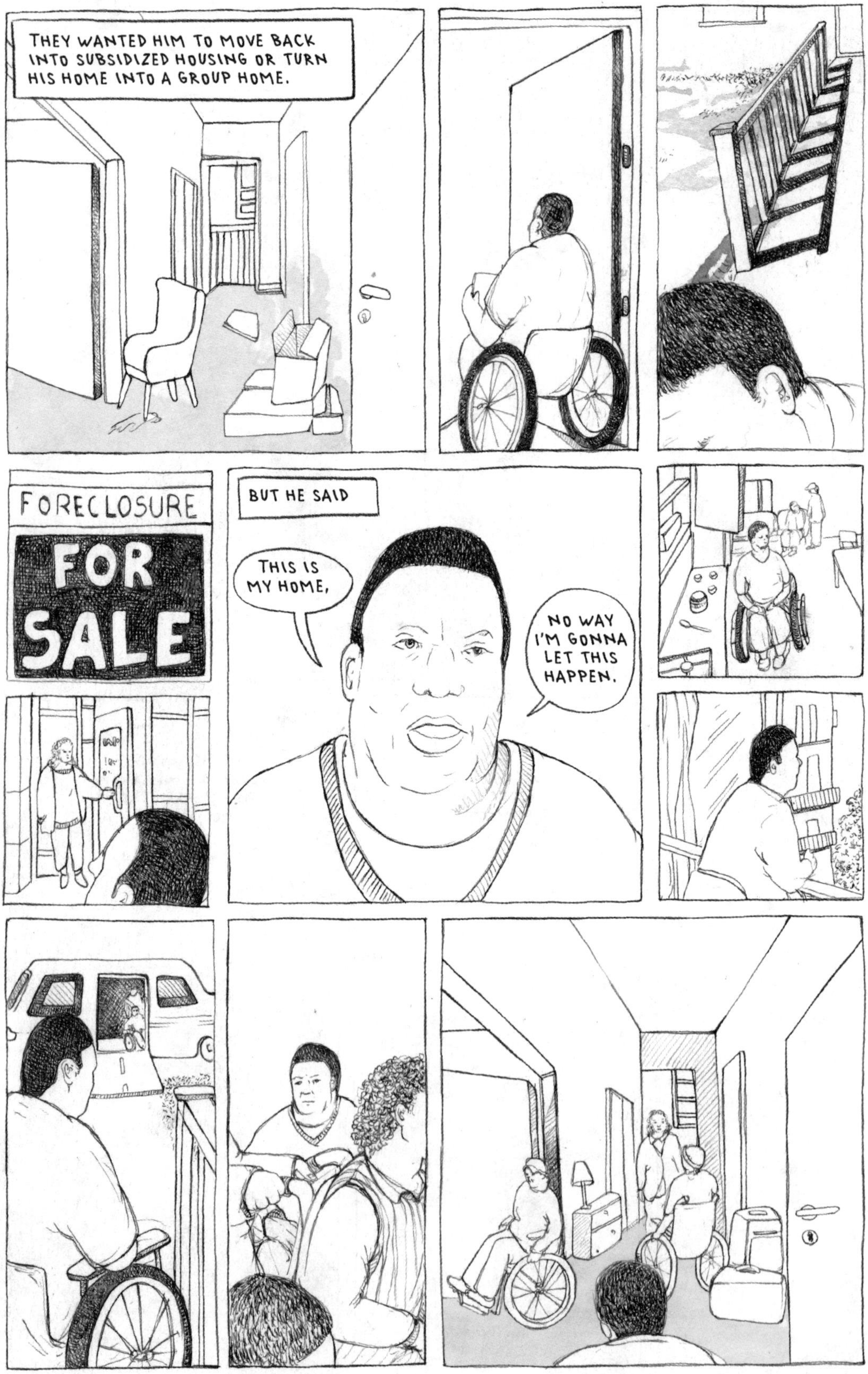
THEY WANTED HIM TO MOVE BACK INTO SUBSIDIZED HOUSING OR TURN HIS HOME INTO A GROUP HOME.
FORECLOSURE
FOR SALE
BUT HE SAID
THIS IS MY HOME,
NO WAY I'M GONNA LET THIS HAPPEN.

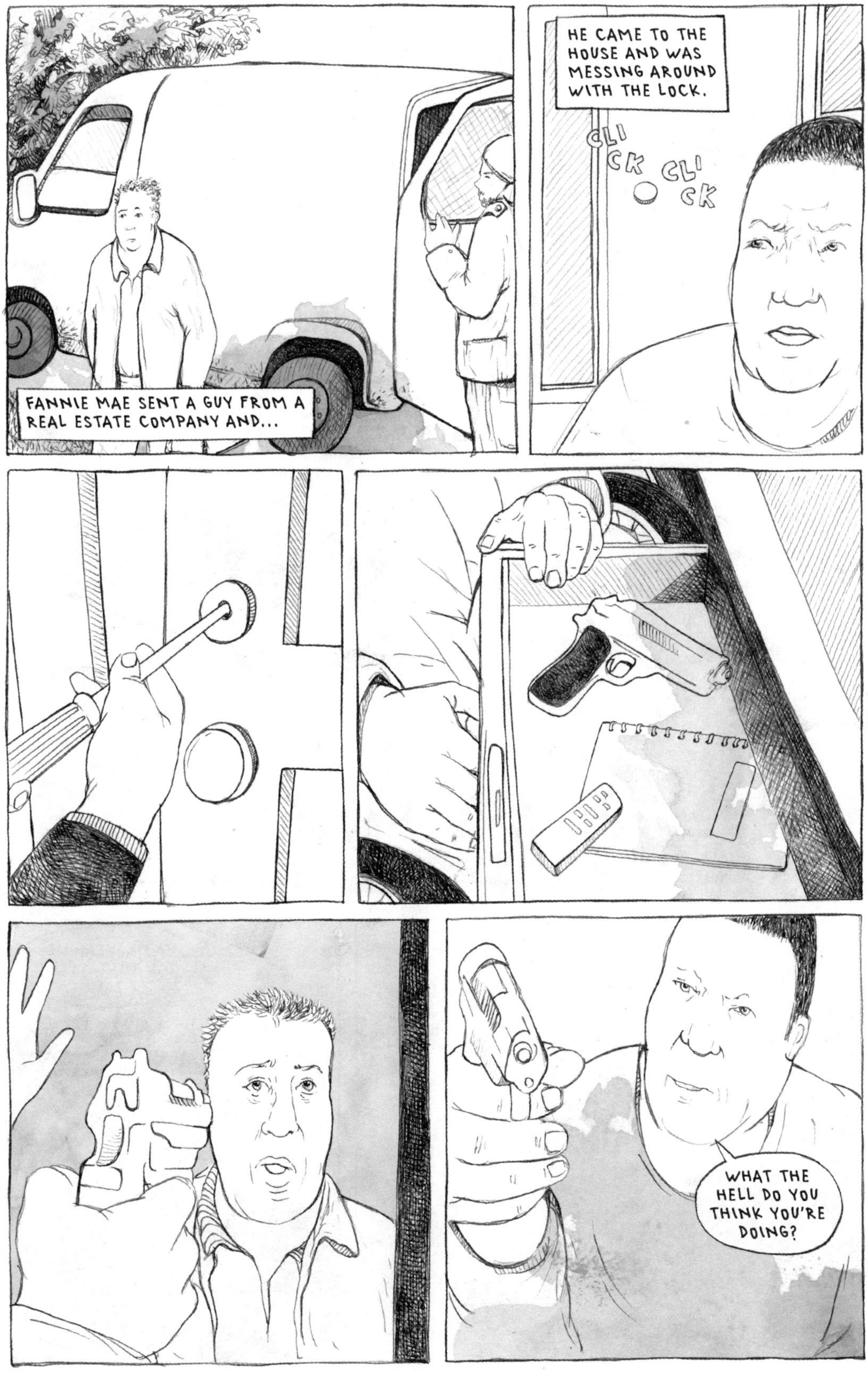
FANNIE MAE SENT A GUY FROM A REAL ESTATE COMPANY AND...
HE CAME TO THE HOUSE AND WAS MESSING AROUND WITH THE LOCK.
CLICK CLICK
WHAT THE HELL DO YOU THINK YOU'RE DOING?

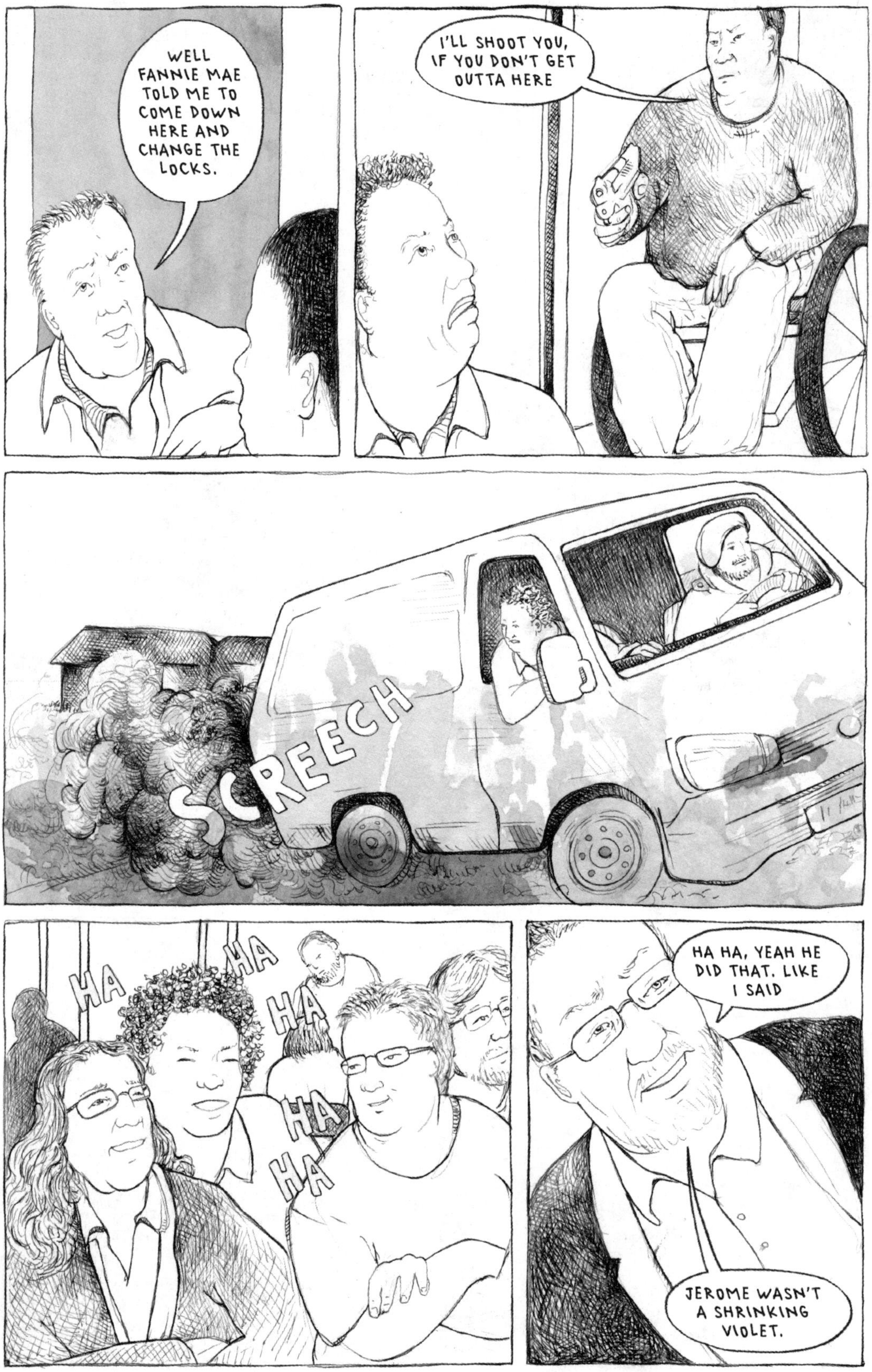
WELL FANNIE MAE TOLD ME TO COME DOWN HERE AND CHANGE THE LOCKS.
I'LL SHOOT YOU, IF YOU DON'T GET OUTTA HERE
SCREECH
HA
HA
HA
HA
HA
HA HA, YEAH HE DID THAT. LIKE I SAID
JEROME WASN'T A SHRINKING VIOLET.

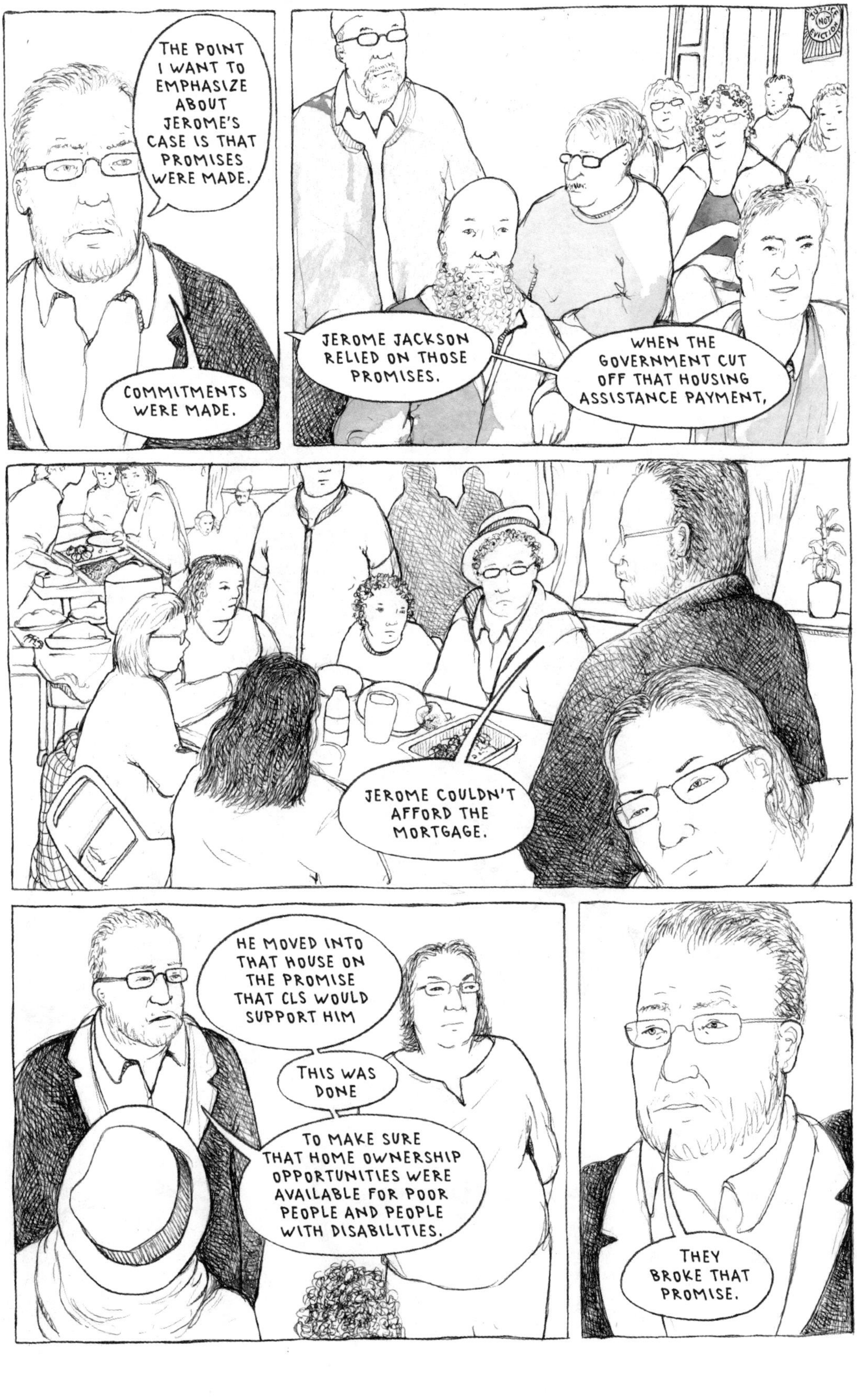
THE POINT I WANT TO EMPHASIZE ABOUT JEROME'S CASE IS THAT PROMISES WERE MADE.
COMMITMENTS WERE MADE.
JUSTICE NOT EVICTION
JEROME JACKSON RELIED ON THOSE PROMISES.
WHEN THE GOVERNMENT CUT OFF THAT HOUSING ASSISTANCE PAYMENT,
JEROME COULDN'T AFFORD THE MORTGAGE.
HE MOVED INTO THAT HOUSE ON THE PROMISE THAT CLS WOULD SUPPORT HIM
THIS WAS DONE
TO MAKE SURE THAT HOME OWNERSHIP OPPORTUNITIES WERE AVAILABLE FOR POOR PEOPLE AND PEOPLE WITH DISABILITIES.
THEY BROKE THAT PROMISE.

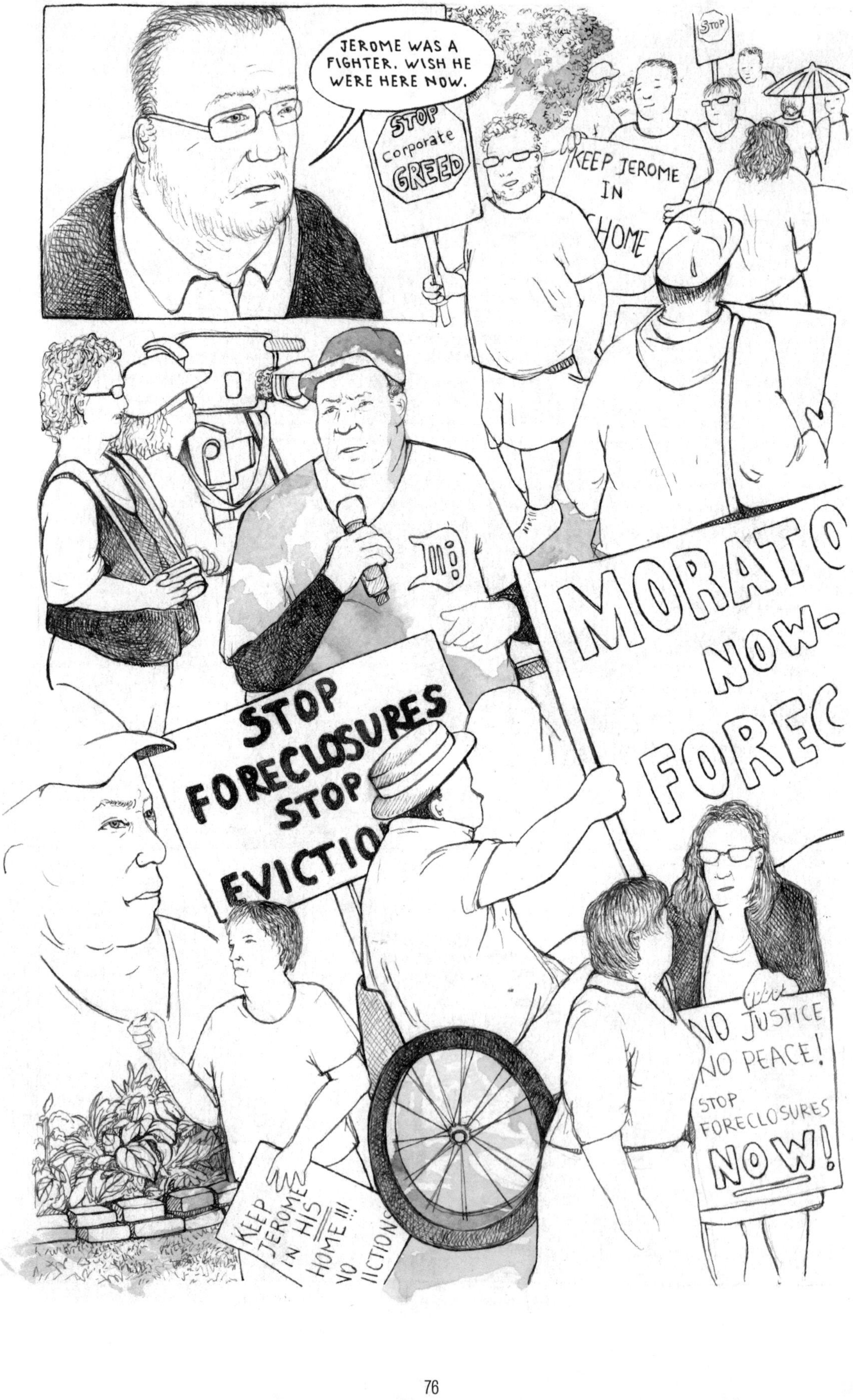
JEROME WAS A FIGHTER. WISH HE WERE HERE NOW.
STOP Corporate GREED
STOP
MORATO NOW- FOREC
STOP FORECLOSURES STOP EVICTIO
NO JUSTICE NO PEACE! STOP FORECLOSURES NOW!
KEEP JEROME IN HIS HOME!!!

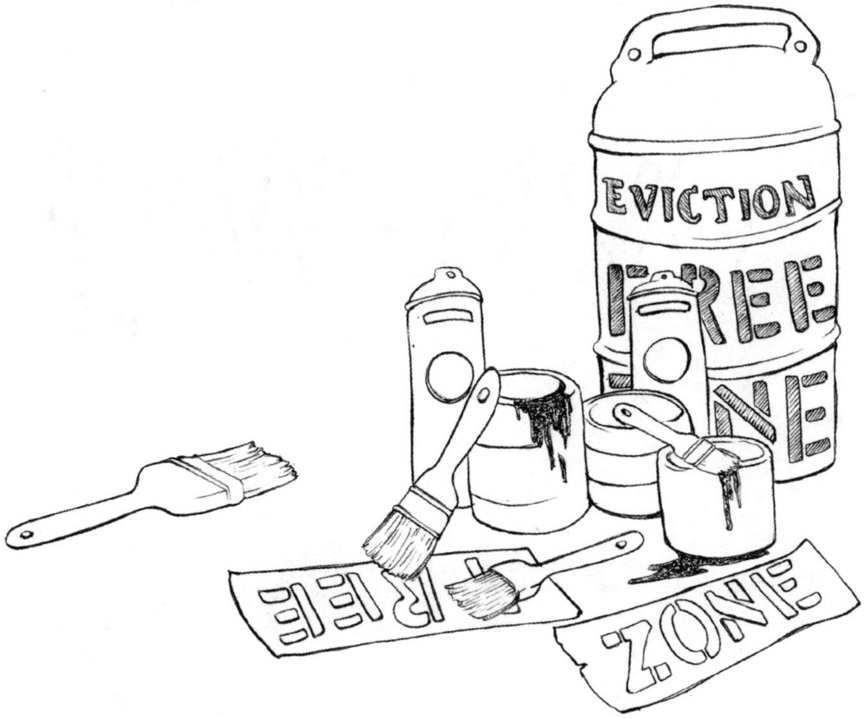
EVICTION
FREE
ZONE
ZONE

we've got to

Fight IT our

Own Way

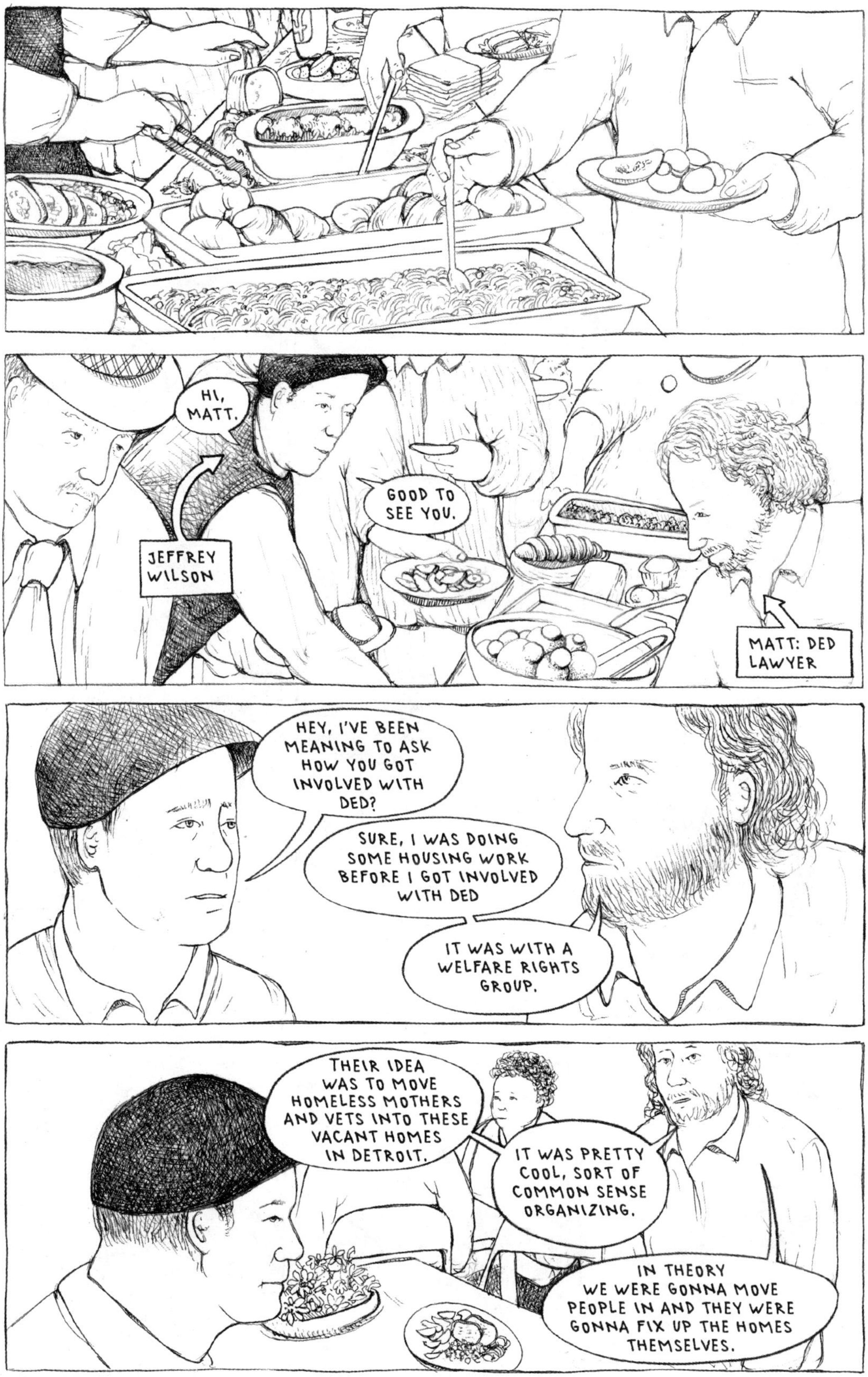
HI, MATT.
JEFFREY WILSON
GOOD TO SEE YOU.
MATT: DED LAWYER
HEY, I'VE BEEN MEANING TO ASK HOW YOU GOT INVOLVED WITH DED?
SURE, I WAS DOING SOME HOUSING WORK BEFORE I GOT INVOLVED WITH DED
IT WAS WITH A WELFARE RIGHTS GROUP.
THEIR IDEA WAS TO MOVE HOMELESS MOTHERS AND VETS INTO THESE VACANT HOMES IN DETROIT.
IT WAS PRETTY COOL, SORT OF COMMON SENSE ORGANIZING.
IN THEORY WE WERE GONNA MOVE PEOPLE IN AND THEY WERE GONNA FIX UP THE HOMES THEMSELVES.

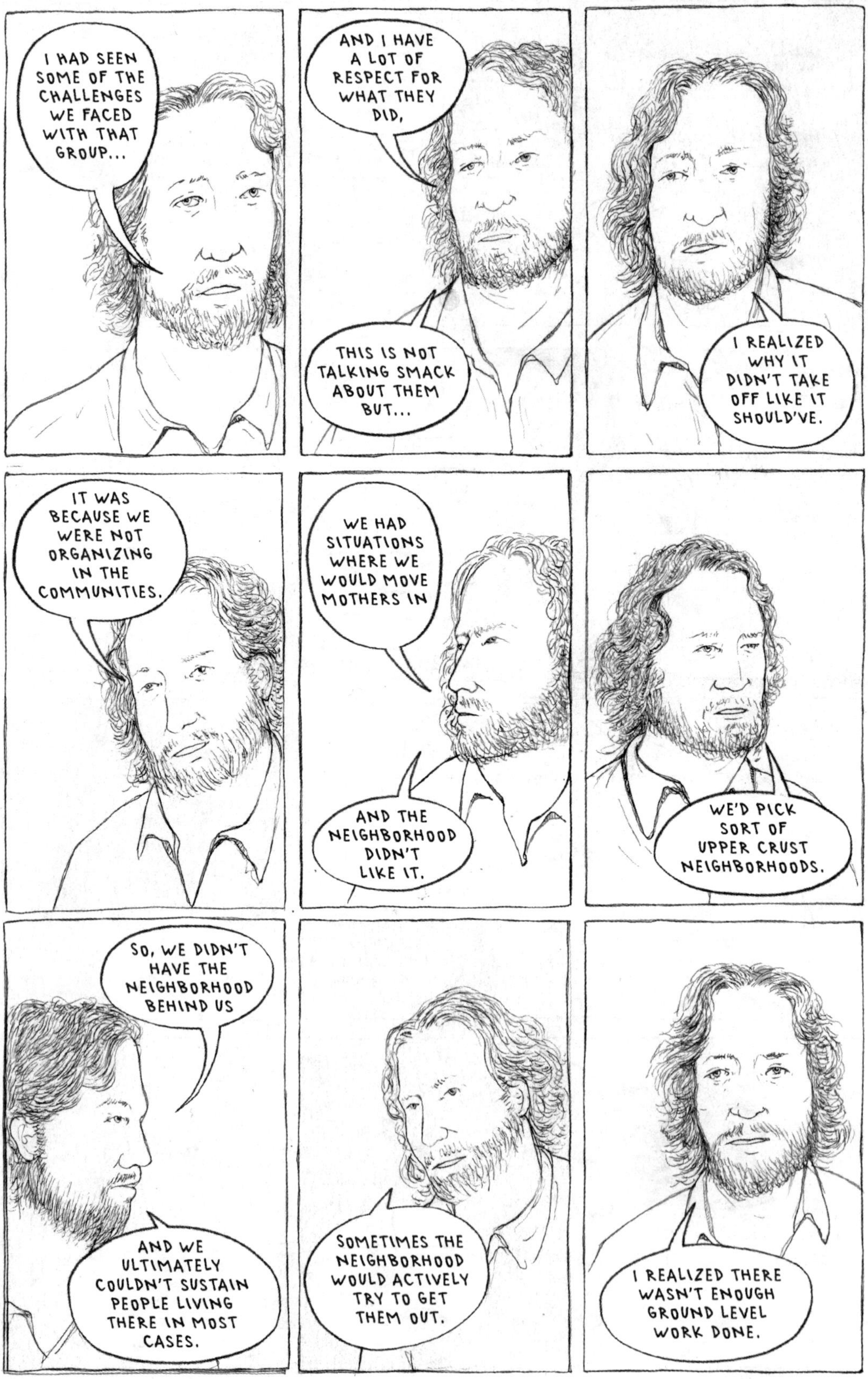
I HAD SEEN SOME OF THE CHALLENGES WE FACED WITH THAT GROUP...
AND I HAVE A LOT OF RESPECT FOR WHAT THEY DID,
THIS IS NOT TALKING SMACK ABOUT THEM BUT...
I REALIZED WHY IT DIDN'T TAKE OFF LIKE IT SHOULD'VE.
IT WAS BECAUSE WE WERE NOT ORGANIZING IN THE COMMUNITIES.
WE HAD SITUATIONS WHERE WE WOULD MOVE MOTHERS IN
AND THE NEIGHBORHOOD DIDN'T LIKE IT.
WE'D PICK SORT OF UPPER CRUST NEIGHBORHOODS.
SO, WE DIDN'T HAVE THE NEIGHBORHOOD BEHIND US
AND WE ULTIMATELY COULDN'T SUSTAIN PEOPLE LIVING THERE IN MOST CASES.
SOMETIMES THE NEIGHBORHOOD WOULD ACTIVELY TRY TO GET THEM OUT.
I REALIZED THERE WASN'T ENOUGH GROUND LEVEL WORK DONE.

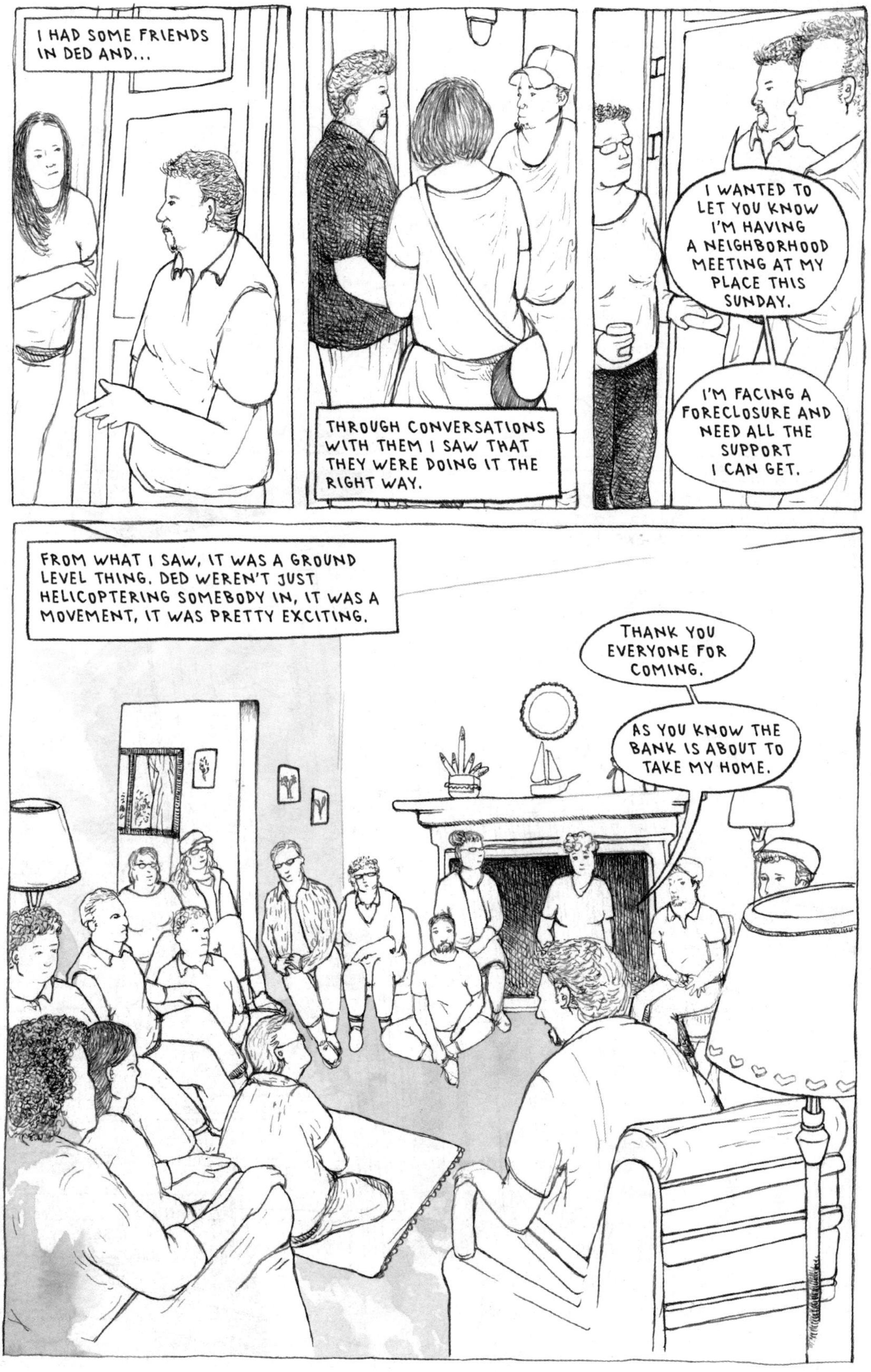
I HAD SOME FRIENDS IN DED AND...
THROUGH CONVERSATIONS WITH THEM I SAW THAT THEY WERE DOING IT THE RIGHT WAY.
I WANTED TO LET YOU KNOW I'M HAVING A NEIGHBORHOOD MEETING AT MY PLACE THIS SUNDAY.
I'M FACING A FORECLOSURE AND NEED ALL THE SUPPORT I CAN GET.
FROM WHAT I SAW, IT WAS A GROUND LEVEL THING. DED WEREN'T JUST HELICOPTERING SOMEBODY IN, IT WAS A MOVEMENT, IT WAS PRETTY EXCITING.
THANK YOU EVERYONE FOR COMING.
AS YOU KNOW THE BANK IS ABOUT TO TAKE MY HOME.

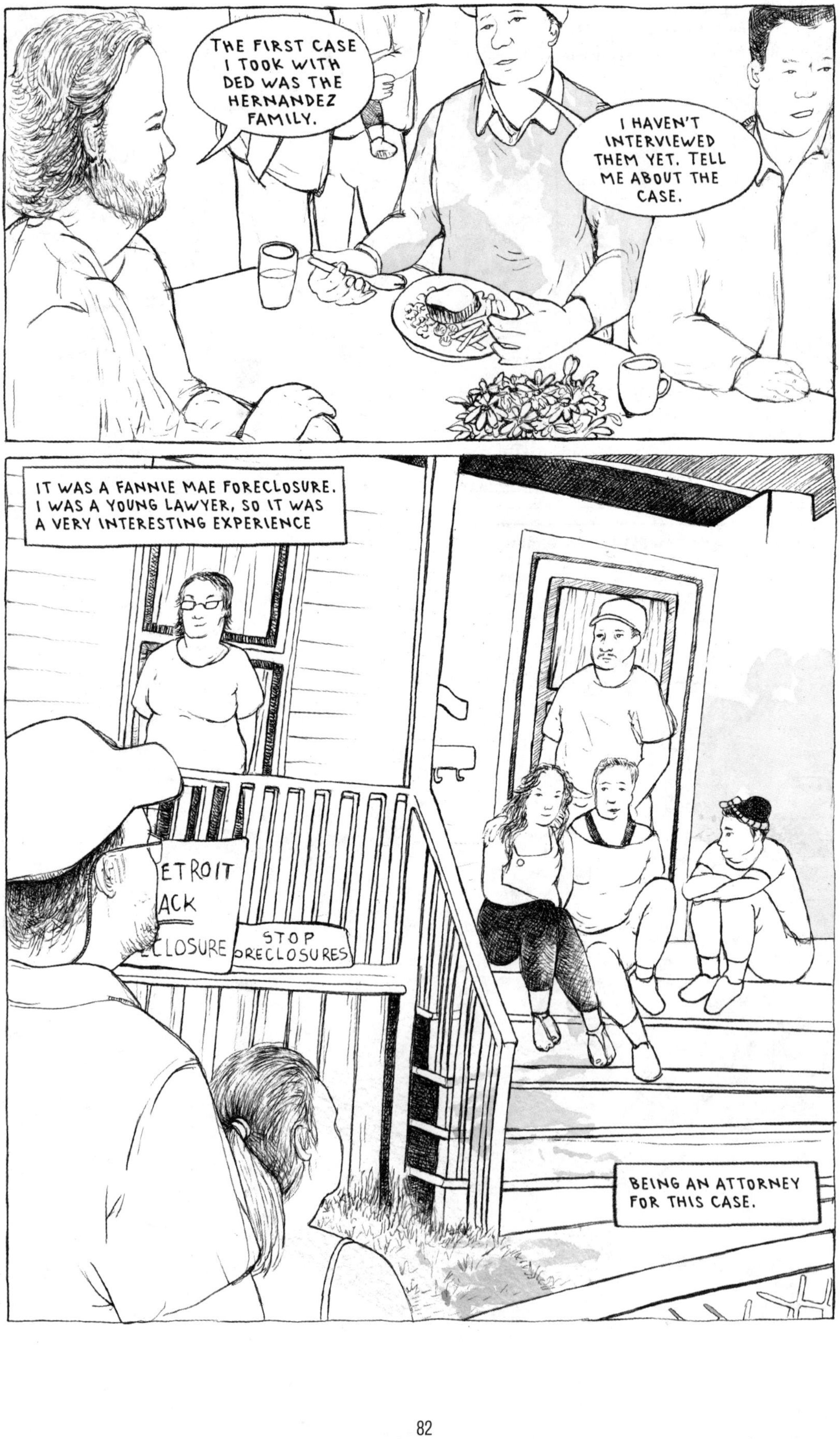
THE FIRST CASE I TOOK WITH DED WAS THE HERNANDEZ FAMILY.
I HAVEN'T INTERVIEWED THEM YET. TELL ME ABOUT THE CASE.
IT WAS A FANNIE MAE FORECLOSURE. I WAS A YOUNG LAWYER, SO IT WAS A VERY INTERESTING EXPERIENCE
STOP
BEING AN ATTORNEY FOR THIS CASE.

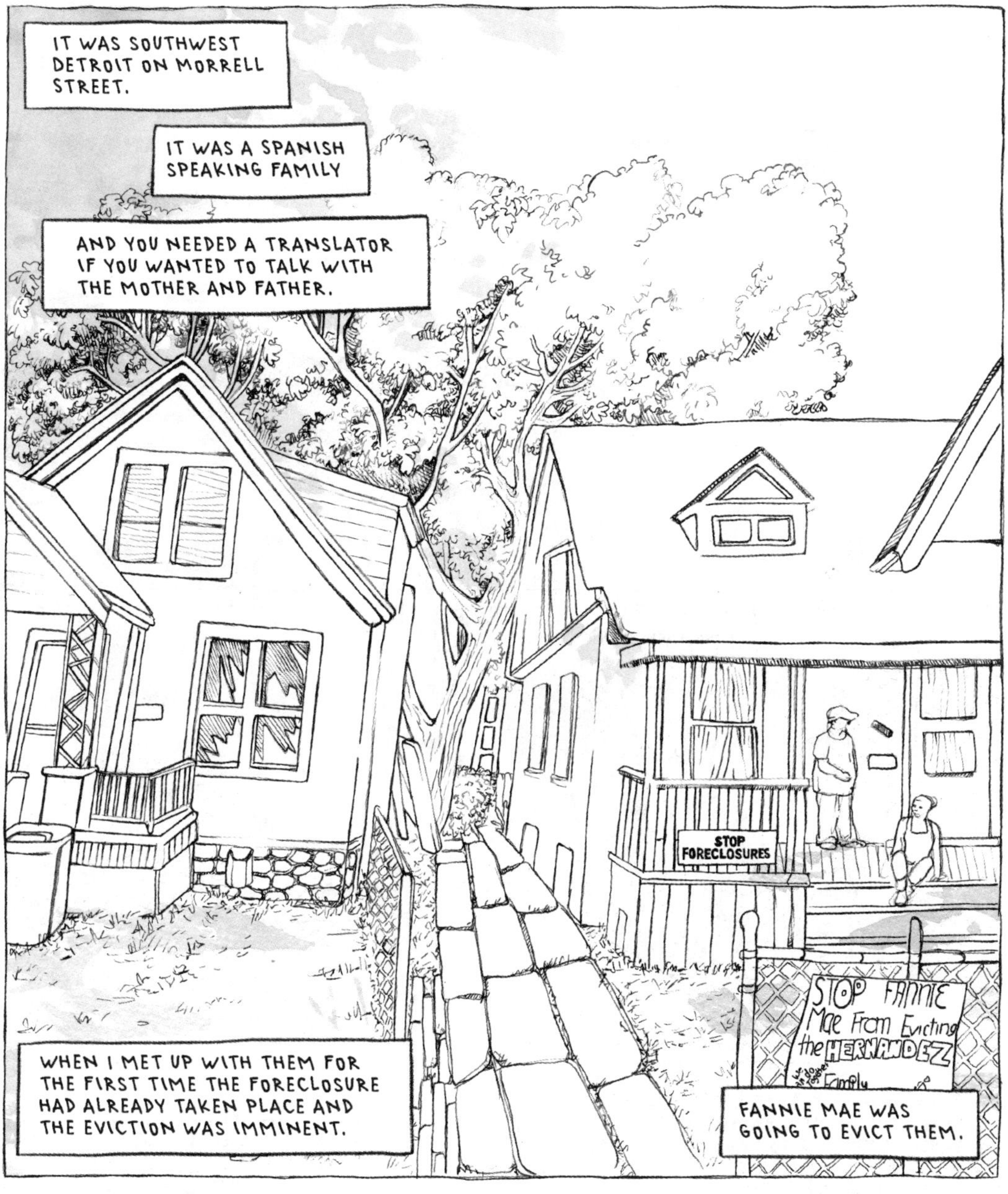
IT WAS SOUTHWEST DETROIT ON MORRELL STREET.
IT WAS A SPANISH SPEAKING FAMILY
AND YOU NEEDED A TRANSLATOR IF YOU WANTED TO TALK WITH THE MOTHER AND FATHER.
STOP FORECLOSURES
STOP FANNIE Mae From Evicting the HERNANDEZ Family
WHEN I MET UP WITH THEM FOR THE FIRST TIME THE FORECLOSURE HAD ALREADY TAKEN PLACE AND THE EVICTION WAS IMMINENT.
FANNIE MAE WAS GOING TO EVICT THEM.

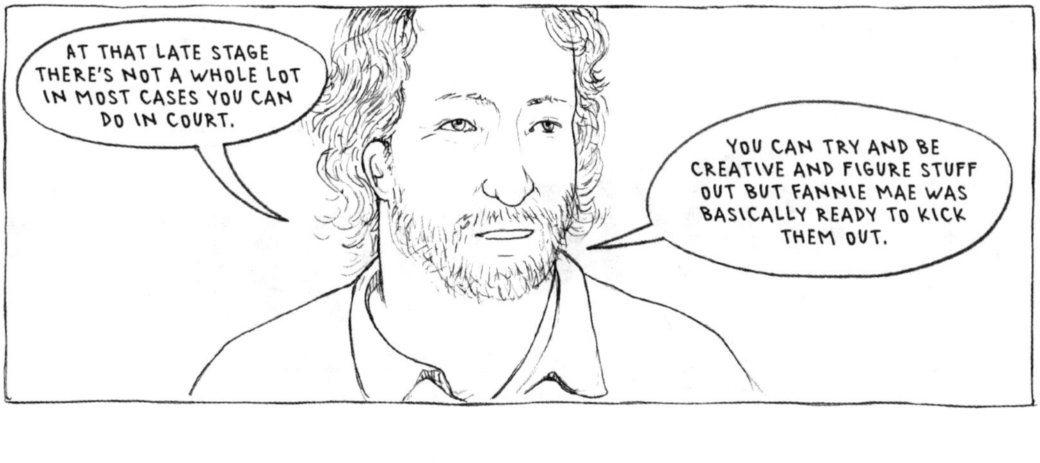
AT THAT LATE STAGE THERE'S NOT A WHOLE LOT IN MOST CASES YOU CAN DO IN COURT.
YOU CAN TRY AND BE CREATIVE AND FIGURE STUFF OUT BUT FANNIE MAE WAS BASICALLY READY TO KICK THEM OUT.

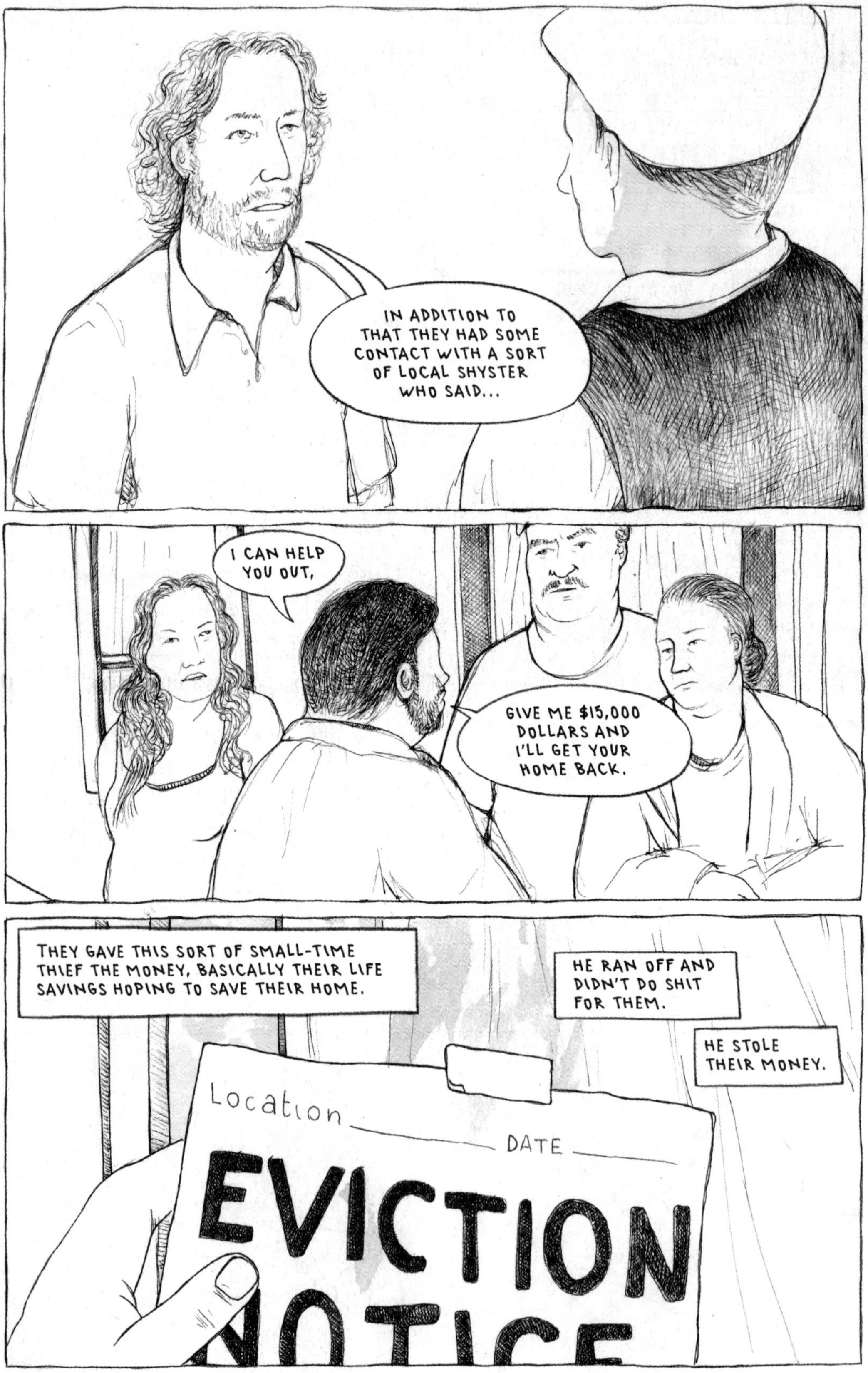

IN ADDITION TO THAT THEY HAD SOME CONTACT WITH A SORT OF LOCAL SHYSTER WHO SAID...
I CAN HELP YOU OUT,
GIVE ME $15,000 DOLLARS AND I'LL GET YOUR HOME BACK.
THEY GAVE THIS SORT OF SMALL-TIME THIEF THE MONEY, BASICALLY THEIR LIFE SAVINGS HOPING TO SAVE THEIR HOME.
HE RAN OFF AND DIDN'T DO SHIT FOR THEM.
HE STOLE THEIR MONEY.
Location
DATE
EVICTION

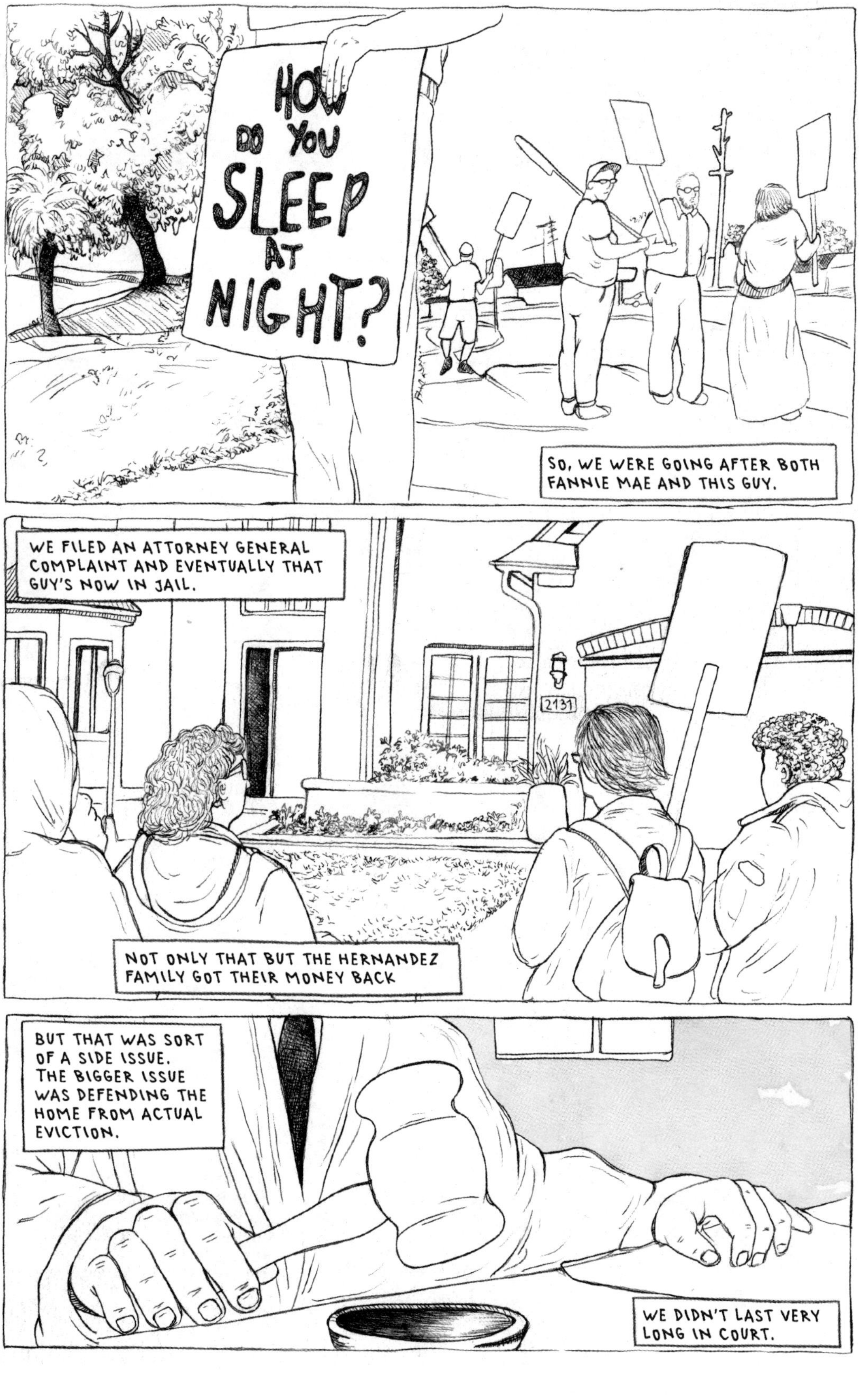
HOW DO YOU SLEEP AT NIGHT?
SO, WE WERE GOING AFTER BOTH FANNIE MAE AND THIS GUY.
WE FILED AN ATTORNEY GENERAL COMPLAINT AND EVENTUALLY THAT GUY'S NOW IN JAIL.
2131
NOT ONLY THAT BUT THE HERNANDEZ FAMILY GOT THEIR MONEY BACK
BUT THAT WAS SORT OF A SIDE ISSUE. THE BIGGER ISSUE WAS DEFENDING THE HOME FROM ACTUAL EVICTION.
WE DIDN'T LAST VERY LONG IN COURT.

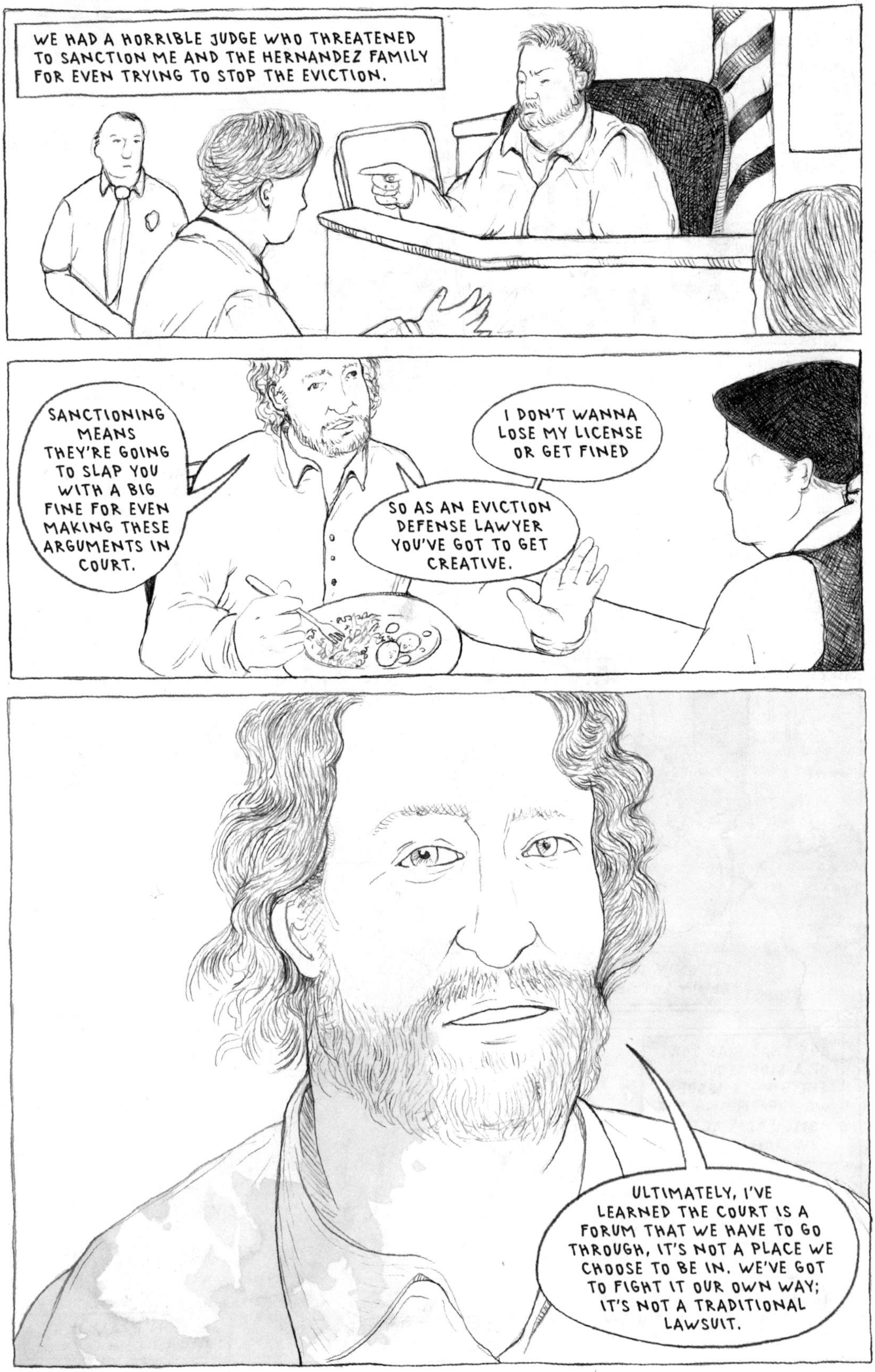
WE HAD A HORRIBLE JUDGE WHO THREATENED TO SANCTION ME AND THE HERNANDEZ FAMILY FOR EVEN TRYING TO STOP THE EVICTION.
SANCTIONING MEANS THEY'RE GOING TO SLAP YOU WITH A BIG FINE FOR EVEN MAKING THESE ARGUMENTS IN COURT.
I DON'T WANNA LOSE MY LICENSE OR GET FINED
SO AS AN EVICTION DEFENSE LAWYER YOU'VE GOT TO GET CREATIVE.
ULTIMATELY, I'VE LEARNED THE COURT IS A FORUM THAT WE HAVE TO GO THROUGH, IT'S NOT A PLACE WE CHOOSE TO BE IN. WE'VE GOT TO FIGHT IT OUR OWN WAY; IT'S NOT A TRADITIONAL LAWSUIT.

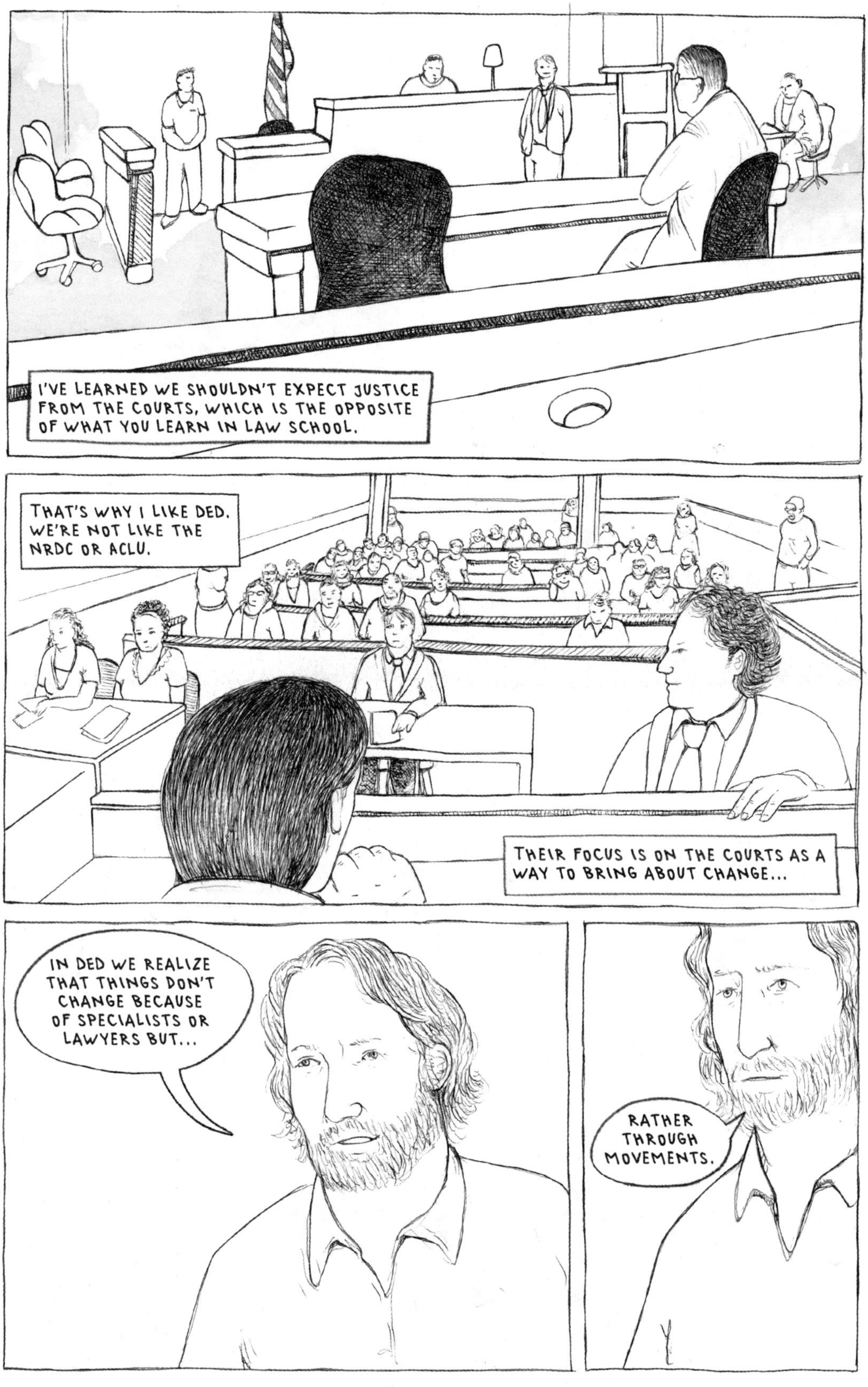
I'VE LEARNED WE SHOULDN'T EXPECT JUSTICE FROM THE COURTS, WHICH IS THE OPPOSITE OF WHAT YOU LEARN IN LAW SCHOOL.
THAT'S WHY I LIKE DED. WE'RE NOT LIKE THE NRDC OR ACLU.
THEIR FOCUS IS ON THE COURTS AS A WAY TO BRING ABOUT CHANGE...
IN DED WE REALIZE THAT THINGS DON'T CHANGE BECAUSE OF SPECIALISTS OR LAWYERS BUT...
RATHER THROUGH MOVEMENTS.

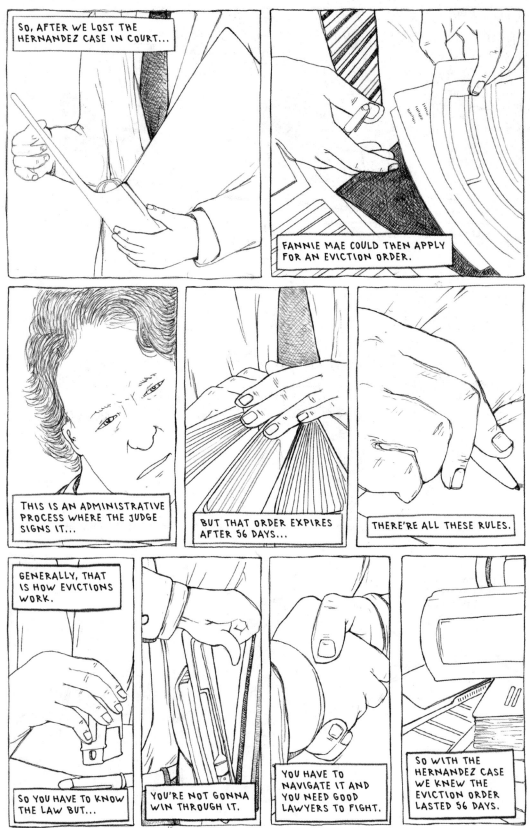

SO, AFTER WE LOST THE HERNANDEZ CASE IN COURT...

FANNIE MAE COULD THEN APPLY FOR AN EVICTION ORDER.

THIS IS AN ADMINISTRATIVE PROCESS WHERE THE JUDGE SIGNS IT...

BUT THAT ORDER EXPIRES AFTER 56 DAYS...

THERE'RE ALL THESE RULES.

GENERALLY, THAT IS HOW EVICTIONS WORK.

SO YOU HAVE TO KNOW THE LAW BUT...

YOU'RE NOT GONNA WIN THROUGH IT.

YOU HAVE TO NAVIGATE IT AND YOU NEED GOOD LAWYERS TO FIGHT.

SO WITH THE HERNANDEZ CASE WE KNEW THE EVICTION ORDER LASTED 56 DAYS.

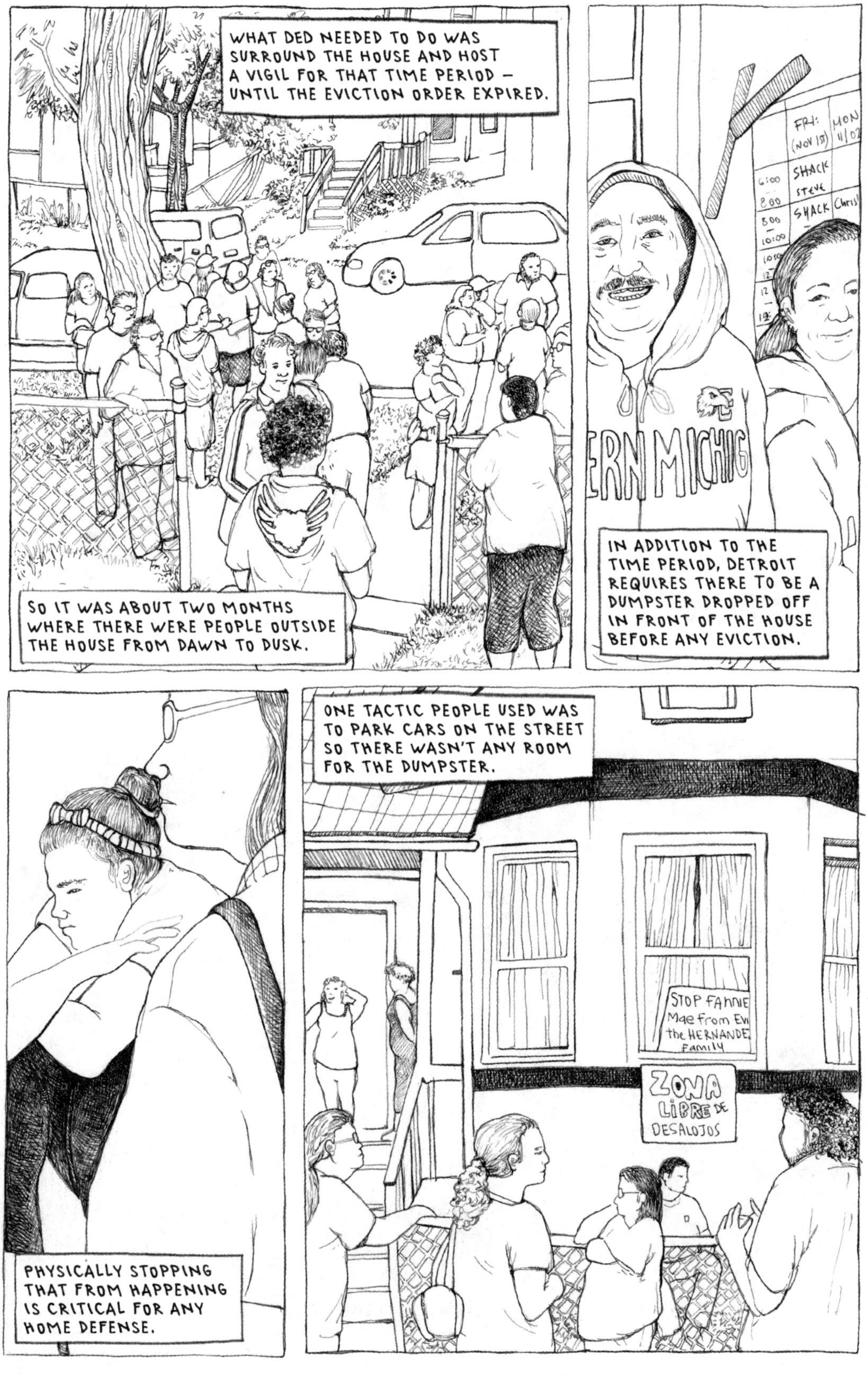
WHAT DED NEEDED TO DO WAS SURROUND THE HOUSE AND HOST A VIGIL FOR THAT TIME PERIOD — UNTIL THE EVICTION ORDER EXPIRED.
SO IT WAS ABOUT TWO MONTHS WHERE THERE WERE PEOPLE OUTSIDE THE HOUSE FROM DAWN TO DUSK.
ERN MICHIG
IN ADDITION TO THE TIME PERIOD, DETROIT REQUIRES THERE TO BE A DUMPSTER DROPPED OFF IN FRONT OF THE HOUSE BEFORE ANY EVICTION.
PHYSICALLY STOPPING THAT FROM HAPPENING IS CRITICAL FOR ANY HOME DEFENSE.
ONE TACTIC PEOPLE USED WAS TO PARK CARS ON THE STREET SO THERE WASN'T ANY ROOM FOR THE DUMPSTER.
STOP FANNIE
Mae From Evi
the HERNANDE
Family
ZONA
LIBRE DE
DESALOJOS

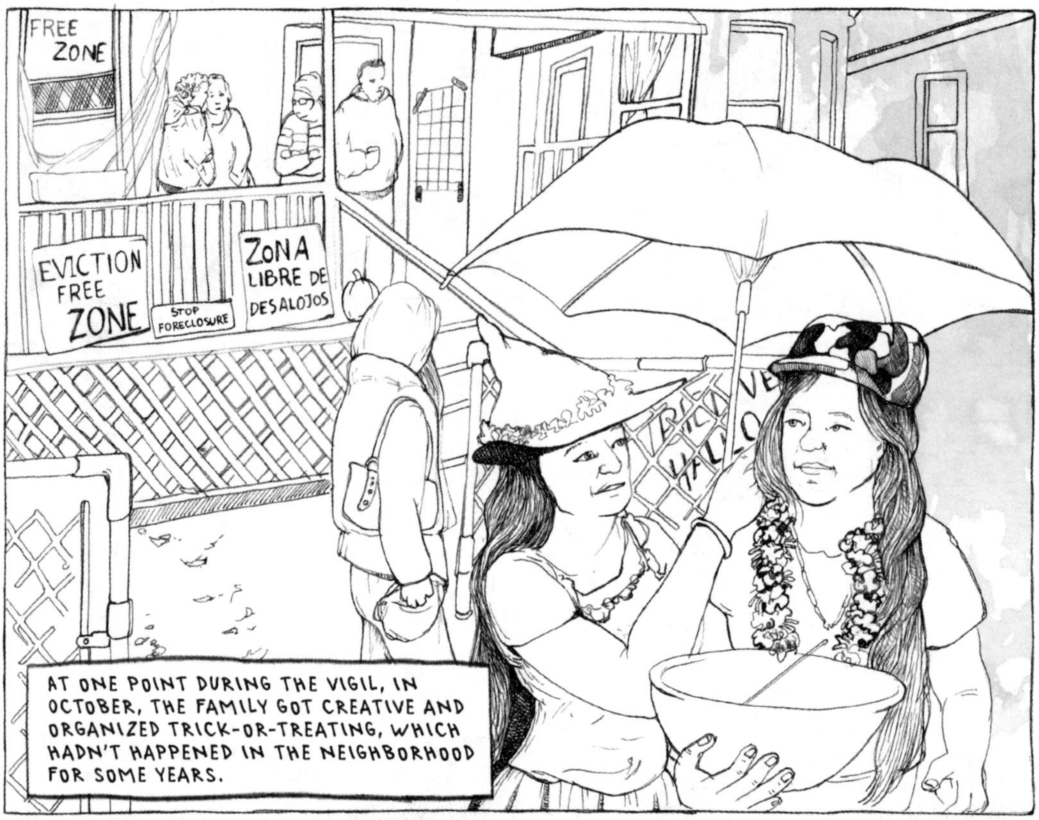
FREE ZONE
EVICTION FREE ZONE
STOP FORECLOSURE
ZONA LIBRE DE DESALOJOS
AT ONE POINT DURING THE VIGIL, IN OCTOBER, THE FAMILY GOT CREATIVE AND ORGANIZED TRICK-OR-TREATING, WHICH HADN'T HAPPENED IN THE NEIGHBORHOOD FOR SOME YEARS.

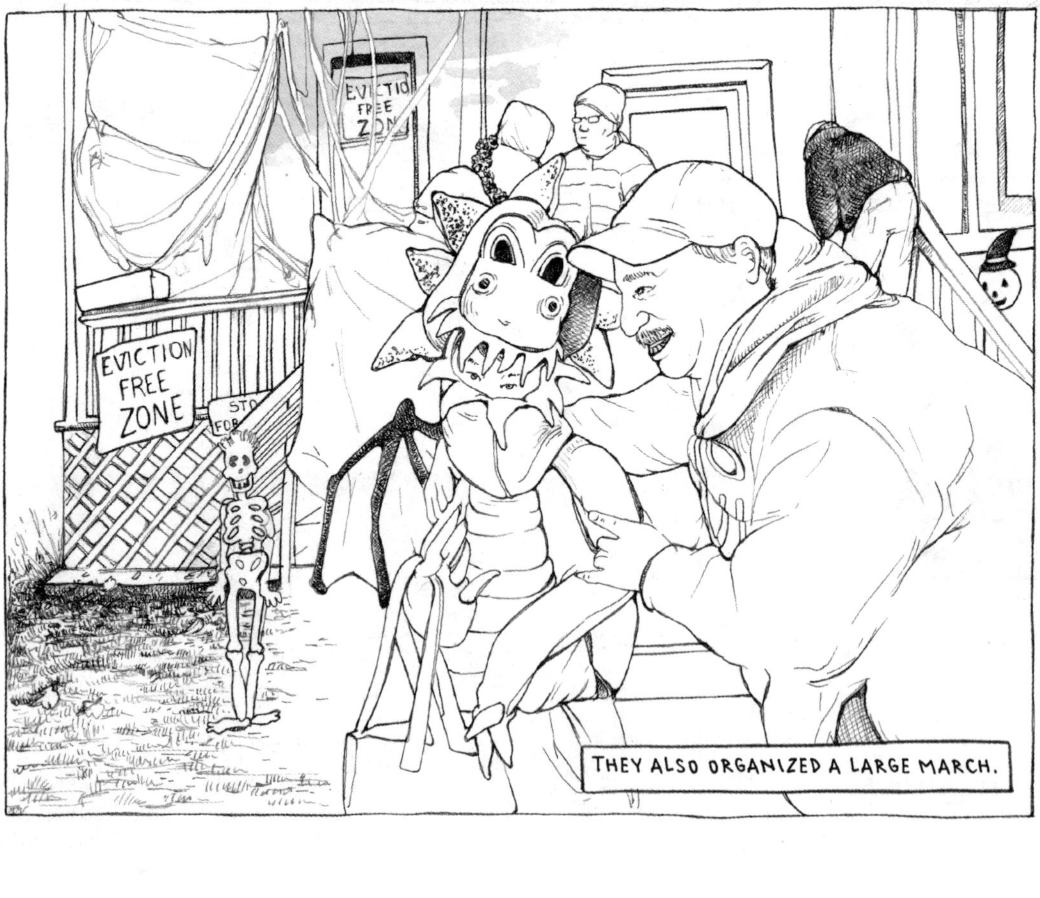
EVICTION FREE ZONE
THEY ALSO ORGANIZED A LARGE MARCH.

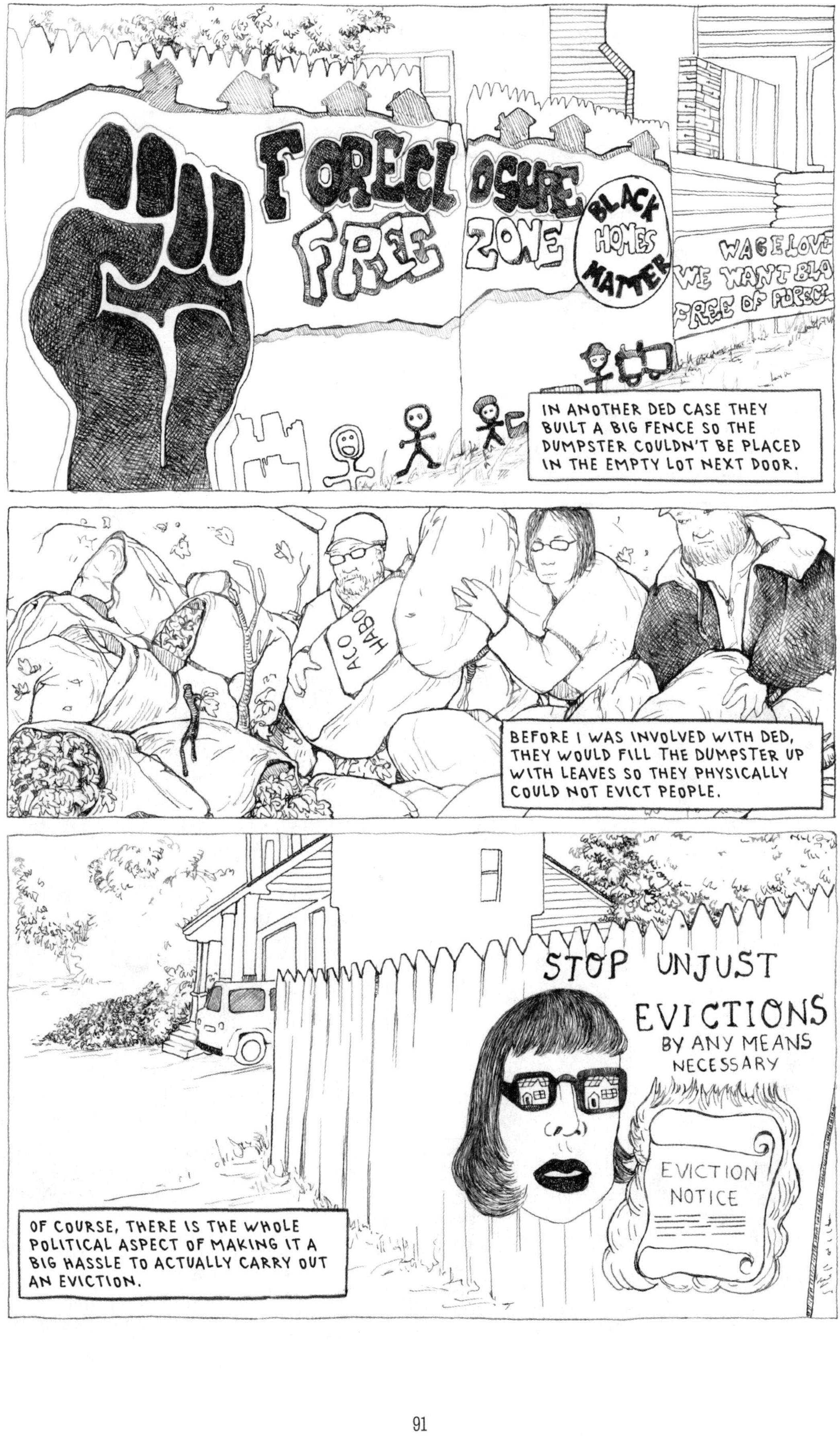
FORECLOSURE FREE ZONE
BLACK HOMES MATTER
WAGE LOVE
IN ANOTHER DED CASE THEY BUILT A BIG FENCE SO THE DUMPSTER COULDN'T BE PLACED IN THE EMPTY LOT NEXT DOOR.
BEFORE I WAS INVOLVED WITH DED, THEY WOULD FILL THE DUMPSTER UP WITH LEAVES SO THEY PHYSICALLY COULD NOT EVICT PEOPLE.
STOP UNJUST EVICTIONS BY ANY MEANS NECESSARY
EVICTION NOTICE
OF COURSE, THERE IS THE WHOLE POLITICAL ASPECT OF MAKING IT A BIG HASSLE TO ACTUALLY CARRY OUT AN EVICTION.

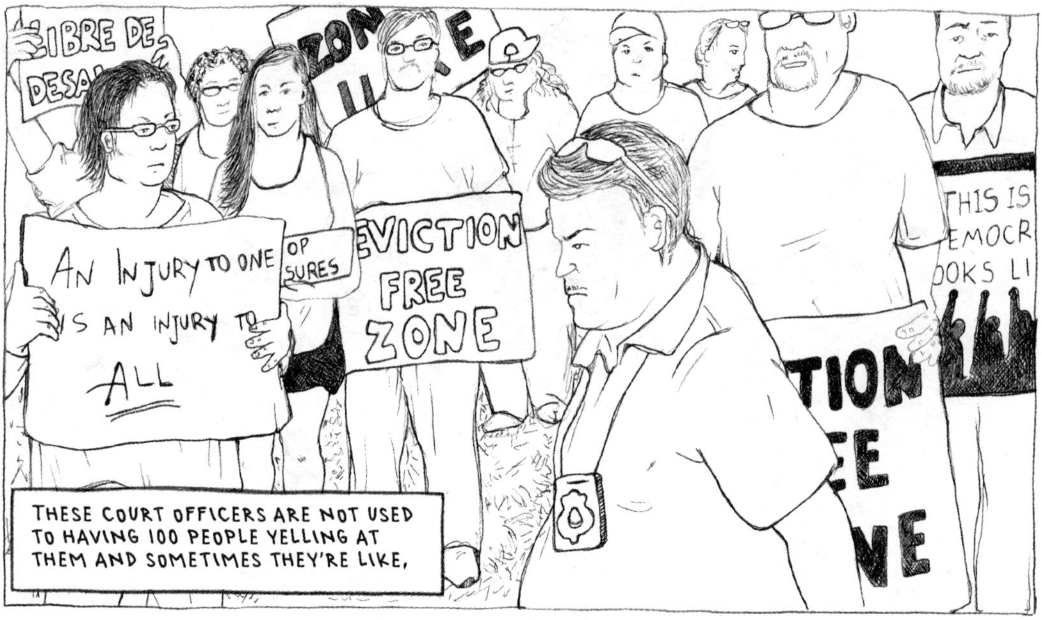

LIBRE DE
DESAL
ZON
EVICTION FREE ZONE
AN INJURY TO ONE IS AN INJURY TO ALL
OP SURES
TION EE NE
THIS IS EMOCR OOKS LI
THESE COURT OFFICERS ARE NOT USED TO HAVING 100 PEOPLE YELLING AT THEM AND SOMETIMES THEY'RE LIKE,

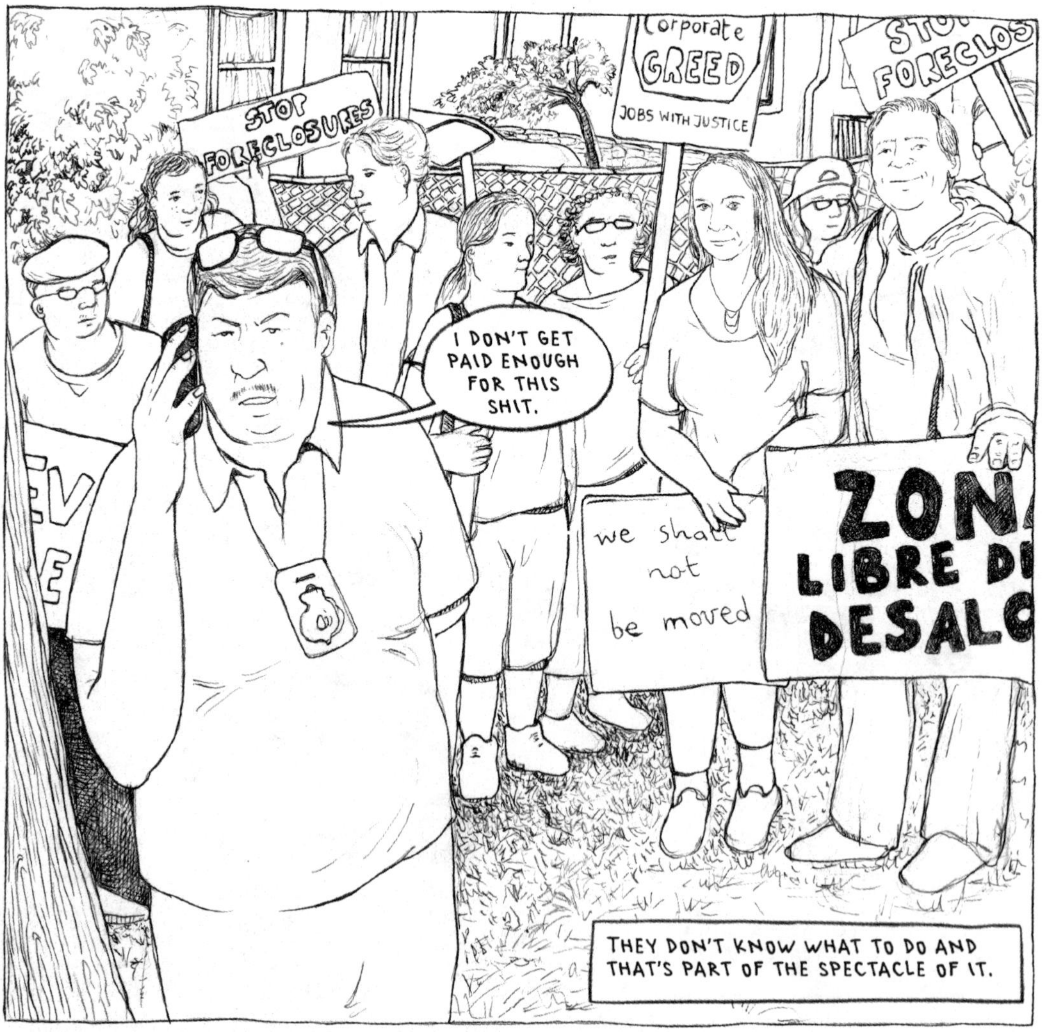

STOP FORECLOSURES
Corporate GREED
JOBS WITH JUSTICE
STOP FORECLOS
EV E
I DON'T GET PAID ENOUGH FOR THIS SHIT.
we shall not be moved
ZONA LIBRE DE DESALO
THEY DON'T KNOW WHAT TO DO AND THAT'S PART OF THE SPECTACLE OF IT.

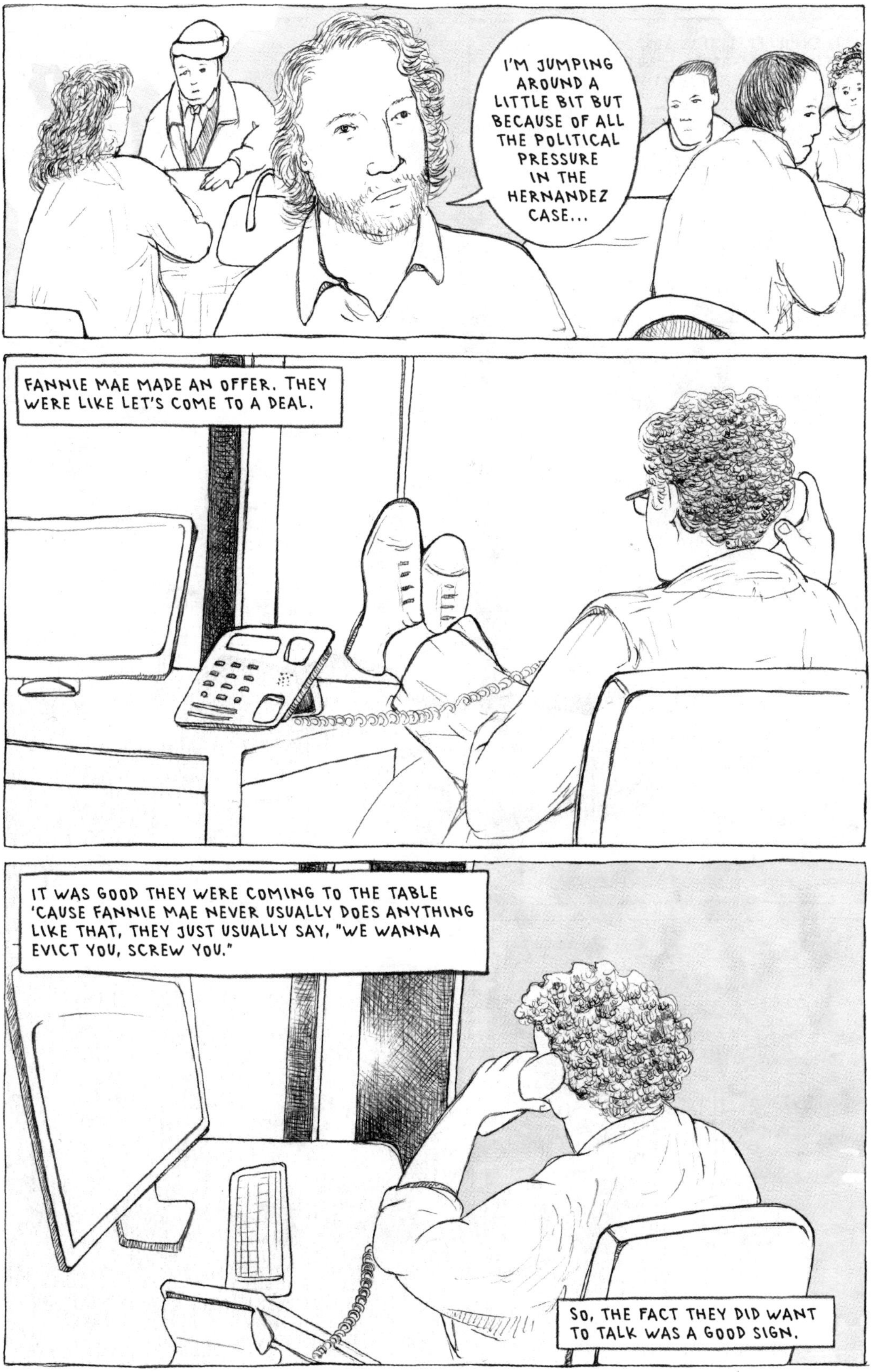
I'M JUMPING AROUND A LITTLE BIT BUT BECAUSE OF ALL THE POLITICAL PRESSURE IN THE HERNANDEZ CASE...
FANNIE MAE MADE AN OFFER. THEY WERE LIKE LET'S COME TO A DEAL.
IT WAS GOOD THEY WERE COMING TO THE TABLE 'CAUSE FANNIE MAE NEVER USUALLY DOES ANYTHING LIKE THAT, THEY JUST USUALLY SAY, "WE WANNA EVICT YOU, SCREW YOU."
SO, THE FACT THEY DID WANT TO TALK WAS A GOOD SIGN.

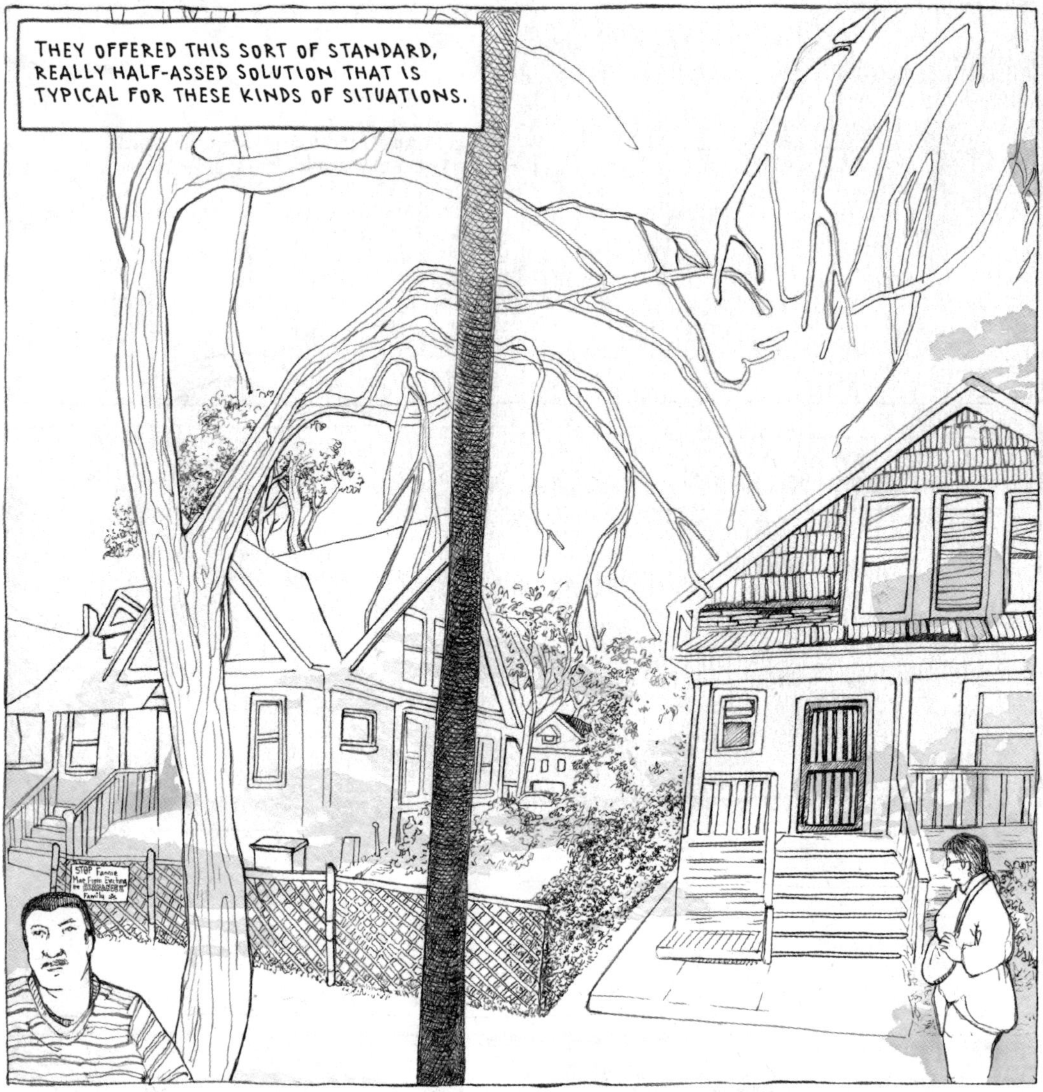
THEY OFFERED THIS SORT OF STANDARD, REALLY HALF-ASSED SOLUTION THAT IS TYPICAL FOR THESE KINDS OF SITUATIONS.

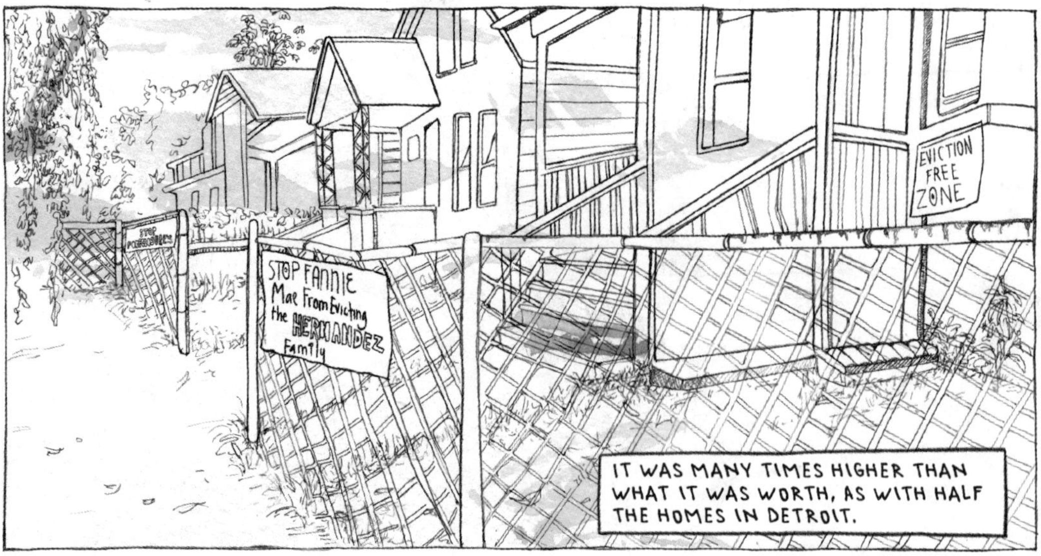
STOP FANNIE Mae From Evicting the HERNANDEZ Family
EVICTION FREE ZONE
IT WAS MANY TIMES HIGHER THAN WHAT IT WAS WORTH, AS WITH HALF THE HOMES IN DETROIT.

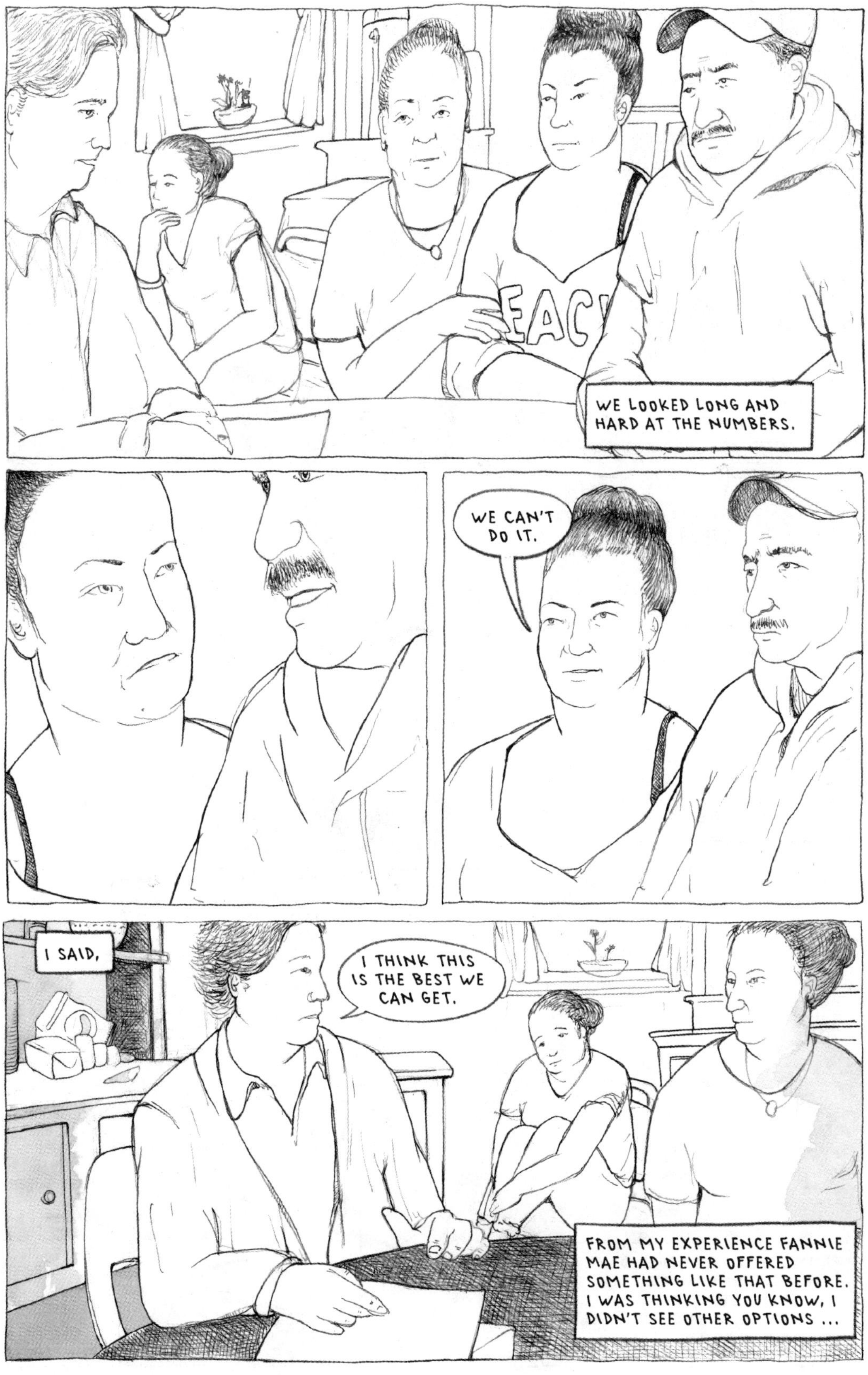
WE LOOKED LONG AND HARD AT THE NUMBERS.
WE CAN'T DO IT.
I SAID,
I THINK THIS IS THE BEST WE CAN GET.
FROM MY EXPERIENCE FANNIE MAE HAD NEVER OFFERED SOMETHING LIKE THAT BEFORE. I WAS THINKING YOU KNOW, I DIDN'T SEE OTHER OPTIONS ...

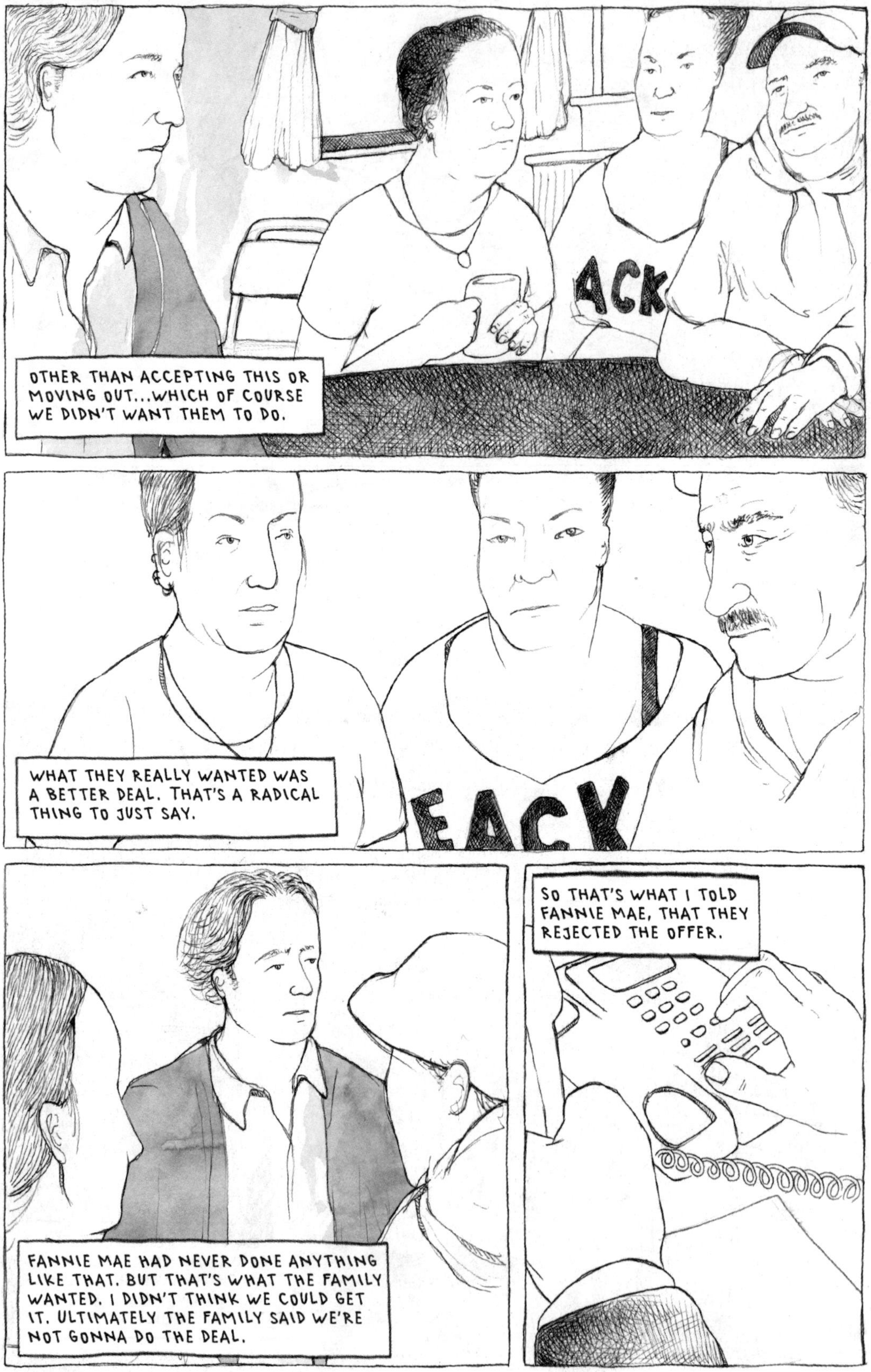
OTHER THAN ACCEPTING THIS OR MOVING OUT...WHICH OF COURSE WE DIDN'T WANT THEM TO DO.
WHAT THEY REALLY WANTED WAS A BETTER DEAL. THAT'S A RADICAL THING TO JUST SAY.
FANNIE MAE HAD NEVER DONE ANYTHING LIKE THAT. BUT THAT'S WHAT THE FAMILY WANTED. I DIDN'T THINK WE COULD GET IT. ULTIMATELY THE FAMILY SAID WE'RE NOT GONNA DO THE DEAL.
SO THAT'S WHAT I TOLD FANNIE MAE, THAT THEY REJECTED THE OFFER.

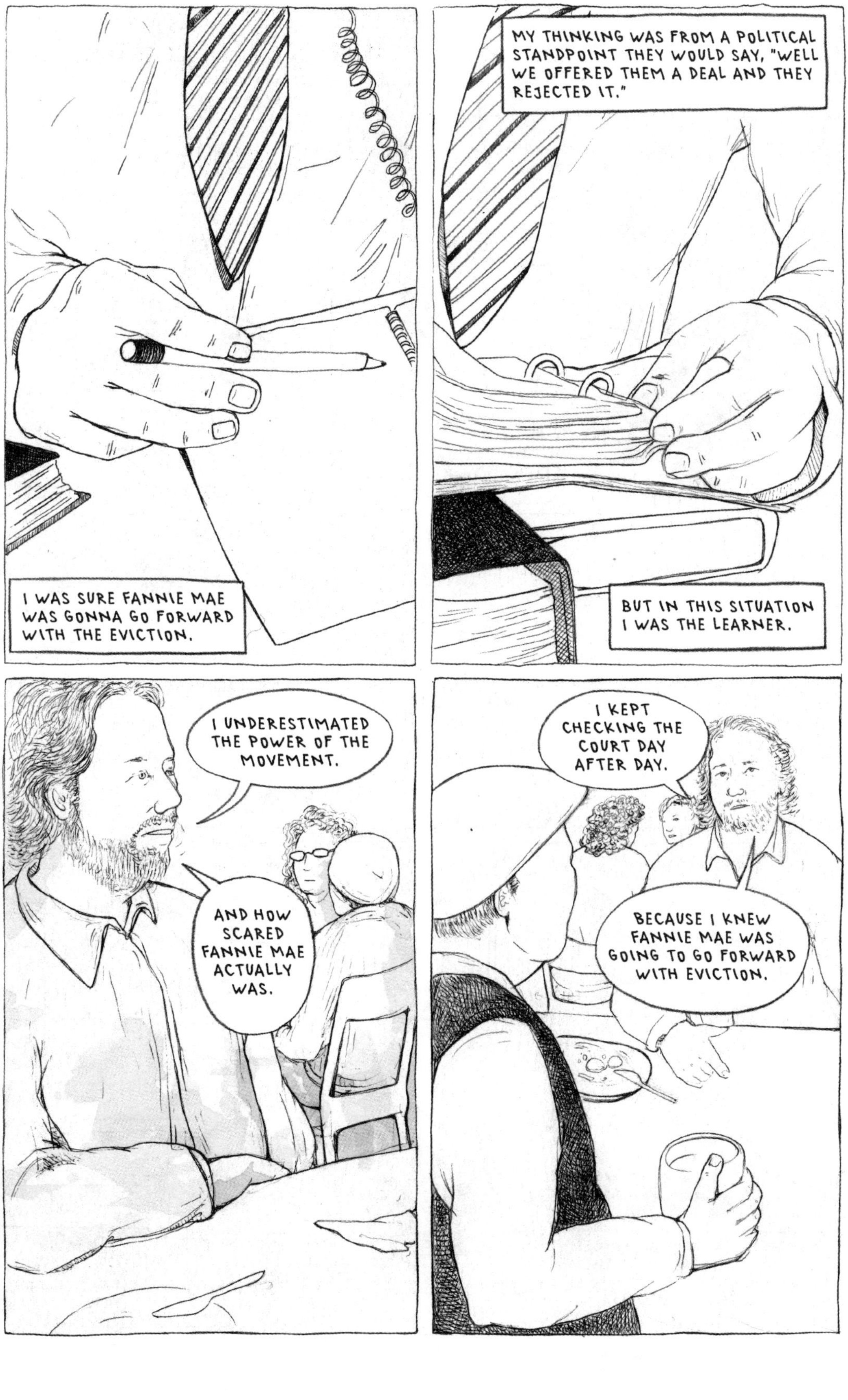
I WAS SURE FANNIE MAE WAS GONNA GO FORWARD WITH THE EVICTION.
MY THINKING WAS FROM A POLITICAL STANDPOINT THEY WOULD SAY, "WELL WE OFFERED THEM A DEAL AND THEY REJECTED IT."
BUT IN THIS SITUATION I WAS THE LEARNER.
I UNDERESTIMATED THE POWER OF THE MOVEMENT.
AND HOW SCARED FANNIE MAE ACTUALLY WAS.
I KEPT CHECKING THE COURT DAY AFTER DAY.
BECAUSE I KNEW FANNIE MAE WAS GOING TO GO FORWARD WITH EVICTION.

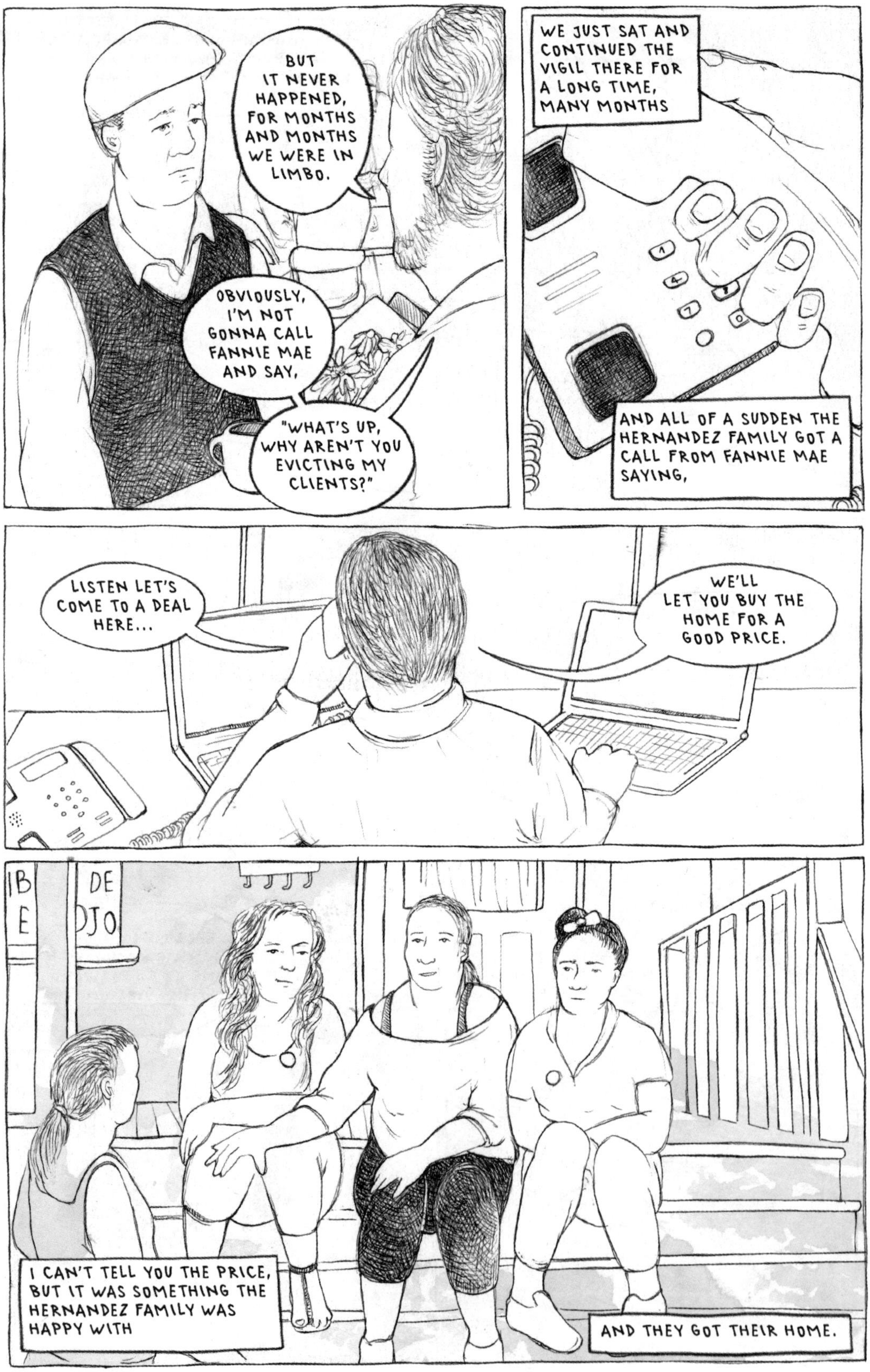
BUT IT NEVER HAPPENED, FOR MONTHS AND MONTHS WE WERE IN LIMBO.
OBVIOUSLY, I'M NOT GONNA CALL FANNIE MAE AND SAY,
"WHAT'S UP, WHY AREN'T YOU EVICTING MY CLIENTS?"
WE JUST SAT AND CONTINUED THE VIGIL THERE FOR A LONG TIME, MANY MONTHS
AND ALL OF A SUDDEN THE HERNANDEZ FAMILY GOT A CALL FROM FANNIE MAE SAYING,
LISTEN LET'S COME TO A DEAL HERE...
WE'LL LET YOU BUY THE HOME FOR A GOOD PRICE.
I CAN'T TELL YOU THE PRICE, BUT IT WAS SOMETHING THE HERNANDEZ FAMILY WAS HAPPY WITH
AND THEY GOT THEIR HOME.

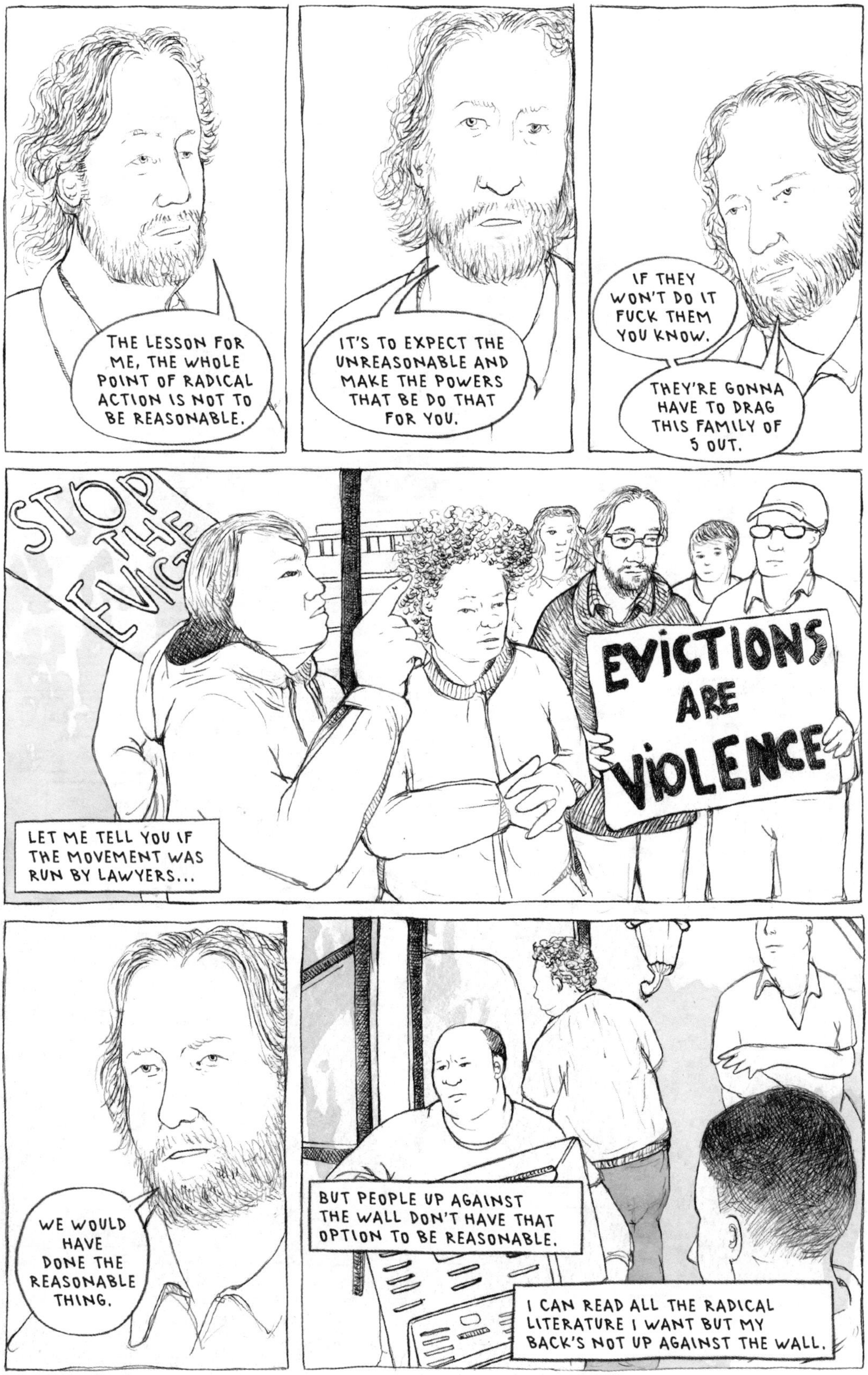
THE LESSON FOR ME, THE WHOLE POINT OF RADICAL ACTION IS NOT TO BE REASONABLE.
IT'S TO EXPECT THE UNREASONABLE AND MAKE THE POWERS THAT BE DO THAT FOR YOU.
IF THEY WON'T DO IT FUCK THEM YOU KNOW.
THEY'RE GONNA HAVE TO DRAG THIS FAMILY OF 5 OUT.
STOP THE EVIC
EVICTIONS ARE VIOLENCE
LET ME TELL YOU IF THE MOVEMENT WAS RUN BY LAWYERS...
WE WOULD HAVE DONE THE REASONABLE THING.
BUT PEOPLE UP AGAINST THE WALL DON'T HAVE THAT OPTION TO BE REASONABLE.
I CAN READ ALL THE RADICAL LITERATURE I WANT BUT MY BACK'S NOT UP AGAINST THE WALL.

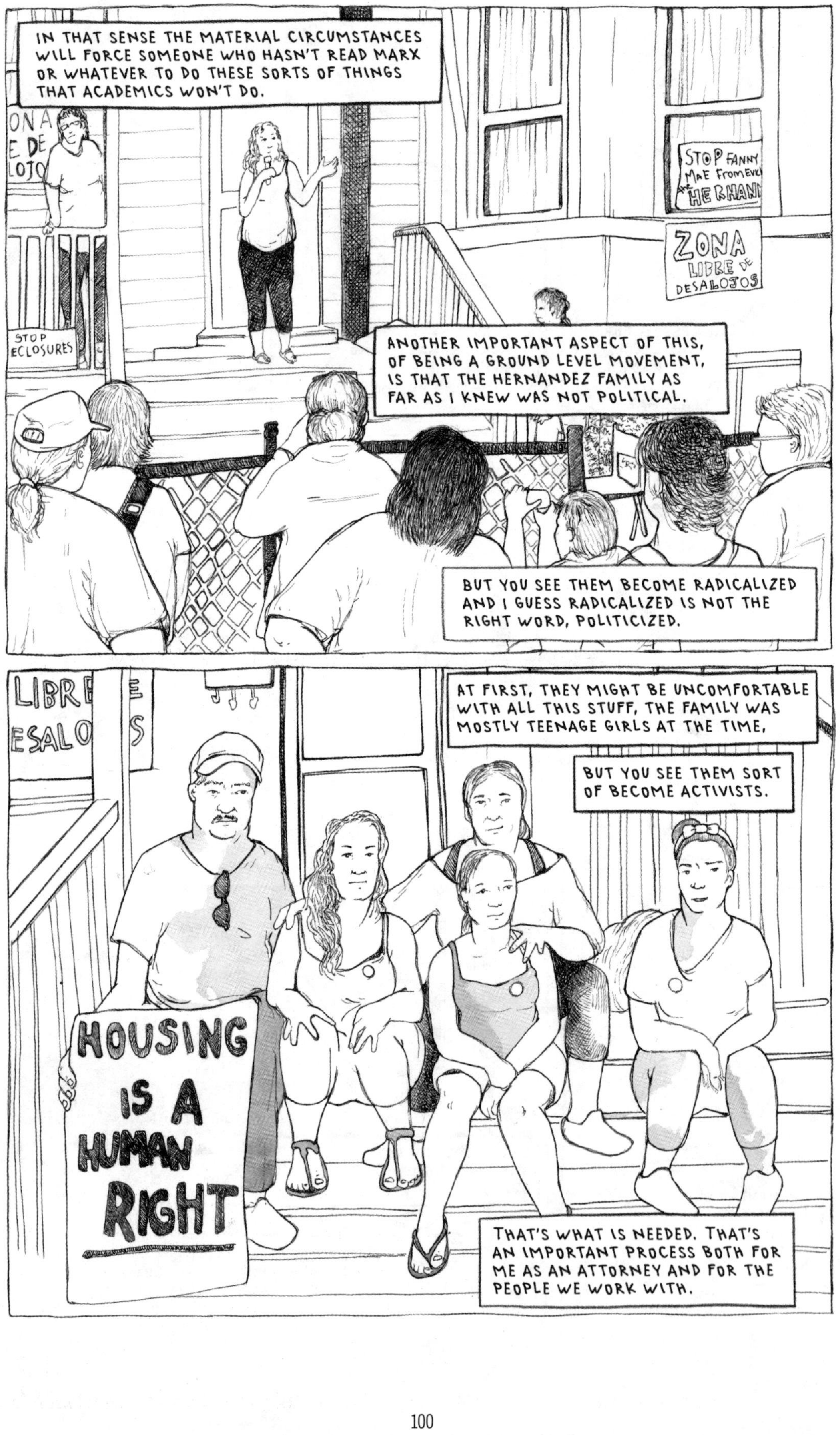
IN THAT SENSE THE MATERIAL CIRCUMSTANCES WILL FORCE SOMEONE WHO HASN'T READ MARX OR WHATEVER TO DO THESE SORTS OF THINGS THAT ACADEMICS WON'T DO.
ZONA LIBRE DE DESALOJOS
STOP ECLOSURES
ANOTHER IMPORTANT ASPECT OF THIS, OF BEING A GROUND LEVEL MOVEMENT, IS THAT THE HERNANDEZ FAMILY AS FAR AS I KNEW WAS NOT POLITICAL.
BUT YOU SEE THEM BECOME RADICALIZED AND I GUESS RADICALIZED IS NOT THE RIGHT WORD, POLITICIZED.
AT FIRST, THEY MIGHT BE UNCOMFORTABLE WITH ALL THIS STUFF, THE FAMILY WAS MOSTLY TEENAGE GIRLS AT THE TIME,
BUT YOU SEE THEM SORT OF BECOME ACTIVISTS.
HOUSING IS A HUMAN RIGHT
THAT'S WHAT IS NEEDED. THAT'S AN IMPORTANT PROCESS BOTH FOR ME AS AN ATTORNEY AND FOR THE PEOPLE WE WORK WITH.

you've got
me as a
member
For life

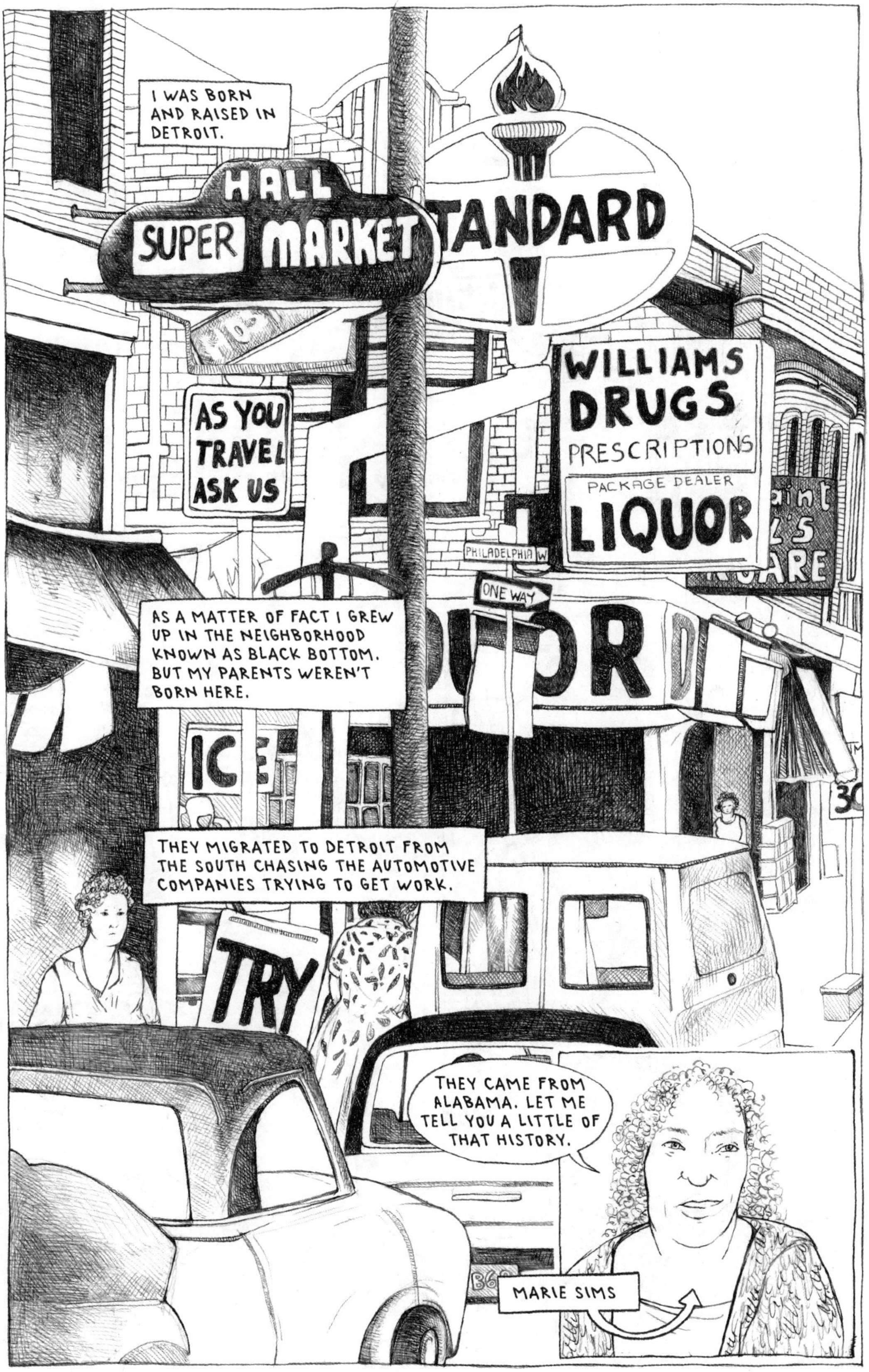
I WAS BORN AND RAISED IN DETROIT.
HALL SUPER MARKET
TANDARD
WILLIAMS DRUGS PRESCRIPTIONS
PACKAGE DEALER LIQUOR
AS YOU TRAVEL ASK US
PHILADELPHIA W
ONE WAY
AS A MATTER OF FACT I GREW UP IN THE NEIGHBORHOOD KNOWN AS BLACK BOTTOM. BUT MY PARENTS WEREN'T BORN HERE.
ICE
THEY MIGRATED TO DETROIT FROM THE SOUTH CHASING THE AUTOMOTIVE COMPANIES TRYING TO GET WORK.
TRY
THEY CAME FROM ALABAMA. LET ME TELL YOU A LITTLE OF THAT HISTORY.
MARIE SIMS

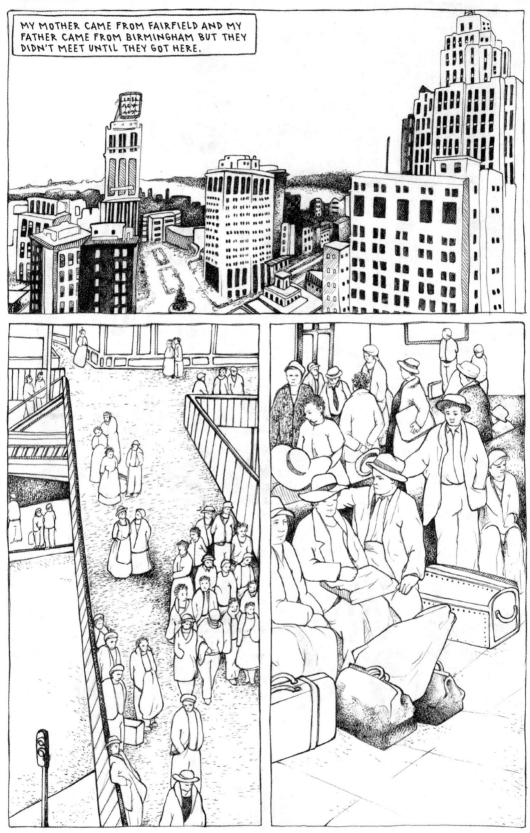

MY MOTHER CAME FROM FAIRFIELD AND MY FATHER CAME FROM BIRMINGHAM BUT THEY DIDN'T MEET UNTIL THEY GOT HERE.

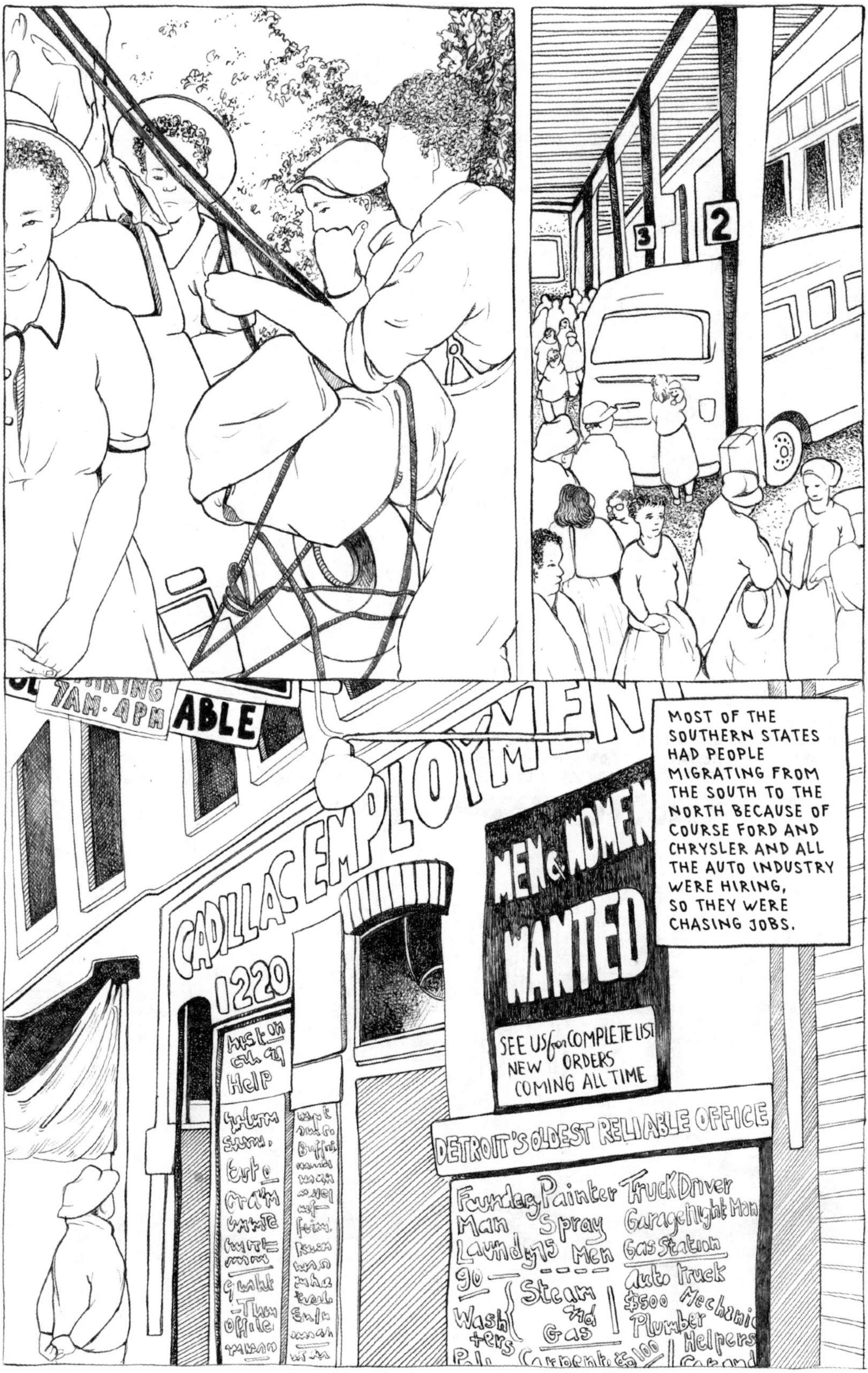

3
2
ABLE
CADILLAC EMPLOYMEN
1220
Help
MEN & WOMEN
WANTED
SEE US for COMPLETE LIST
NEW ORDERS
COMING ALL TIME
DETROIT'S OLDEST RELIABLE OFFICE
Painter Truck Driver
Man Spray Garage Night Man
Men Gas Station
Steam Auto Truck
Gas $500 Mechanic
Plumber
Helpers
MOST OF THE SOUTHERN STATES HAD PEOPLE MIGRATING FROM THE SOUTH TO THE NORTH BECAUSE OF COURSE FORD AND CHRYSLER AND ALL THE AUTO INDUSTRY WERE HIRING, SO THEY WERE CHASING JOBS.

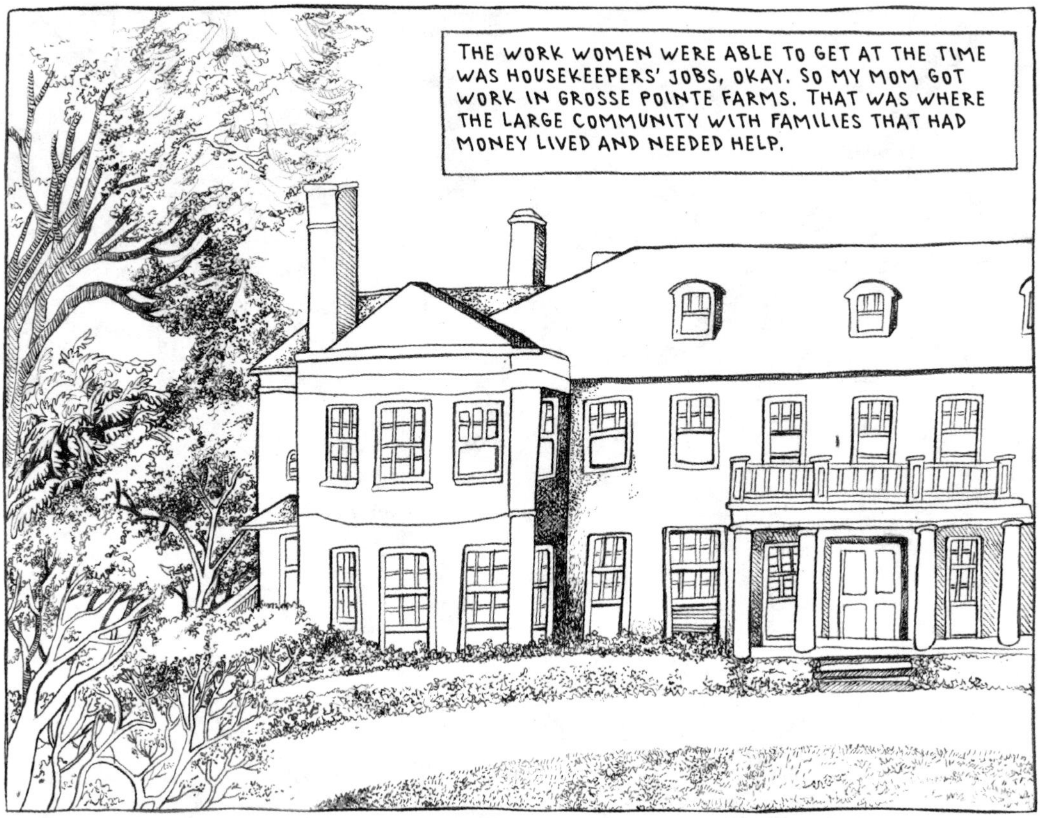
THE WORK WOMEN WERE ABLE TO GET AT THE TIME WAS HOUSEKEEPERS' JOBS, OKAY. SO MY MOM GOT WORK IN GROSSE POINTE FARMS. THAT WAS WHERE THE LARGE COMMUNITY WITH FAMILIES THAT HAD MONEY LIVED AND NEEDED HELP.

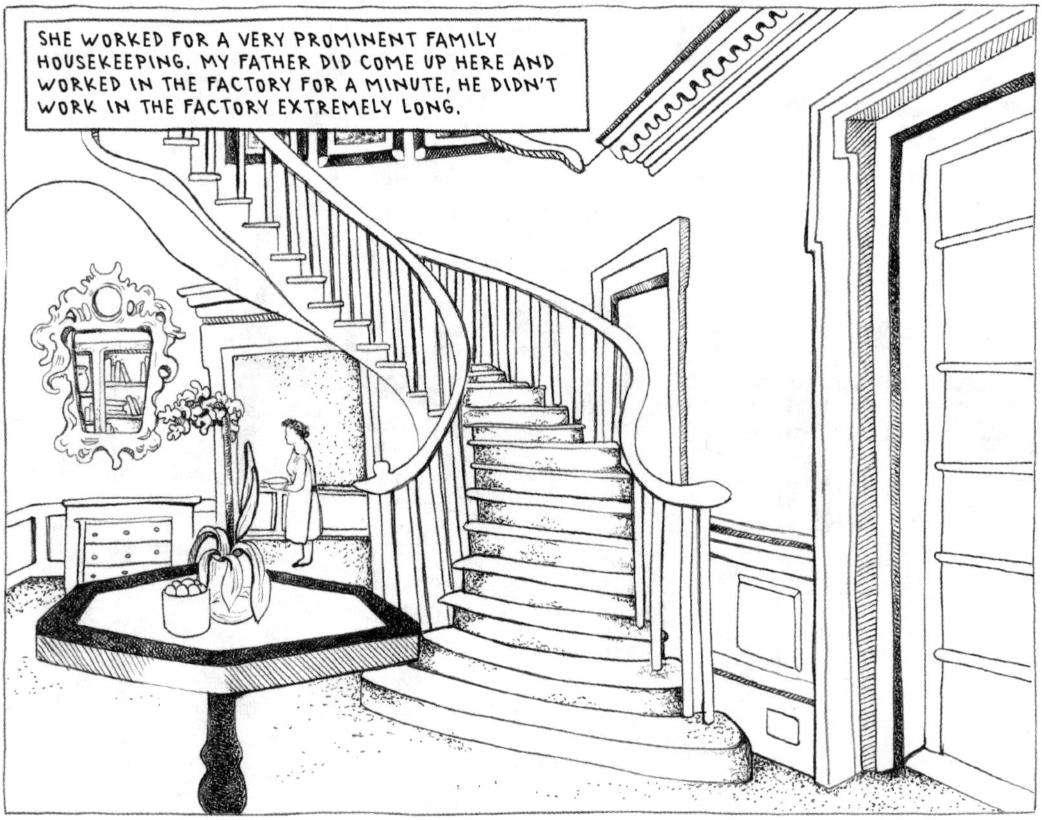
SHE WORKED FOR A VERY PROMINENT FAMILY HOUSEKEEPING. MY FATHER DID COME UP HERE AND WORKED IN THE FACTORY FOR A MINUTE, HE DIDN'T WORK IN THE FACTORY EXTREMELY LONG.

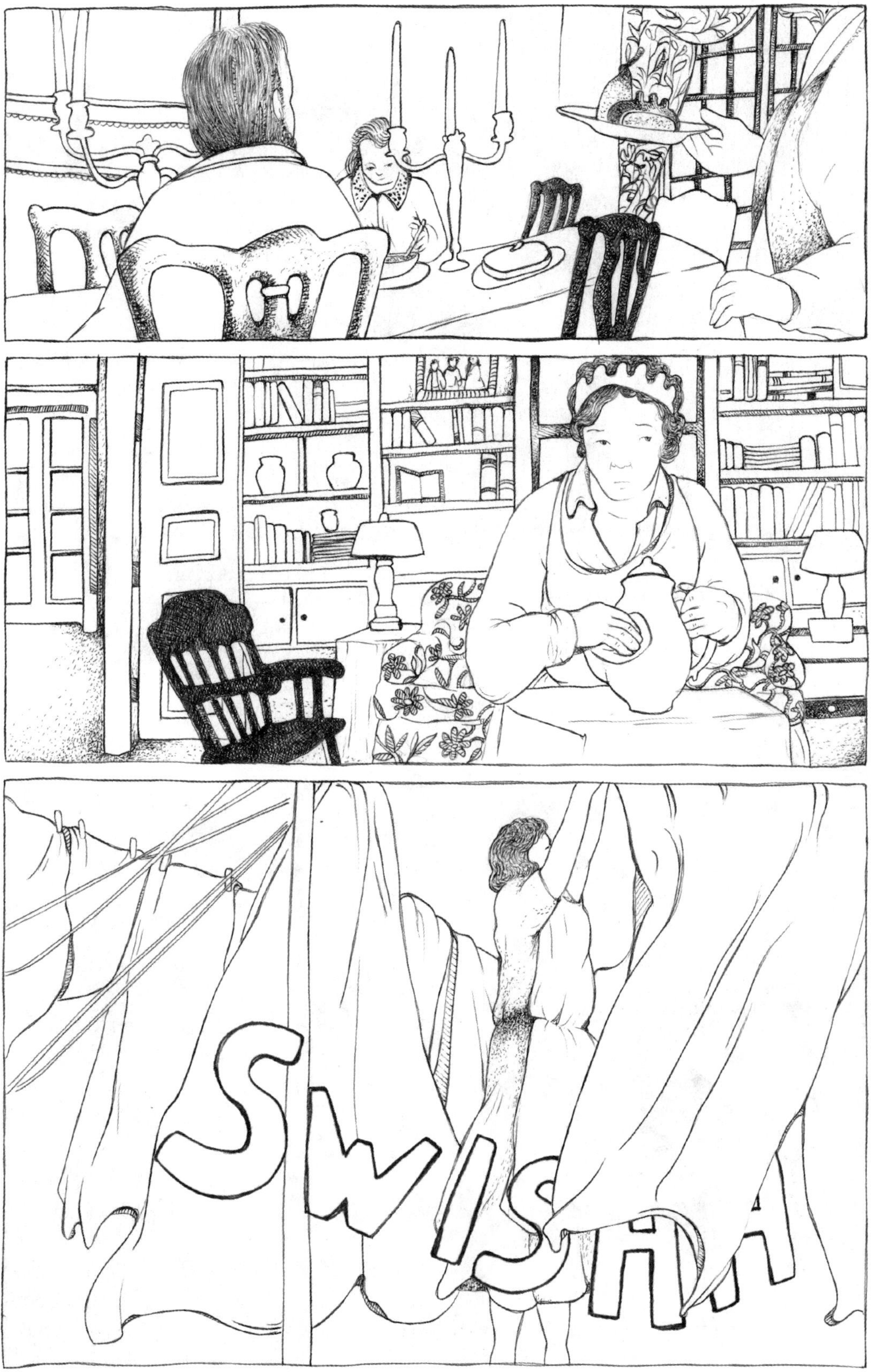
SWISHH

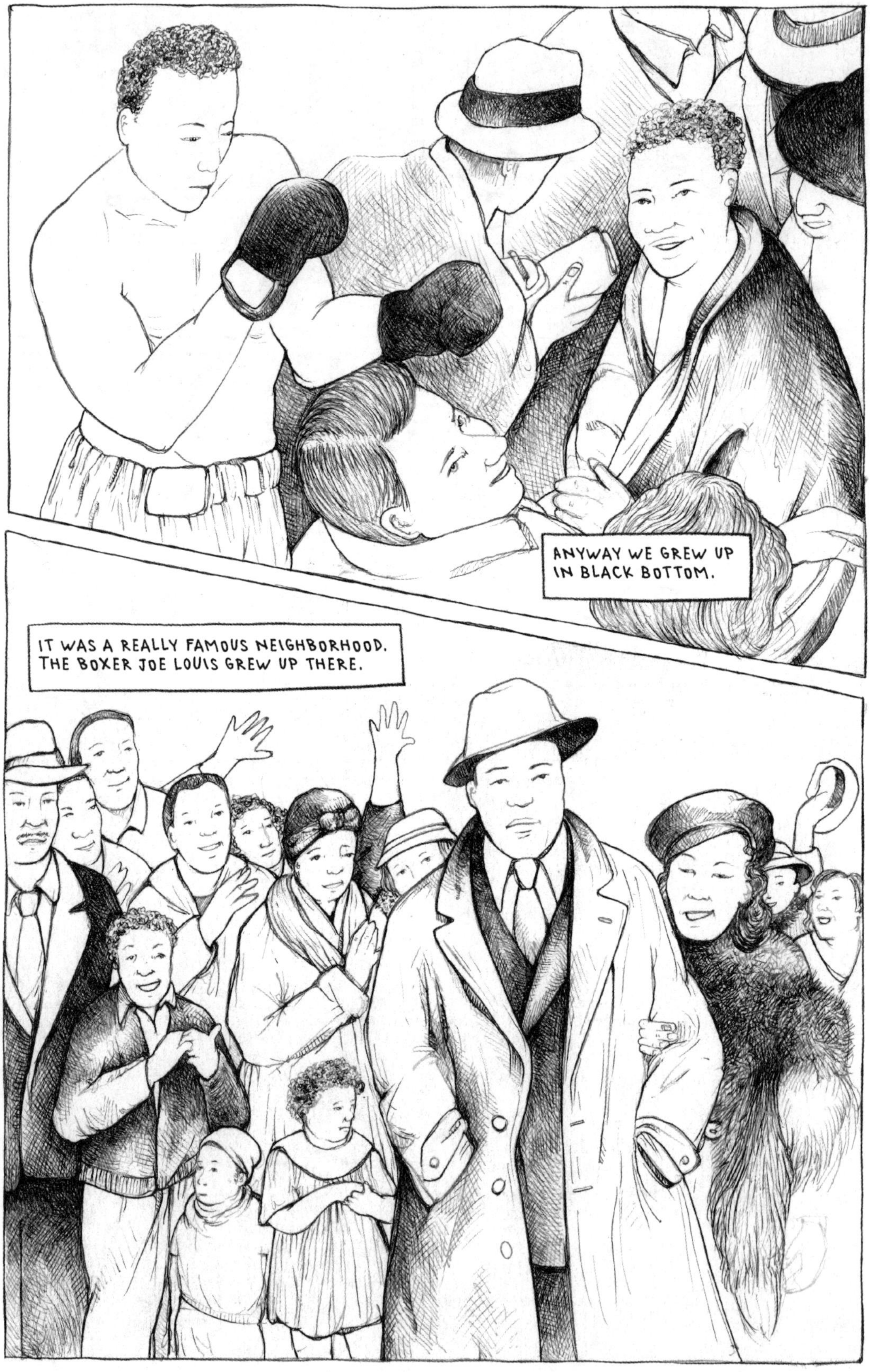
ANYWAY WE GREW UP IN BLACK BOTTOM.
IT WAS A REALLY FAMOUS NEIGHBORHOOD. THE BOXER JOE LOUIS GREW UP THERE.

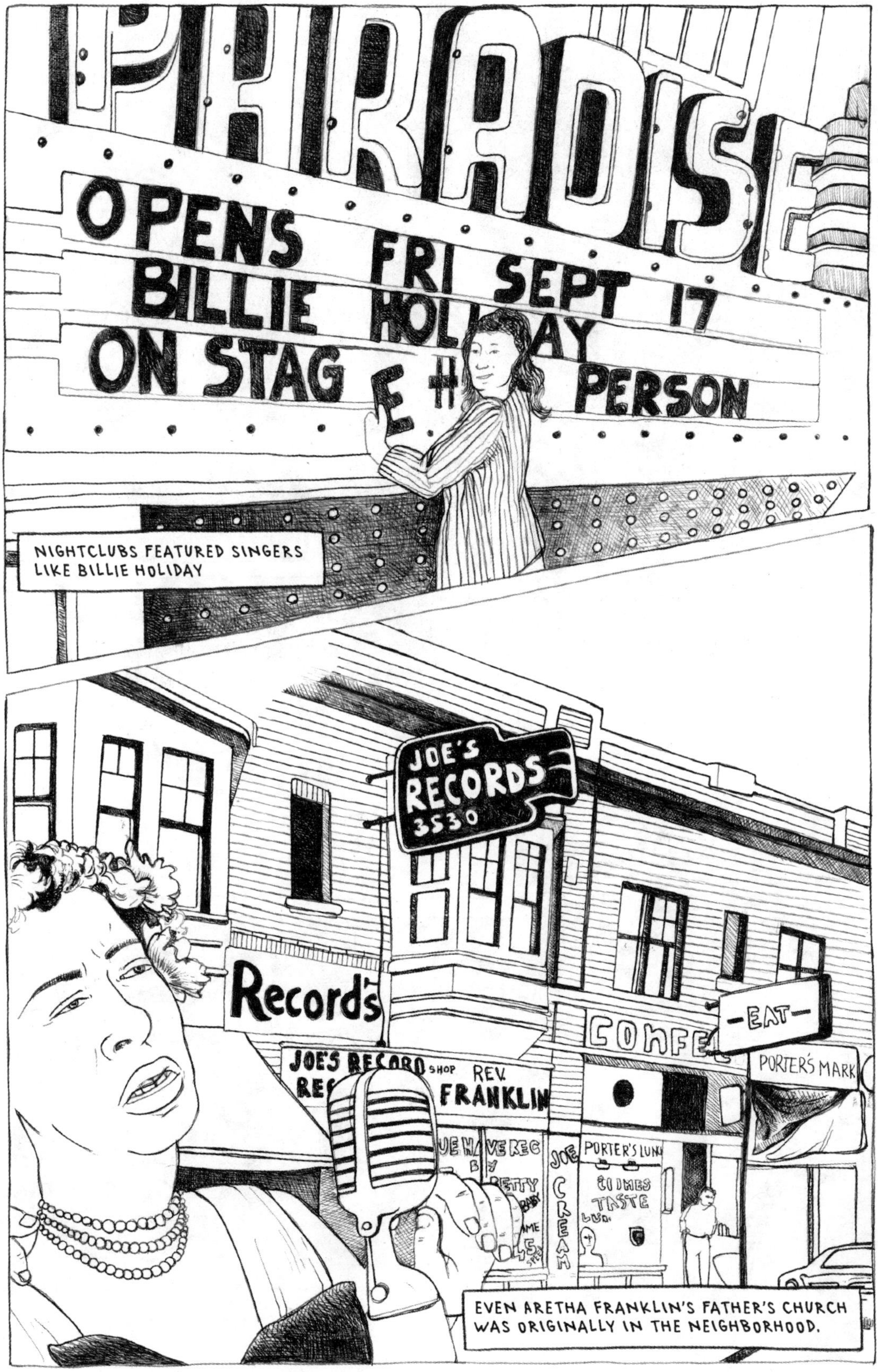
OPENS FRI SEPT 17
NIGHTCLUBS FEATURED SINGERS LIKE BILLIE HOLIDAY
JOE'S RECORDS 3530
Record's
REV. FRANKLIN
-EAT-
PORTER'S MARK
EVEN ARETHA FRANKLIN'S FATHER'S CHURCH WAS ORIGINALLY IN THE NEIGHBORHOOD.

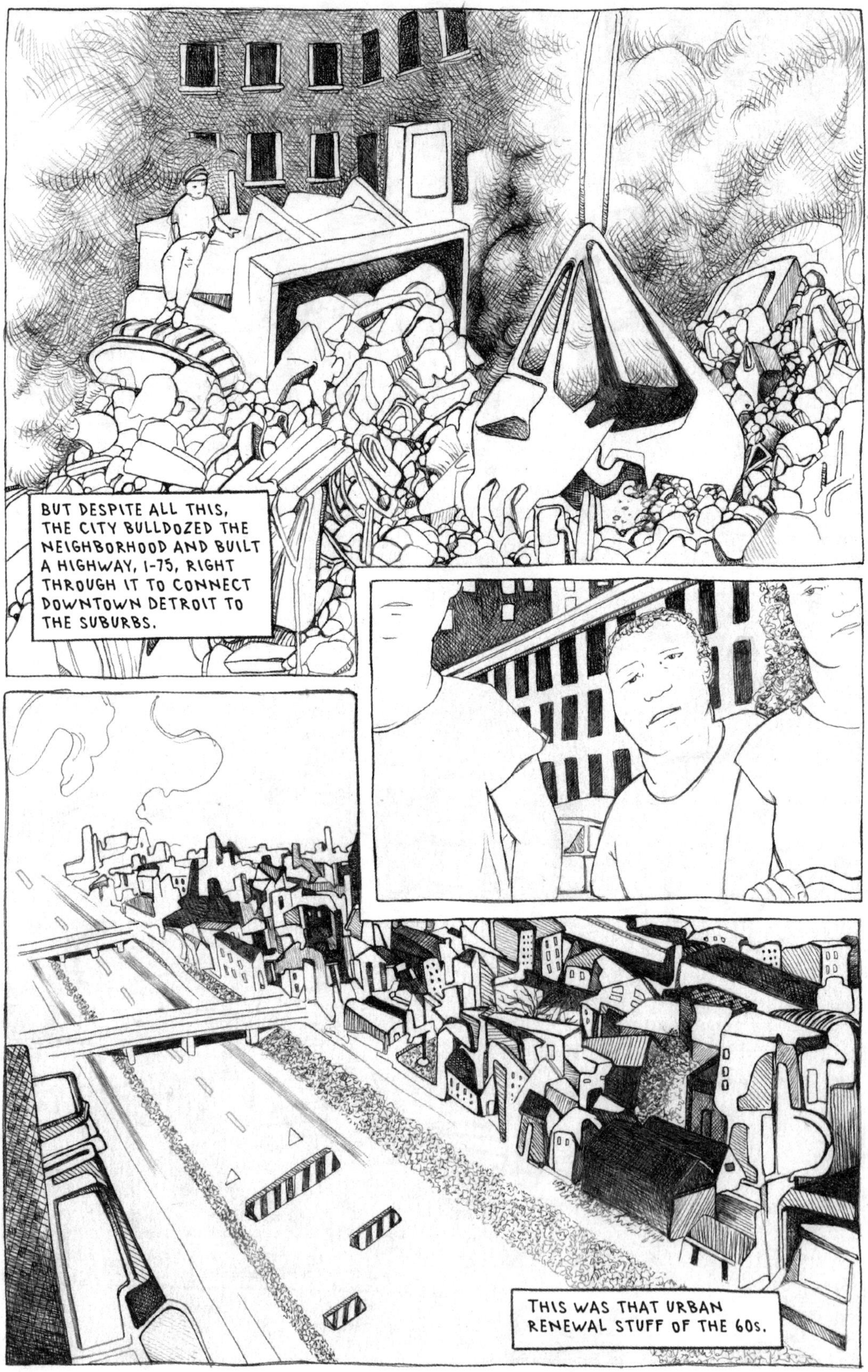
BUT DESPITE ALL THIS, THE CITY BULLDOZED THE NEIGHBORHOOD AND BUILT A HIGHWAY, I-75, RIGHT THROUGH IT TO CONNECT DOWNTOWN DETROIT TO THE SUBURBS.
THIS WAS THAT URBAN RENEWAL STUFF OF THE 60s.

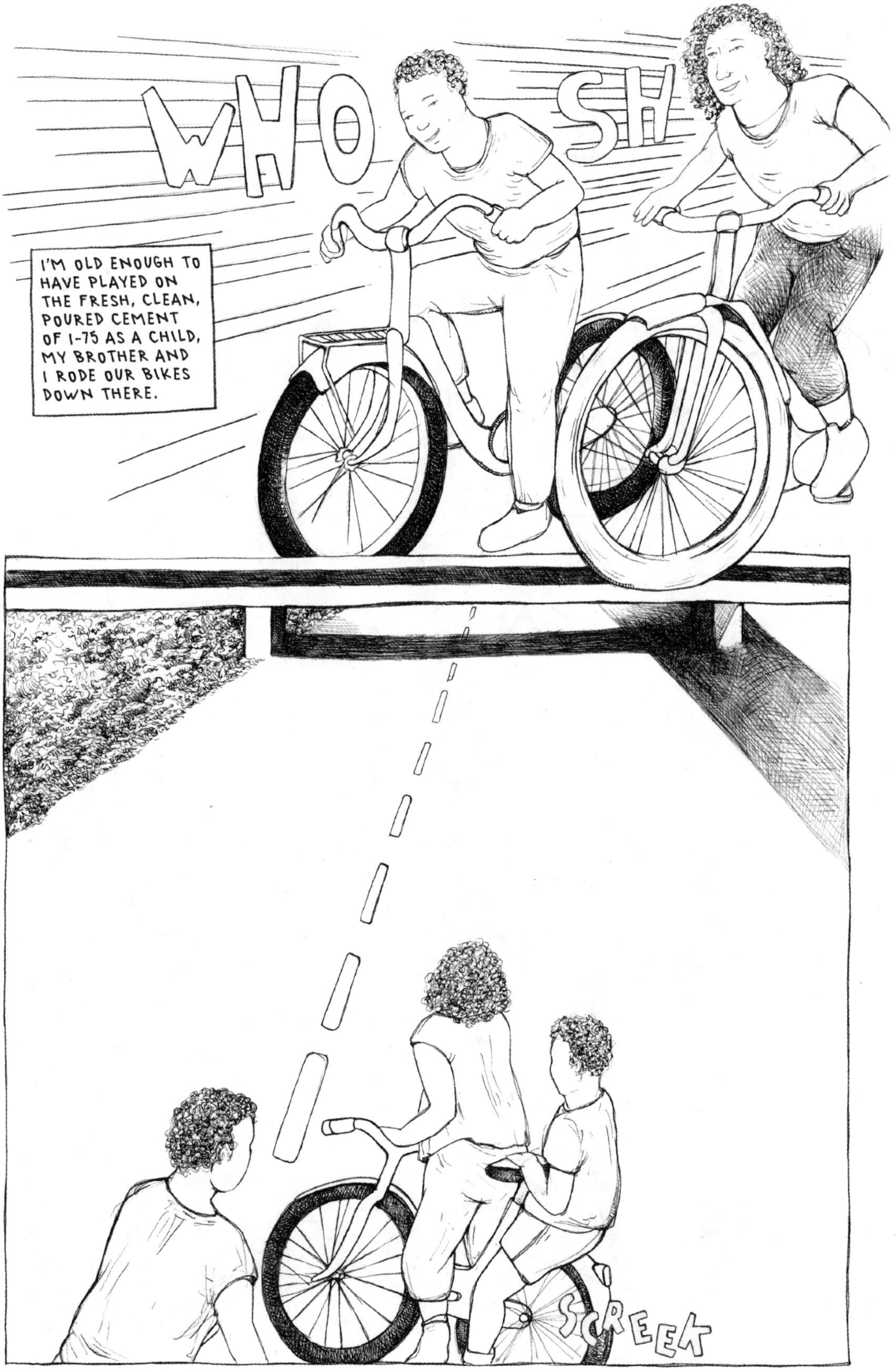
WHOOSH
I'M OLD ENOUGH TO HAVE PLAYED ON THE FRESH, CLEAN, POURED CEMENT OF I-75 AS A CHILD, MY BROTHER AND I RODE OUR BIKES DOWN THERE.
SCREEK

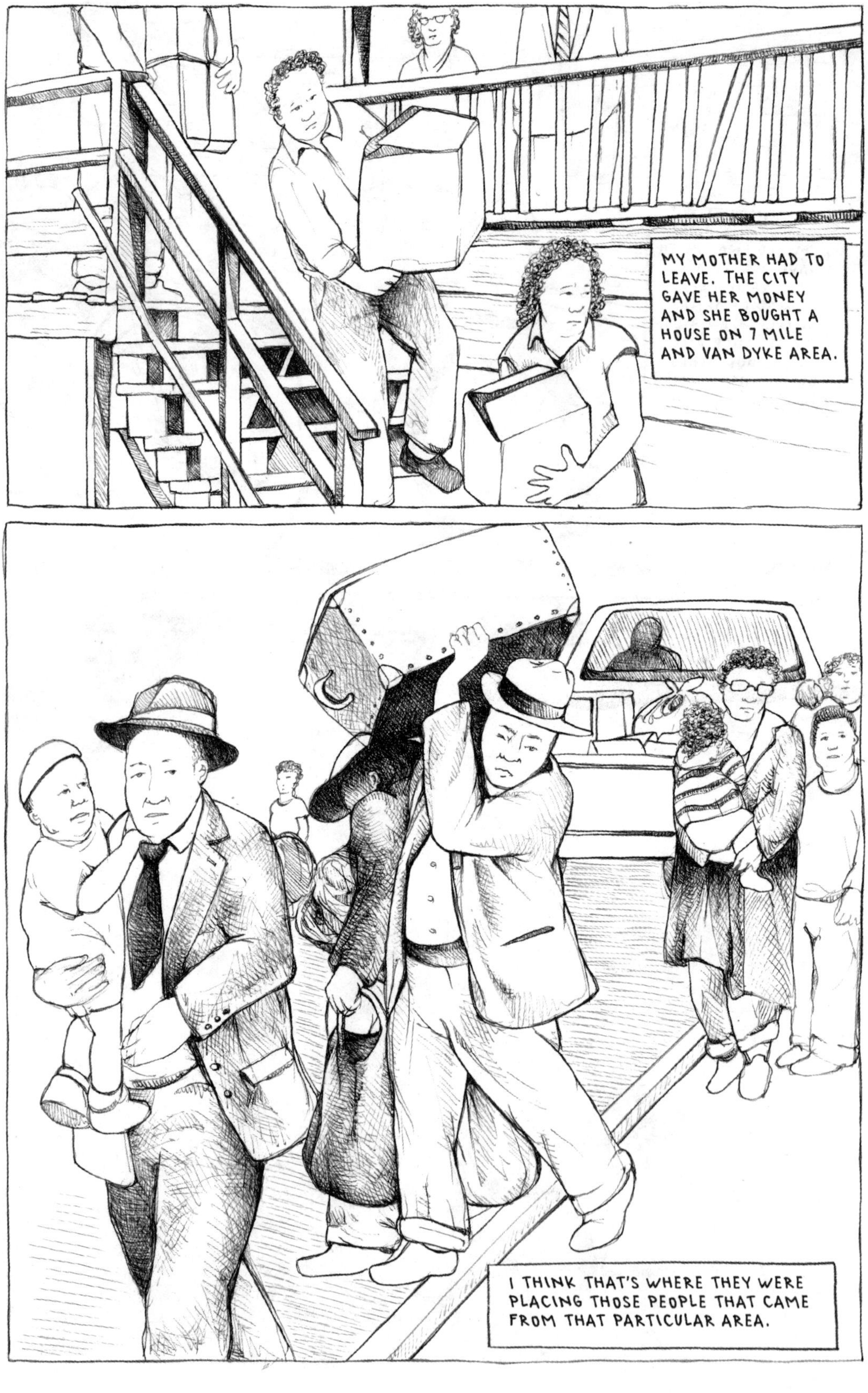
MY MOTHER HAD TO LEAVE. THE CITY GAVE HER MONEY AND SHE BOUGHT A HOUSE ON 7 MILE AND VAN DYKE AREA.
I THINK THAT'S WHERE THEY WERE PLACING THOSE PEOPLE THAT CAME FROM THAT PARTICULAR AREA.

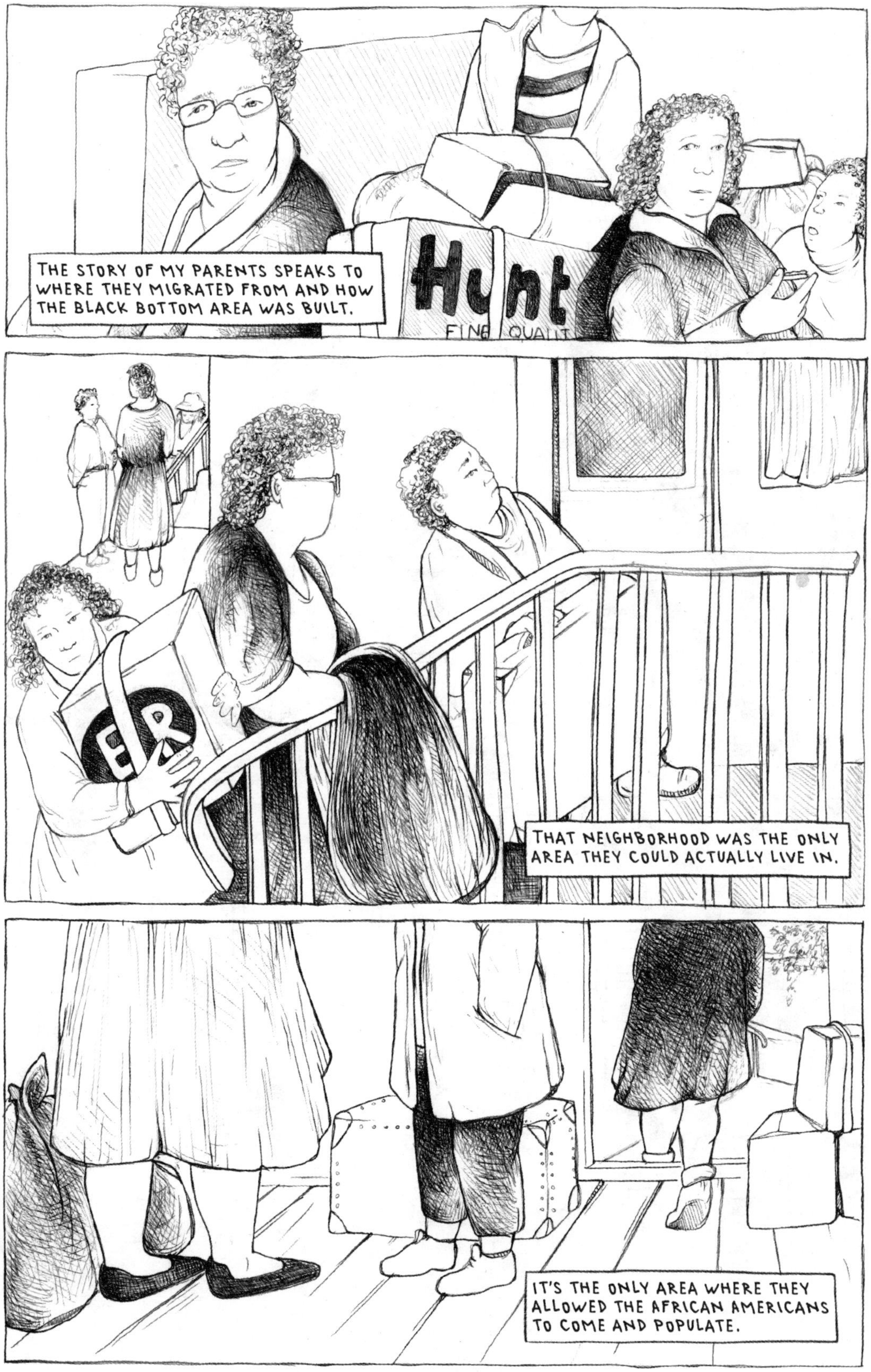
THE STORY OF MY PARENTS SPEAKS TO WHERE THEY MIGRATED FROM AND HOW THE BLACK BOTTOM AREA WAS BUILT.
Hunt
ER
THAT NEIGHBORHOOD WAS THE ONLY AREA THEY COULD ACTUALLY LIVE IN.
IT'S THE ONLY AREA WHERE THEY ALLOWED THE AFRICAN AMERICANS TO COME AND POPULATE.

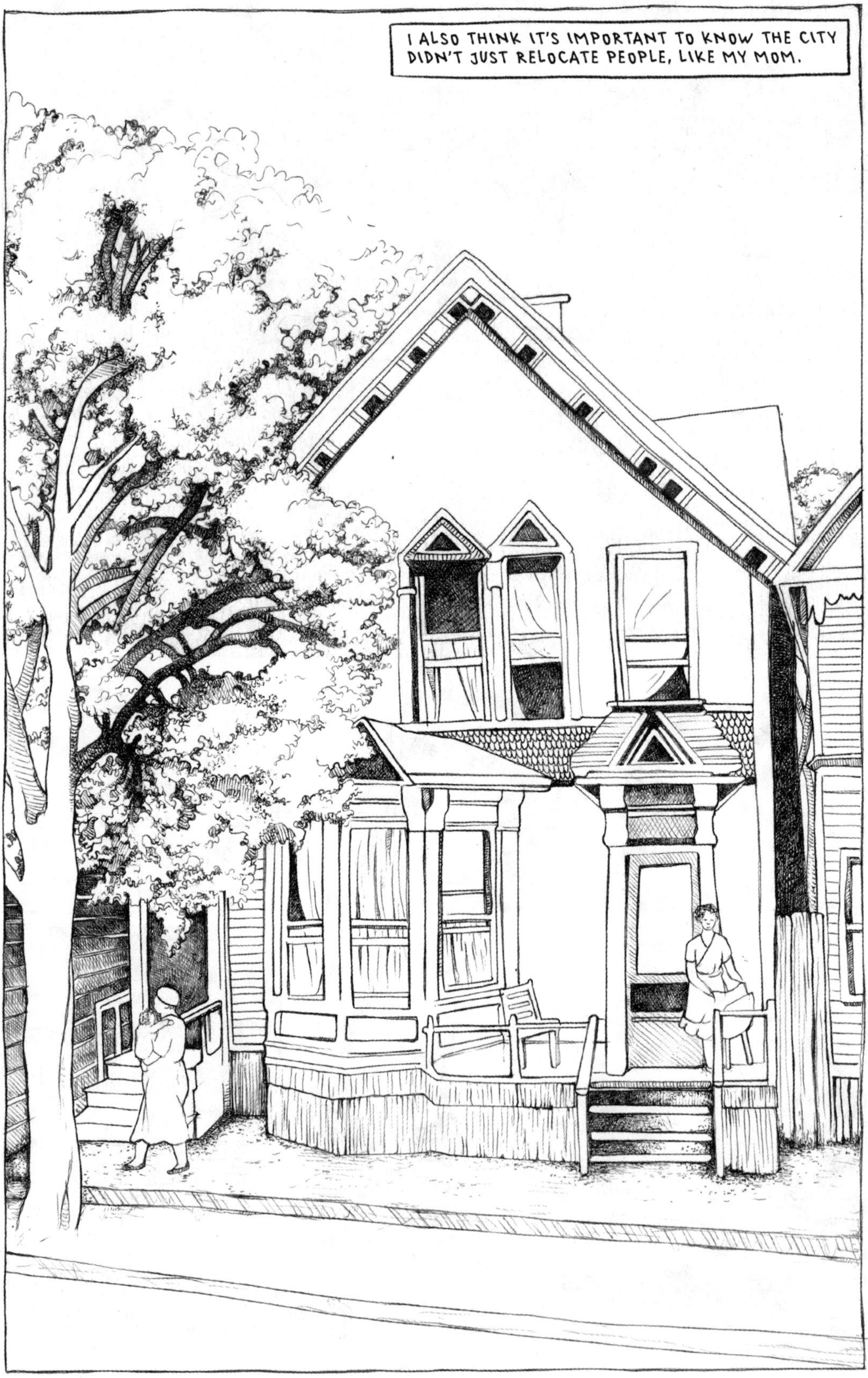
I ALSO THINK IT'S IMPORTANT TO KNOW THE CITY DIDN'T JUST RELOCATE PEOPLE, LIKE MY MOM.

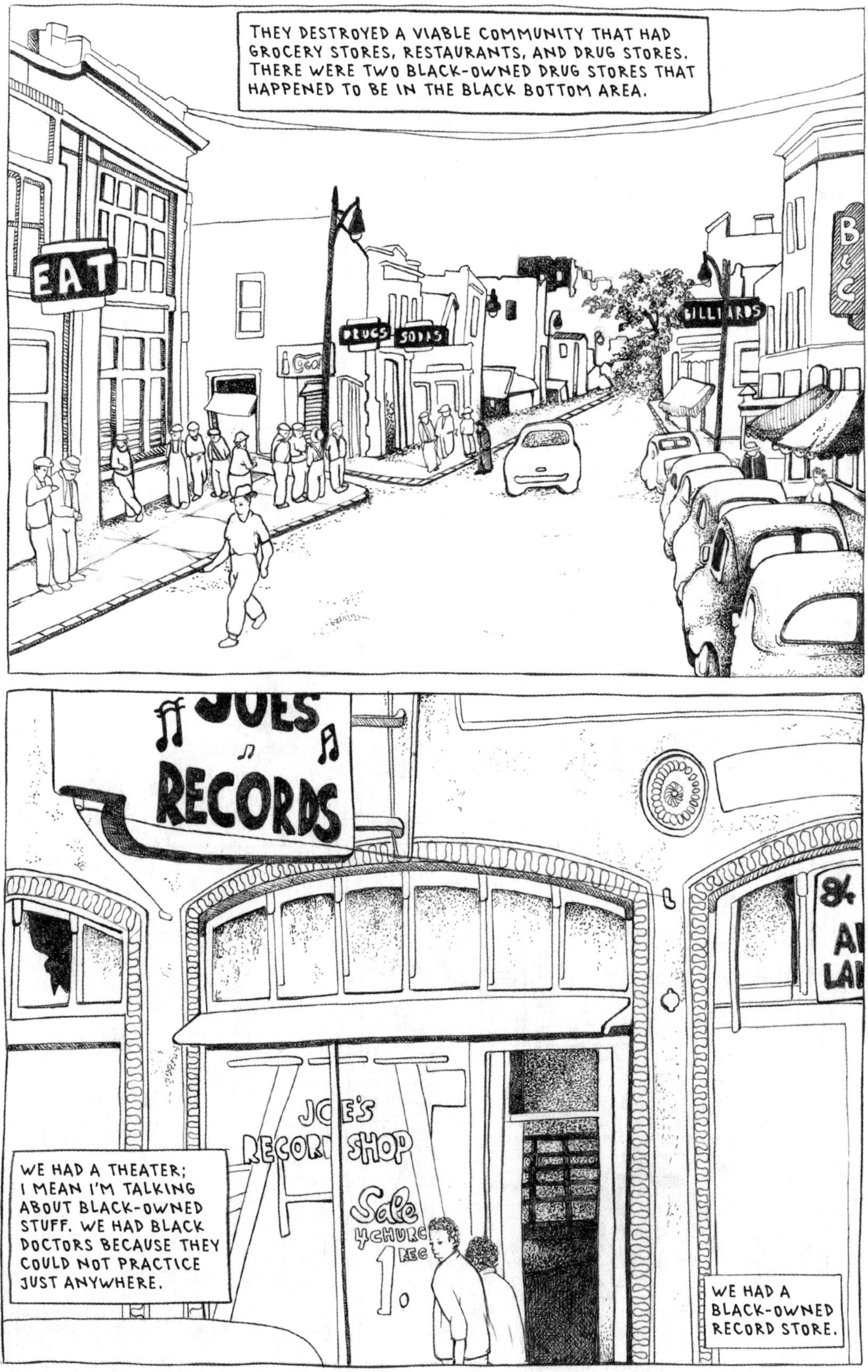
THEY DESTROYED A VIABLE COMMUNITY THAT HAD GROCERY STORES, RESTAURANTS, AND DRUG STORES. THERE WERE TWO BLACK-OWNED DRUG STORES THAT HAPPENED TO BE IN THE BLACK BOTTOM AREA.
EAT
DRUGS
SODAS
BILLIARDS
RECORDS
JOE'S
Sale
WE HAD A THEATER; I MEAN I'M TALKING ABOUT BLACK-OWNED STUFF. WE HAD BLACK DOCTORS BECAUSE THEY COULD NOT PRACTICE JUST ANYWHERE.
WE HAD A BLACK-OWNED RECORD STORE.

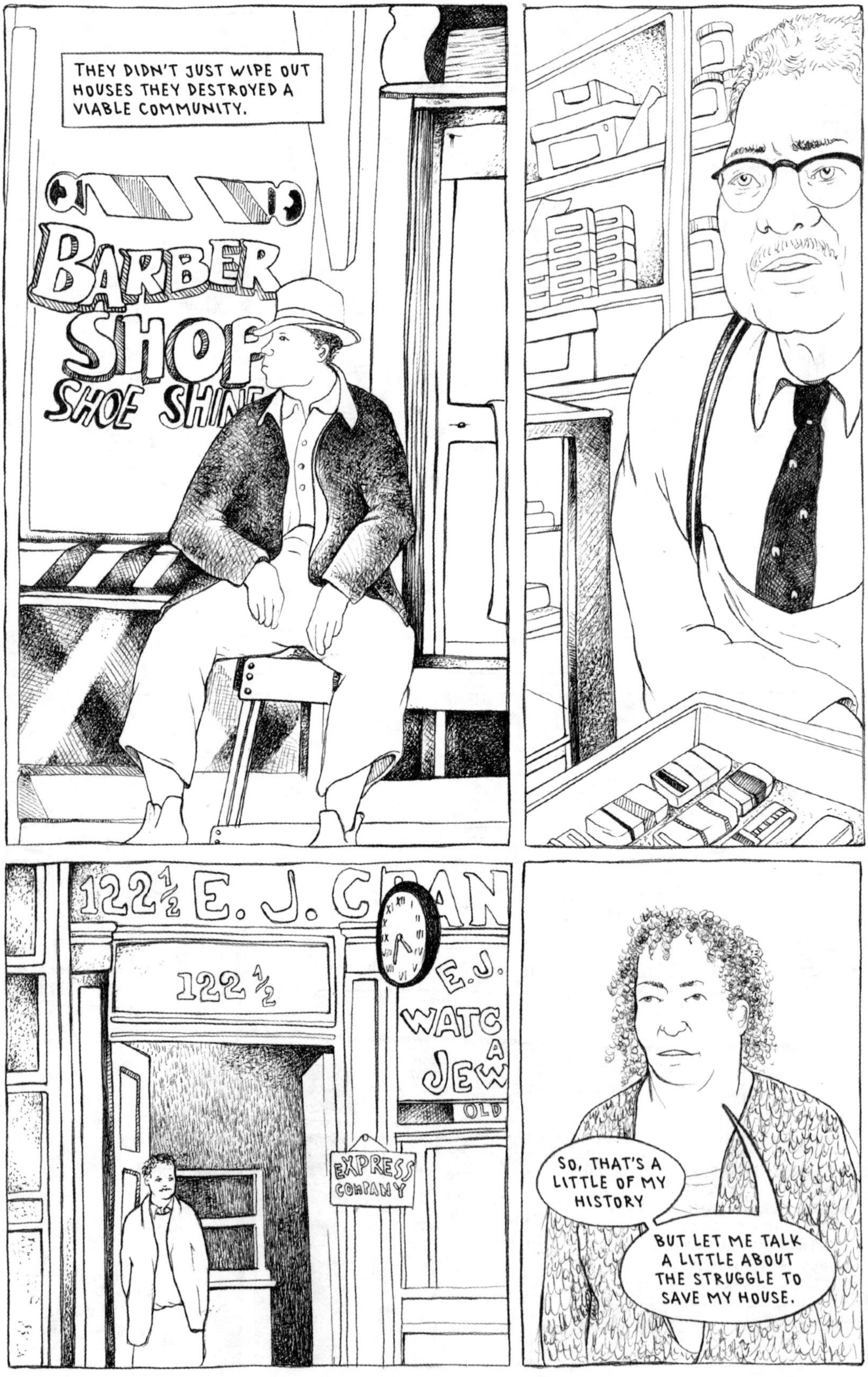
THEY DIDN'T JUST WIPE OUT HOUSES THEY DESTROYED A VIABLE COMMUNITY.
BARBER SHOP
122 1/2
EXPRESS COMPANY
SO, THAT'S A LITTLE OF MY HISTORY
BUT LET ME TALK A LITTLE ABOUT THE STRUGGLE TO SAVE MY HOUSE.

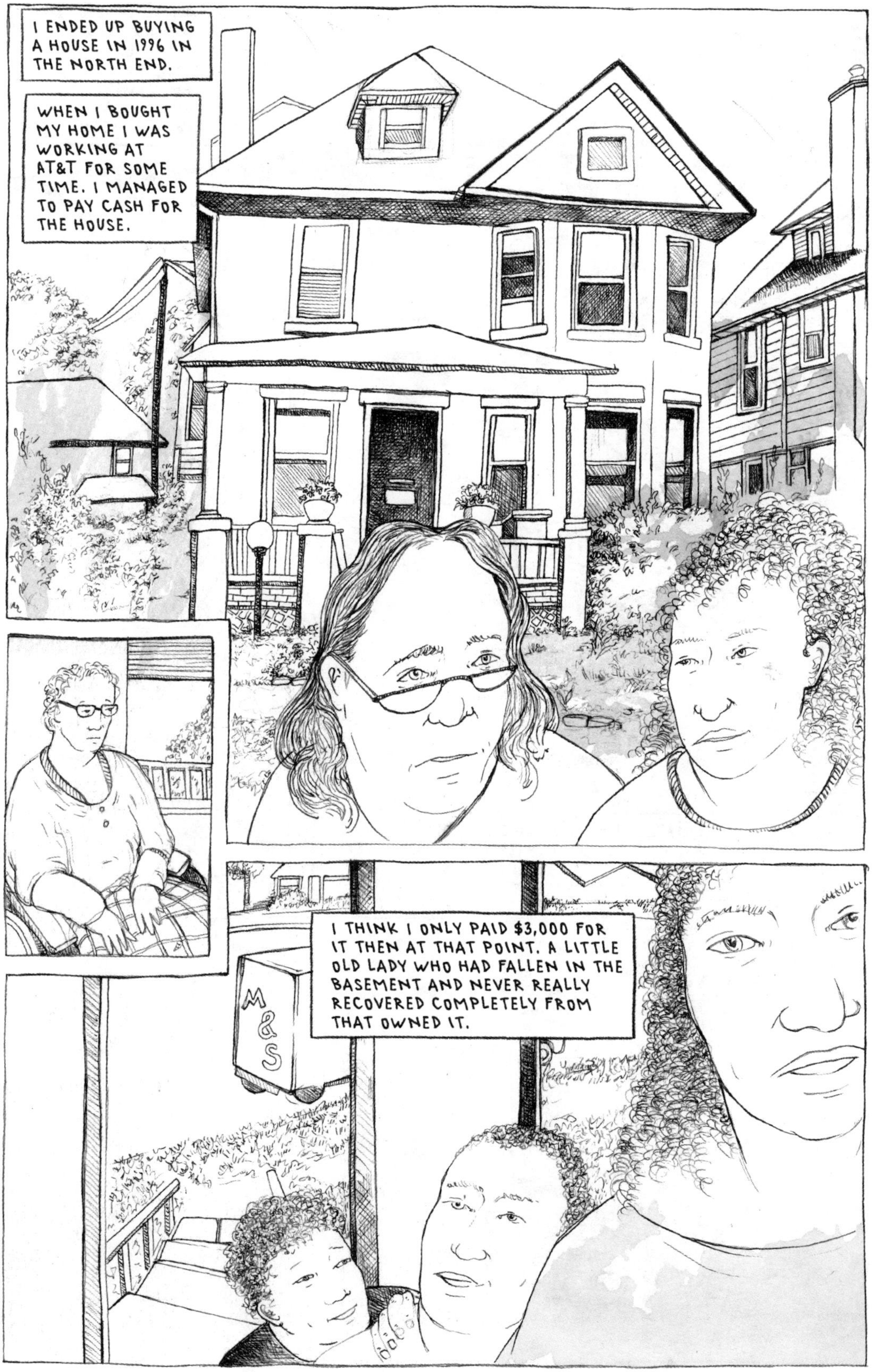
I ENDED UP BUYING A HOUSE IN 1996 IN THE NORTH END.
WHEN I BOUGHT MY HOME I WAS WORKING AT AT&T FOR SOME TIME. I MANAGED TO PAY CASH FOR THE HOUSE.
I THINK I ONLY PAID $3,000 FOR IT THEN AT THAT POINT. A LITTLE OLD LADY WHO HAD FALLEN IN THE BASEMENT AND NEVER REALLY RECOVERED COMPLETELY FROM THAT OWNED IT.
M&S

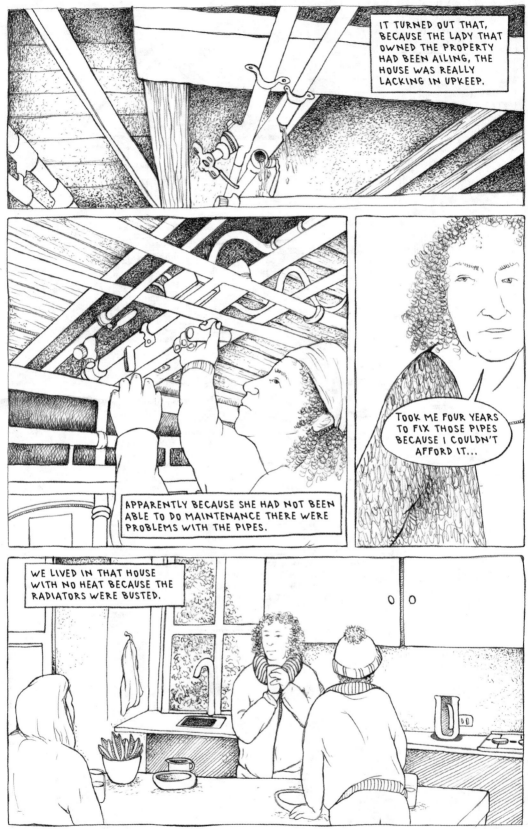

IT TURNED OUT THAT, BECAUSE THE LADY THAT OWNED THE PROPERTY HAD BEEN AILING, THE HOUSE WAS REALLY LACKING IN UPKEEP.

TOOK ME FOUR YEARS TO FIX THOSE PIPES BECAUSE I COULDN'T AFFORD IT...

APPARENTLY BECAUSE SHE HAD NOT BEEN ABLE TO DO MAINTENANCE THERE WERE PROBLEMS WITH THE PIPES.

WE LIVED IN THAT HOUSE WITH NO HEAT BECAUSE THE RADIATORS WERE BUSTED.

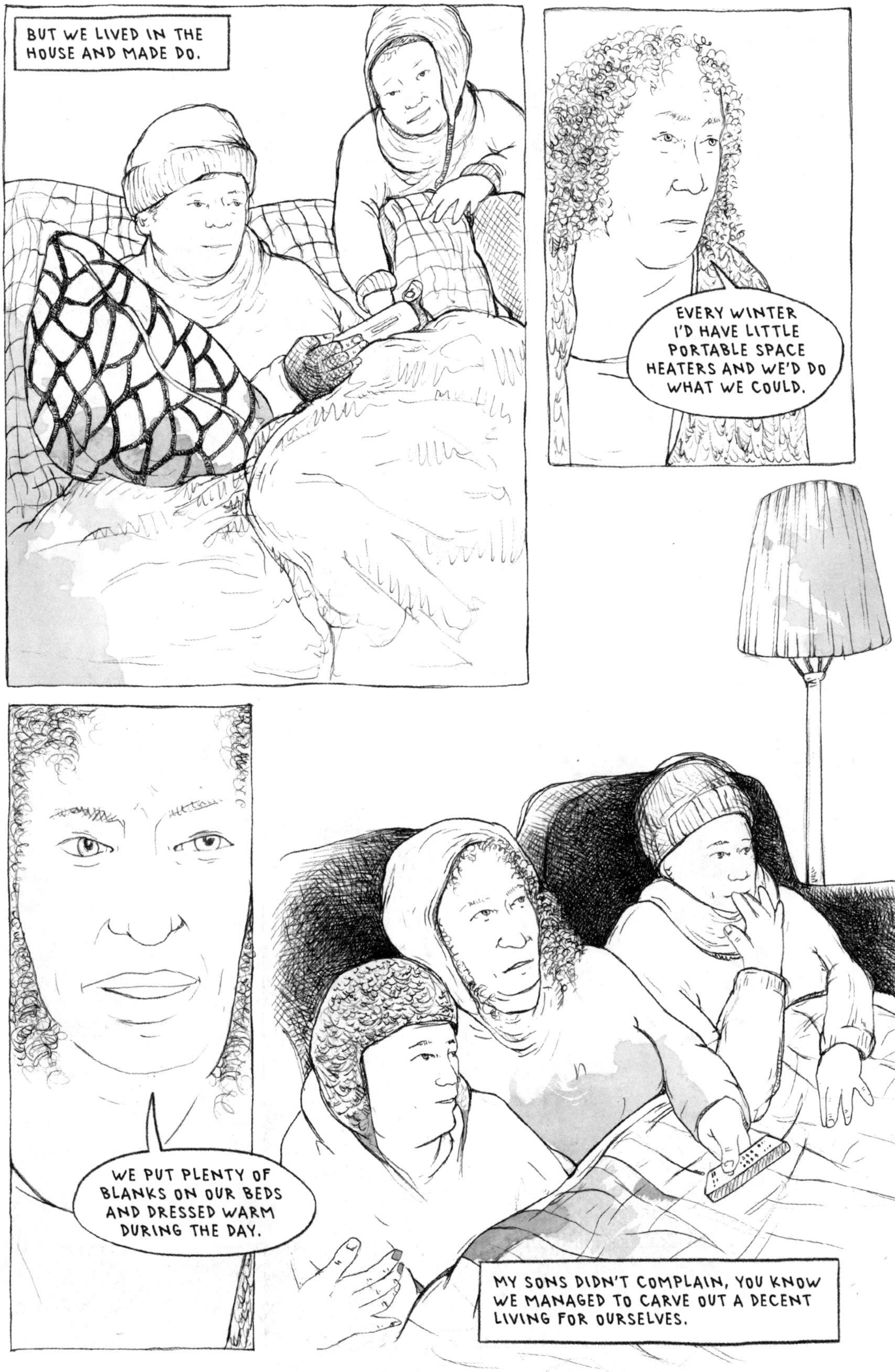
BUT WE LIVED IN THE HOUSE AND MADE DO.
EVERY WINTER I'D HAVE LITTLE PORTABLE SPACE HEATERS AND WE'D DO WHAT WE COULD.
WE PUT PLENTY OF BLANKS ON OUR BEDS AND DRESSED WARM DURING THE DAY.
MY SONS DIDN'T COMPLAIN, YOU KNOW WE MANAGED TO CARVE OUT A DECENT LIVING FOR OURSELVES.

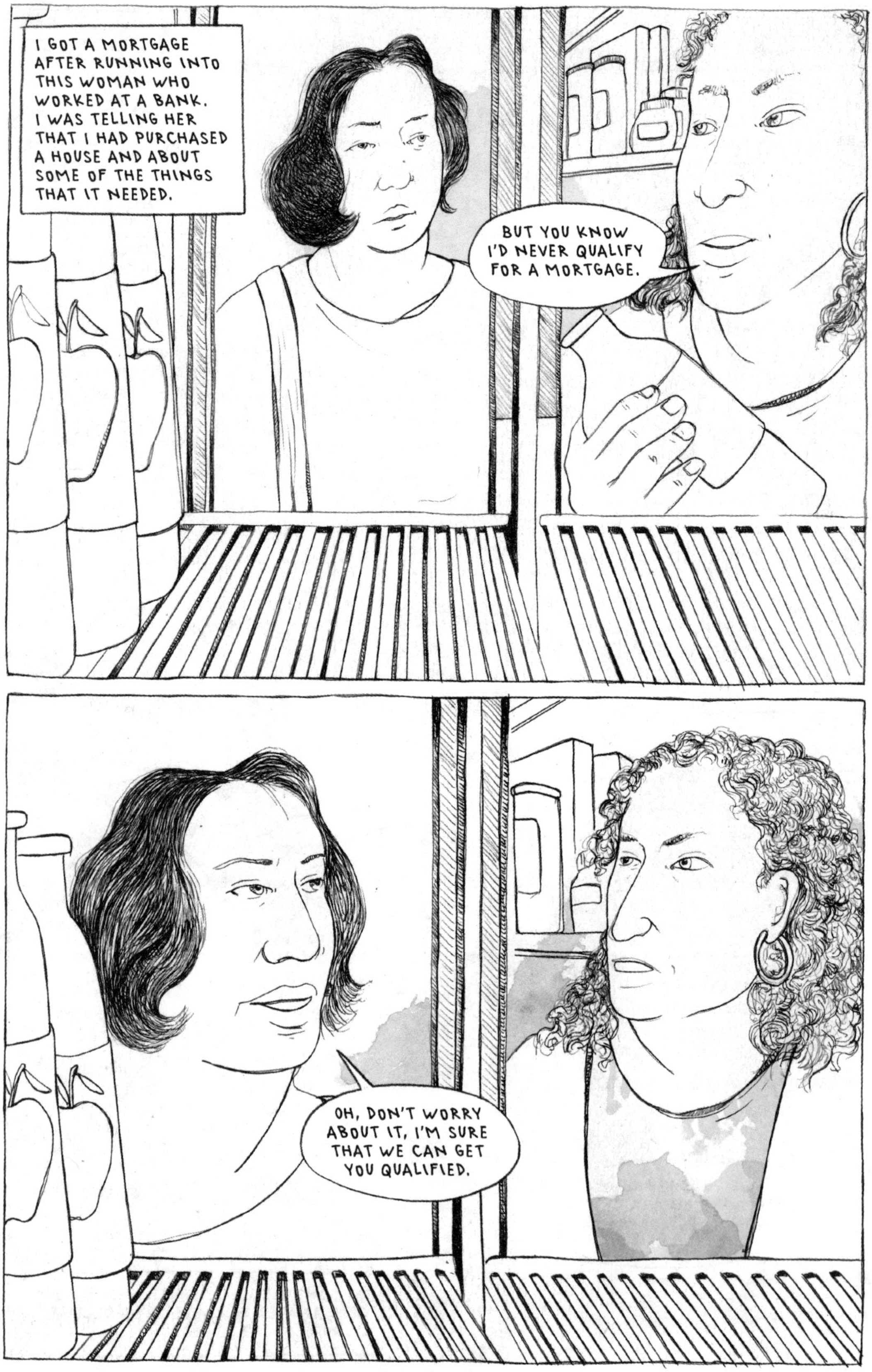
I GOT A MORTGAGE AFTER RUNNING INTO THIS WOMAN WHO WORKED AT A BANK. I WAS TELLING HER THAT I HAD PURCHASED A HOUSE AND ABOUT SOME OF THE THINGS THAT IT NEEDED.
BUT YOU KNOW I'D NEVER QUALIFY FOR A MORTGAGE.
OH, DON'T WORRY ABOUT IT, I'M SURE THAT WE CAN GET YOU QUALIFIED.

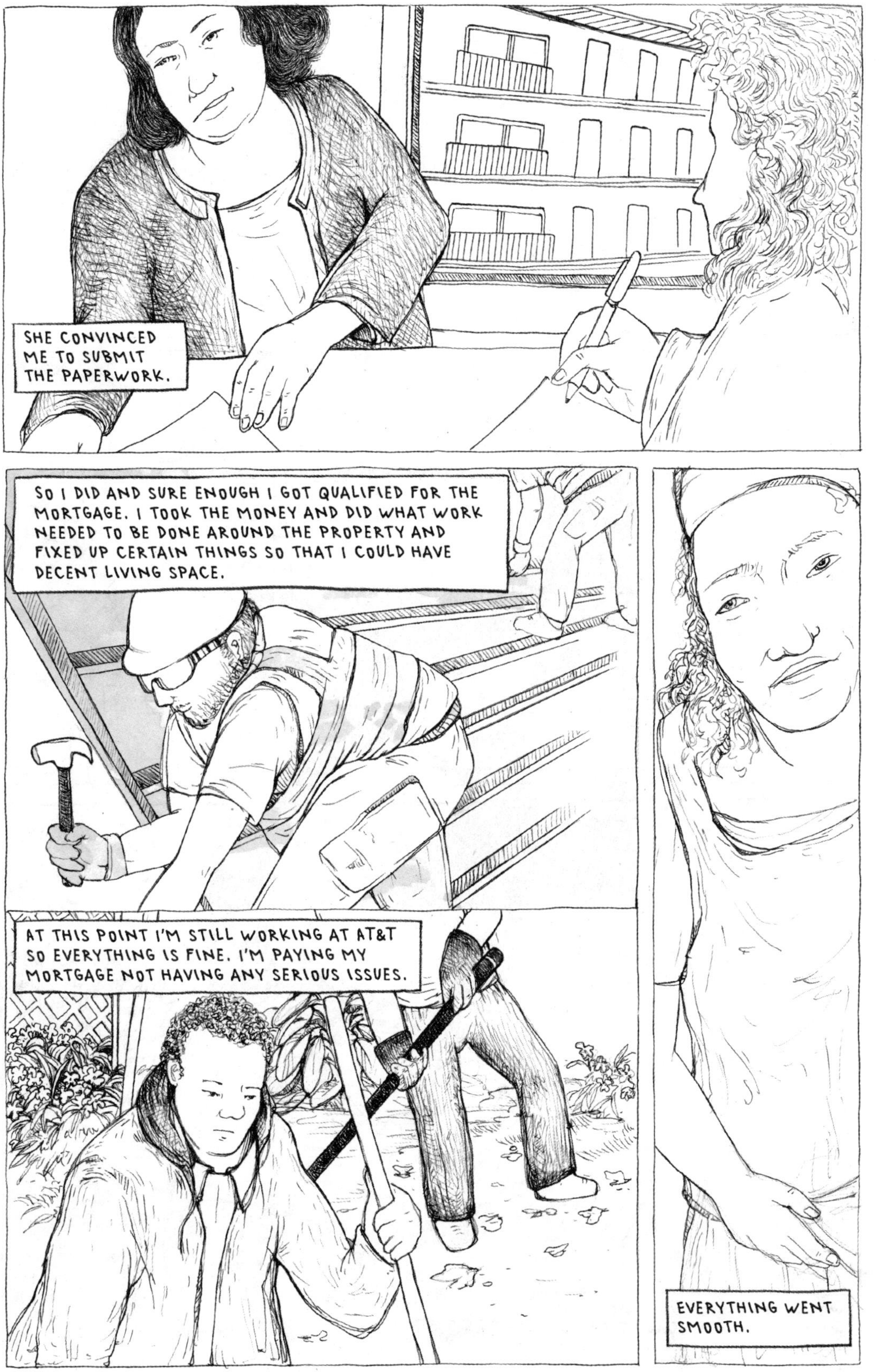
SHE CONVINCED ME TO SUBMIT THE PAPERWORK.
SO I DID AND SURE ENOUGH I GOT QUALIFIED FOR THE MORTGAGE. I TOOK THE MONEY AND DID WHAT WORK NEEDED TO BE DONE AROUND THE PROPERTY AND FIXED UP CERTAIN THINGS SO THAT I COULD HAVE DECENT LIVING SPACE.
AT THIS POINT I'M STILL WORKING AT AT&T SO EVERYTHING IS FINE. I'M PAYING MY MORTGAGE NOT HAVING ANY SERIOUS ISSUES.
EVERYTHING WENT SMOOTH.

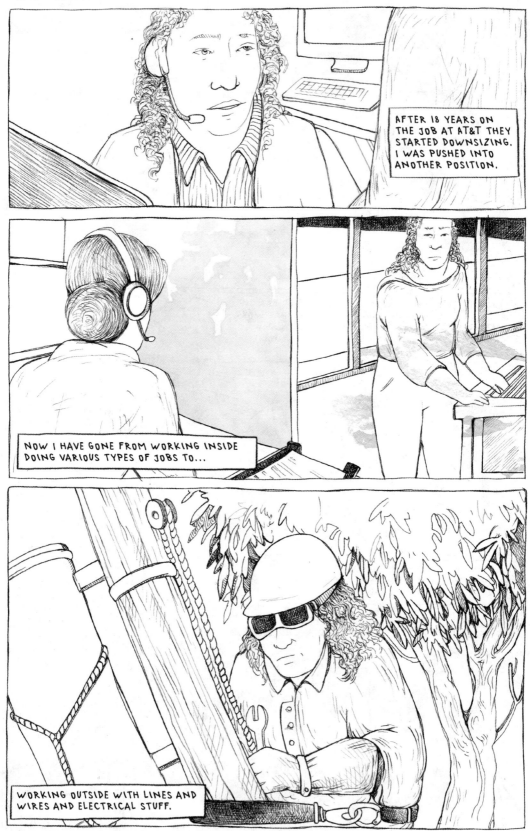

AFTER 18 YEARS ON THE JOB AT AT&T THEY STARTED DOWNSIZING. I WAS PUSHED INTO ANOTHER POSITION.

NOW I HAVE GONE FROM WORKING INSIDE DOING VARIOUS TYPES OF JOBS TO...

WORKING OUTSIDE WITH LINES AND WIRES AND ELECTRICAL STUFF.

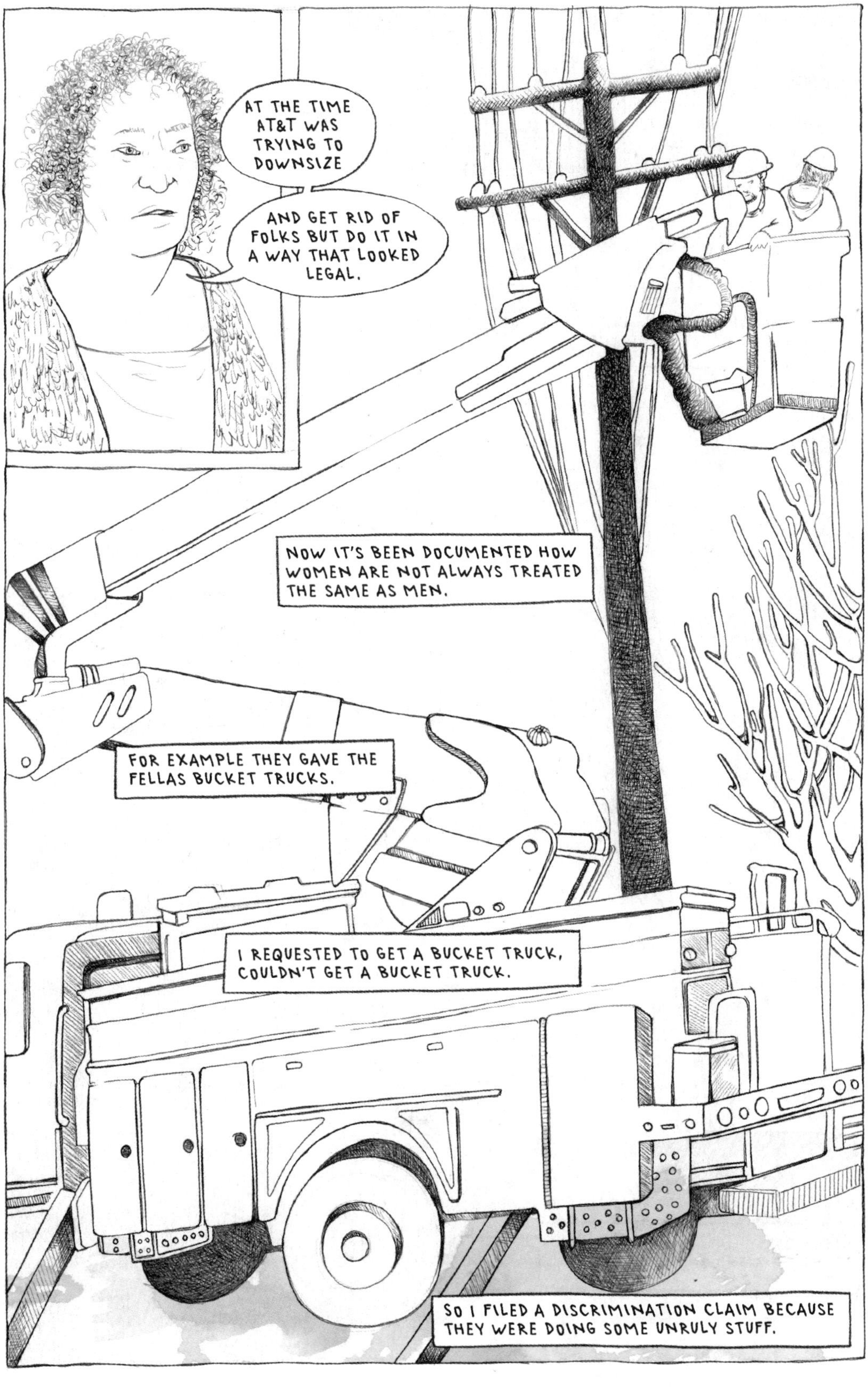
AT THE TIME AT&T WAS TRYING TO DOWNSIZE
AND GET RID OF FOLKS BUT DO IT IN A WAY THAT LOOKED LEGAL.
NOW IT'S BEEN DOCUMENTED HOW WOMEN ARE NOT ALWAYS TREATED THE SAME AS MEN.
FOR EXAMPLE THEY GAVE THE FELLAS BUCKET TRUCKS.
I REQUESTED TO GET A BUCKET TRUCK, COULDN'T GET A BUCKET TRUCK.
SO I FILED A DISCRIMINATION CLAIM BECAUSE THEY WERE DOING SOME UNRULY STUFF.

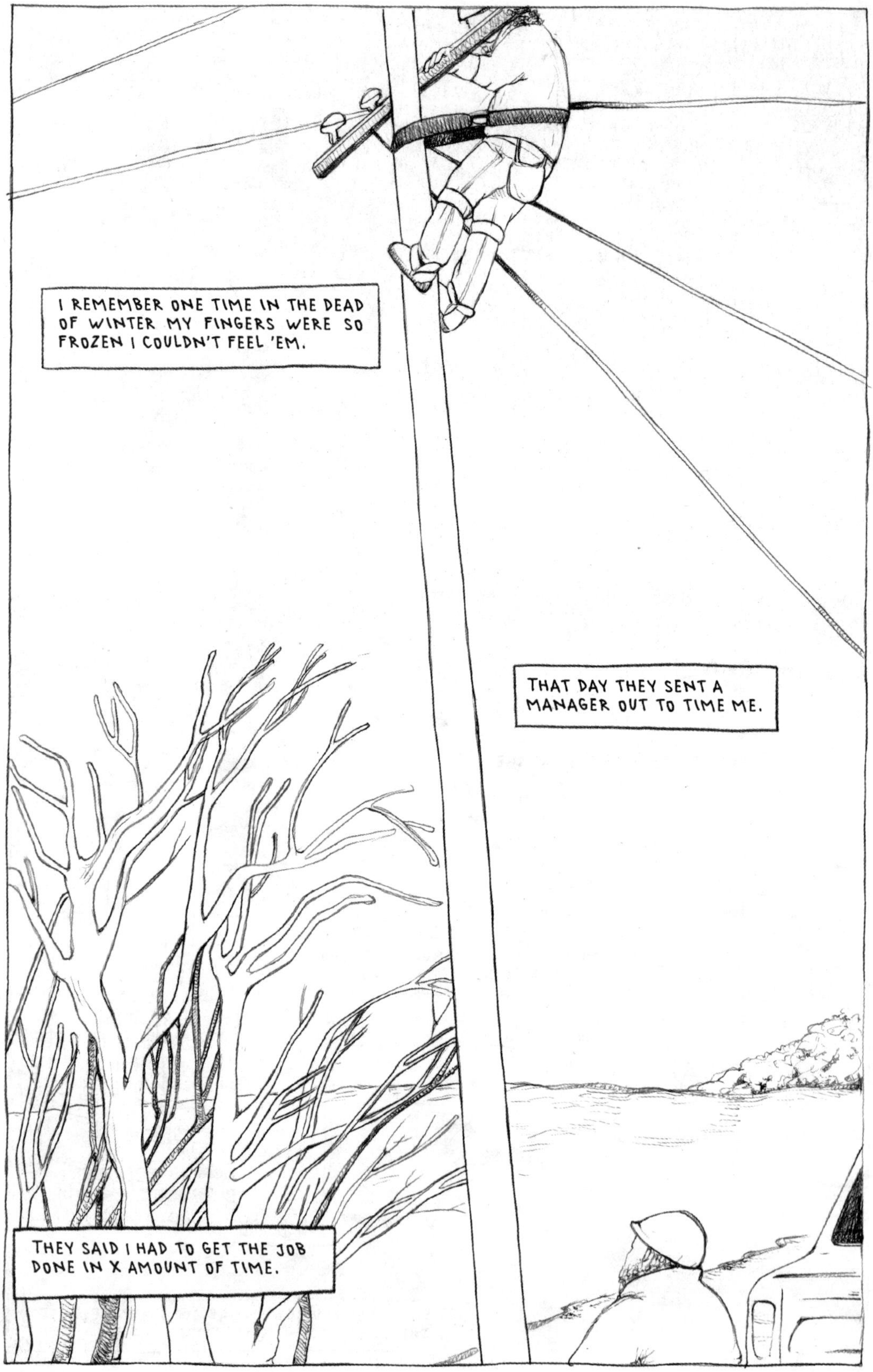
I REMEMBER ONE TIME IN THE DEAD OF WINTER MY FINGERS WERE SO FROZEN I COULDN'T FEEL 'EM.
THAT DAY THEY SENT A MANAGER OUT TO TIME ME.
THEY SAID I HAD TO GET THE JOB DONE IN X AMOUNT OF TIME.

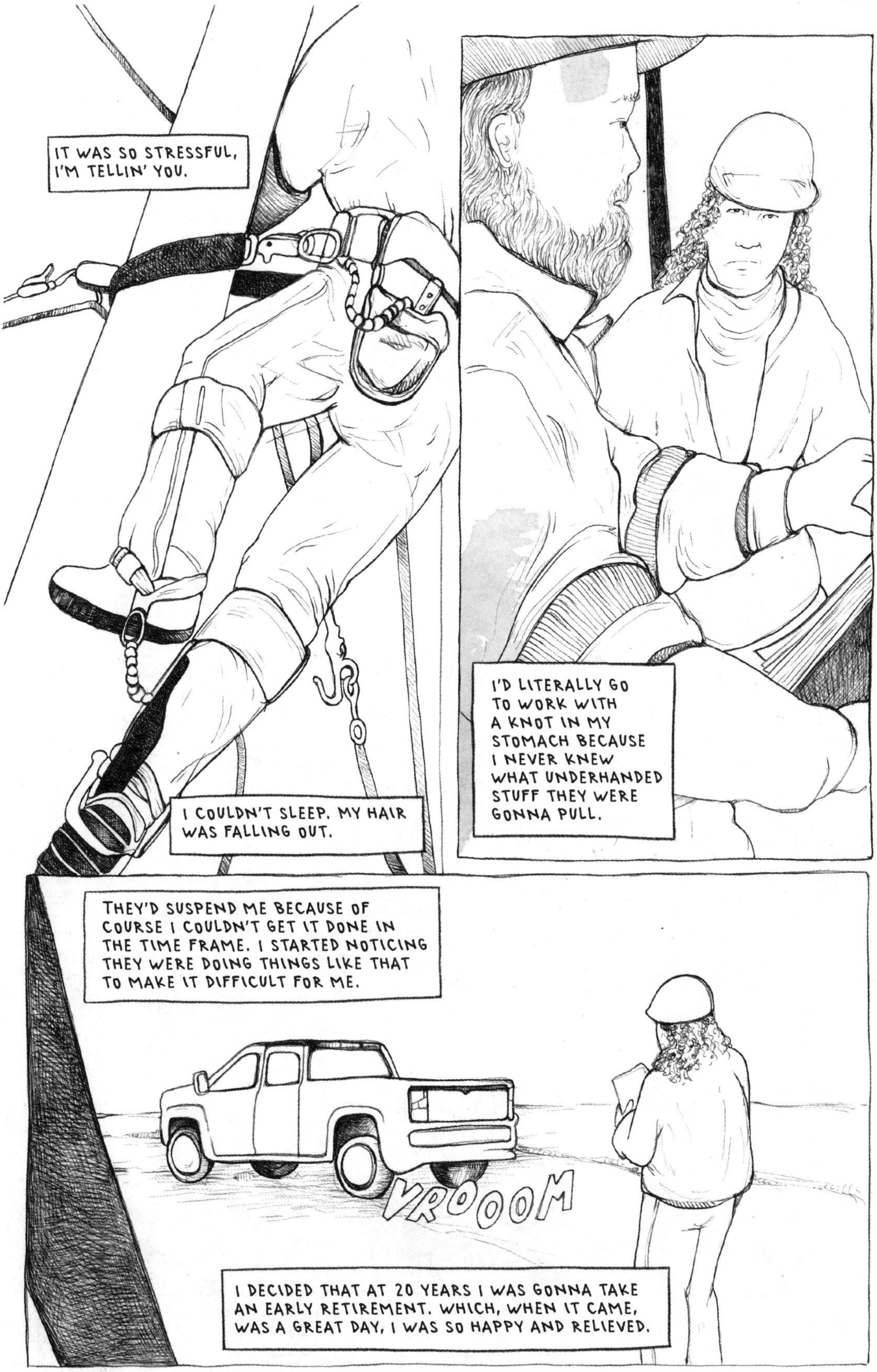
IT WAS SO STRESSFUL, I'M TELLIN' YOU.
I COULDN'T SLEEP. MY HAIR WAS FALLING OUT.
I'D LITERALLY GO TO WORK WITH A KNOT IN MY STOMACH BECAUSE I NEVER KNEW WHAT UNDERHANDED STUFF THEY WERE GONNA PULL.
THEY'D SUSPEND ME BECAUSE OF COURSE I COULDN'T GET IT DONE IN THE TIME FRAME. I STARTED NOTICING THEY WERE DOING THINGS LIKE THAT TO MAKE IT DIFFICULT FOR ME.
VROOOM
I DECIDED THAT AT 20 YEARS I WAS GONNA TAKE AN EARLY RETIREMENT. WHICH, WHEN IT CAME, WAS A GREAT DAY, I WAS SO HAPPY AND RELIEVED.

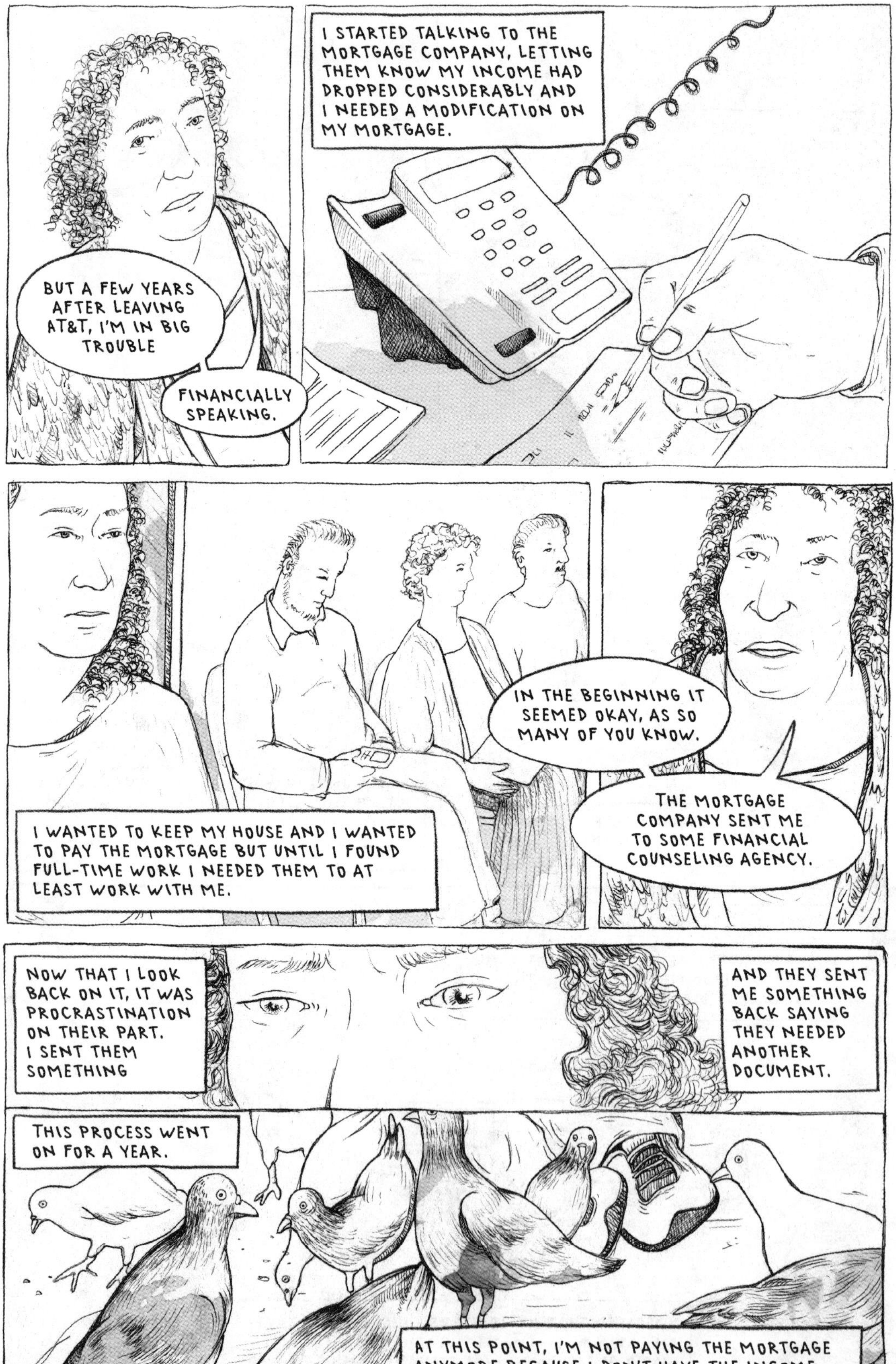
BUT A FEW YEARS AFTER LEAVING AT&T, I'M IN BIG TROUBLE
FINANCIALLY SPEAKING.
I STARTED TALKING TO THE MORTGAGE COMPANY, LETTING THEM KNOW MY INCOME HAD DROPPED CONSIDERABLY AND I NEEDED A MODIFICATION ON MY MORTGAGE.
I WANTED TO KEEP MY HOUSE AND I WANTED TO PAY THE MORTGAGE BUT UNTIL I FOUND FULL-TIME WORK I NEEDED THEM TO AT LEAST WORK WITH ME.
IN THE BEGINNING IT SEEMED OKAY, AS SO MANY OF YOU KNOW.
THE MORTGAGE COMPANY SENT ME TO SOME FINANCIAL COUNSELING AGENCY.
NOW THAT I LOOK BACK ON IT, IT WAS PROCRASTINATION ON THEIR PART. I SENT THEM SOMETHING
AND THEY SENT ME SOMETHING BACK SAYING THEY NEEDED ANOTHER DOCUMENT.
THIS PROCESS WENT ON FOR A YEAR.
AT THIS POINT, I'M NOT PAYING THE MORTGAGE ANYMORE BECAUSE I DON'T HAVE THE INCOME.

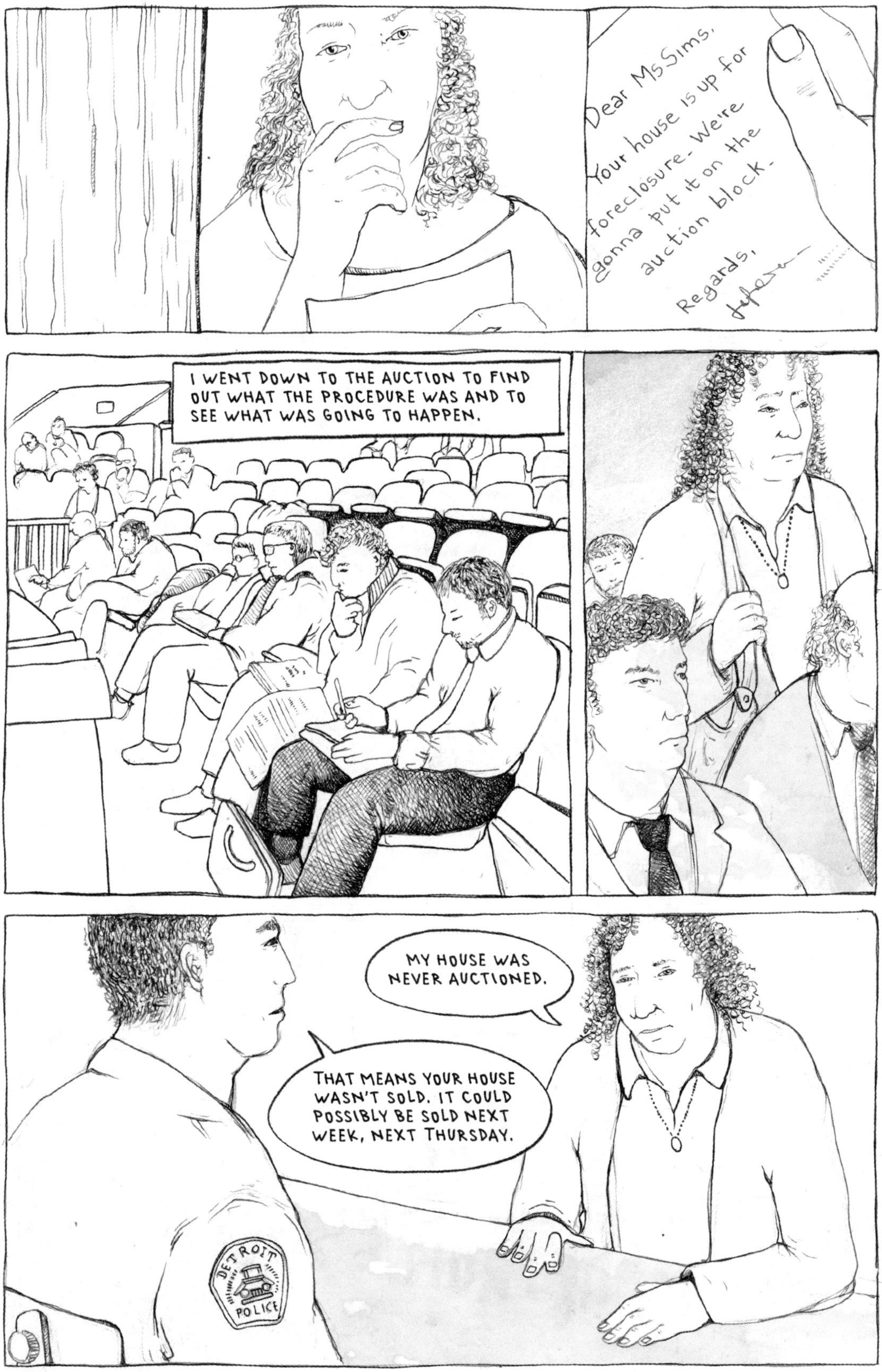
Dear Ms Sims,
Your house is up for foreclosure. We're gonna put it on the auction block.
Regards,
I WENT DOWN TO THE AUCTION TO FIND OUT WHAT THE PROCEDURE WAS AND TO SEE WHAT WAS GOING TO HAPPEN.
MY HOUSE WAS NEVER AUCTIONED.
THAT MEANS YOUR HOUSE WASN'T SOLD. IT COULD POSSIBLY BE SOLD NEXT WEEK, NEXT THURSDAY.
DETROIT POLICE

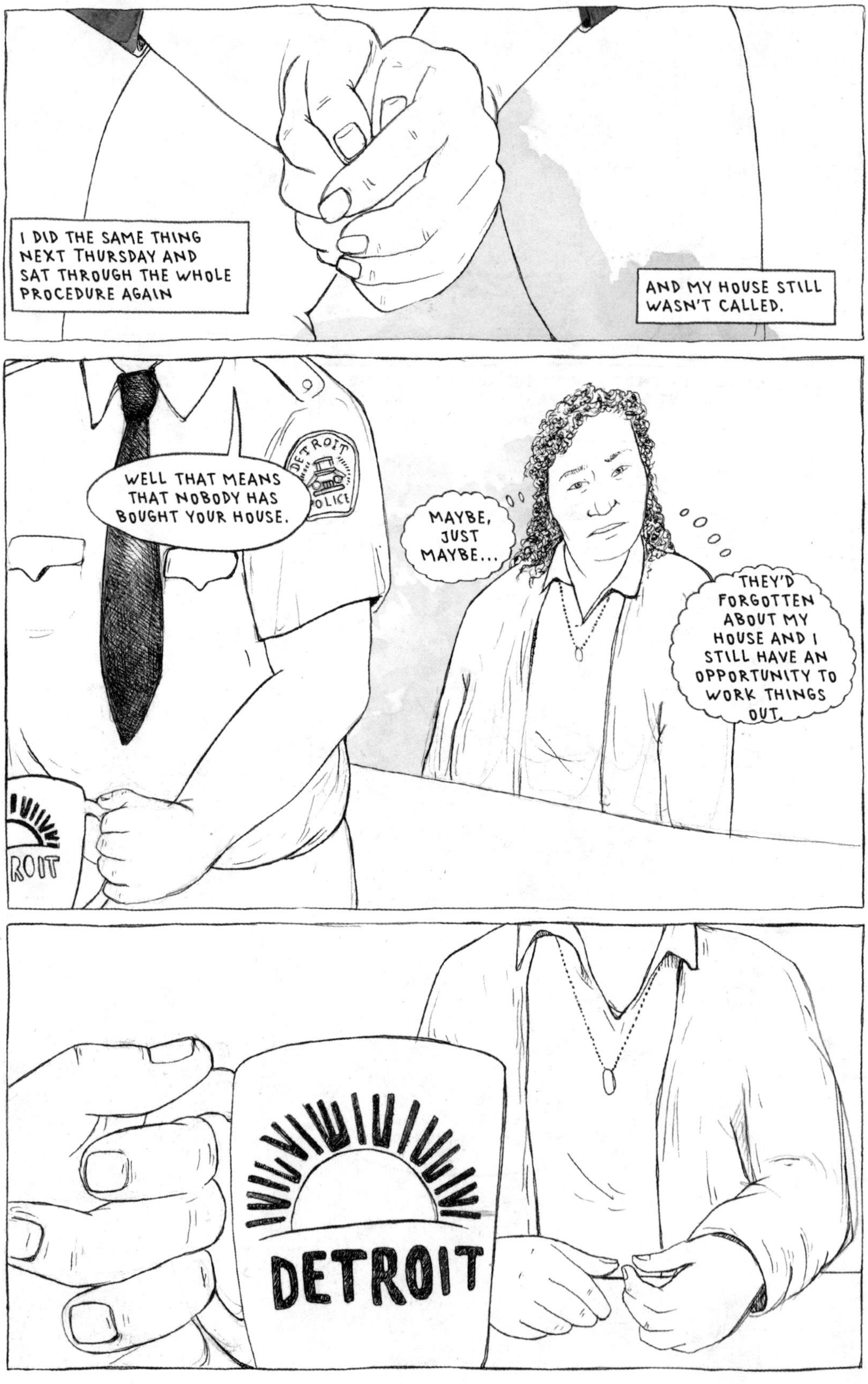
I DID THE SAME THING NEXT THURSDAY AND SAT THROUGH THE WHOLE PROCEDURE AGAIN
AND MY HOUSE STILL WASN'T CALLED.
DETROIT POLICE
WELL THAT MEANS THAT NOBODY HAS BOUGHT YOUR HOUSE.
MAYBE, JUST MAYBE...
THEY'D FORGOTTEN ABOUT MY HOUSE AND I STILL HAVE AN OPPORTUNITY TO WORK THINGS OUT.
DETROIT

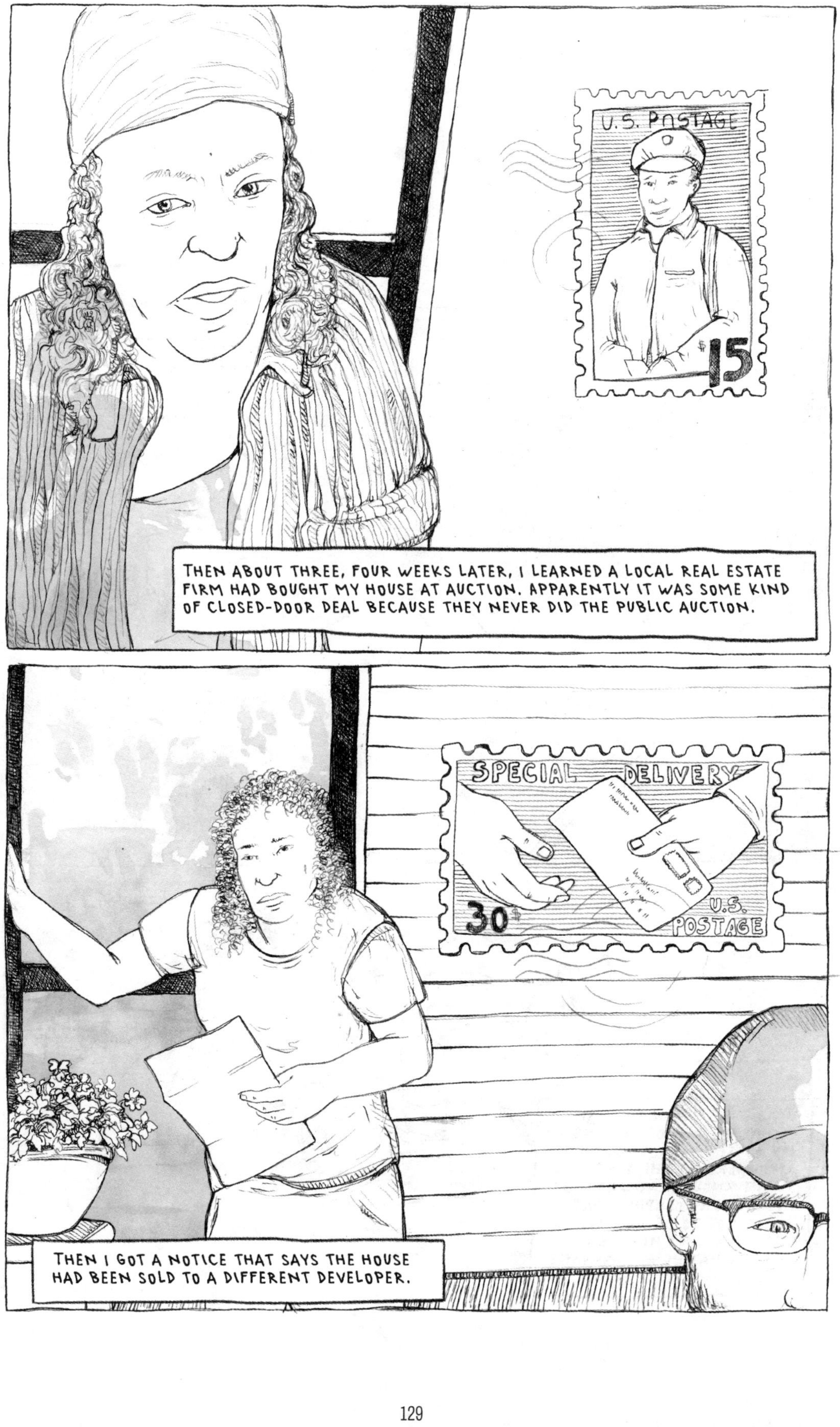
U.S. POSTAGE
15
THEN ABOUT THREE, FOUR WEEKS LATER, I LEARNED A LOCAL REAL ESTATE FIRM HAD BOUGHT MY HOUSE AT AUCTION. APPARENTLY IT WAS SOME KIND OF CLOSED-DOOR DEAL BECAUSE THEY NEVER DID THE PUBLIC AUCTION.
SPECIAL DELIVERY
30¢
U.S. POSTAGE
THEN I GOT A NOTICE THAT SAYS THE HOUSE HAD BEEN SOLD TO A DIFFERENT DEVELOPER.

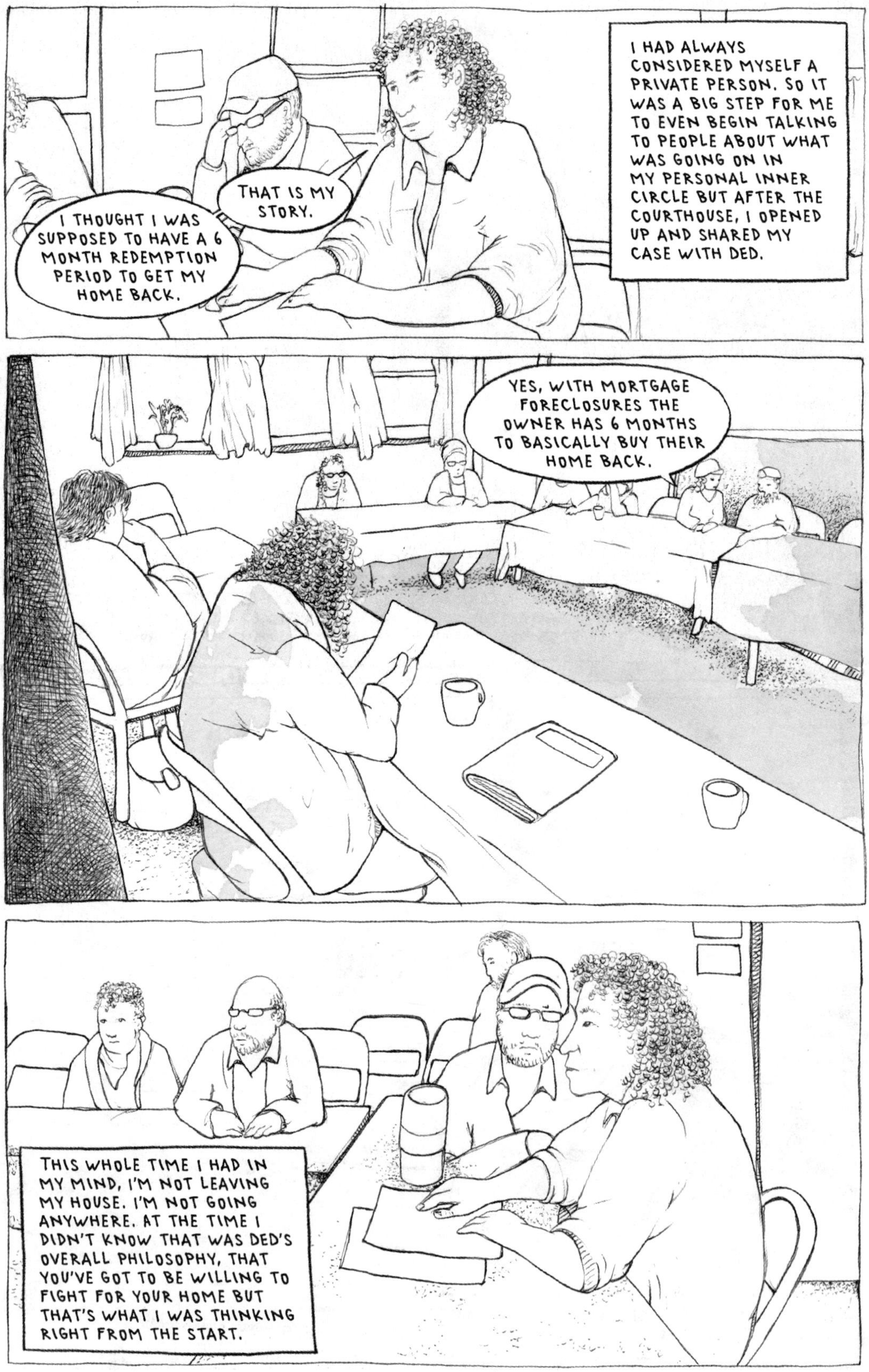
I THOUGHT I WAS SUPPOSED TO HAVE A 6 MONTH REDEMPTION PERIOD TO GET MY HOME BACK.
THAT IS MY STORY.
I HAD ALWAYS CONSIDERED MYSELF A PRIVATE PERSON. SO IT WAS A BIG STEP FOR ME TO EVEN BEGIN TALKING TO PEOPLE ABOUT WHAT WAS GOING ON IN MY PERSONAL INNER CIRCLE BUT AFTER THE COURTHOUSE, I OPENED UP AND SHARED MY CASE WITH DED.
YES, WITH MORTGAGE FORECLOSURES THE OWNER HAS 6 MONTHS TO BASICALLY BUY THEIR HOME BACK.
THIS WHOLE TIME I HAD IN MY MIND, I'M NOT LEAVING MY HOUSE. I'M NOT GOING ANYWHERE. AT THE TIME I DIDN'T KNOW THAT WAS DED'S OVERALL PHILOSOPHY, THAT YOU'VE GOT TO BE WILLING TO FIGHT FOR YOUR HOME BUT THAT'S WHAT I WAS THINKING RIGHT FROM THE START.

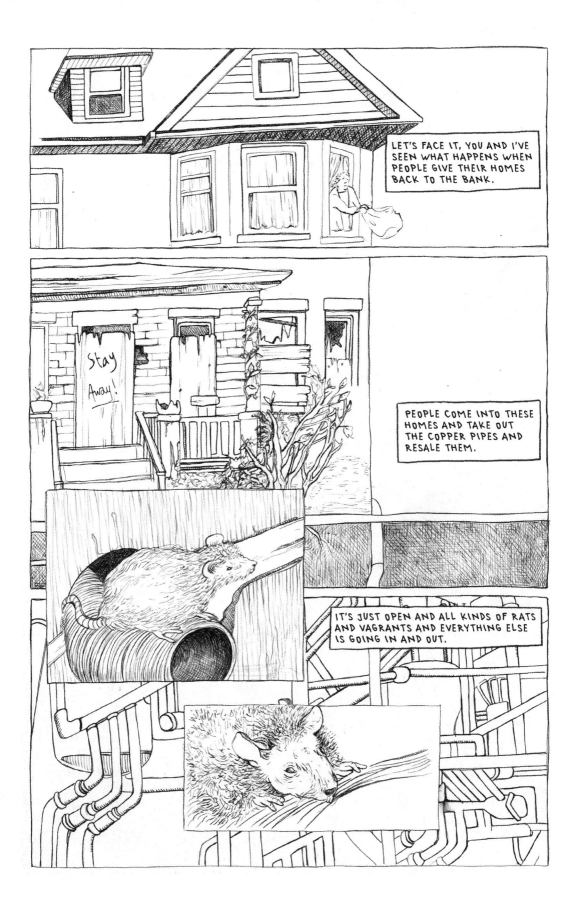

LET'S FACE IT, YOU AND I'VE SEEN WHAT HAPPENS WHEN PEOPLE GIVE THEIR HOMES BACK TO THE BANK.

Stay Away!

PEOPLE COME INTO THESE HOMES AND TAKE OUT THE COPPER PIPES AND RESALE THEM.

IT'S JUST OPEN AND ALL KINDS OF RATS AND VAGRANTS AND EVERYTHING ELSE IS GOING IN AND OUT.

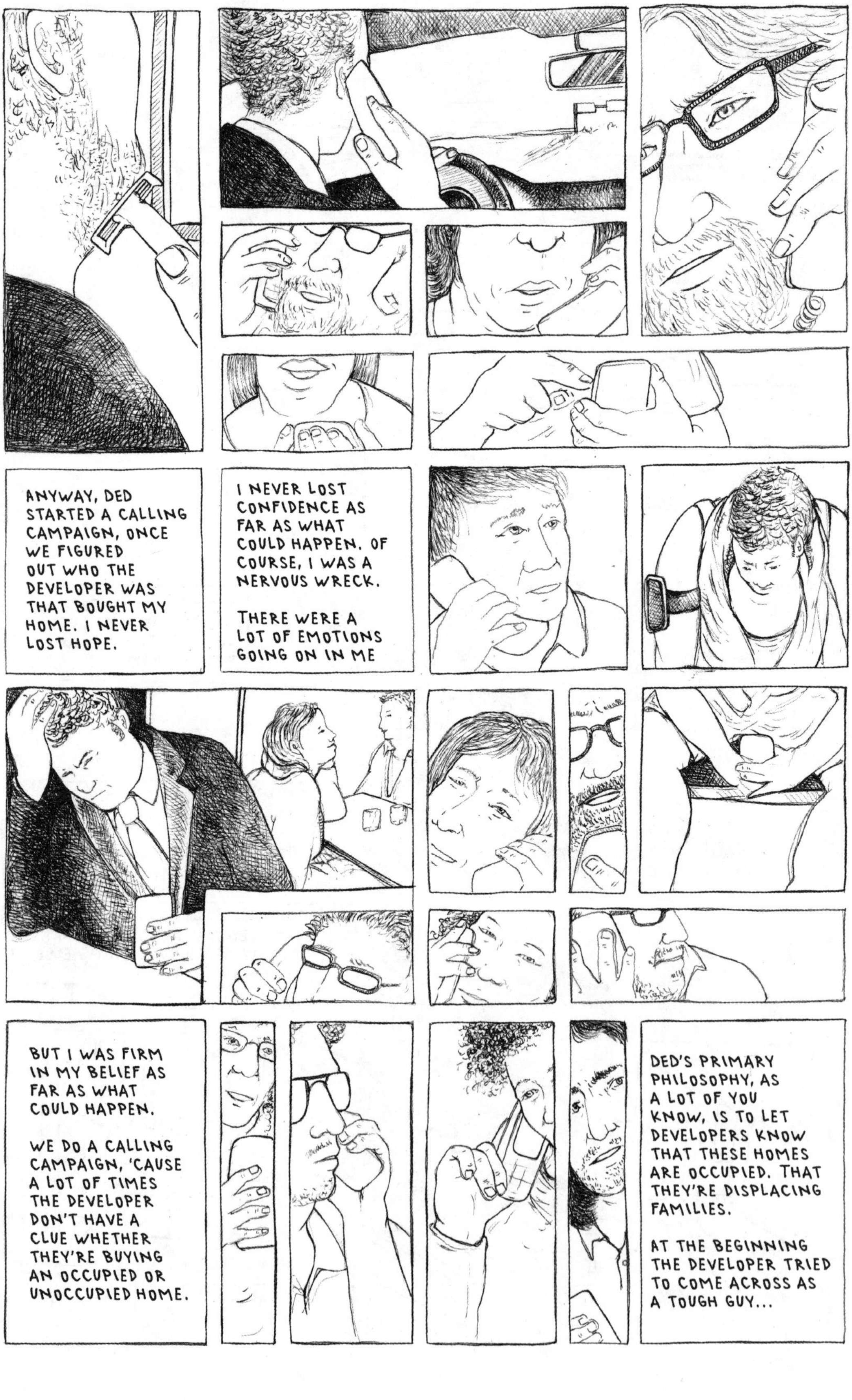
ANYWAY, DED STARTED A CALLING CAMPAIGN, ONCE WE FIGURED OUT WHO THE DEVELOPER WAS THAT BOUGHT MY HOME. I NEVER LOST HOPE.
I NEVER LOST CONFIDENCE AS FAR AS WHAT COULD HAPPEN. OF COURSE, I WAS A NERVOUS WRECK.
THERE WERE A LOT OF EMOTIONS GOING ON IN ME
BUT I WAS FIRM IN MY BELIEF AS FAR AS WHAT COULD HAPPEN.
WE DO A CALLING CAMPAIGN, 'CAUSE A LOT OF TIMES THE DEVELOPER DON'T HAVE A CLUE WHETHER THEY'RE BUYING AN OCCUPIED OR UNOCCUPIED HOME.
DED'S PRIMARY PHILOSOPHY, AS A LOT OF YOU KNOW, IS TO LET DEVELOPERS KNOW THAT THESE HOMES ARE OCCUPIED. THAT THEY'RE DISPLACING FAMILIES.
AT THE BEGINNING THE DEVELOPER TRIED TO COME ACROSS AS A TOUGH GUY...

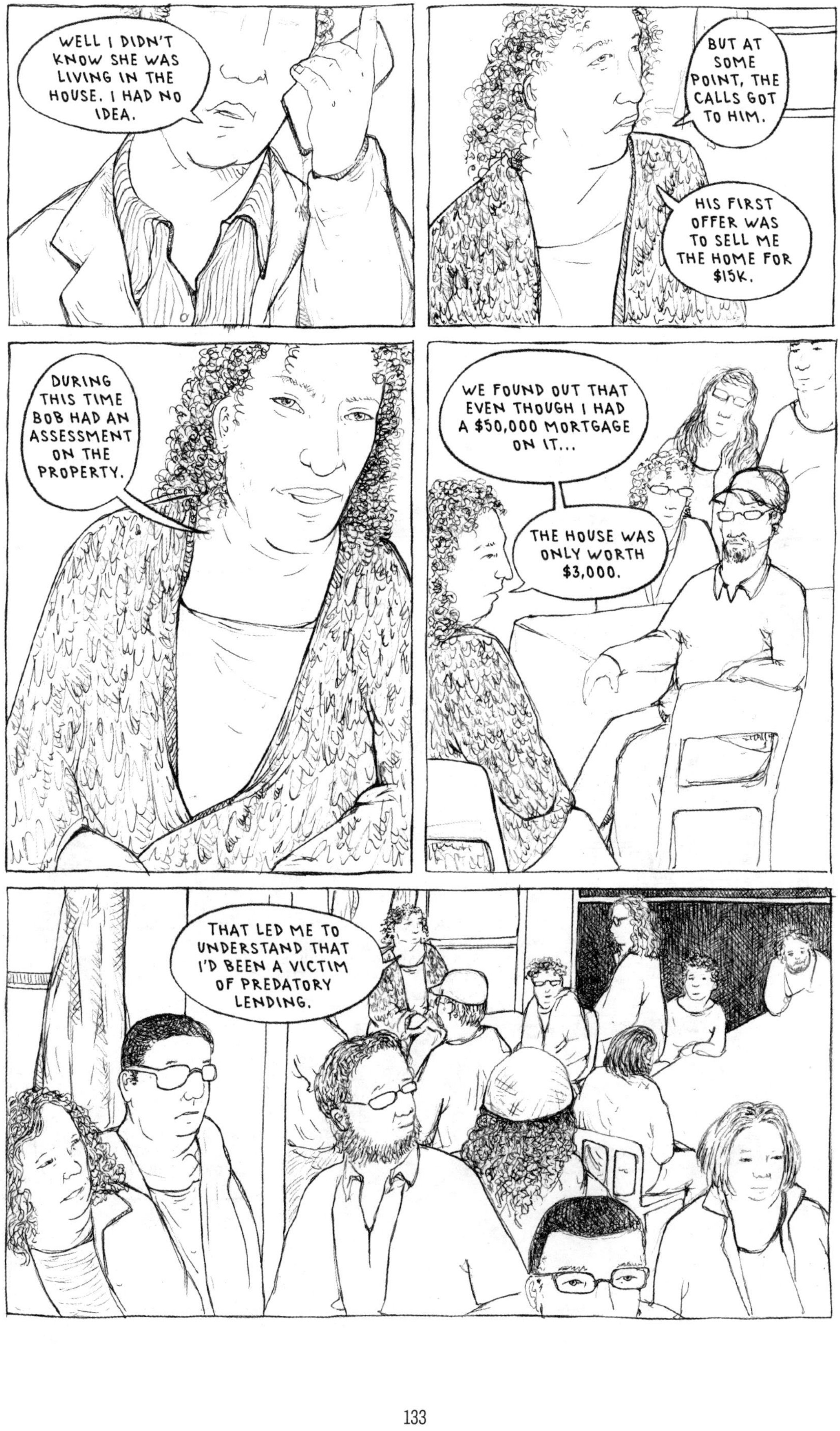
WELL I DIDN'T KNOW SHE WAS LIVING IN THE HOUSE. I HAD NO IDEA.
BUT AT SOME POINT, THE CALLS GOT TO HIM.
HIS FIRST OFFER WAS TO SELL ME THE HOME FOR $15K.
DURING THIS TIME BOB HAD AN ASSESSMENT ON THE PROPERTY.
WE FOUND OUT THAT EVEN THOUGH I HAD A $50,000 MORTGAGE ON IT...
THE HOUSE WAS ONLY WORTH $3,000.
THAT LED ME TO UNDERSTAND THAT I'D BEEN A VICTIM OF PREDATORY LENDING.

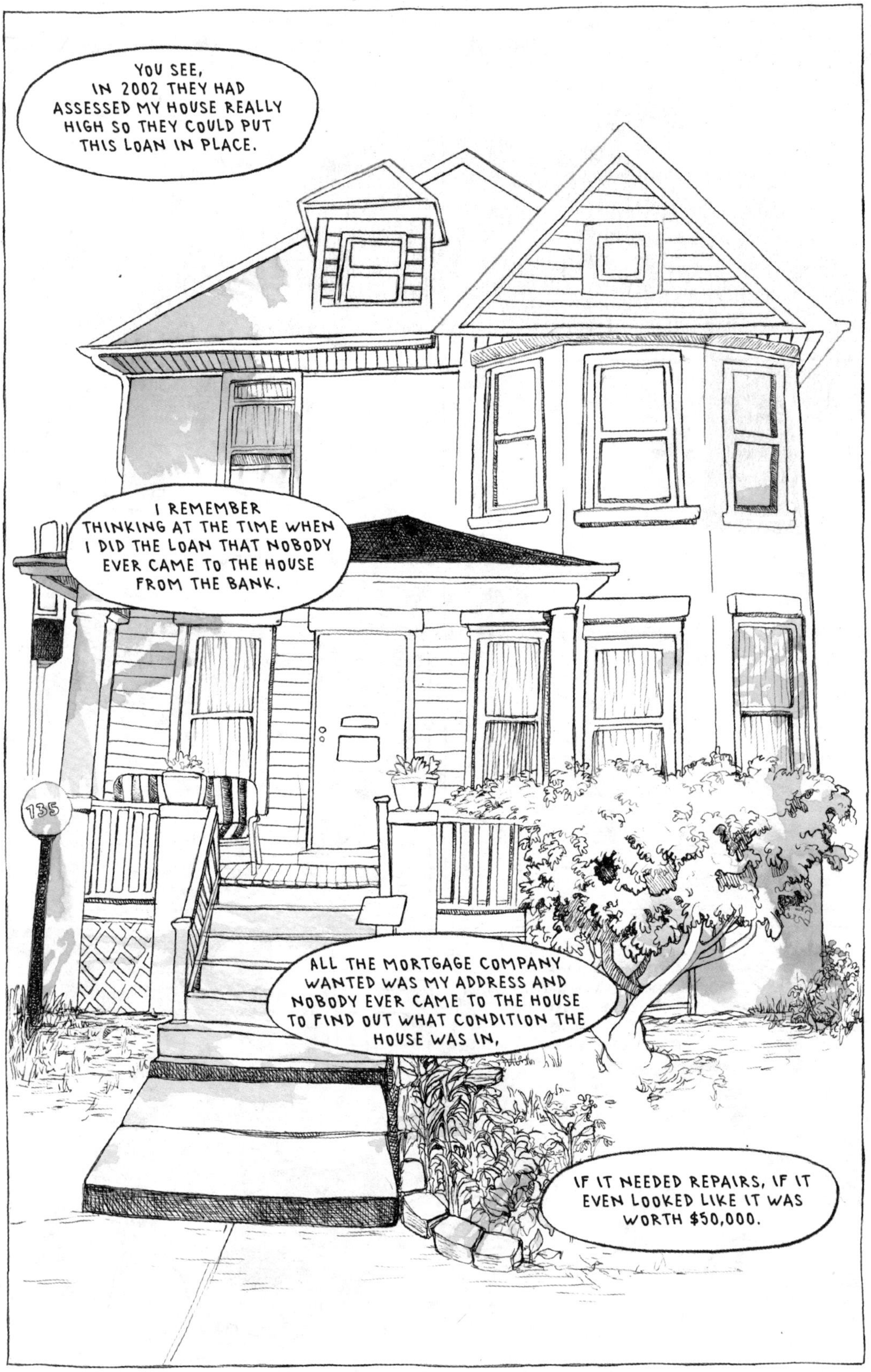
YOU SEE, IN 2002 THEY HAD ASSESSED MY HOUSE REALLY HIGH SO THEY COULD PUT THIS LOAN IN PLACE.
I REMEMBER THINKING AT THE TIME WHEN I DID THE LOAN THAT NOBODY EVER CAME TO THE HOUSE FROM THE BANK.
135
ALL THE MORTGAGE COMPANY WANTED WAS MY ADDRESS AND NOBODY EVER CAME TO THE HOUSE TO FIND OUT WHAT CONDITION THE HOUSE WAS IN,
IF IT NEEDED REPAIRS, IF IT EVEN LOOKED LIKE IT WAS WORTH $50,000.

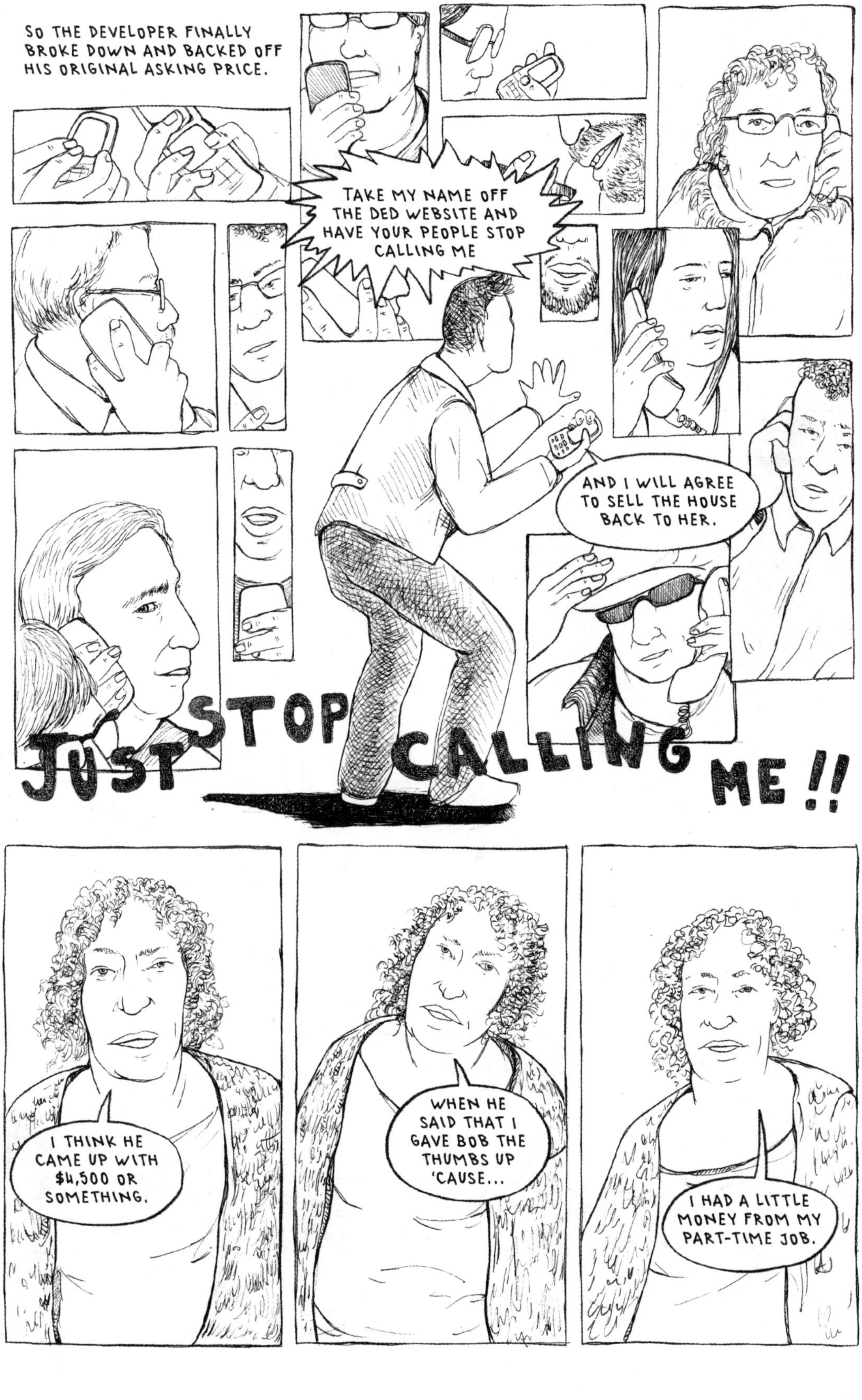
SO THE DEVELOPER FINALLY BROKE DOWN AND BACKED OFF HIS ORIGINAL ASKING PRICE.
TAKE MY NAME OFF THE DED WEBSITE AND HAVE YOUR PEOPLE STOP CALLING ME
AND I WILL AGREE TO SELL THE HOUSE BACK TO HER.
JUST STOP CALLING ME!!
I THINK HE CAME UP WITH $4,500 OR SOMETHING.
WHEN HE SAID THAT I GAVE BOB THE THUMBS UP 'CAUSE...
I HAD A LITTLE MONEY FROM MY PART-TIME JOB.

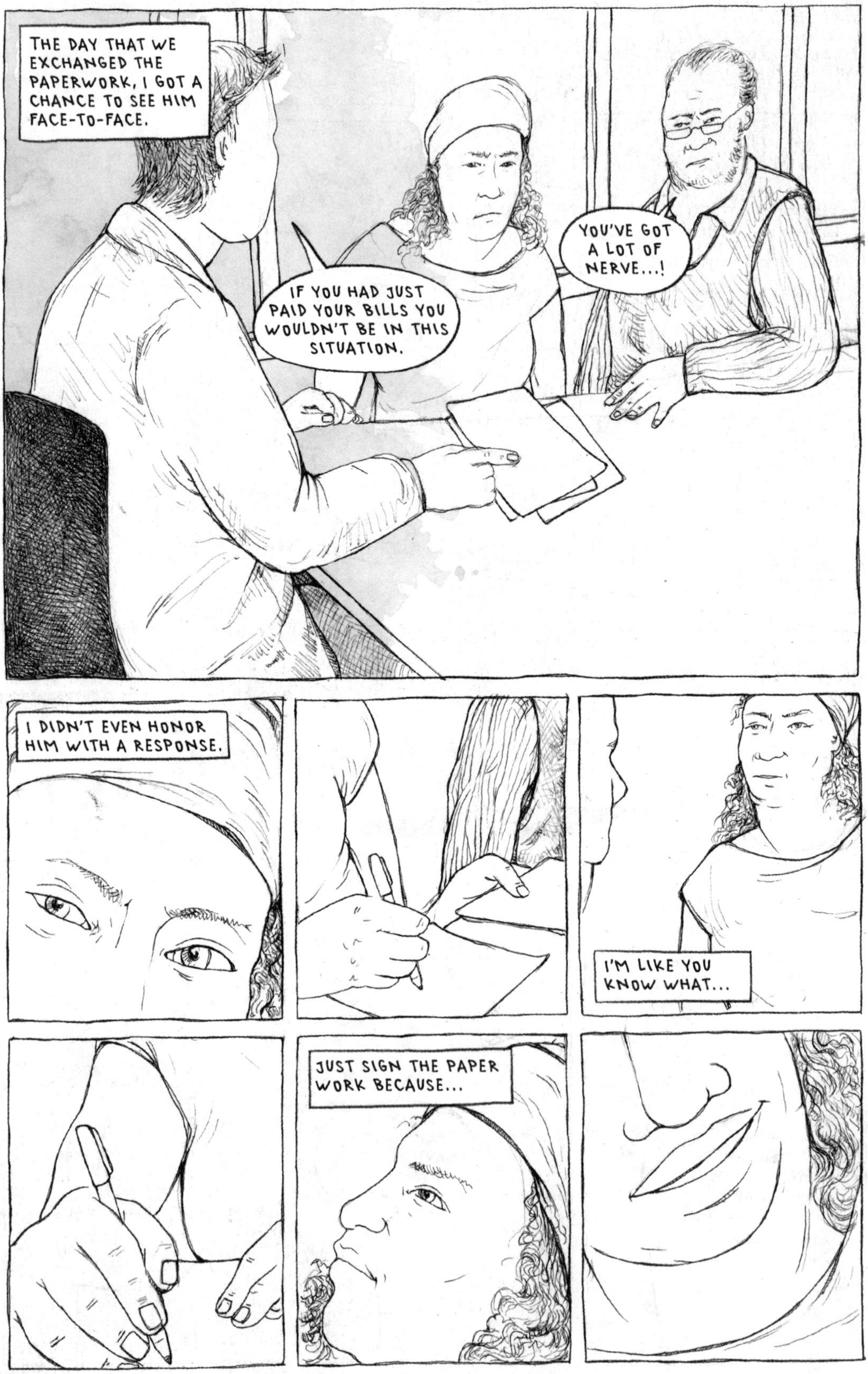
THE DAY THAT WE EXCHANGED THE PAPERWORK, I GOT A CHANCE TO SEE HIM FACE-TO-FACE.
YOU'VE GOT A LOT OF NERVE...!
IF YOU HAD JUST PAID YOUR BILLS YOU WOULDN'T BE IN THIS SITUATION.
I DIDN'T EVEN HONOR HIM WITH A RESPONSE.
I'M LIKE YOU KNOW WHAT...
JUST SIGN THE PAPER WORK BECAUSE...

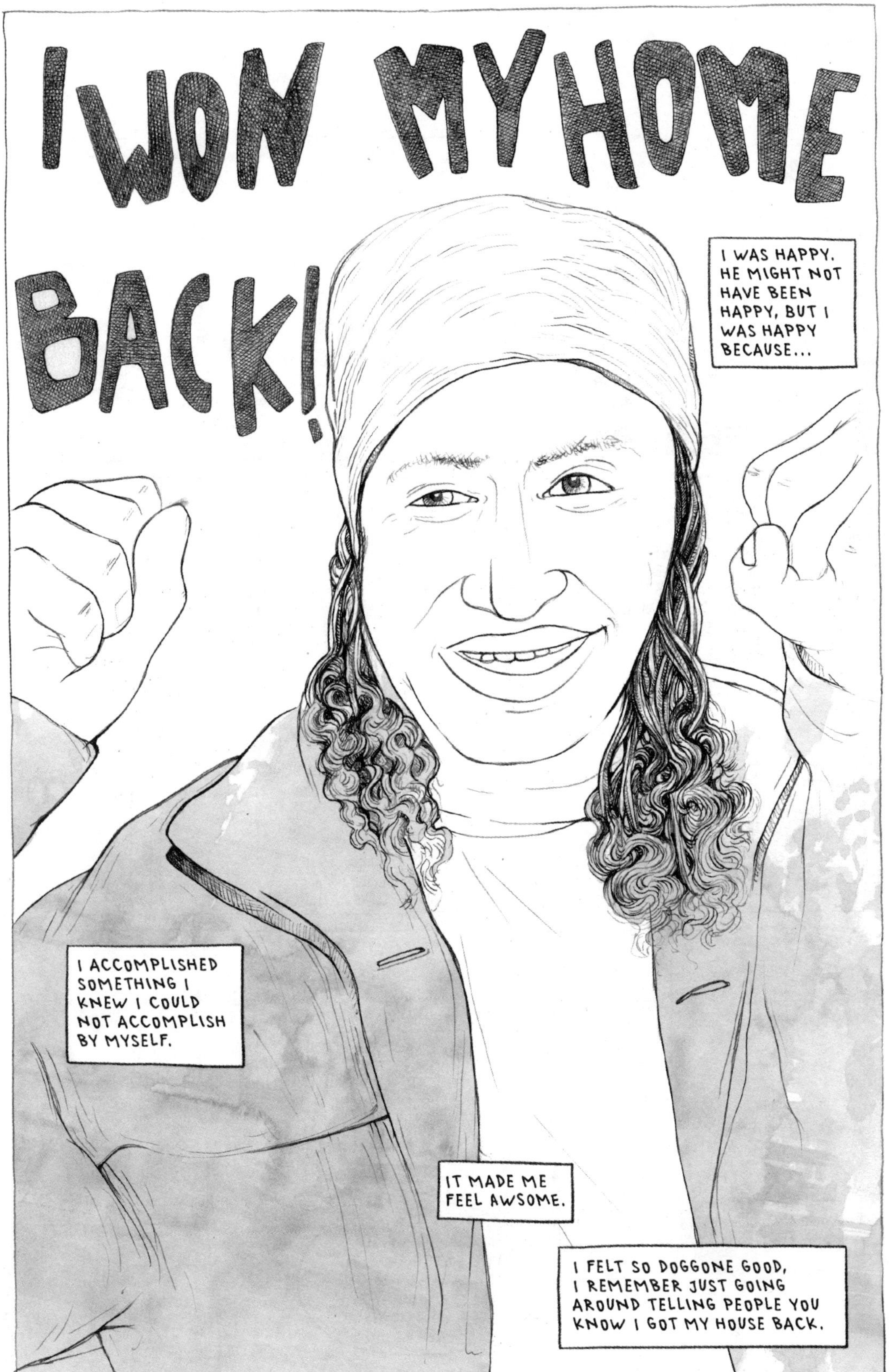
I WON MY HOME BACK!
I WAS HAPPY. HE MIGHT NOT HAVE BEEN HAPPY, BUT I WAS HAPPY BECAUSE...
I ACCOMPLISHED SOMETHING I KNEW I COULD NOT ACCOMPLISH BY MYSELF.
IT MADE ME FEEL AWSOME.
I FELT SO DOGGONE GOOD, I REMEMBER JUST GOING AROUND TELLING PEOPLE YOU KNOW I GOT MY HOUSE BACK.

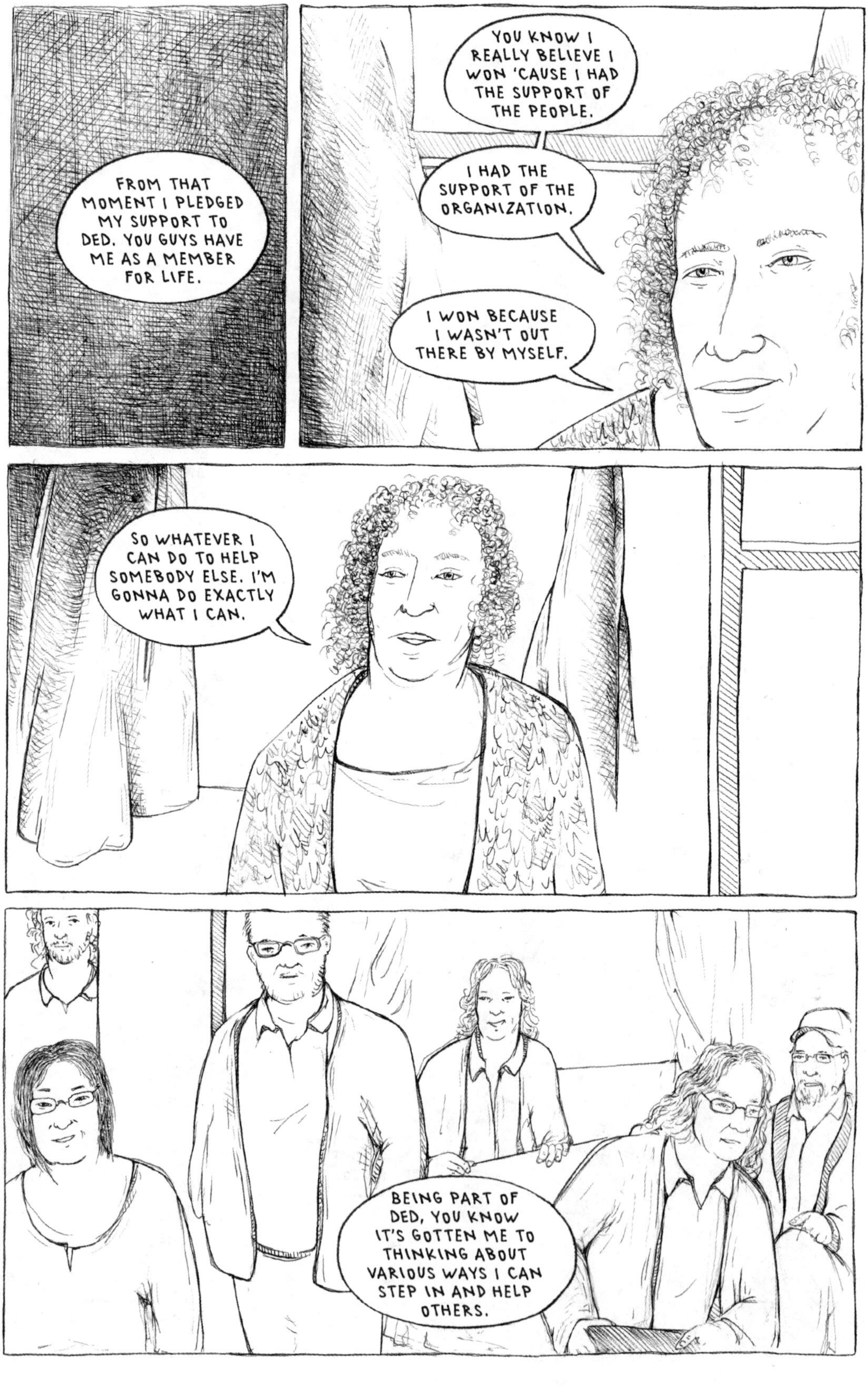
FROM THAT MOMENT I PLEDGED MY SUPPORT TO DED. YOU GUYS HAVE ME AS A MEMBER FOR LIFE.
YOU KNOW I REALLY BELIEVE I WON 'CAUSE I HAD THE SUPPORT OF THE PEOPLE.
I HAD THE SUPPORT OF THE ORGANIZATION.
I WON BECAUSE I WASN'T OUT THERE BY MYSELF.
SO WHATEVER I CAN DO TO HELP SOMEBODY ELSE. I'M GONNA DO EXACTLY WHAT I CAN.
BEING PART OF DED, YOU KNOW IT'S GOTTEN ME TO THINKING ABOUT VARIOUS WAYS I CAN STEP IN AND HELP OTHERS.

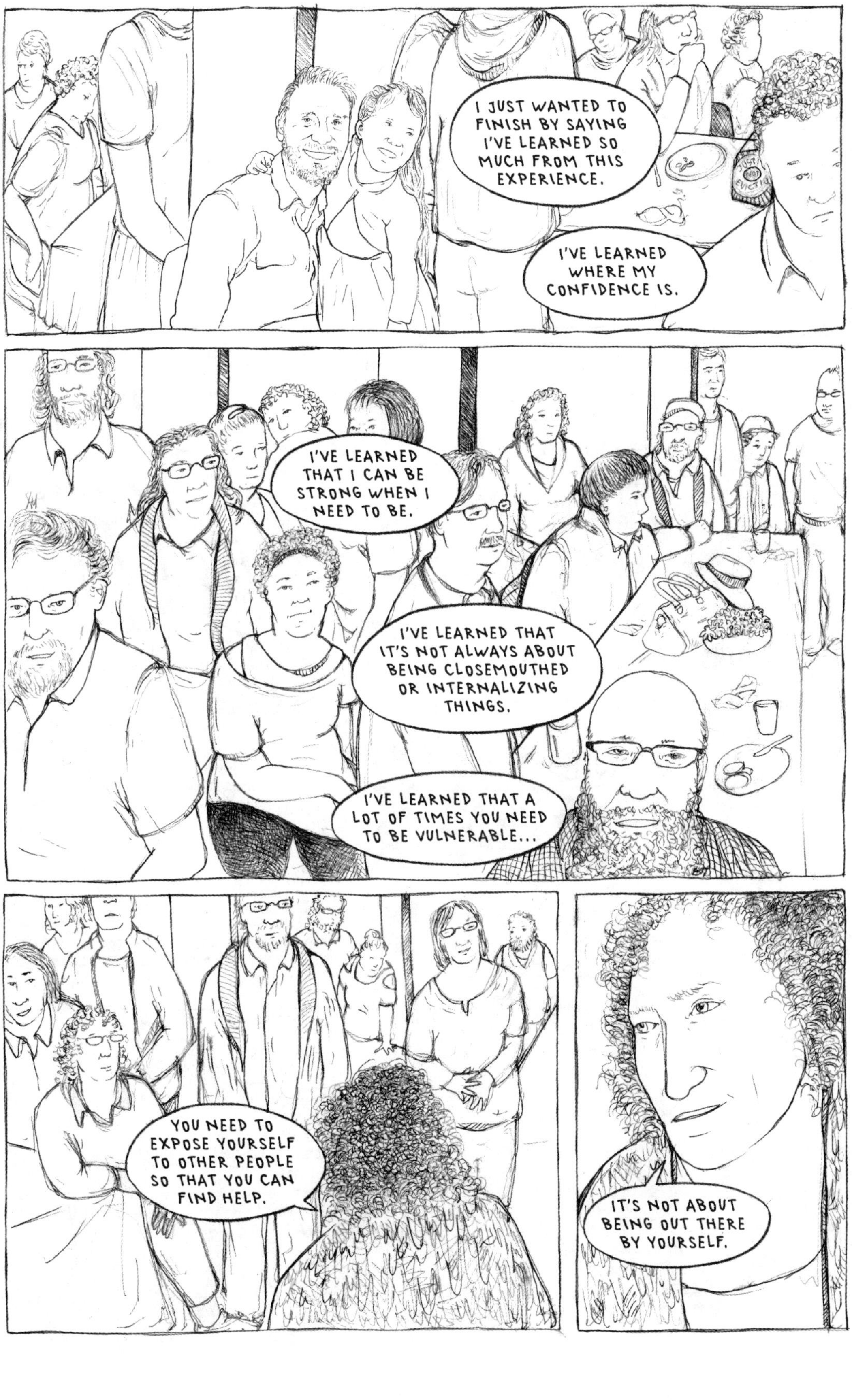
I JUST WANTED TO FINISH BY SAYING I'VE LEARNED SO MUCH FROM THIS EXPERIENCE.
I'VE LEARNED WHERE MY CONFIDENCE IS.
I'VE LEARNED THAT I CAN BE STRONG WHEN I NEED TO BE.
I'VE LEARNED THAT IT'S NOT ALWAYS ABOUT BEING CLOSEMOUTHED OR INTERNALIZING THINGS.
I'VE LEARNED THAT A LOT OF TIMES YOU NEED TO BE VULNERABLE...
YOU NEED TO EXPOSE YOURSELF TO OTHER PEOPLE SO THAT YOU CAN FIND HELP.
IT'S NOT ABOUT BEING OUT THERE BY YOURSELF.

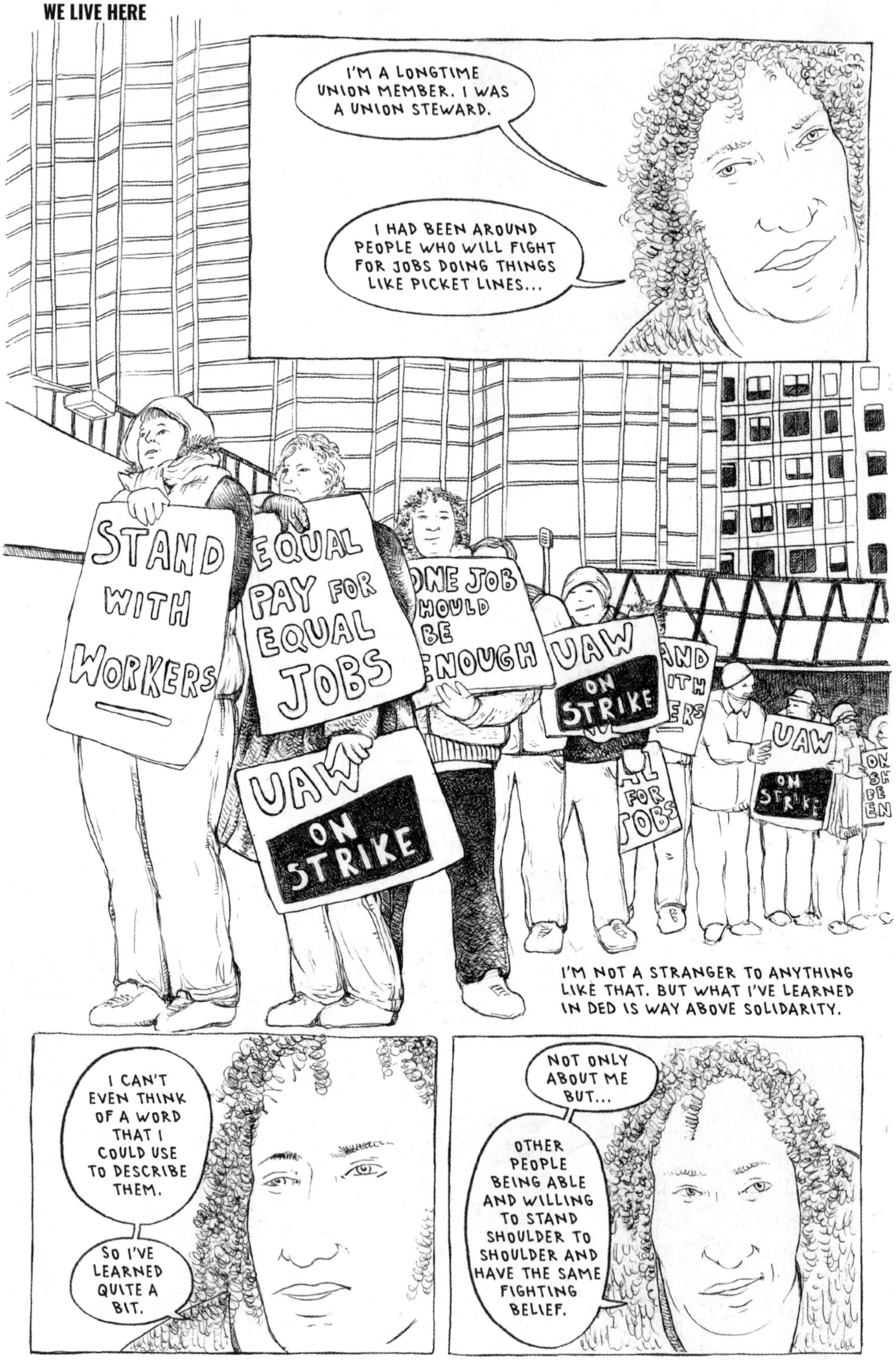
I'M A LONGTIME UNION MEMBER. I WAS A UNION STEWARD.
I HAD BEEN AROUND PEOPLE WHO WILL FIGHT FOR JOBS DOING THINGS LIKE PICKET LINES...
STAND WITH WORKERS
EQUAL PAY FOR EQUAL JOBS
UAW ON STRIKE
I'M NOT A STRANGER TO ANYTHING LIKE THAT. BUT WHAT I'VE LEARNED IN DED IS WAY ABOVE SOLIDARITY.
I CAN'T EVEN THINK OF A WORD THAT I COULD USE TO DESCRIBE THEM.
SO I'VE LEARNED QUITE A BIT.
NOT ONLY ABOUT ME BUT...
OTHER PEOPLE BEING ABLE AND WILLING TO STAND SHOULDER TO SHOULDER AND HAVE THE SAME FIGHTING BELIEF.

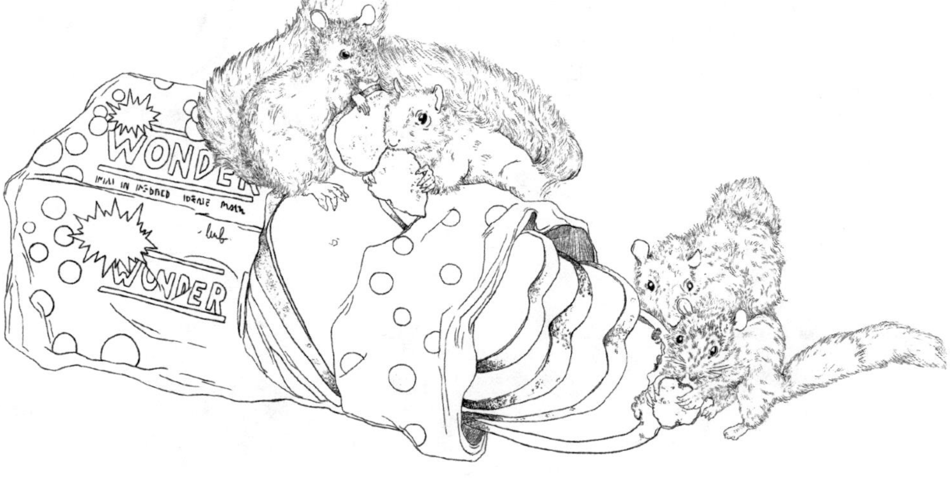
WONDER
WONDER

giving us
the possibility
to fight

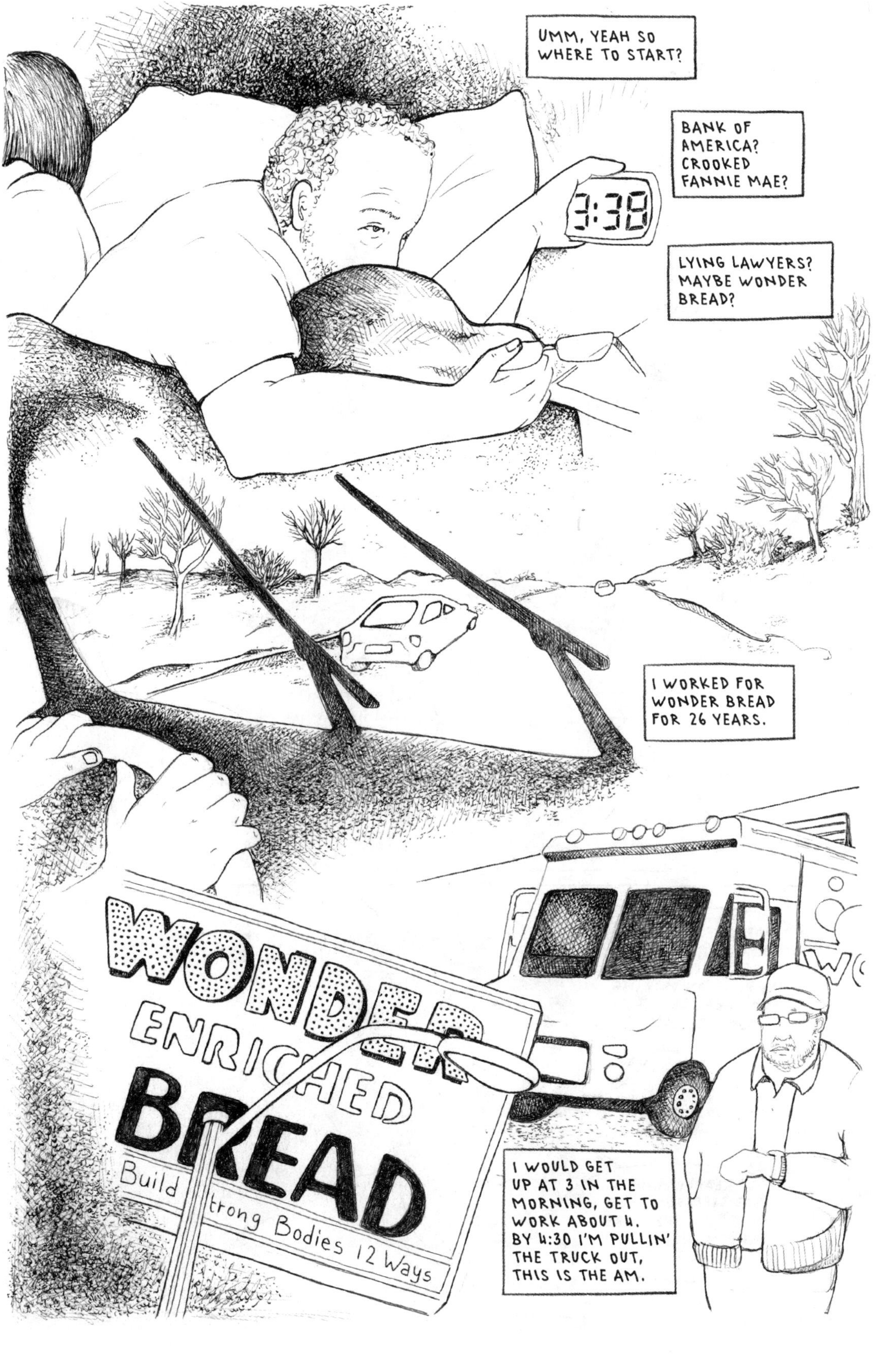
UMM, YEAH SO WHERE TO START?
BANK OF AMERICA? CROOKED FANNIE MAE?
3:38
LYING LAWYERS? MAYBE WONDER BREAD?
I WORKED FOR WONDER BREAD FOR 26 YEARS.
WONDER
ENRICHED
BREAD
Build Strong Bodies 12 Ways
I WOULD GET UP AT 3 IN THE MORNING, GET TO WORK ABOUT 4. BY 4:30 I'M PULLIN' THE TRUCK OUT, THIS IS THE AM.

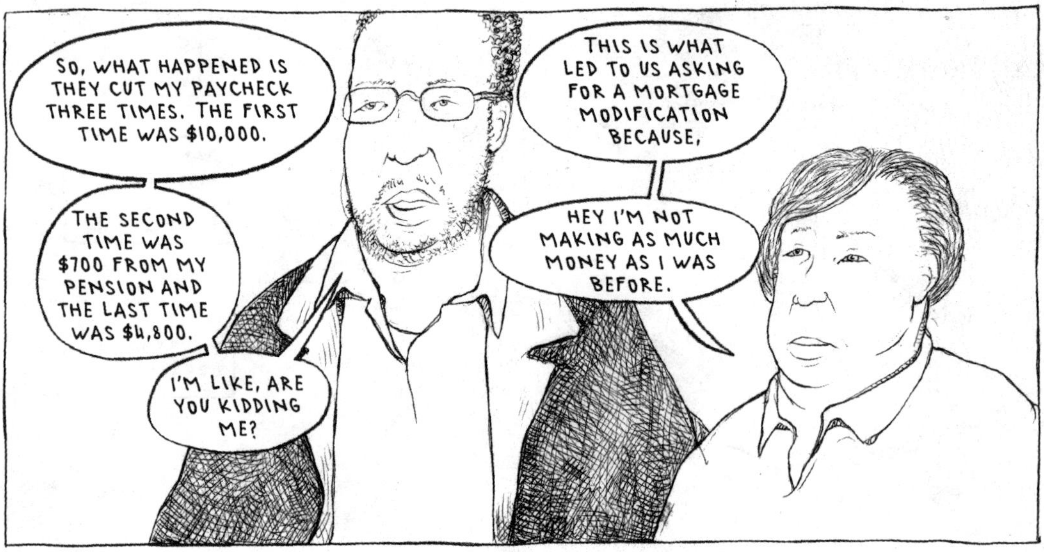
SO, WHAT HAPPENED IS THEY CUT MY PAYCHECK THREE TIMES. THE FIRST TIME WAS $10,000.
THE SECOND TIME WAS $700 FROM MY PENSION AND THE LAST TIME WAS $4,800.
I'M LIKE, ARE YOU KIDDING ME?
THIS IS WHAT LED TO US ASKING FOR A MORTGAGE MODIFICATION BECAUSE,
HEY I'M NOT MAKING AS MUCH MONEY AS I WAS BEFORE.

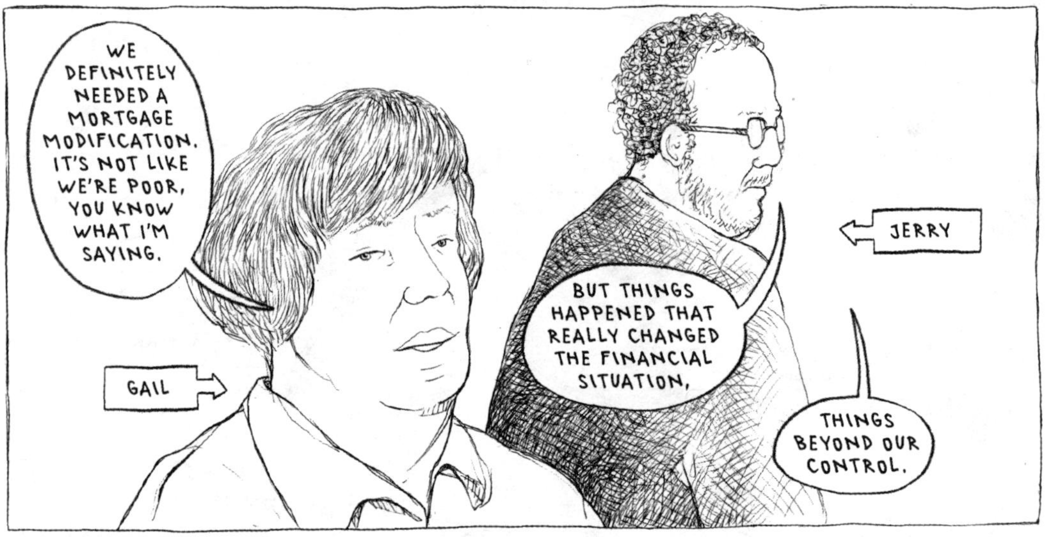
WE DEFINITELY NEEDED A MORTGAGE MODIFICATION. IT'S NOT LIKE WE'RE POOR, YOU KNOW WHAT I'M SAYING.
GAIL
JERRY
BUT THINGS HAPPENED THAT REALLY CHANGED THE FINANCIAL SITUATION,
THINGS BEYOND OUR CONTROL.

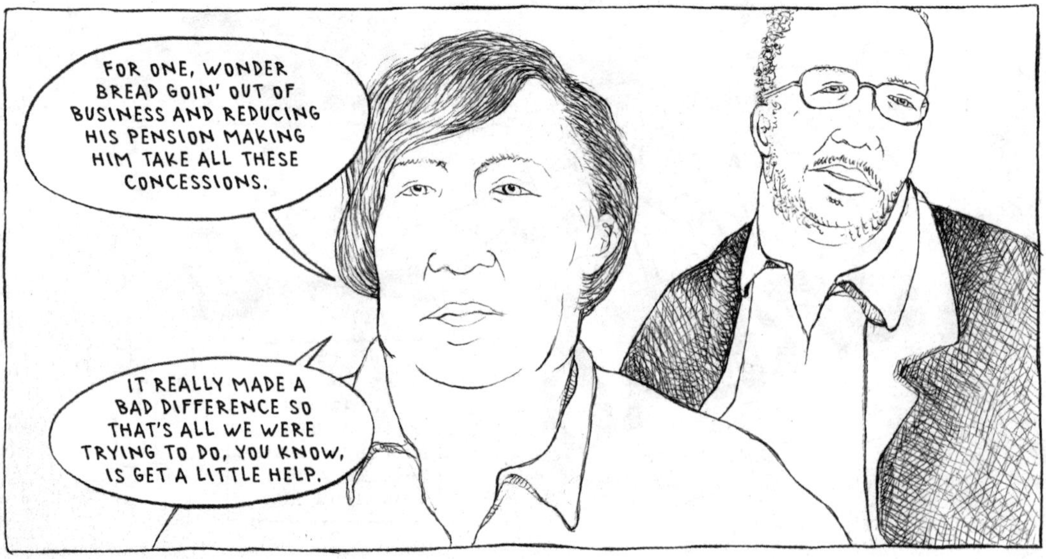
FOR ONE, WONDER BREAD GOIN' OUT OF BUSINESS AND REDUCING HIS PENSION MAKING HIM TAKE ALL THESE CONCESSIONS.
IT REALLY MADE A BAD DIFFERENCE SO THAT'S ALL WE WERE TRYING TO DO, YOU KNOW, IS GET A LITTLE HELP.

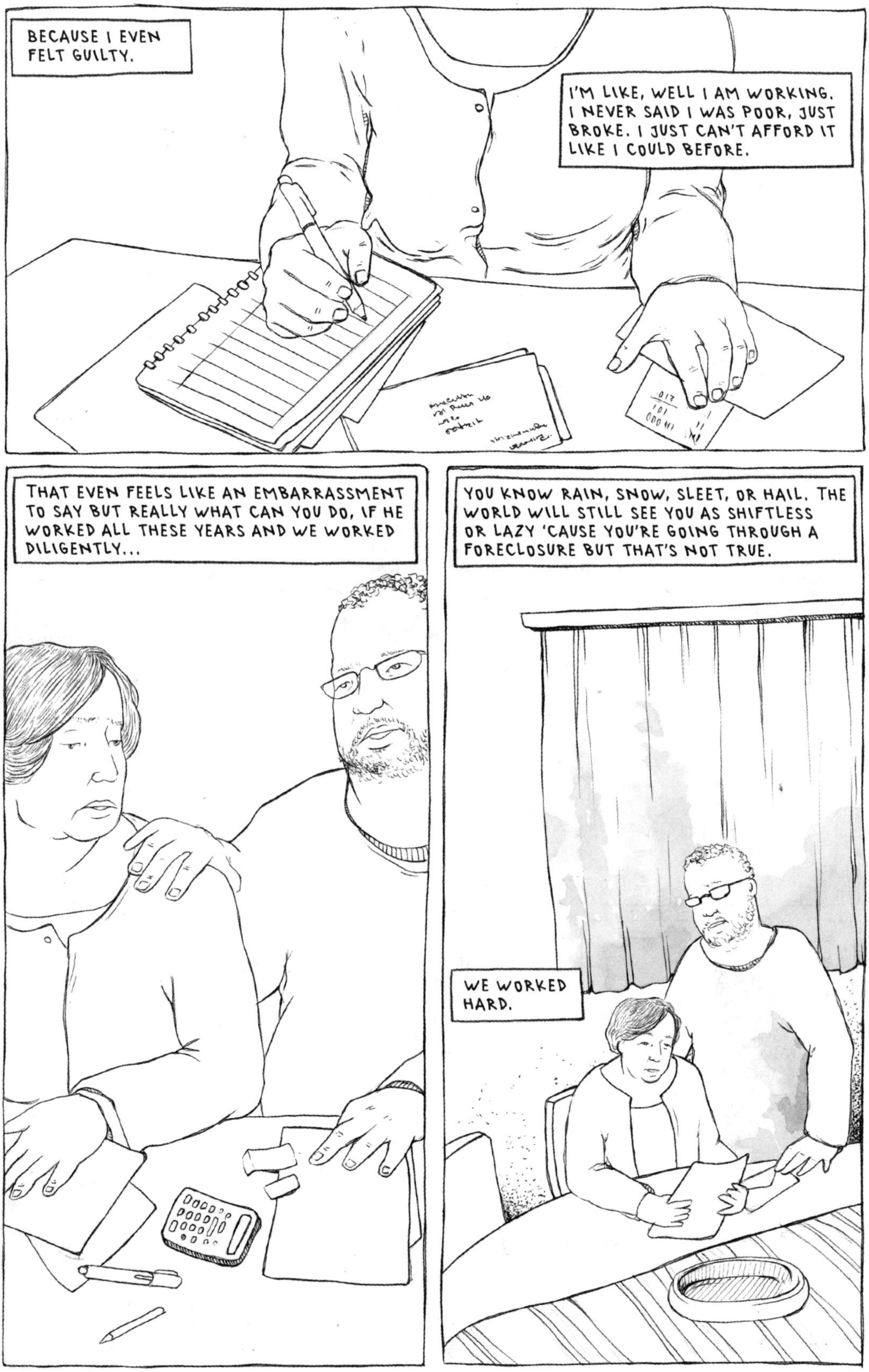
BECAUSE I EVEN FELT GUILTY.
I'M LIKE, WELL I AM WORKING. I NEVER SAID I WAS POOR, JUST BROKE. I JUST CAN'T AFFORD IT LIKE I COULD BEFORE.
THAT EVEN FEELS LIKE AN EMBARRASSMENT TO SAY BUT REALLY WHAT CAN YOU DO, IF HE WORKED ALL THESE YEARS AND WE WORKED DILIGENTLY...
YOU KNOW RAIN, SNOW, SLEET, OR HAIL. THE WORLD WILL STILL SEE YOU AS SHIFTLESS OR LAZY 'CAUSE YOU'RE GOING THROUGH A FORECLOSURE BUT THAT'S NOT TRUE.
WE WORKED HARD.

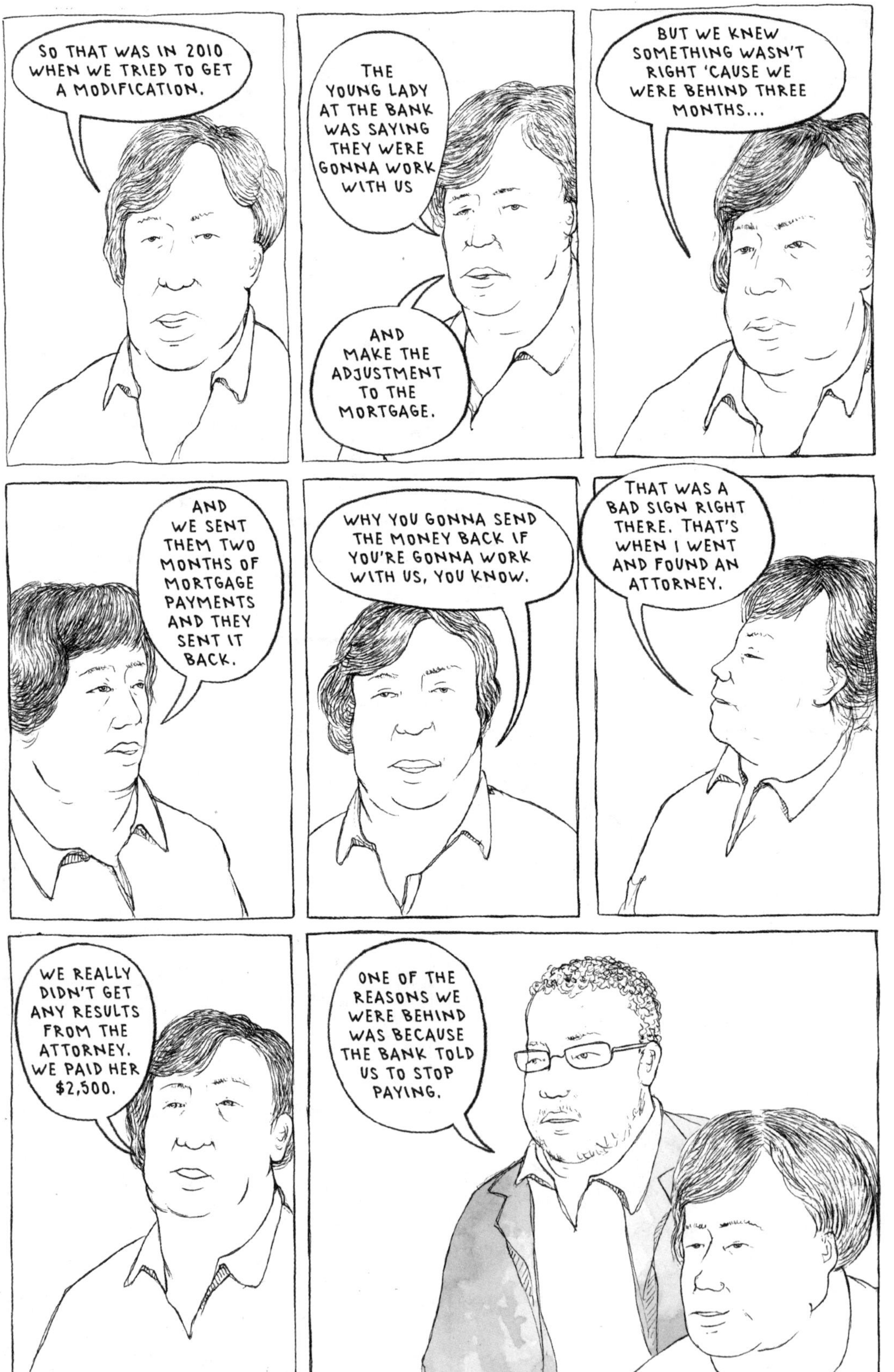
SO THAT WAS IN 2010 WHEN WE TRIED TO GET A MODIFICATION.
THE YOUNG LADY AT THE BANK WAS SAYING THEY WERE GONNA WORK WITH US
AND MAKE THE ADJUSTMENT TO THE MORTGAGE.
BUT WE KNEW SOMETHING WASN'T RIGHT 'CAUSE WE WERE BEHIND THREE MONTHS...
AND WE SENT THEM TWO MONTHS OF MORTGAGE PAYMENTS AND THEY SENT IT BACK.
WHY YOU GONNA SEND THE MONEY BACK IF YOU'RE GONNA WORK WITH US, YOU KNOW.
THAT WAS A BAD SIGN RIGHT THERE. THAT'S WHEN I WENT AND FOUND AN ATTORNEY.
WE REALLY DIDN'T GET ANY RESULTS FROM THE ATTORNEY. WE PAID HER $2,500.
ONE OF THE REASONS WE WERE BEHIND WAS BECAUSE THE BANK TOLD US TO STOP PAYING.

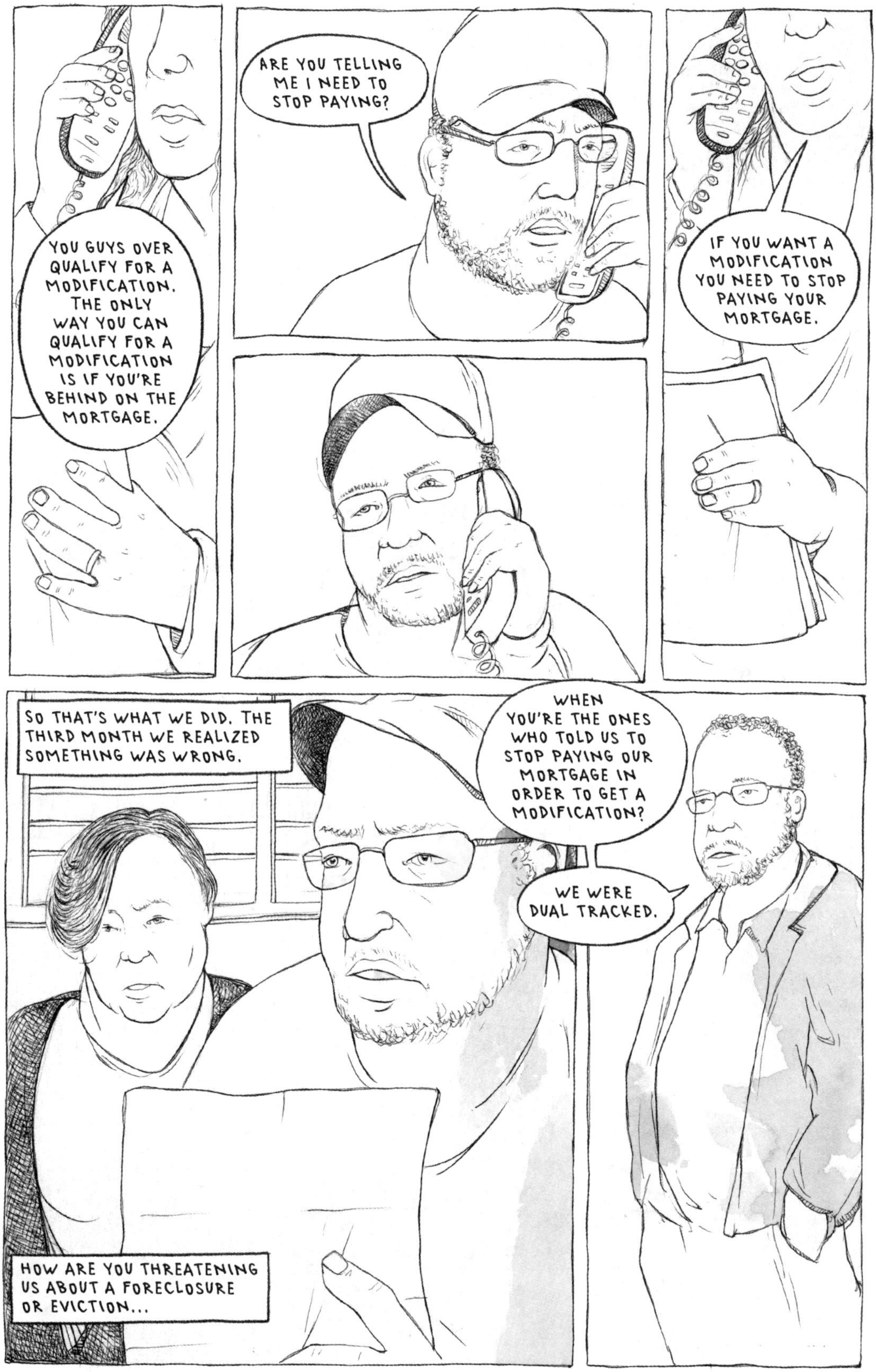
YOU GUYS OVER QUALIFY FOR A MODIFICATION. THE ONLY WAY YOU CAN QUALIFY FOR A MODIFICATION IS IF YOU'RE BEHIND ON THE MORTGAGE.
ARE YOU TELLING ME I NEED TO STOP PAYING?
IF YOU WANT A MODIFICATION YOU NEED TO STOP PAYING YOUR MORTGAGE.
SO THAT'S WHAT WE DID. THE THIRD MONTH WE REALIZED SOMETHING WAS WRONG.
HOW ARE YOU THREATENING US ABOUT A FORECLOSURE OR EVICTION...
WHEN YOU'RE THE ONES WHO TOLD US TO STOP PAYING OUR MORTGAGE IN ORDER TO GET A MODIFICATION?
WE WERE DUAL TRACKED.

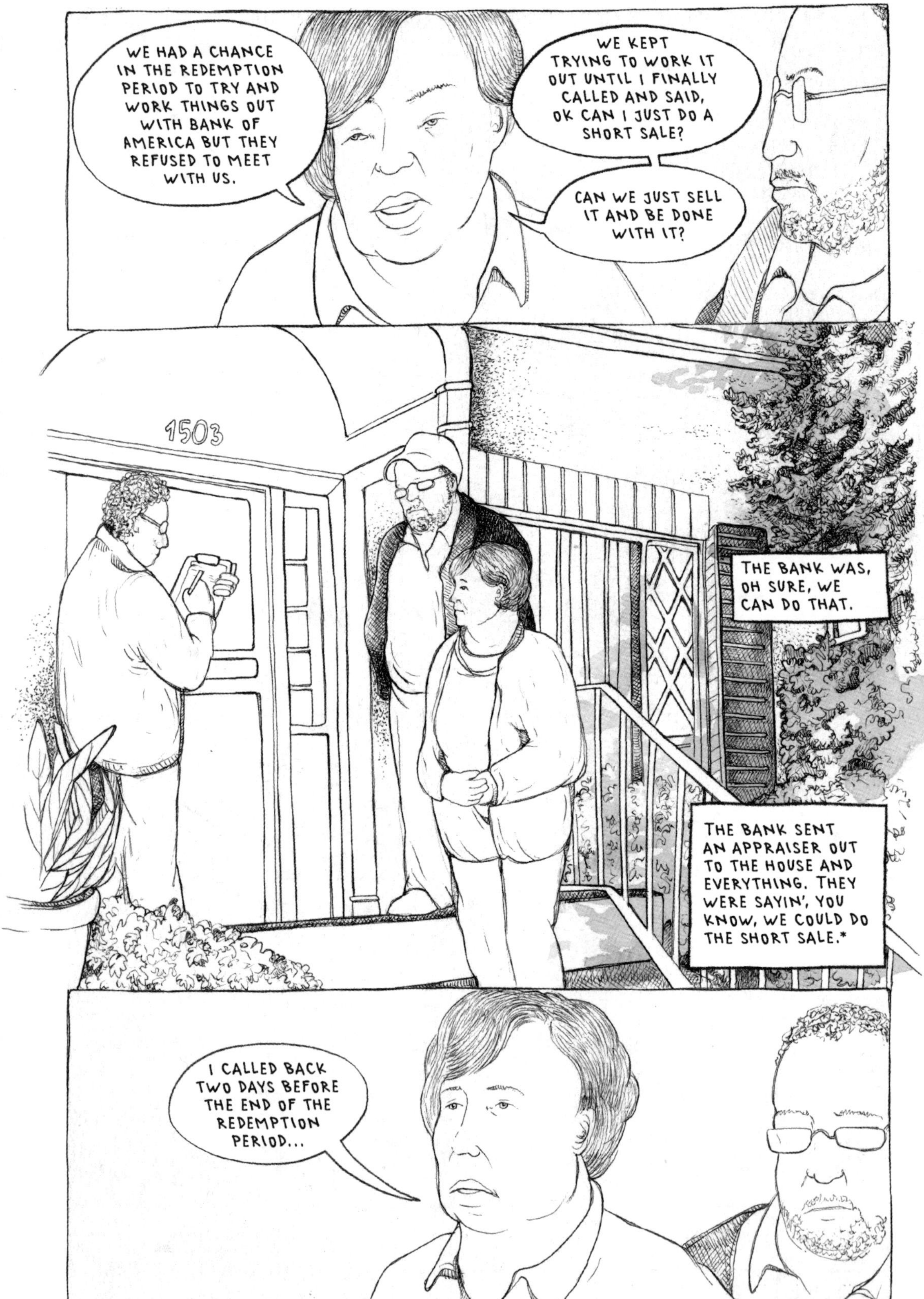
WE HAD A CHANCE IN THE REDEMPTION PERIOD TO TRY AND WORK THINGS OUT WITH BANK OF AMERICA BUT THEY REFUSED TO MEET WITH US.
WE KEPT TRYING TO WORK IT OUT UNTIL I FINALLY CALLED AND SAID, OK CAN I JUST DO A SHORT SALE?
CAN WE JUST SELL IT AND BE DONE WITH IT?
1503
THE BANK WAS, OH SURE, WE CAN DO THAT.
THE BANK SENT AN APPRAISER OUT TO THE HOUSE AND EVERYTHING. THEY WERE SAYIN', YOU KNOW, WE COULD DO THE SHORT SALE.*
I CALLED BACK TWO DAYS BEFORE THE END OF THE REDEMPTION PERIOD...

*A SHORT SALE IS WHEN A MORTGAGE COMPANY ACCEPTS A PAYOFF AMOUNT LESS THAN WHAT IS OWED.

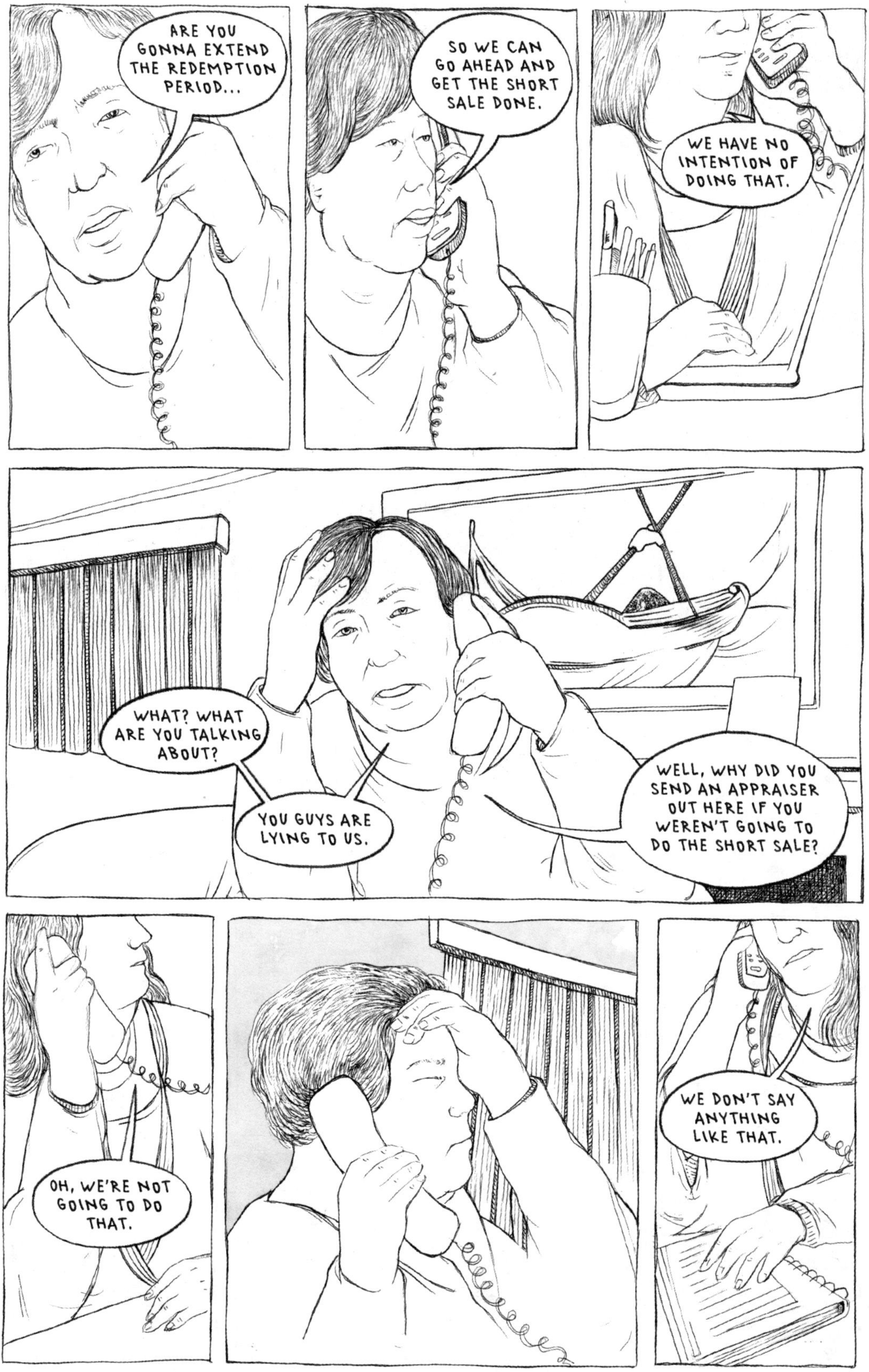
ARE YOU GONNA EXTEND THE REDEMPTION PERIOD...
SO WE CAN GO AHEAD AND GET THE SHORT SALE DONE.
WE HAVE NO INTENTION OF DOING THAT.
WHAT? WHAT ARE YOU TALKING ABOUT?
YOU GUYS ARE LYING TO US.
WELL, WHY DID YOU SEND AN APPRAISER OUT HERE IF YOU WEREN'T GOING TO DO THE SHORT SALE?
OH, WE'RE NOT GOING TO DO THAT.
WE DON'T SAY ANYTHING LIKE THAT.

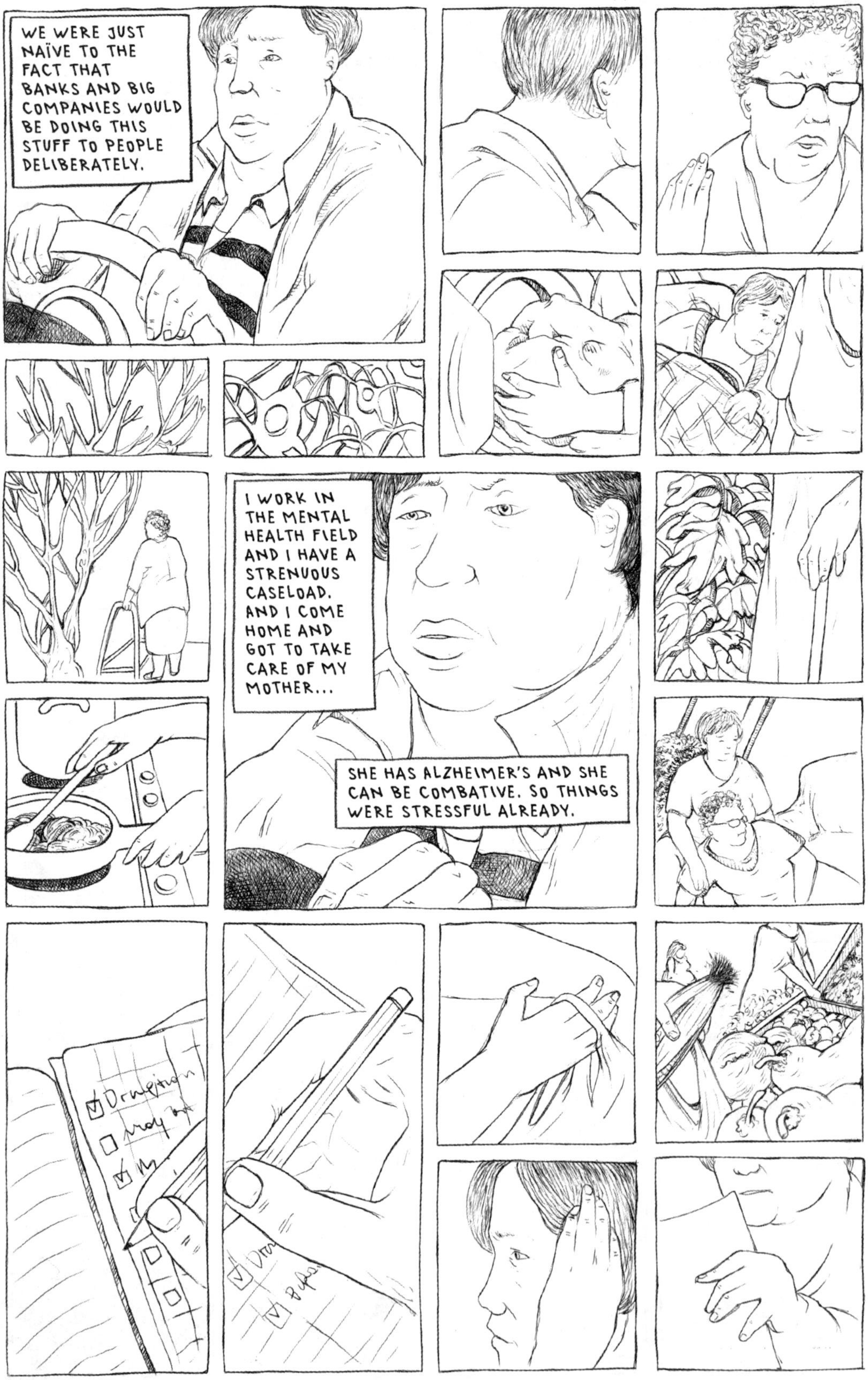
WE WERE JUST NAÏVE TO THE FACT THAT BANKS AND BIG COMPANIES WOULD BE DOING THIS STUFF TO PEOPLE DELIBERATELY.
I WORK IN THE MENTAL HEALTH FIELD AND I HAVE A STRENUOUS CASELOAD. AND I COME HOME AND GOT TO TAKE CARE OF MY MOTHER...
SHE HAS ALZHEIMER'S AND SHE CAN BE COMBATIVE. SO THINGS WERE STRESSFUL ALREADY.

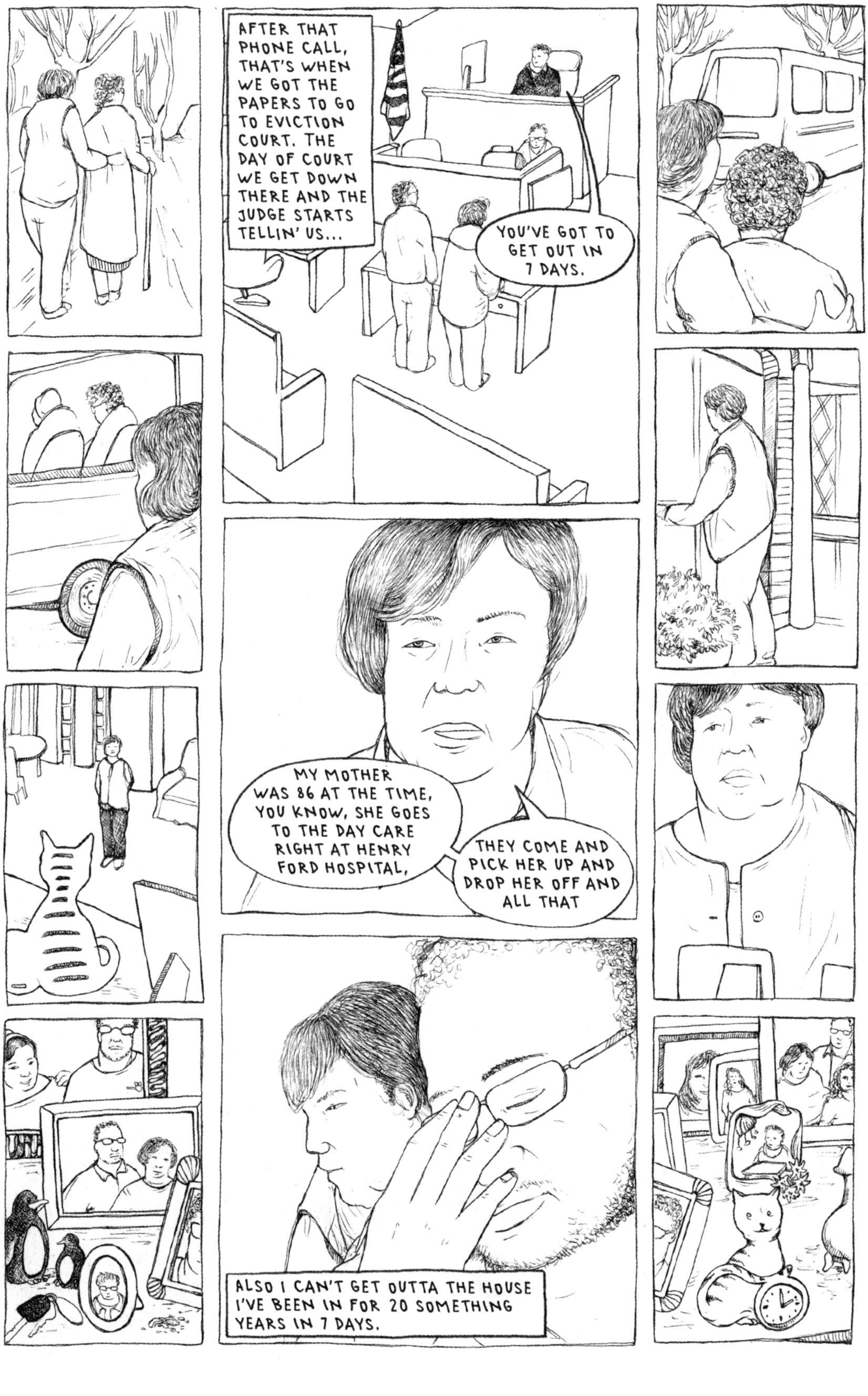
AFTER THAT PHONE CALL, THAT'S WHEN WE GOT THE PAPERS TO GO TO EVICTION COURT. THE DAY OF COURT WE GET DOWN THERE AND THE JUDGE STARTS TELLIN' US...
YOU'VE GOT TO GET OUT IN 7 DAYS.
MY MOTHER WAS 86 AT THE TIME, YOU KNOW, SHE GOES TO THE DAY CARE RIGHT AT HENRY FORD HOSPITAL,
THEY COME AND PICK HER UP AND DROP HER OFF AND ALL THAT
ALSO I CAN'T GET OUTTA THE HOUSE I'VE BEEN IN FOR 20 SOMETHING YEARS IN 7 DAYS.

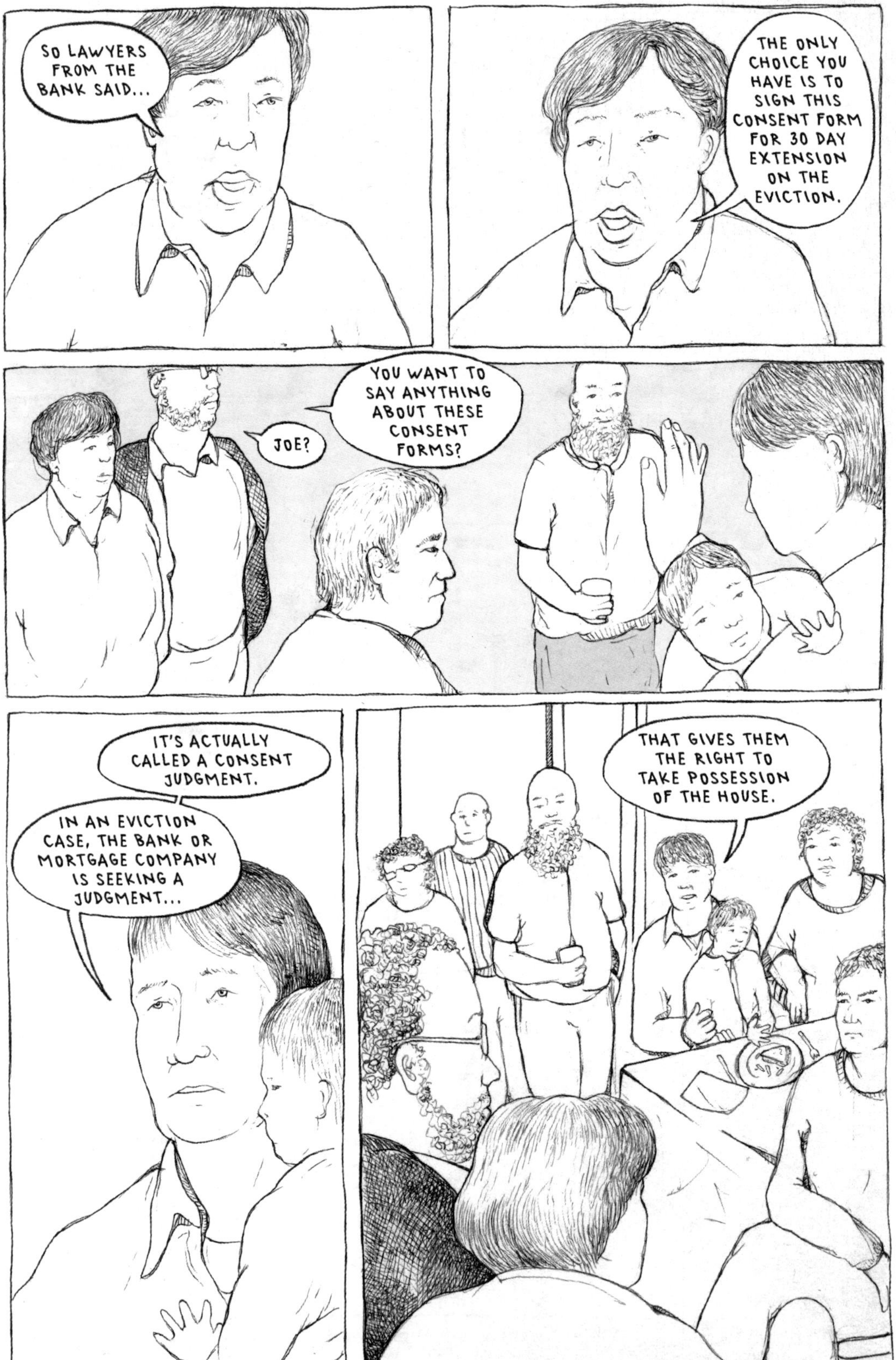
SO LAWYERS FROM THE BANK SAID...
THE ONLY CHOICE YOU HAVE IS TO SIGN THIS CONSENT FORM FOR 30 DAY EXTENSION ON THE EVICTION.
JOE?
YOU WANT TO SAY ANYTHING ABOUT THESE CONSENT FORMS?
IT'S ACTUALLY CALLED A CONSENT JUDGMENT.
IN AN EVICTION CASE, THE BANK OR MORTGAGE COMPANY IS SEEKING A JUDGMENT...
THAT GIVES THEM THE RIGHT TO TAKE POSSESSION OF THE HOUSE.

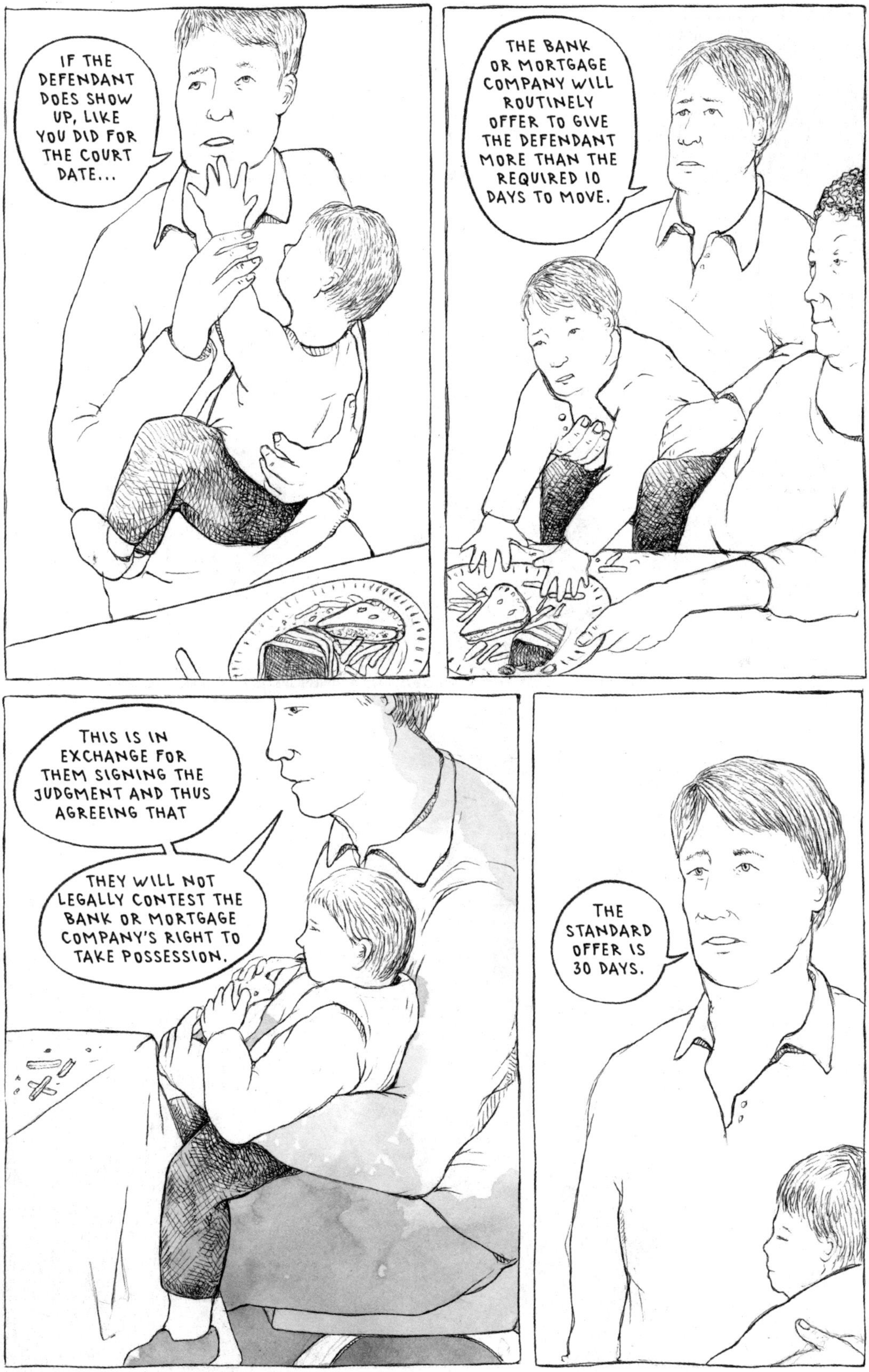
IF THE DEFENDANT DOES SHOW UP, LIKE YOU DID FOR THE COURT DATE...
THE BANK OR MORTGAGE COMPANY WILL ROUTINELY OFFER TO GIVE THE DEFENDANT MORE THAN THE REQUIRED 10 DAYS TO MOVE.
THIS IS IN EXCHANGE FOR THEM SIGNING THE JUDGMENT AND THUS AGREEING THAT
THEY WILL NOT LEGALLY CONTEST THE BANK OR MORTGAGE COMPANY'S RIGHT TO TAKE POSSESSION.
THE STANDARD OFFER IS 30 DAYS.

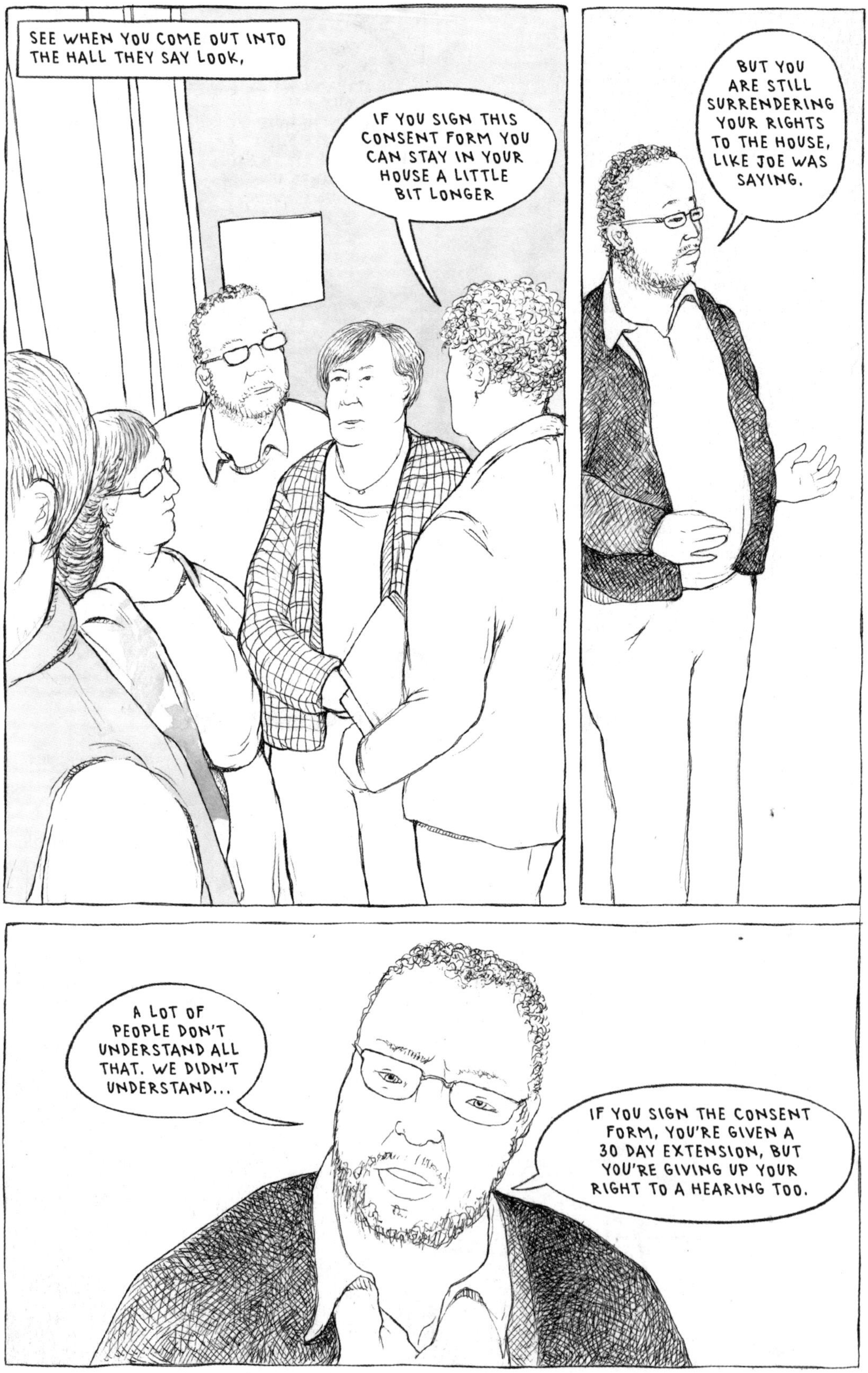
SEE WHEN YOU COME OUT INTO THE HALL THEY SAY LOOK,
IF YOU SIGN THIS CONSENT FORM YOU CAN STAY IN YOUR HOUSE A LITTLE BIT LONGER
BUT YOU ARE STILL SURRENDERING YOUR RIGHTS TO THE HOUSE, LIKE JOE WAS SAYING.
A LOT OF PEOPLE DON'T UNDERSTAND ALL THAT. WE DIDN'T UNDERSTAND...
IF YOU SIGN THE CONSENT FORM, YOU'RE GIVEN A 30 DAY EXTENSION, BUT YOU'RE GIVING UP YOUR RIGHT TO A HEARING TOO.

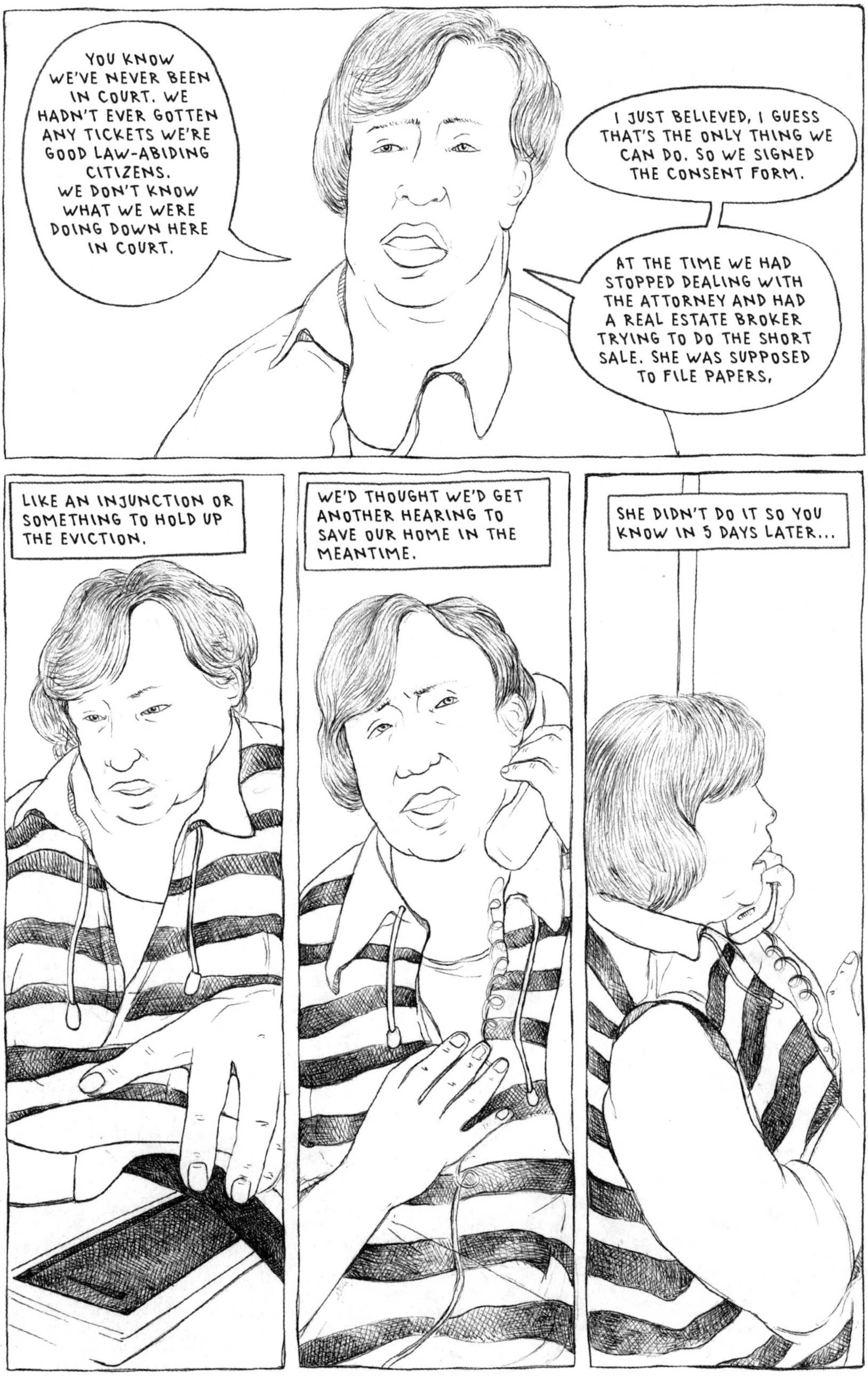
YOU KNOW WE'VE NEVER BEEN IN COURT. WE HADN'T EVER GOTTEN ANY TICKETS WE'RE GOOD LAW-ABIDING CITIZENS. WE DON'T KNOW WHAT WE WERE DOING DOWN HERE IN COURT.
I JUST BELIEVED, I GUESS THAT'S THE ONLY THING WE CAN DO. SO WE SIGNED THE CONSENT FORM.
AT THE TIME WE HAD STOPPED DEALING WITH THE ATTORNEY AND HAD A REAL ESTATE BROKER TRYING TO DO THE SHORT SALE. SHE WAS SUPPOSED TO FILE PAPERS,
LIKE AN INJUNCTION OR SOMETHING TO HOLD UP THE EVICTION.
WE'D THOUGHT WE'D GET ANOTHER HEARING TO SAVE OUR HOME IN THE MEANTIME.
SHE DIDN'T DO IT SO YOU KNOW IN 5 DAYS LATER...

THERE WAS A DUMPSTER OUT FRONT OF OUR HOUSE.

SEEING THAT, IT WAS SHOCKING.

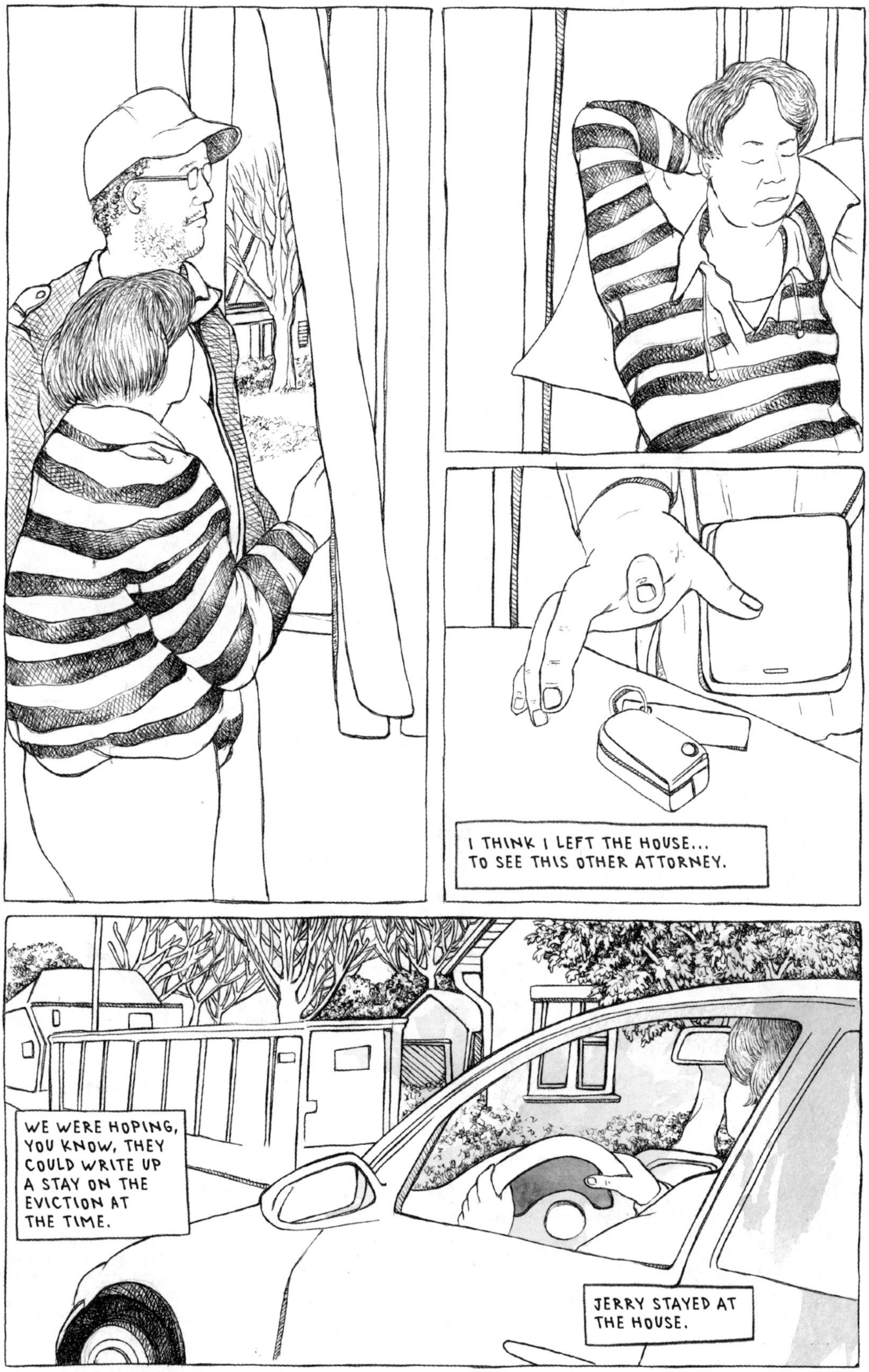
I THINK I LEFT THE HOUSE...
TO SEE THIS OTHER ATTORNEY.
WE WERE HOPING, YOU KNOW, THEY COULD WRITE UP A STAY ON THE EVICTION AT THE TIME.
JERRY STAYED AT THE HOUSE.

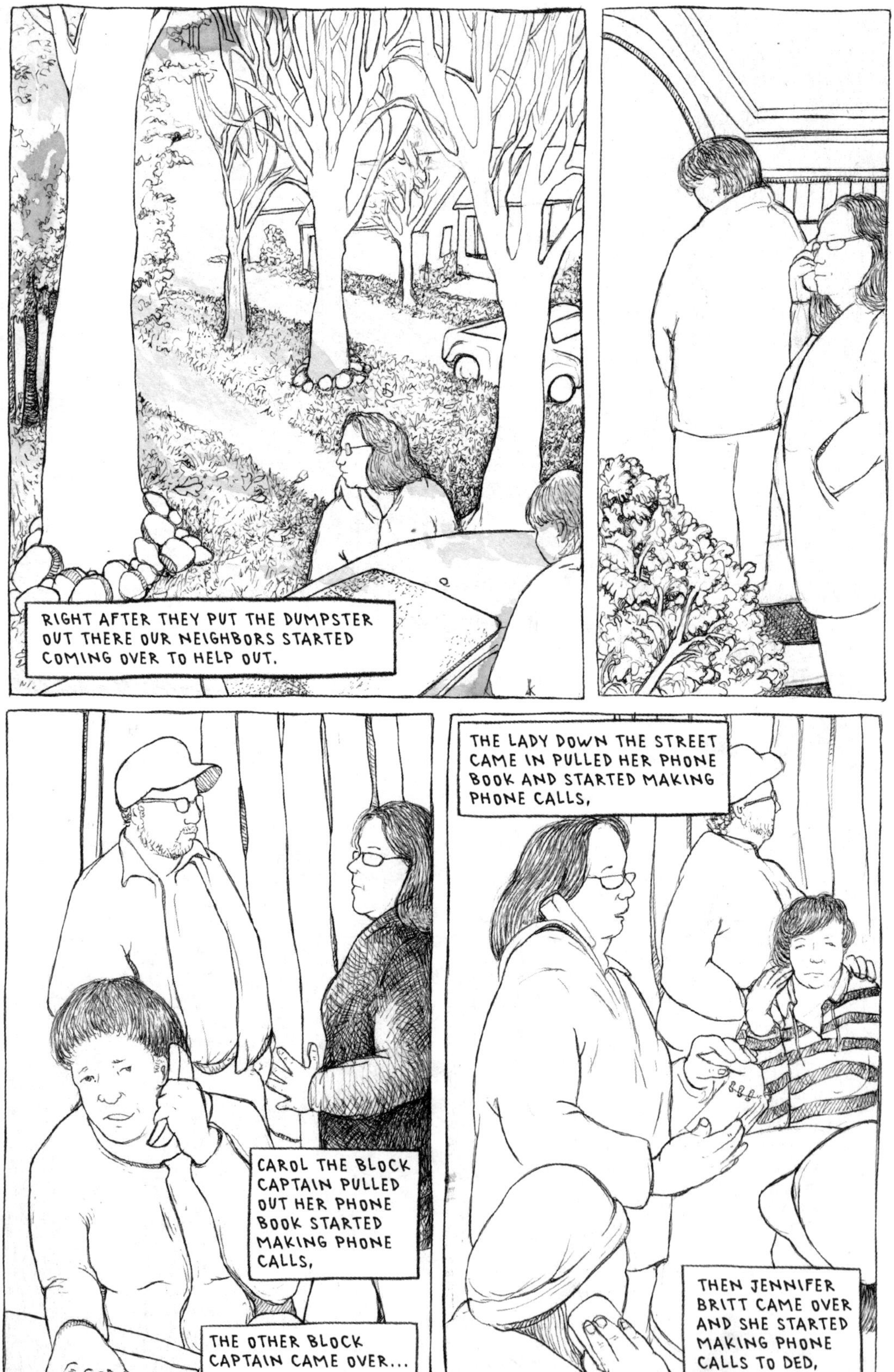
RIGHT AFTER THEY PUT THE DUMPSTER OUT THERE OUR NEIGHBORS STARTED COMING OVER TO HELP OUT.
CAROL THE BLOCK CAPTAIN PULLED OUT HER PHONE BOOK STARTED MAKING PHONE CALLS,
THE OTHER BLOCK CAPTAIN CAME OVER...
THE LADY DOWN THE STREET CAME IN PULLED HER PHONE BOOK AND STARTED MAKING PHONE CALLS,
THEN JENNIFER BRITT CAME OVER AND SHE STARTED MAKING PHONE CALLS TO DED,

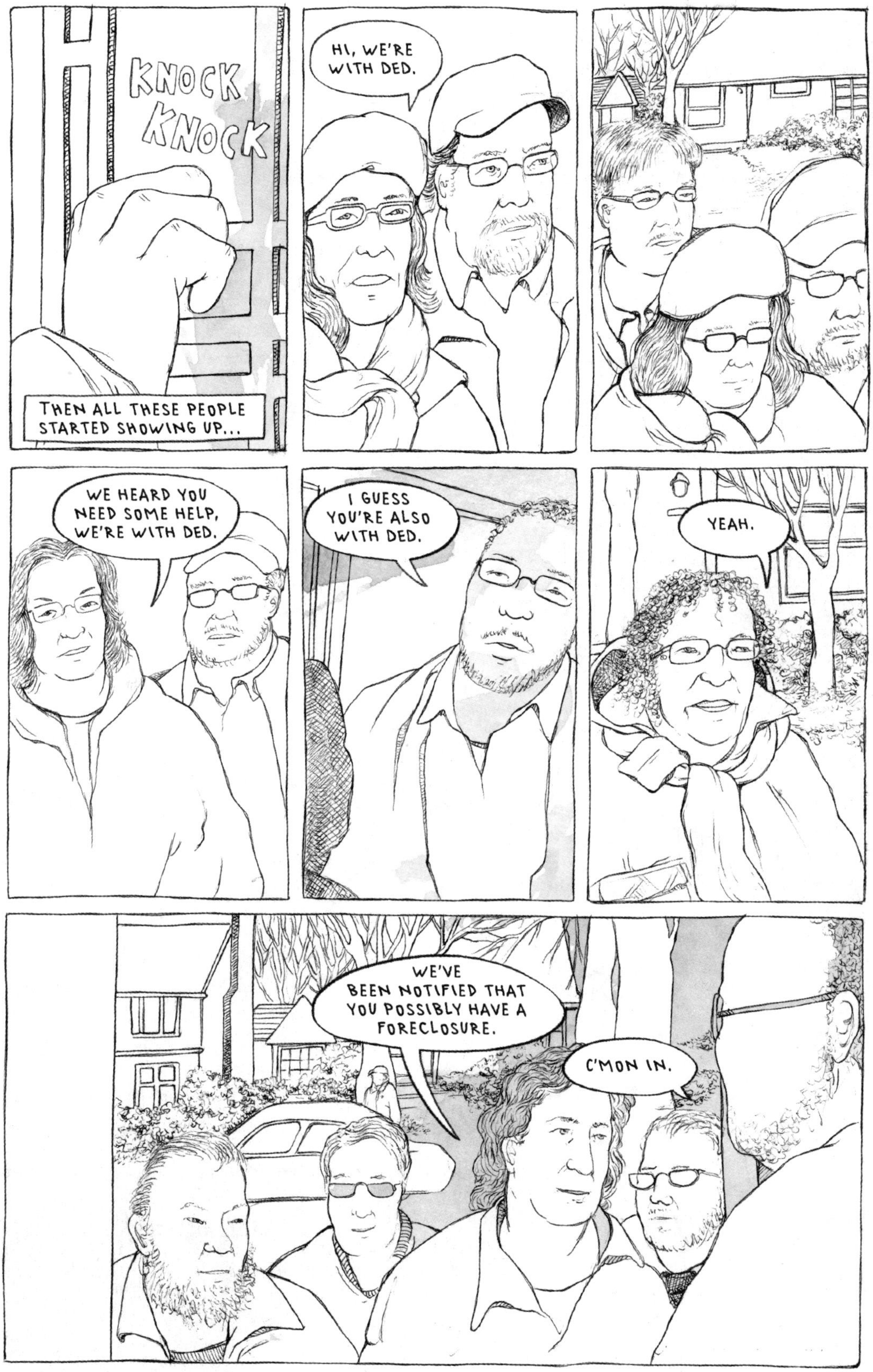

KNOCK KNOCK
THEN ALL THESE PEOPLE STARTED SHOWING UP...
HI, WE'RE WITH DED.
WE HEARD YOU NEED SOME HELP, WE'RE WITH DED.
I GUESS YOU'RE ALSO WITH DED.
YEAH.
WE'VE BEEN NOTIFIED THAT YOU POSSIBLY HAVE A FORECLOSURE.
C'MON IN.

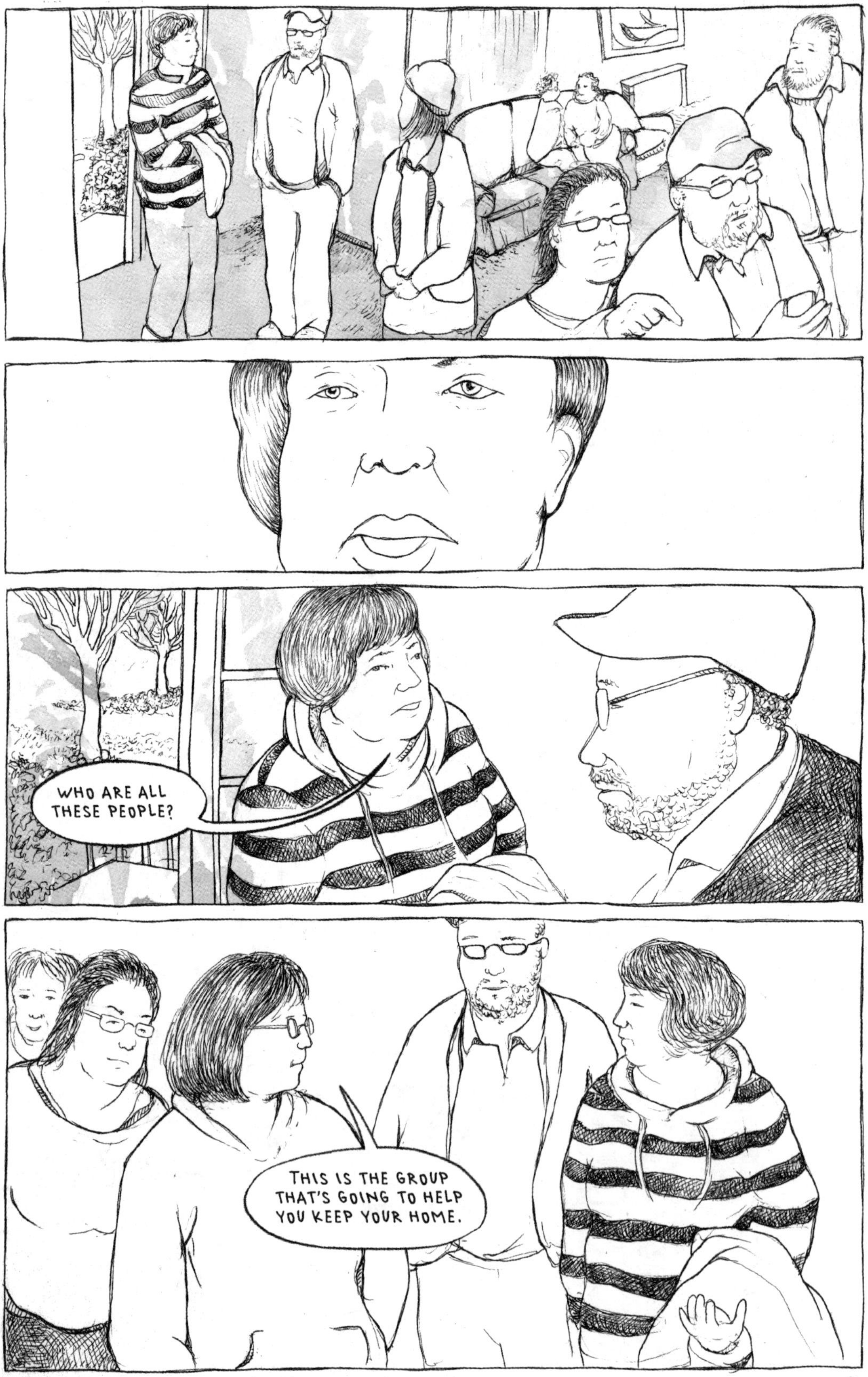
WHO ARE ALL THESE PEOPLE?
THIS IS THE GROUP THAT'S GOING TO HELP YOU KEEP YOUR HOME.

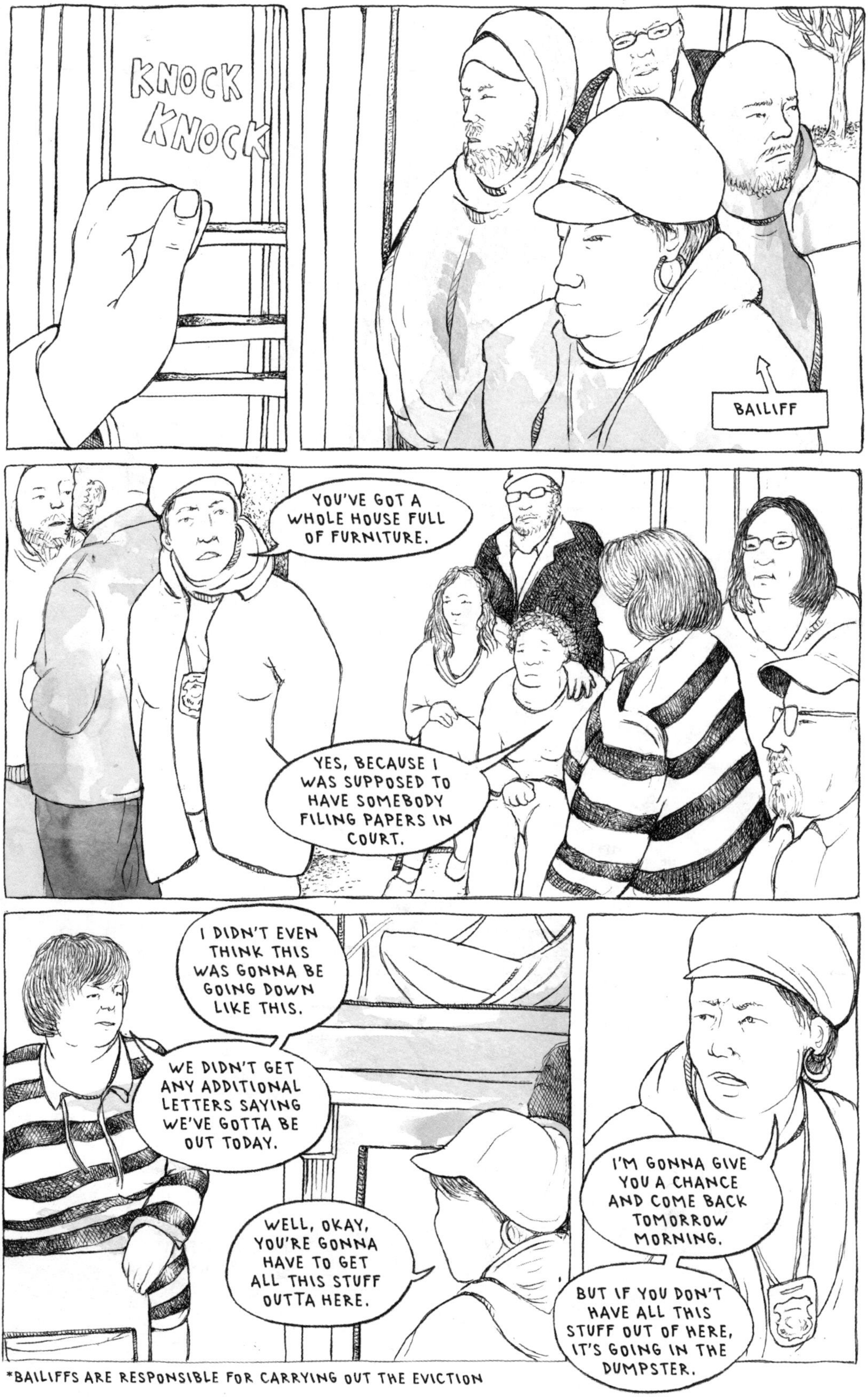
KNOCK KNOCK
BAILIFF
YOU'VE GOT A WHOLE HOUSE FULL OF FURNITURE.
YES, BECAUSE I WAS SUPPOSED TO HAVE SOMEBODY FILING PAPERS IN COURT.
I DIDN'T EVEN THINK THIS WAS GONNA BE GOING DOWN LIKE THIS.
WE DIDN'T GET ANY ADDITIONAL LETTERS SAYING WE'VE GOTTA BE OUT TODAY.
WELL, OKAY, YOU'RE GONNA HAVE TO GET ALL THIS STUFF OUTTA HERE.
I'M GONNA GIVE YOU A CHANCE AND COME BACK TOMORROW MORNING.
BUT IF YOU DON'T HAVE ALL THIS STUFF OUT OF HERE, IT'S GOING IN THE DUMPSTER.

*BAILIFFS ARE RESPONSIBLE FOR CARRYING OUT THE EVICTION

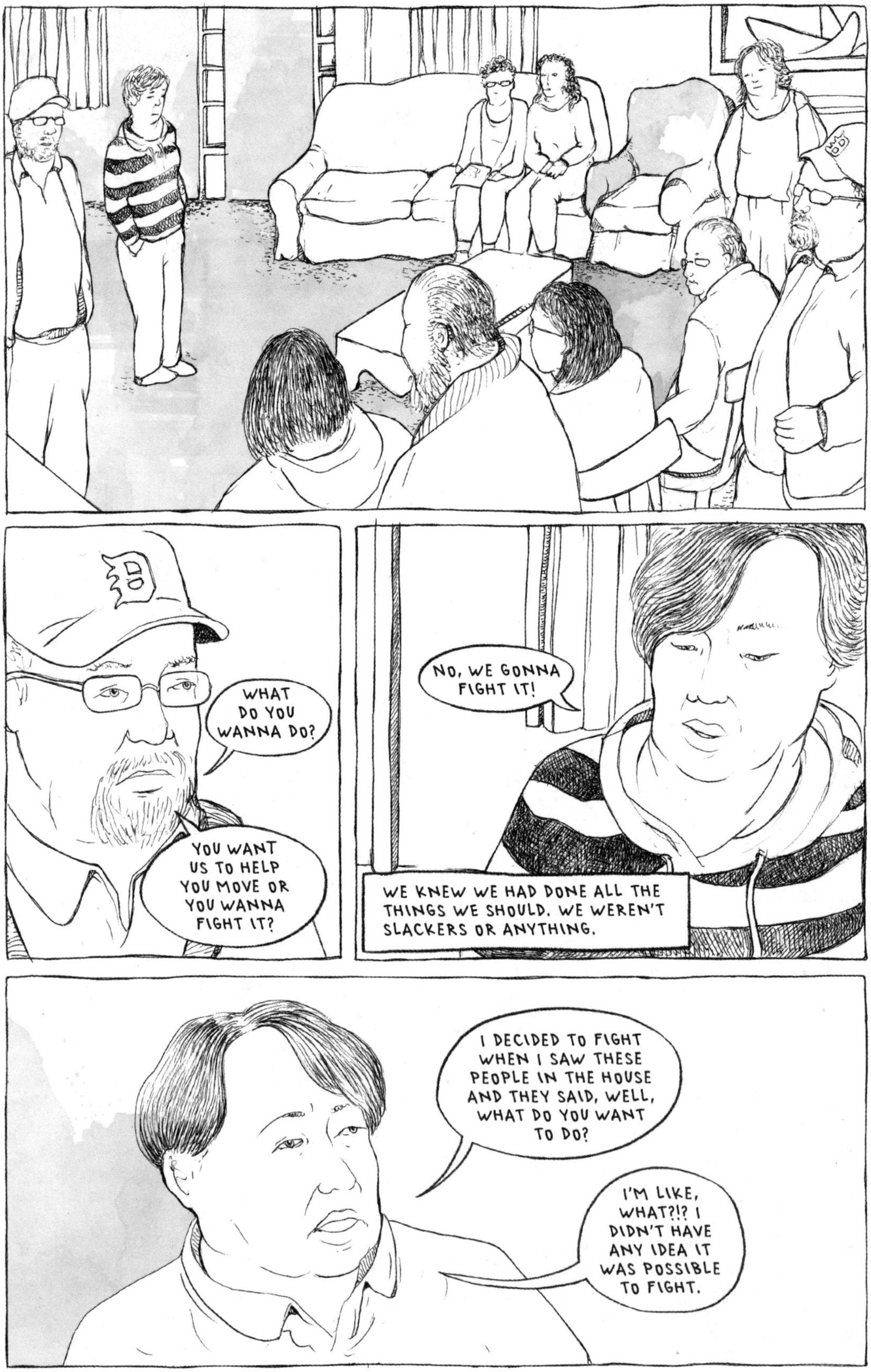
WHAT DO YOU WANNA DO?
YOU WANT US TO HELP YOU MOVE OR YOU WANNA FIGHT IT?
NO, WE GONNA FIGHT IT!
WE KNEW WE HAD DONE ALL THE THINGS WE SHOULD. WE WEREN'T SLACKERS OR ANYTHING.
I DECIDED TO FIGHT WHEN I SAW THESE PEOPLE IN THE HOUSE AND THEY SAID, WELL, WHAT DO YOU WANT TO DO?
I'M LIKE, WHAT?!? I DIDN'T HAVE ANY IDEA IT WAS POSSIBLE TO FIGHT.

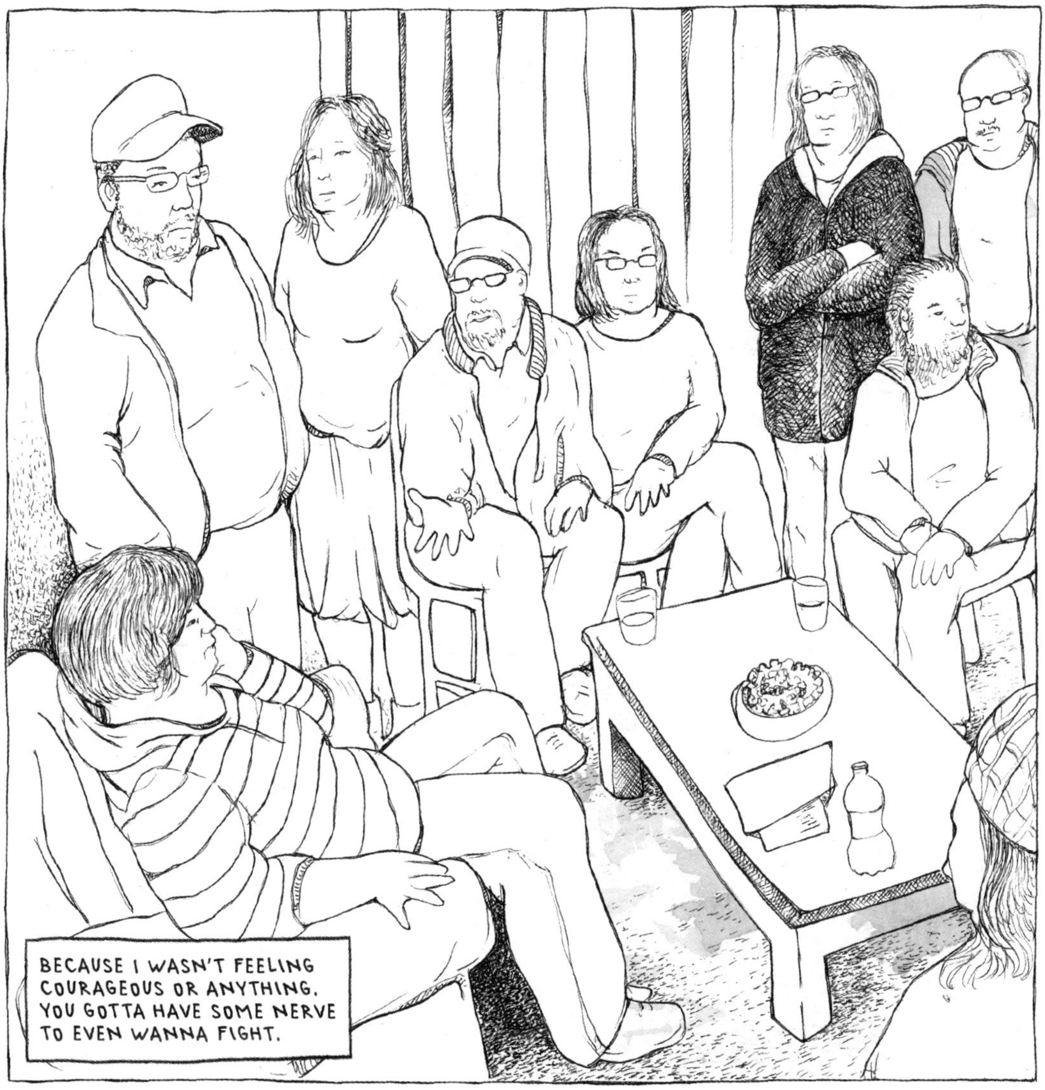
BECAUSE I WASN'T FEELING COURAGEOUS OR ANYTHING. YOU GOTTA HAVE SOME NERVE TO EVEN WANNA FIGHT.

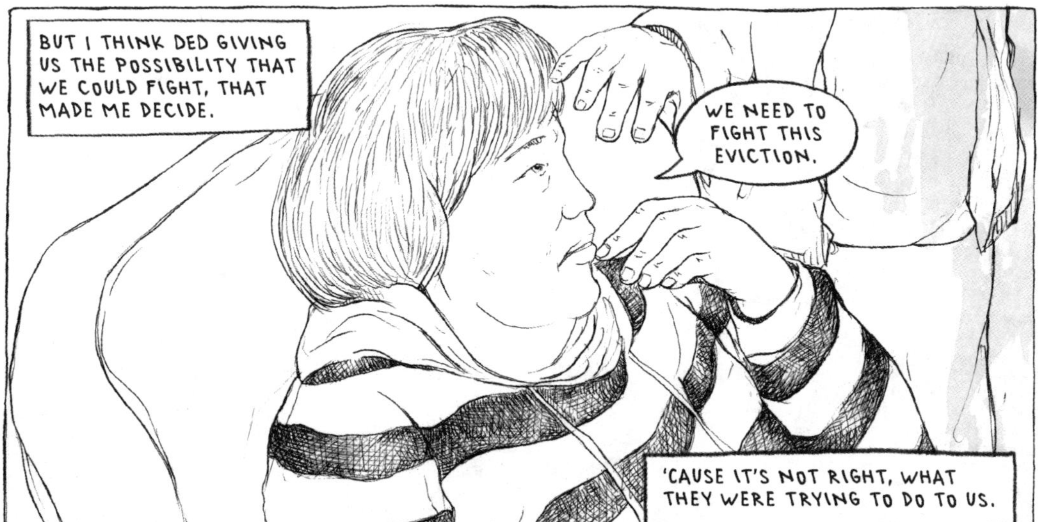
BUT I THINK DED GIVING US THE POSSIBILITY THAT WE COULD FIGHT, THAT MADE ME DECIDE.
WE NEED TO FIGHT THIS EVICTION.
'CAUSE IT'S NOT RIGHT, WHAT THEY WERE TRYING TO DO TO US.

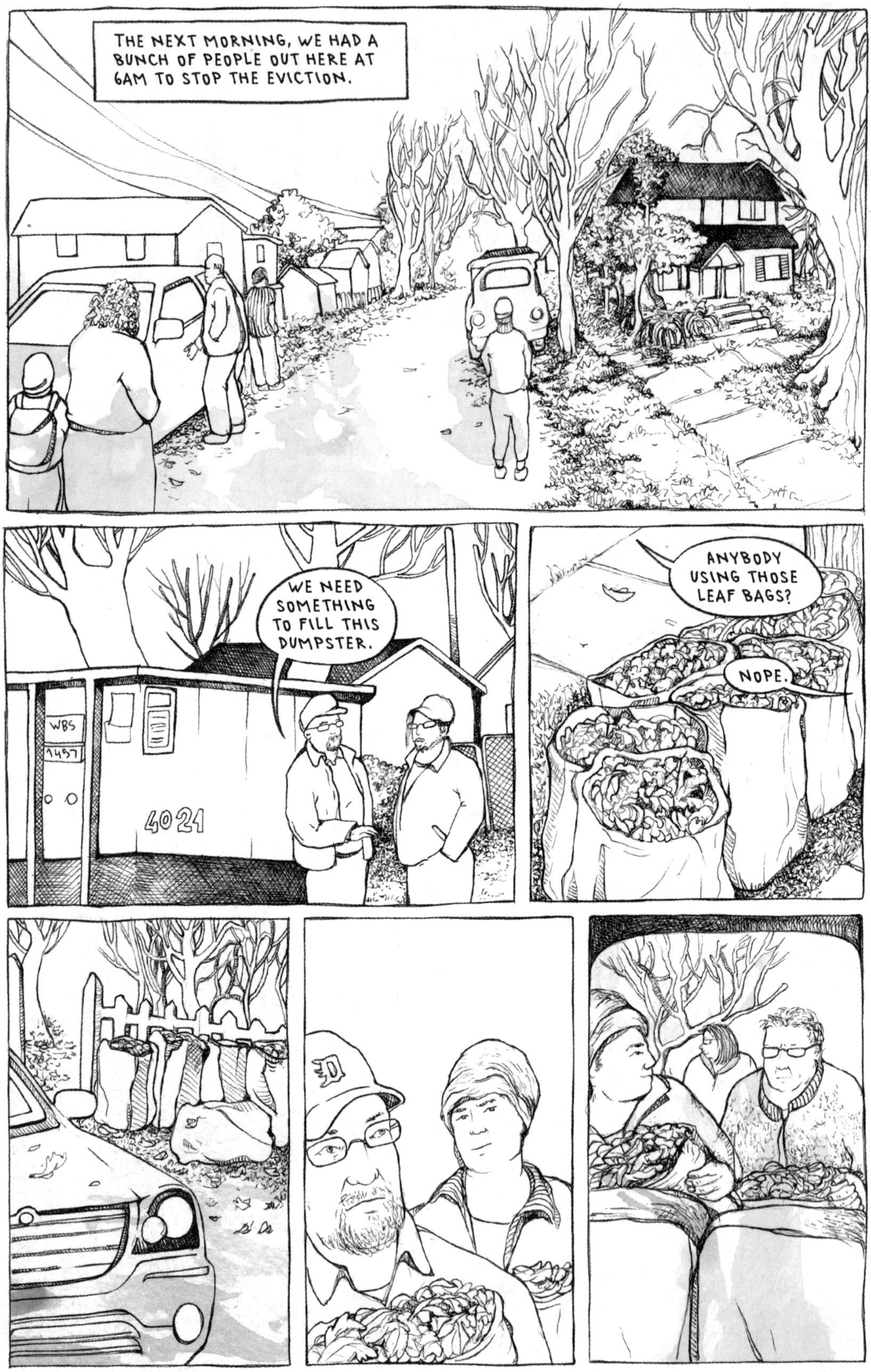
THE NEXT MORNING, WE HAD A BUNCH OF PEOPLE OUT HERE AT 6AM TO STOP THE EVICTION.
WBS
4021
WE NEED SOMETHING TO FILL THIS DUMPSTER.
ANYBODY USING THOSE LEAF BAGS?
NOPE.

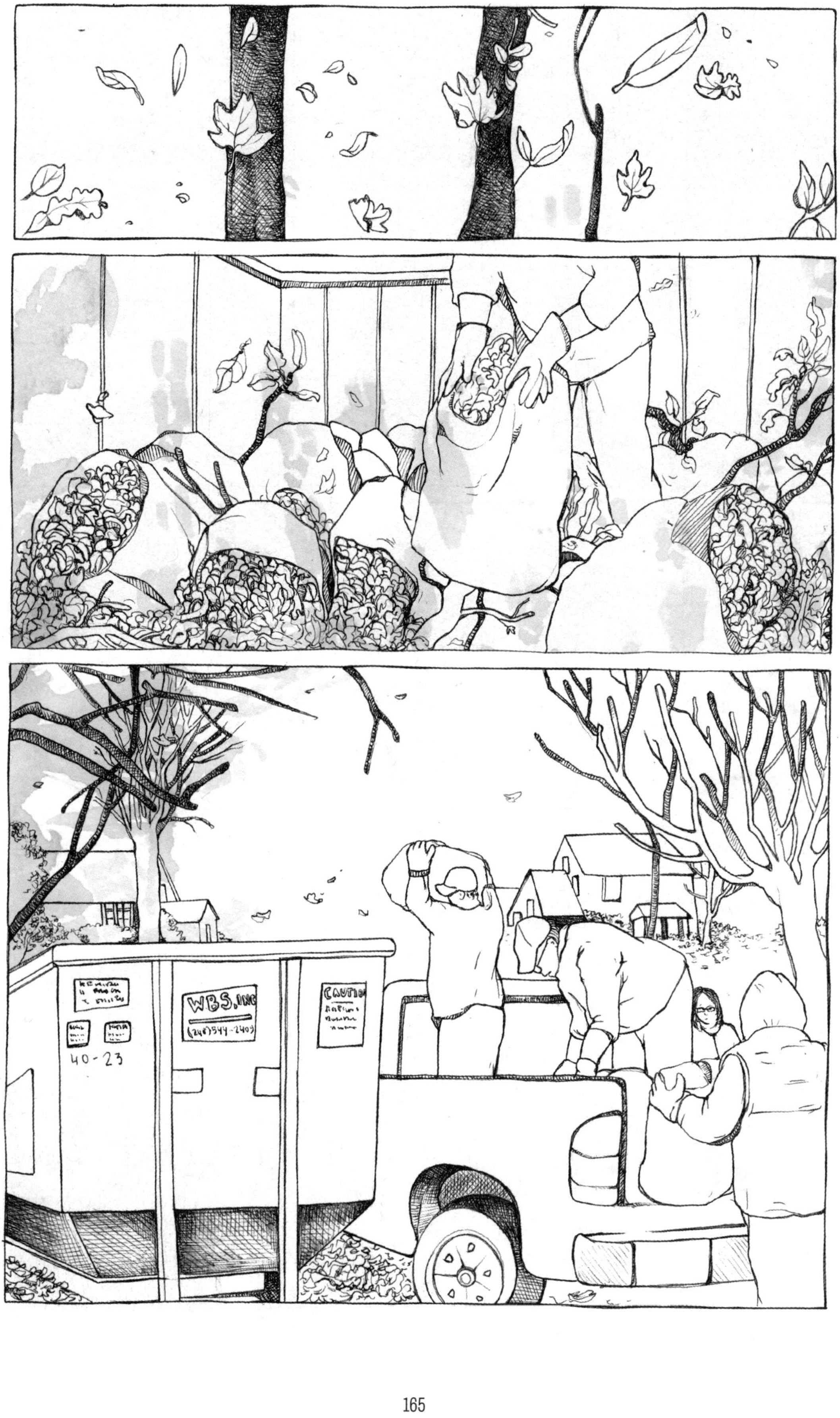
WBS, INC
(248)544-2409
CAUTION
40-23

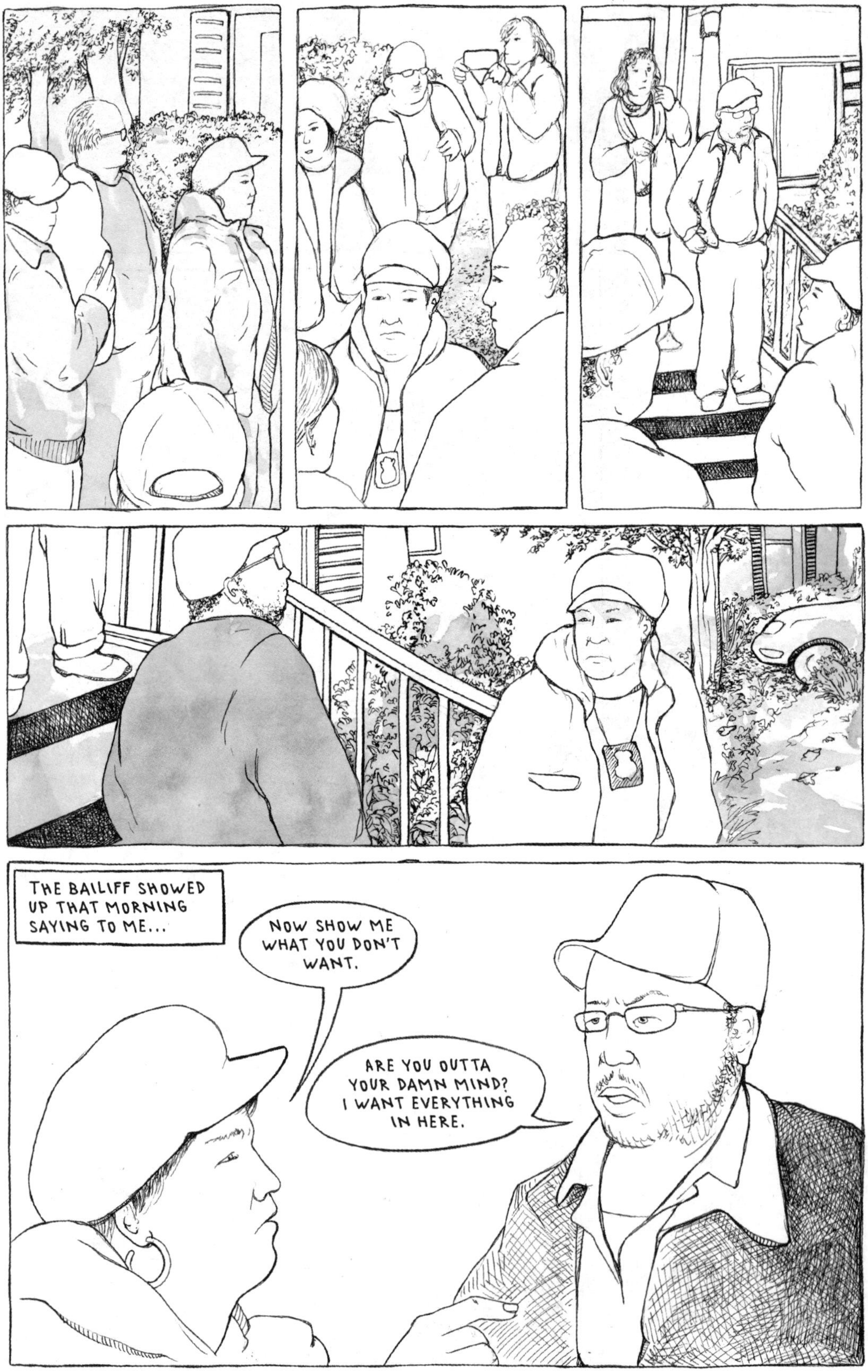
THE BAILIFF SHOWED UP THAT MORNING SAYING TO ME...
NOW SHOW ME WHAT YOU DON'T WANT.
ARE YOU OUTTA YOUR DAMN MIND? I WANT EVERYTHING IN HERE.

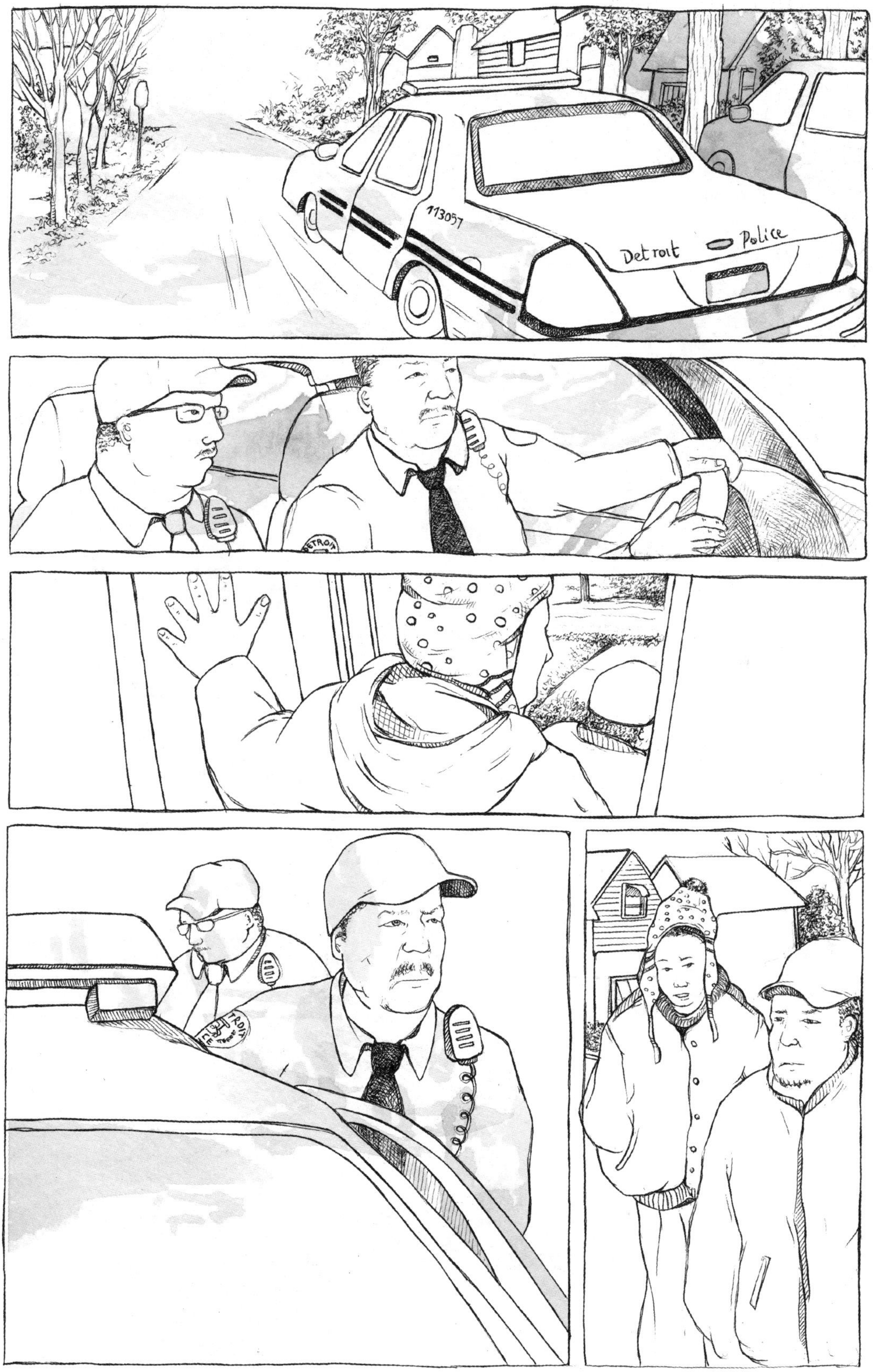
113057
Detroit
Police

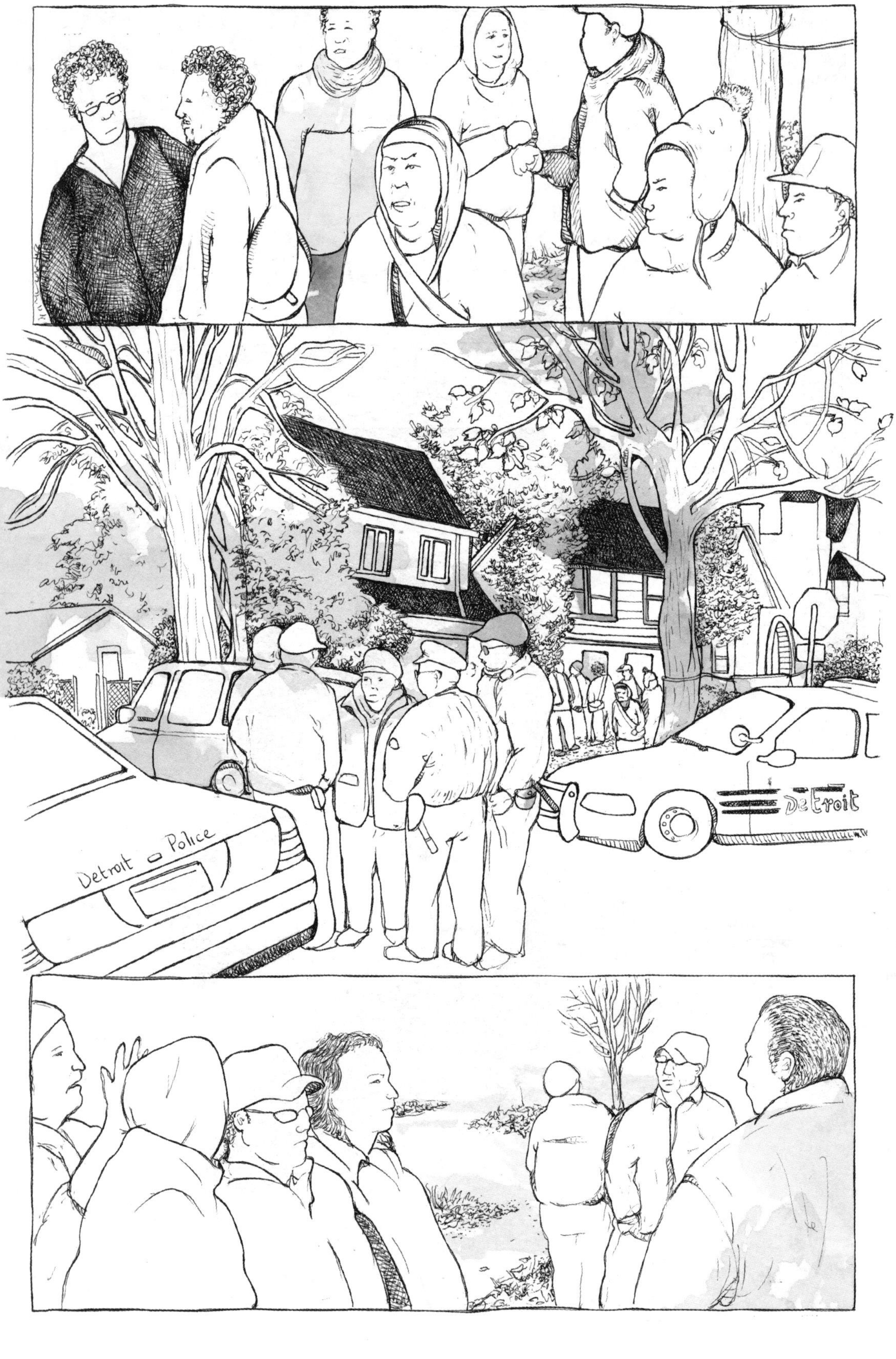
Detroit Police
Detroit

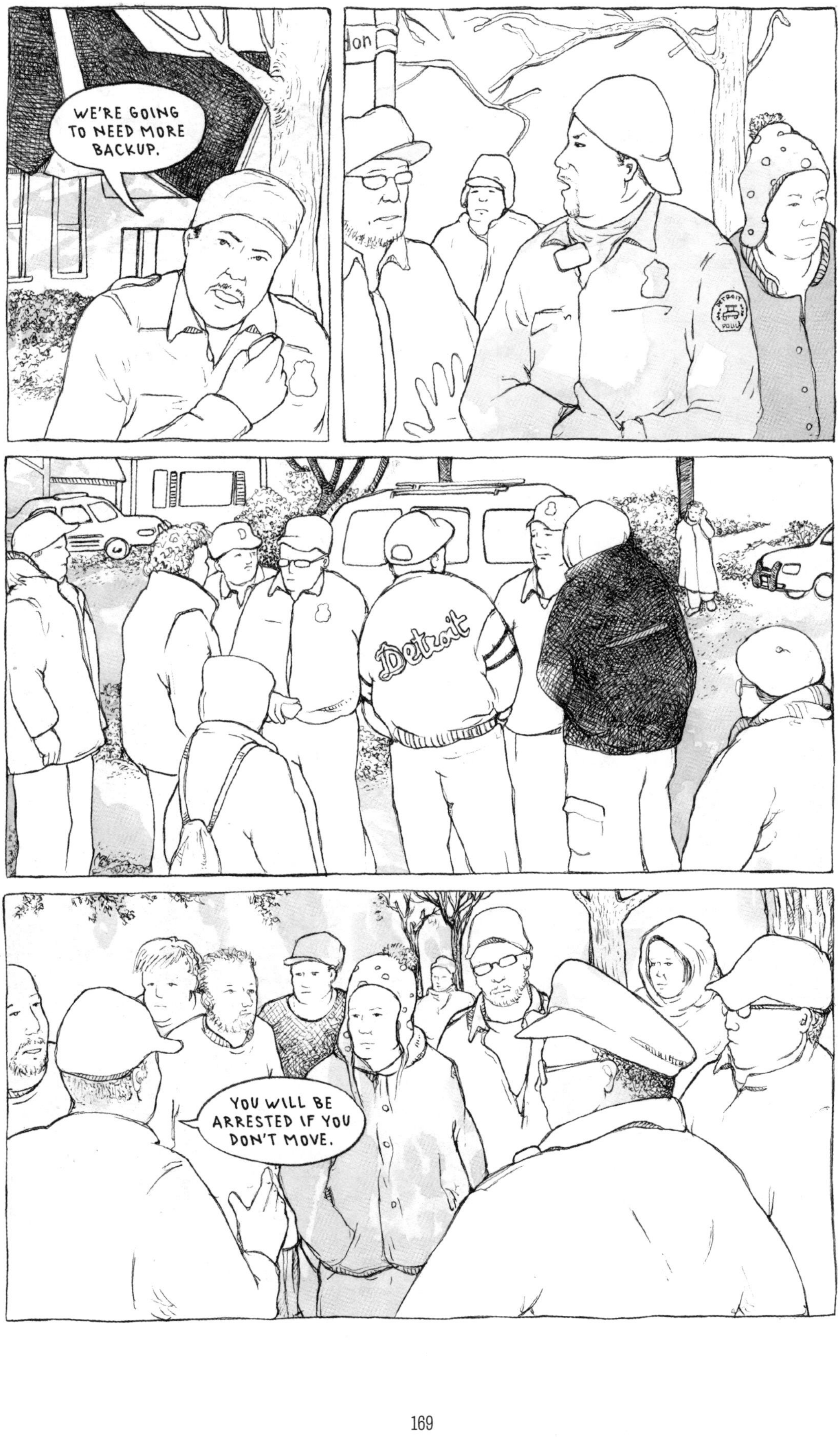
WE'RE GOING TO NEED MORE BACKUP.
Detroit
YOU WILL BE ARRESTED IF YOU DON'T MOVE.

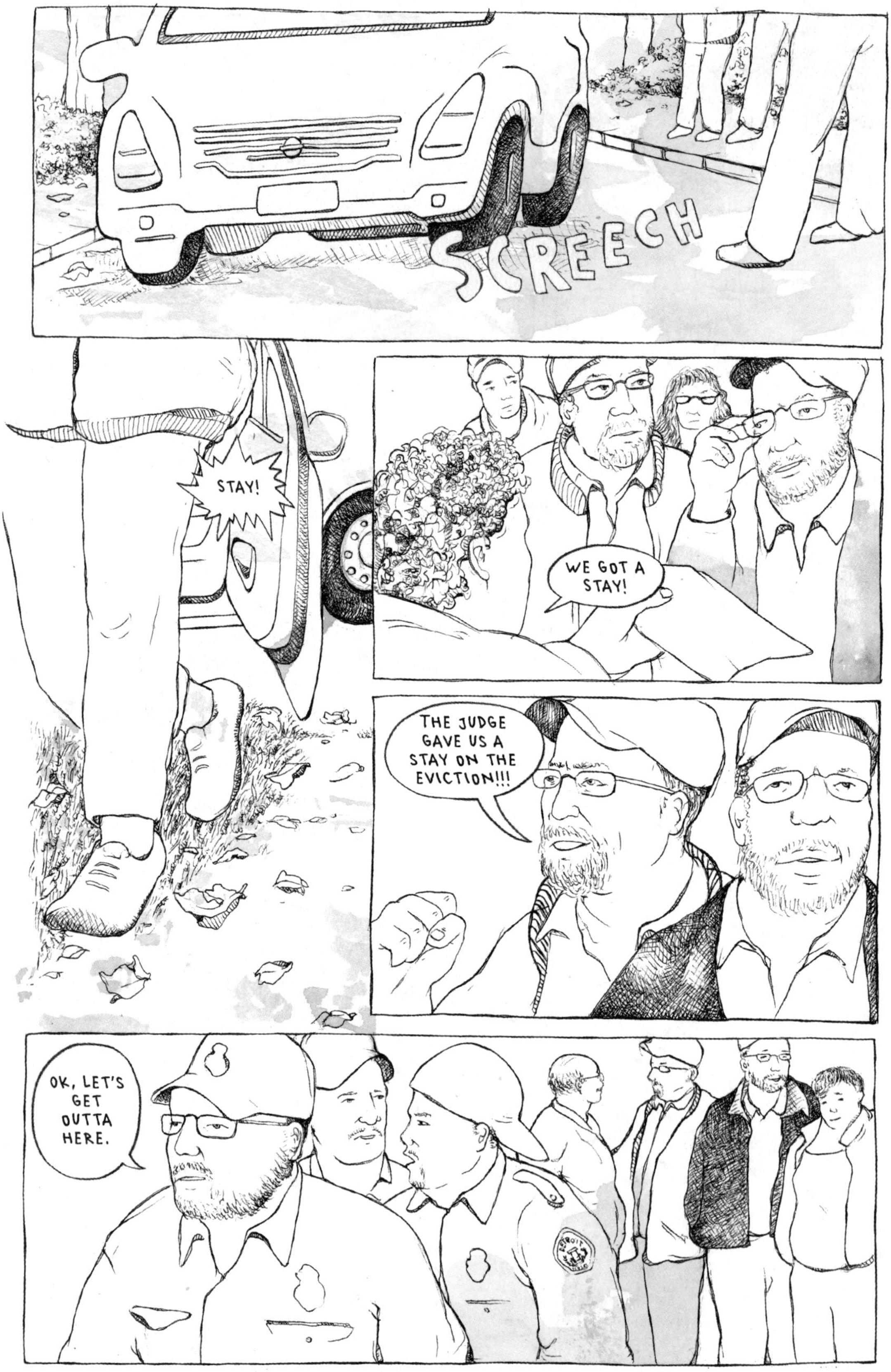
SCREECH
STAY!
WE GOT A STAY!
THE JUDGE GAVE US A STAY ON THE EVICTION!!!
OK, LET'S GET OUTTA HERE.

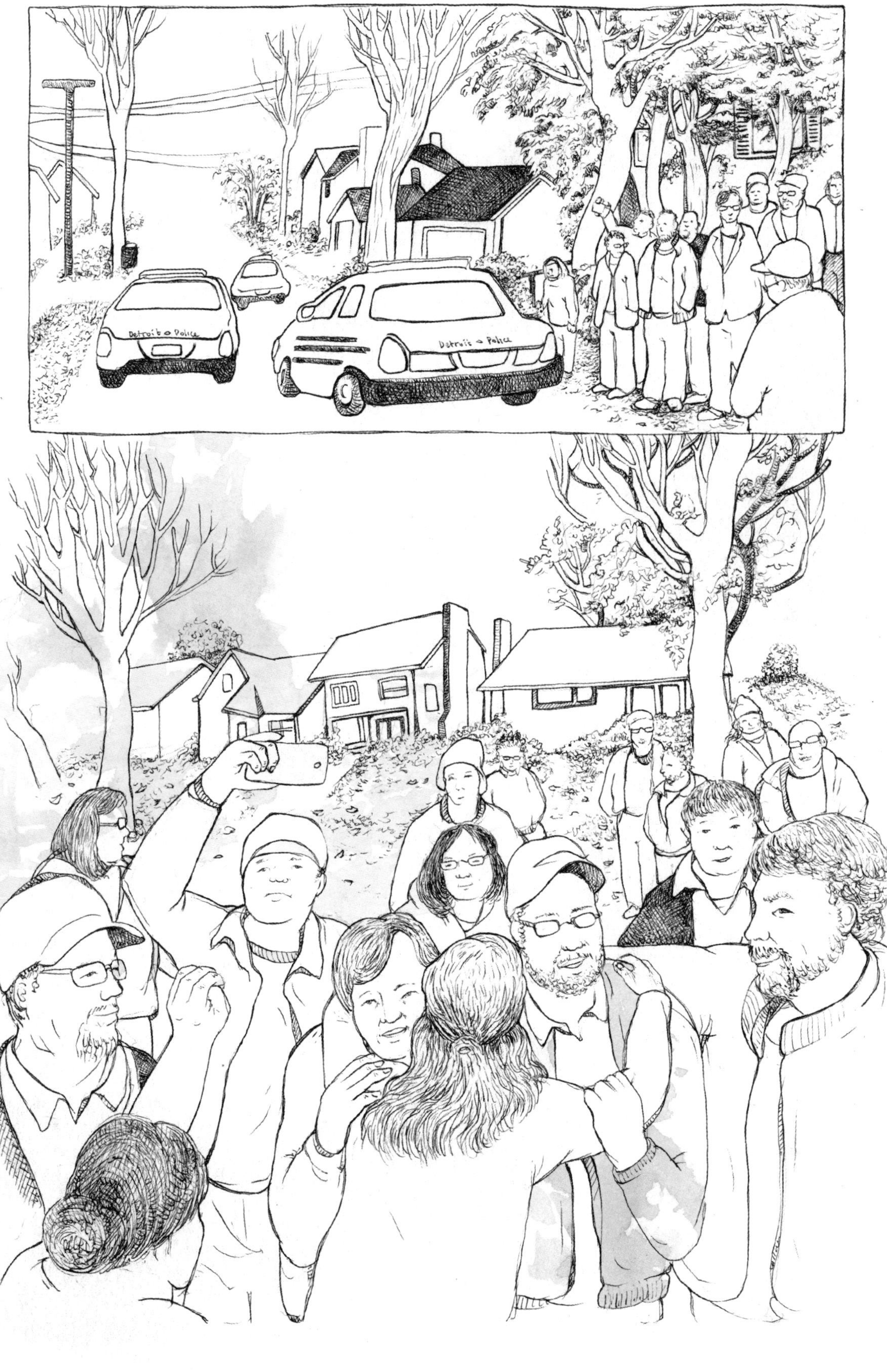
Detroit Police
Detroit Police

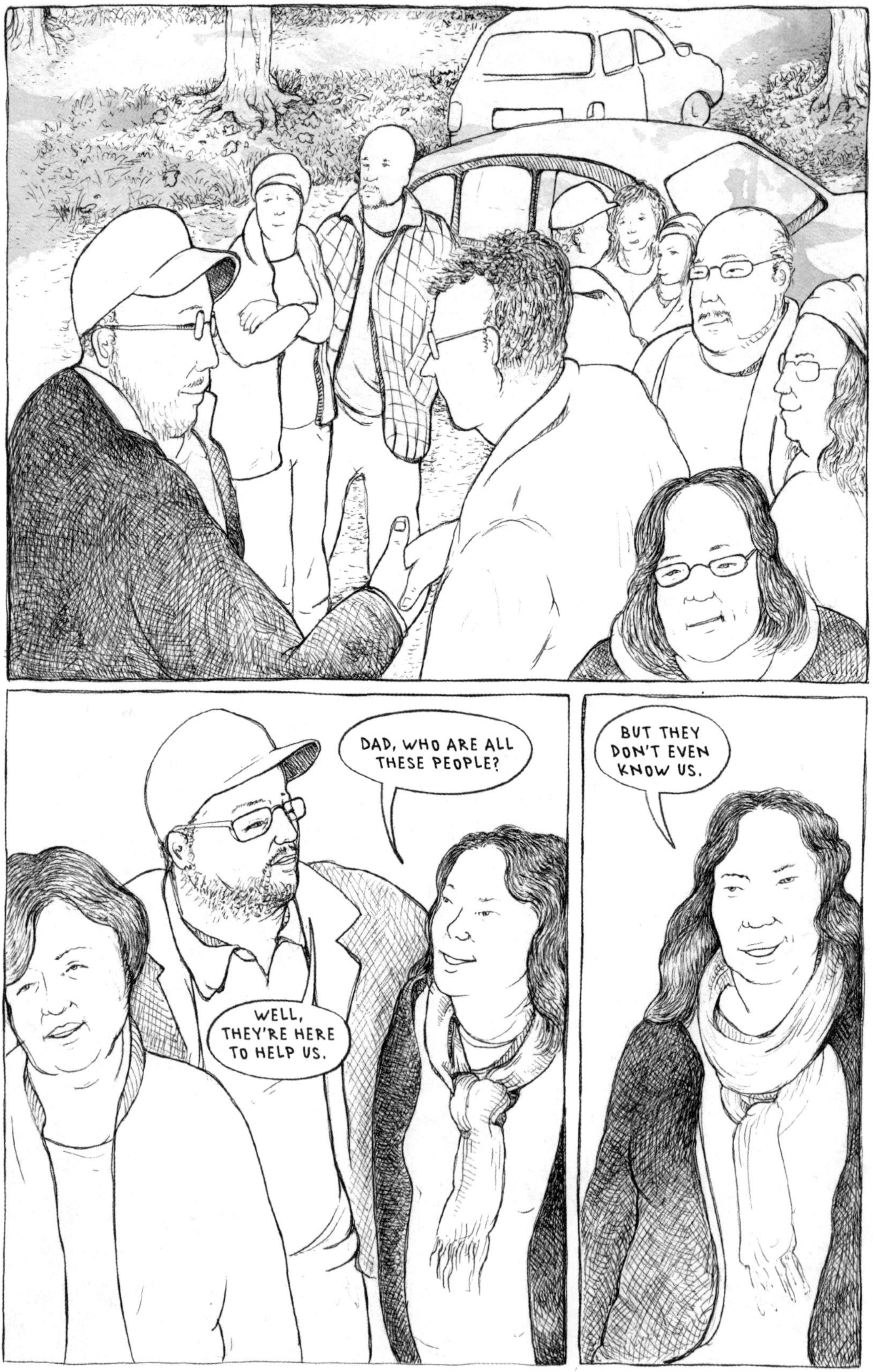
DAD, WHO ARE ALL THESE PEOPLE?
WELL, THEY'RE HERE TO HELP US.
BUT THEY DON'T EVEN KNOW US.

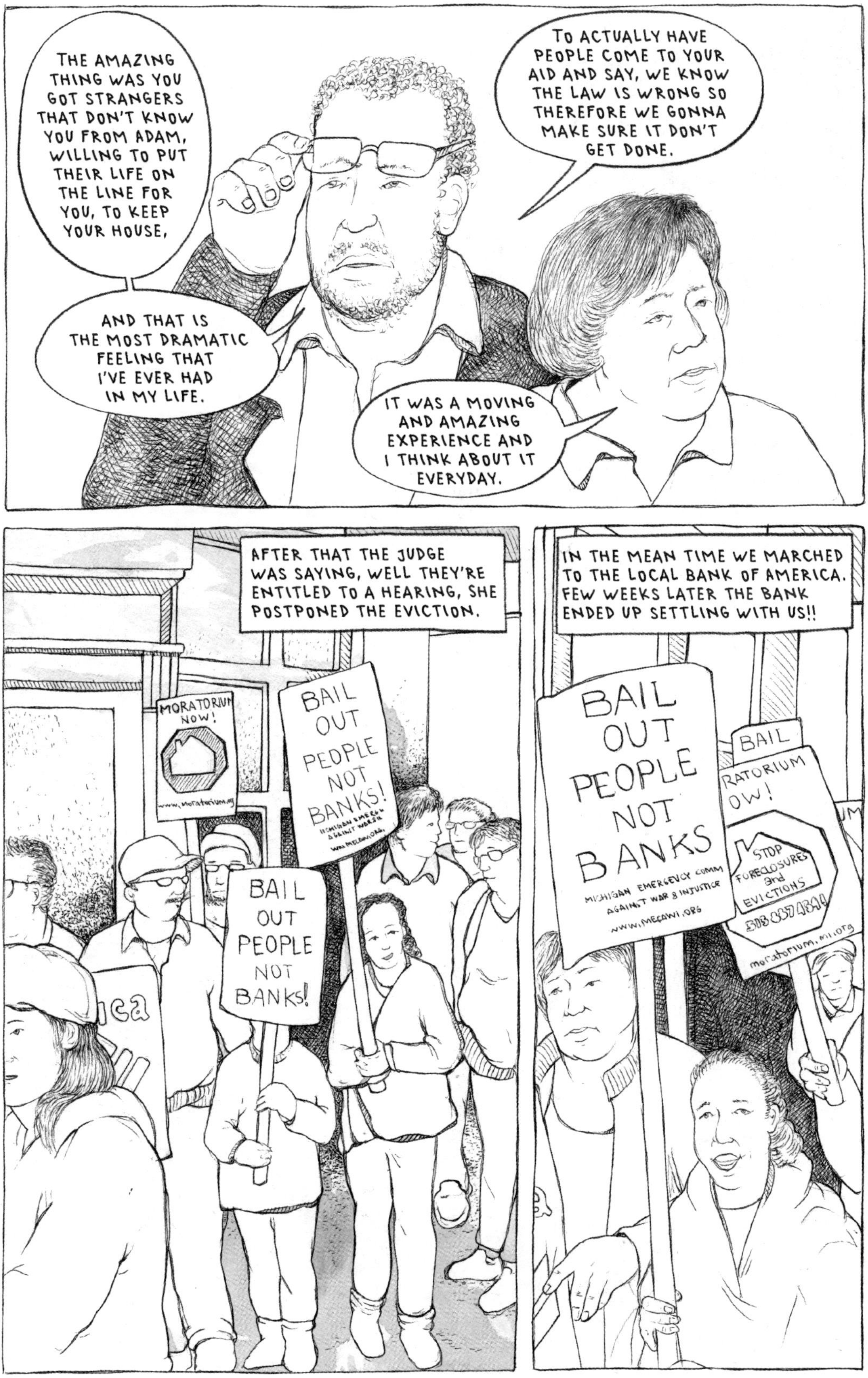
THE AMAZING THING WAS YOU GOT STRANGERS THAT DON'T KNOW YOU FROM ADAM, WILLING TO PUT THEIR LIFE ON THE LINE FOR YOU, TO KEEP YOUR HOUSE,
AND THAT IS THE MOST DRAMATIC FEELING THAT I'VE EVER HAD IN MY LIFE.
TO ACTUALLY HAVE PEOPLE COME TO YOUR AID AND SAY, WE KNOW THE LAW IS WRONG SO THEREFORE WE GONNA MAKE SURE IT DON'T GET DONE.
IT WAS A MOVING AND AMAZING EXPERIENCE AND I THINK ABOUT IT EVERYDAY.
AFTER THAT THE JUDGE WAS SAYING, WELL THEY'RE ENTITLED TO A HEARING, SHE POSTPONED THE EVICTION.
MORATORIUM NOW!
BAIL OUT PEOPLE NOT BANKS!
BAIL OUT PEOPLE NOT BANKS!
IN THE MEAN TIME WE MARCHED TO THE LOCAL BANK OF AMERICA. FEW WEEKS LATER THE BANK ENDED UP SETTLING WITH US!!
BAIL OUT PEOPLE NOT BANKS
MICHIGAN EMERGENCY COMM AGAINST WAR & INJUSTICE
WWW.MECAWI.ORG
BAIL
STOP FORECLOSURES and EVICTIONS
moratorium.mi.org

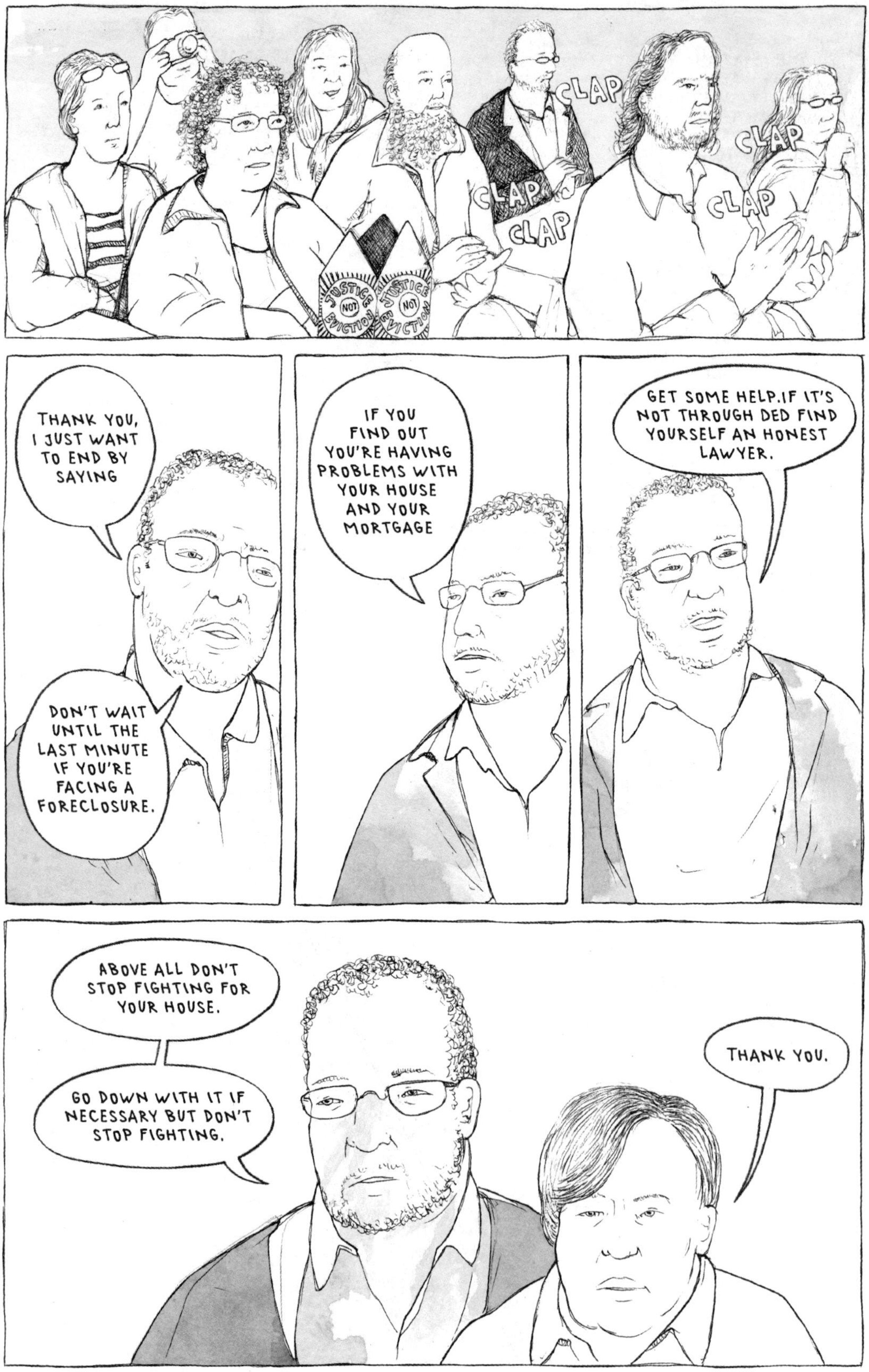

JUSTICE NOT EVICTION
JUSTICE NOT EVICTION
CLAP
CLAP
CLAP
CLAP
CLAP
THANK YOU, I JUST WANT TO END BY SAYING
DON'T WAIT UNTIL THE LAST MINUTE IF YOU'RE FACING A FORECLOSURE.
IF YOU FIND OUT YOU'RE HAVING PROBLEMS WITH YOUR HOUSE AND YOUR MORTGAGE
GET SOME HELP. IF IT'S NOT THROUGH DED FIND YOURSELF AN HONEST LAWYER.
ABOVE ALL DON'T STOP FIGHTING FOR YOUR HOUSE.
GO DOWN WITH IT IF NECESSARY BUT DON'T STOP FIGHTING.
THANK YOU.

I'm not
leaving
my home

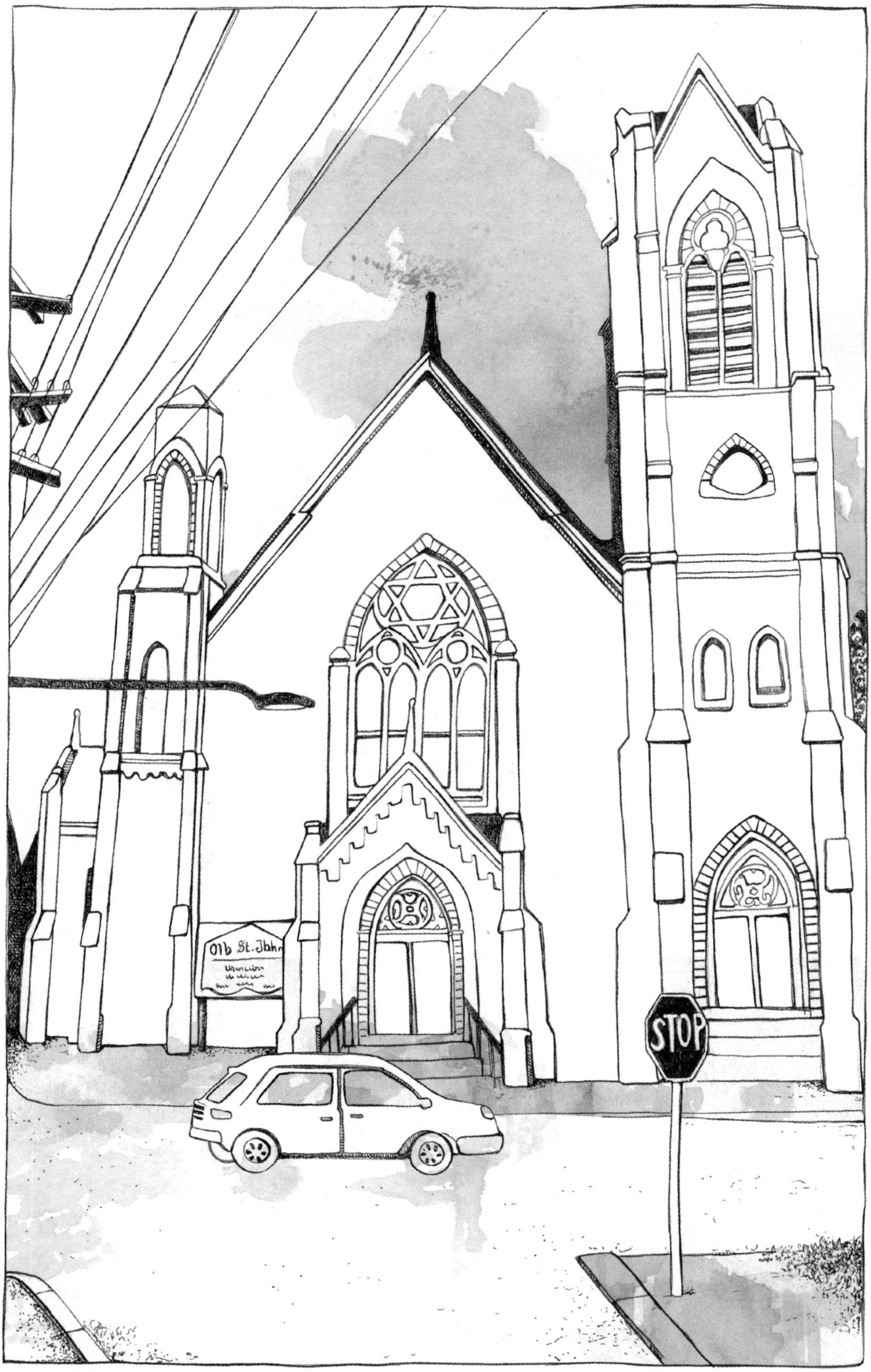
STOP

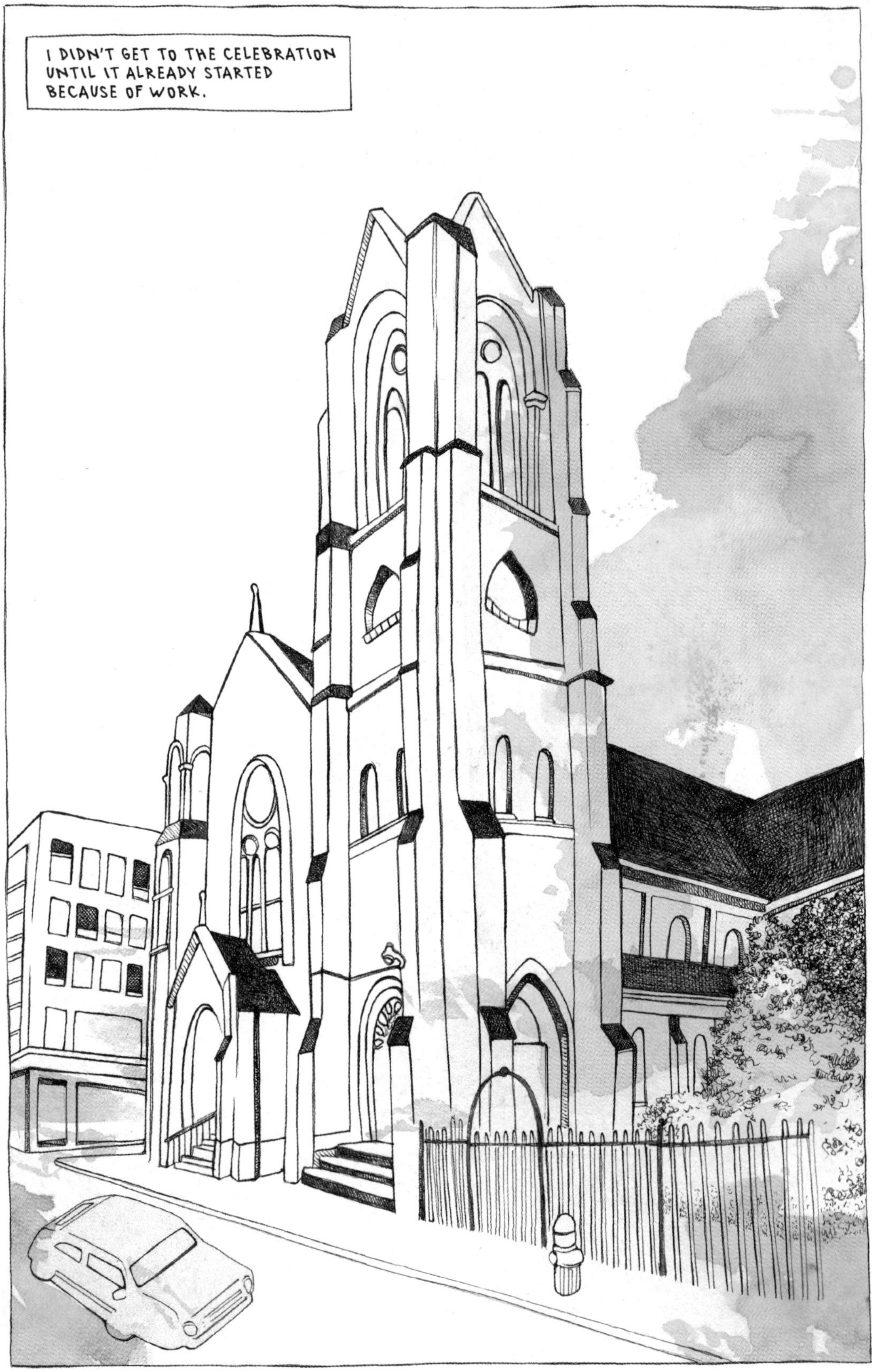
I DIDN'T GET TO THE CELEBRATION UNTIL IT ALREADY STARTED BECAUSE OF WORK.

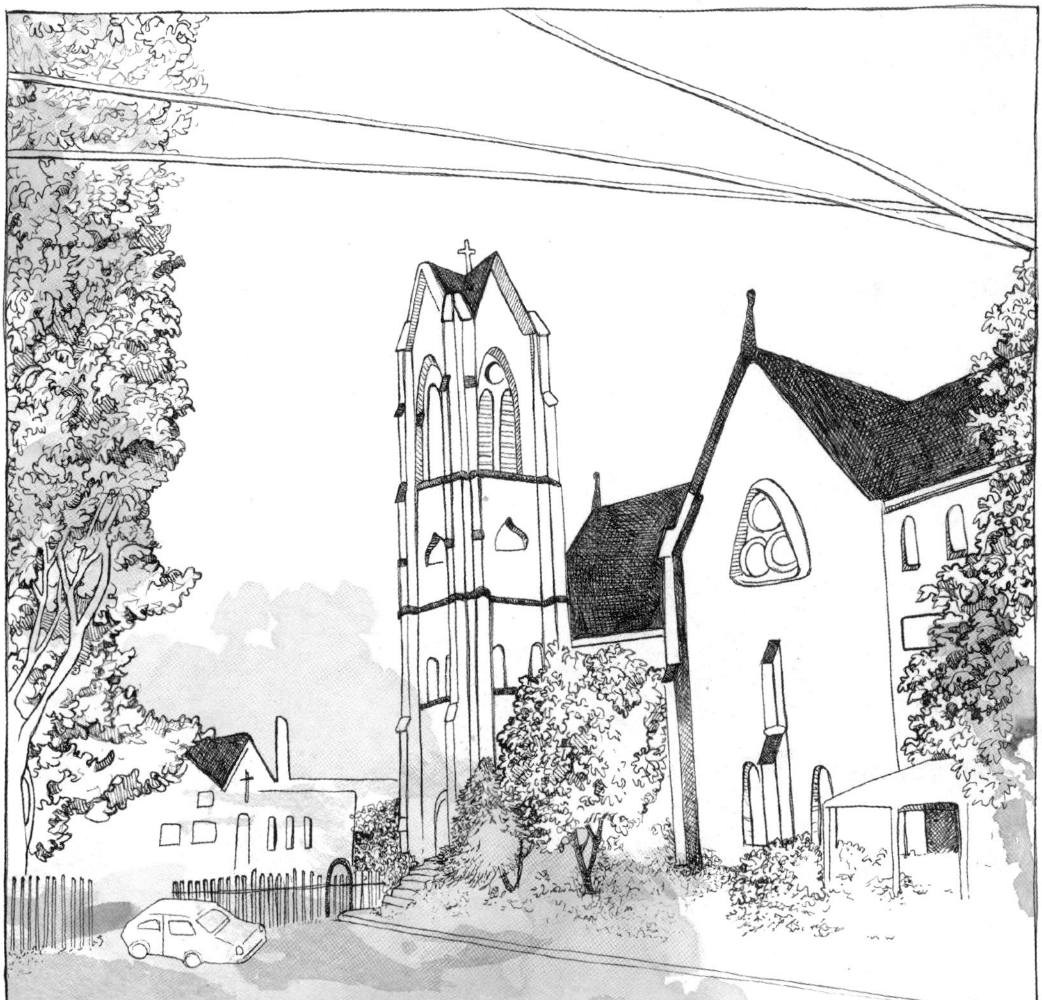

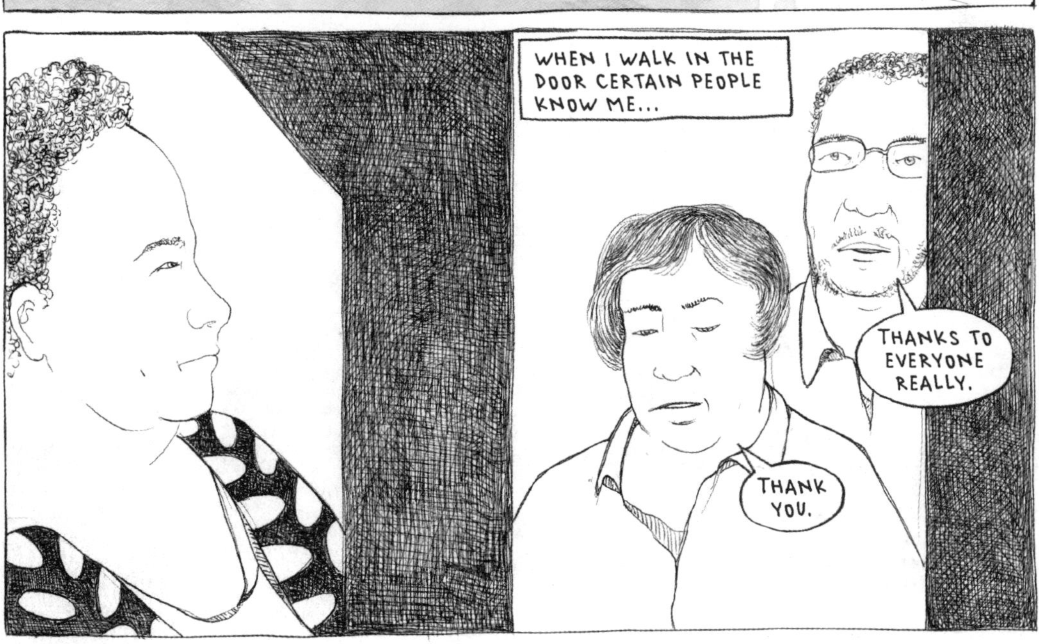
WHEN I WALK IN THE DOOR CERTAIN PEOPLE KNOW ME...
THANKS TO EVERYONE REALLY.
THANK YOU.

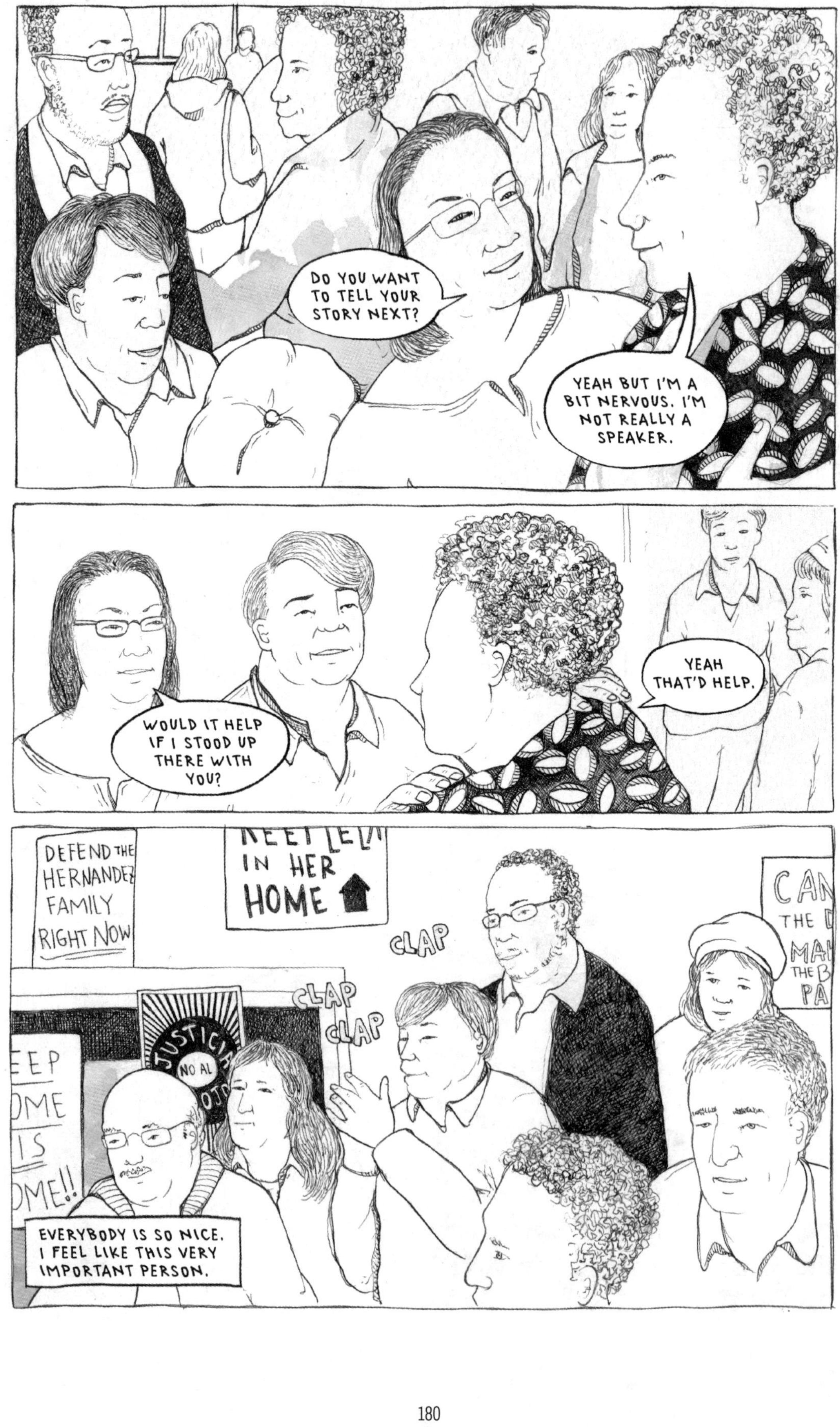
DO YOU WANT TO TELL YOUR STORY NEXT?
YEAH BUT I'M A BIT NERVOUS. I'M NOT REALLY A SPEAKER.
WOULD IT HELP IF I STOOD UP THERE WITH YOU?
YEAH THAT'D HELP.
DEFEND THE HERNANDEZ FAMILY RIGHT NOW
IN HER HOME
CLAP
CLAP
CLAP
NO AL
EVERYBODY IS SO NICE. I FEEL LIKE THIS VERY IMPORTANT PERSON.

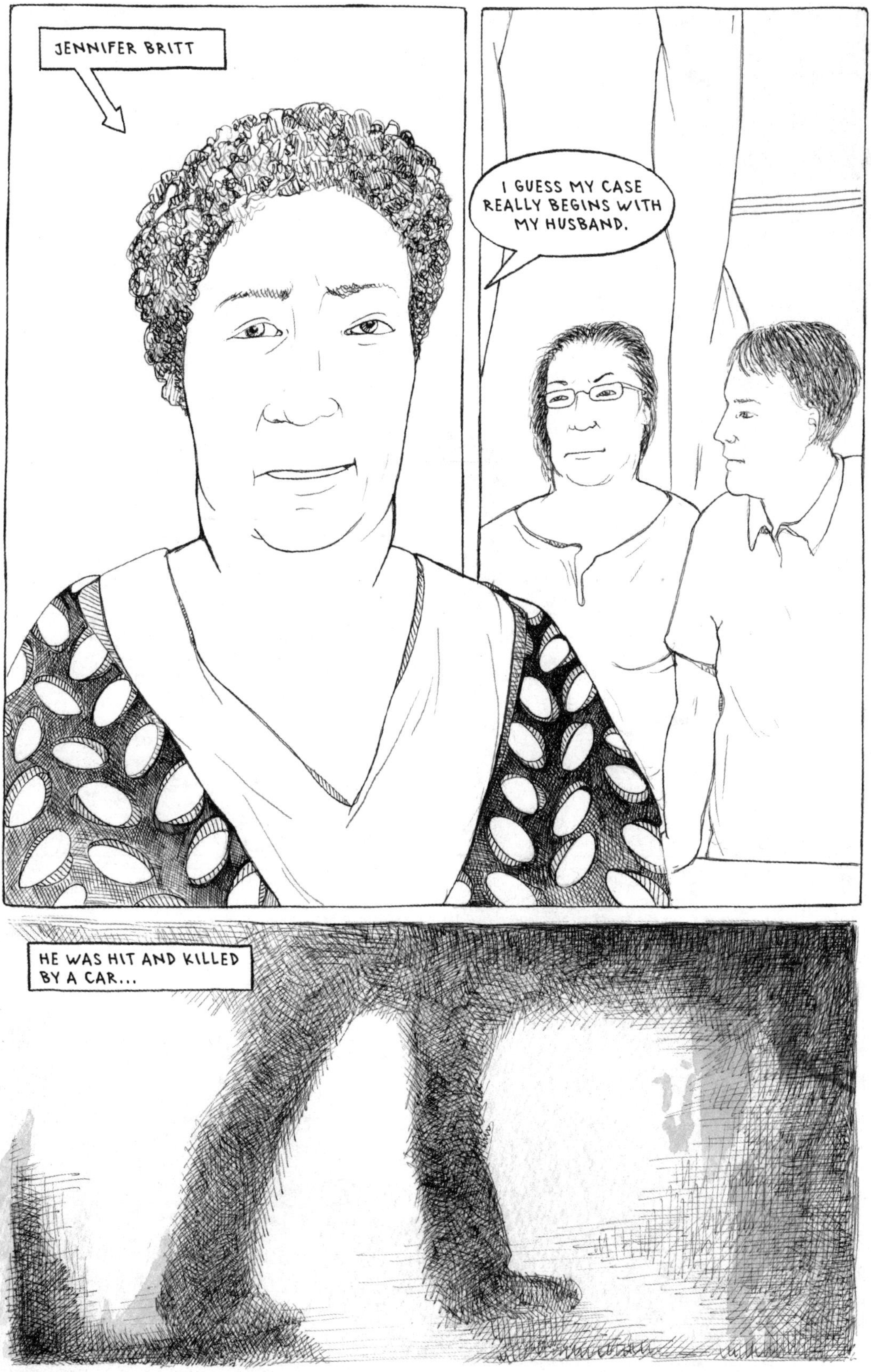
JENNIFER BRITT
I GUESS MY CASE REALLY BEGINS WITH MY HUSBAND.
HE WAS HIT AND KILLED BY A CAR...

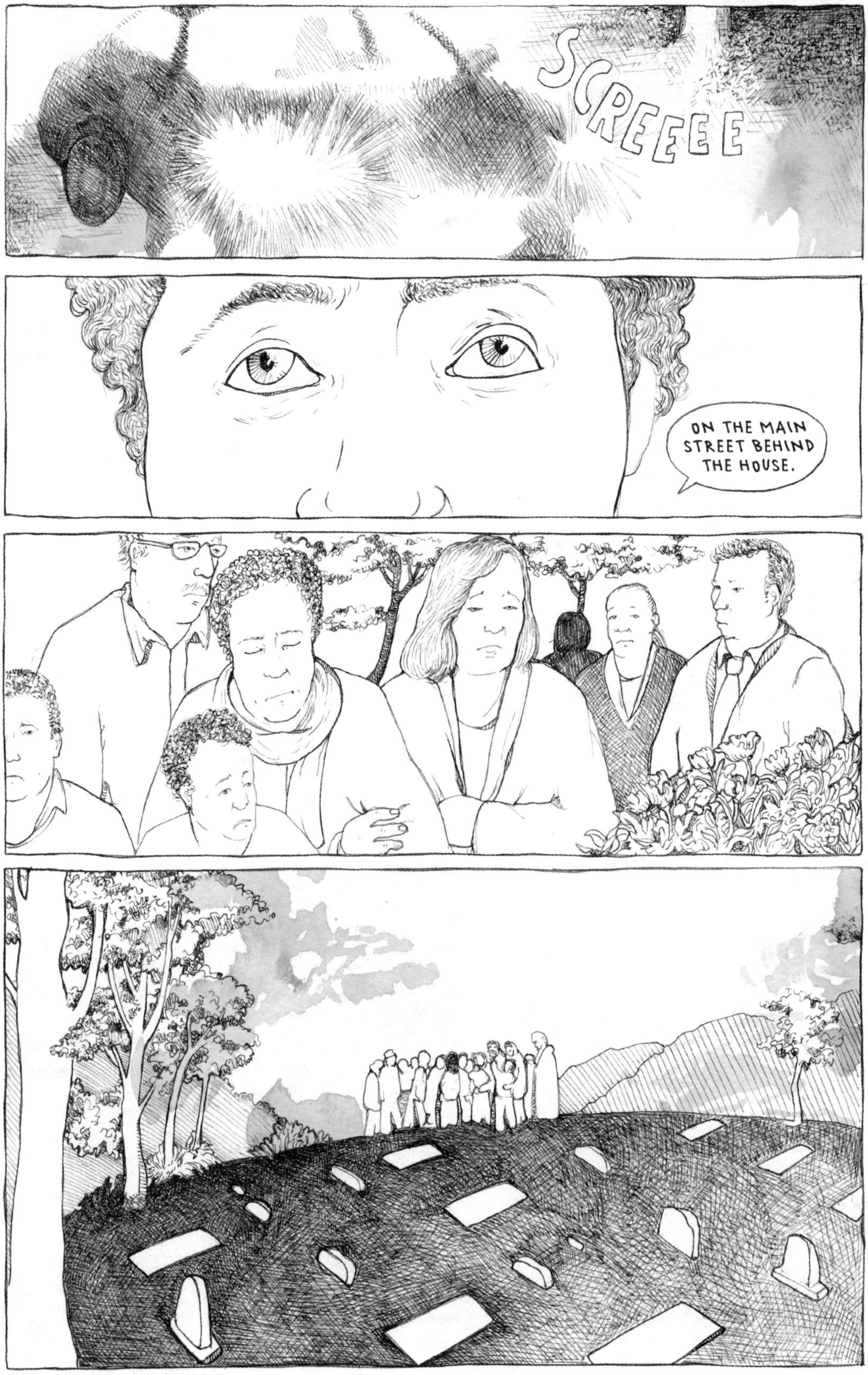
SCREEEE
ON THE MAIN STREET BEHIND THE HOUSE.

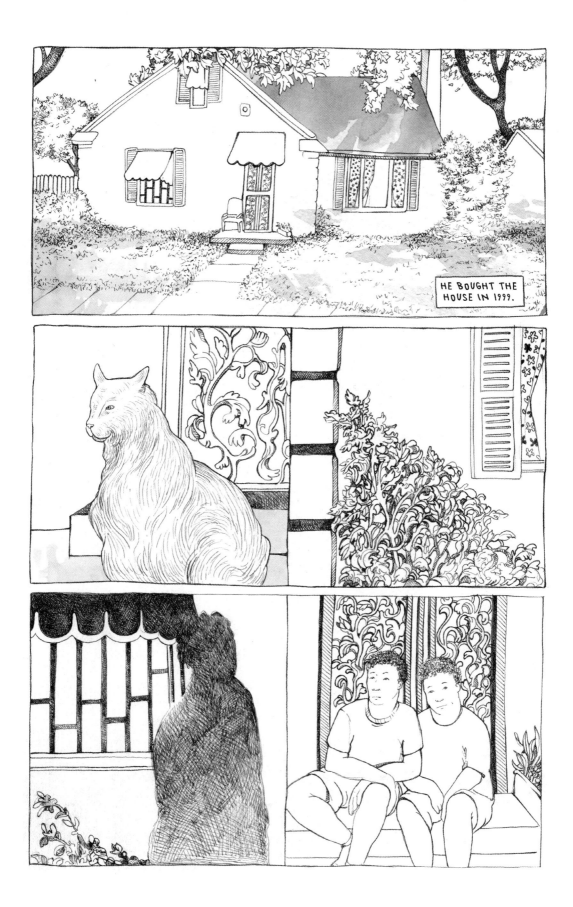

HE BOUGHT THE HOUSE IN 1999.

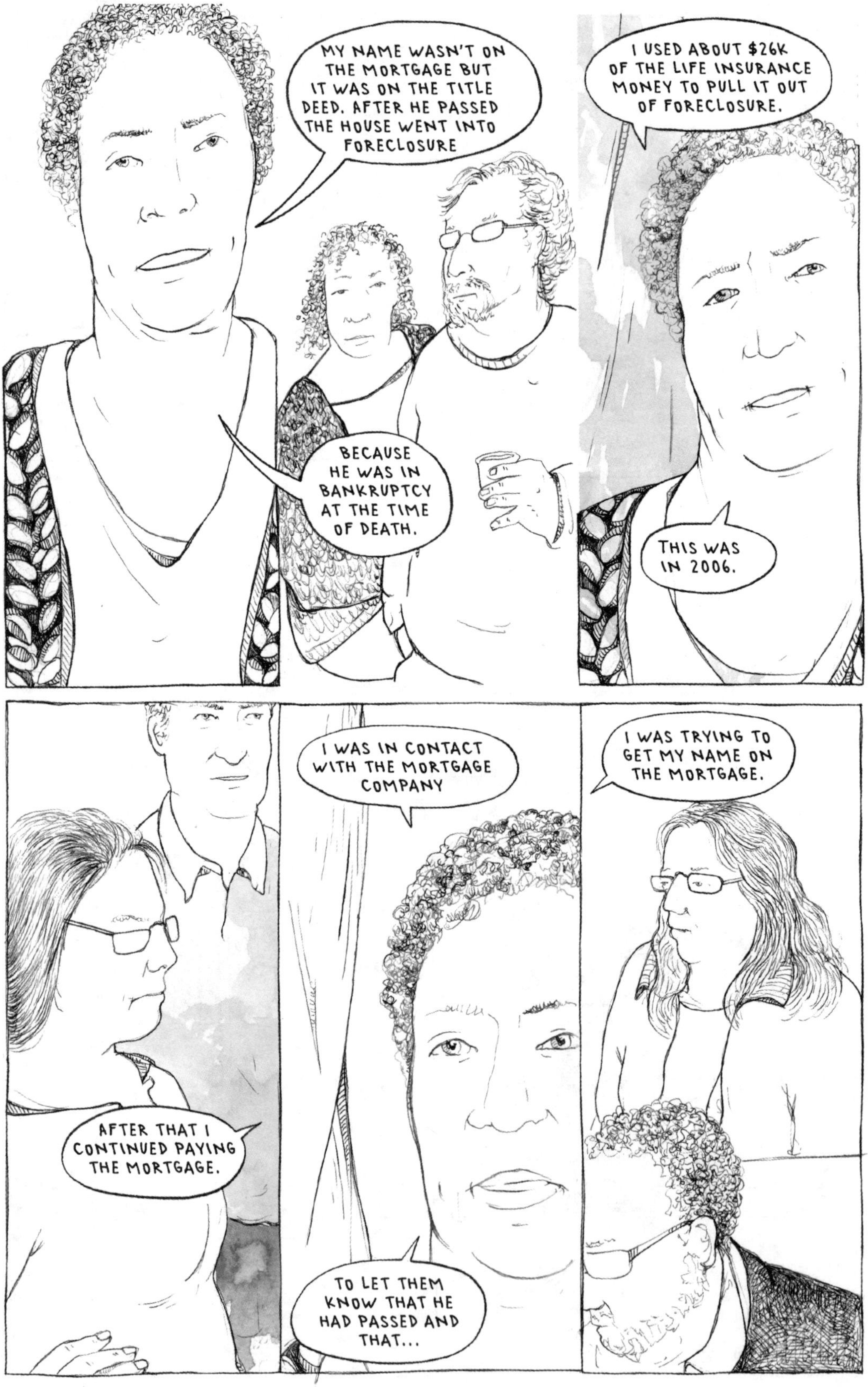
MY NAME WASN'T ON THE MORTGAGE BUT IT WAS ON THE TITLE DEED. AFTER HE PASSED THE HOUSE WENT INTO FORECLOSURE
BECAUSE HE WAS IN BANKRUPTCY AT THE TIME OF DEATH.
I USED ABOUT $26K OF THE LIFE INSURANCE MONEY TO PULL IT OUT OF FORECLOSURE.
THIS WAS IN 2006.
AFTER THAT I CONTINUED PAYING THE MORTGAGE.
I WAS IN CONTACT WITH THE MORTGAGE COMPANY
TO LET THEM KNOW THAT HE HAD PASSED AND THAT...
I WAS TRYING TO GET MY NAME ON THE MORTGAGE.

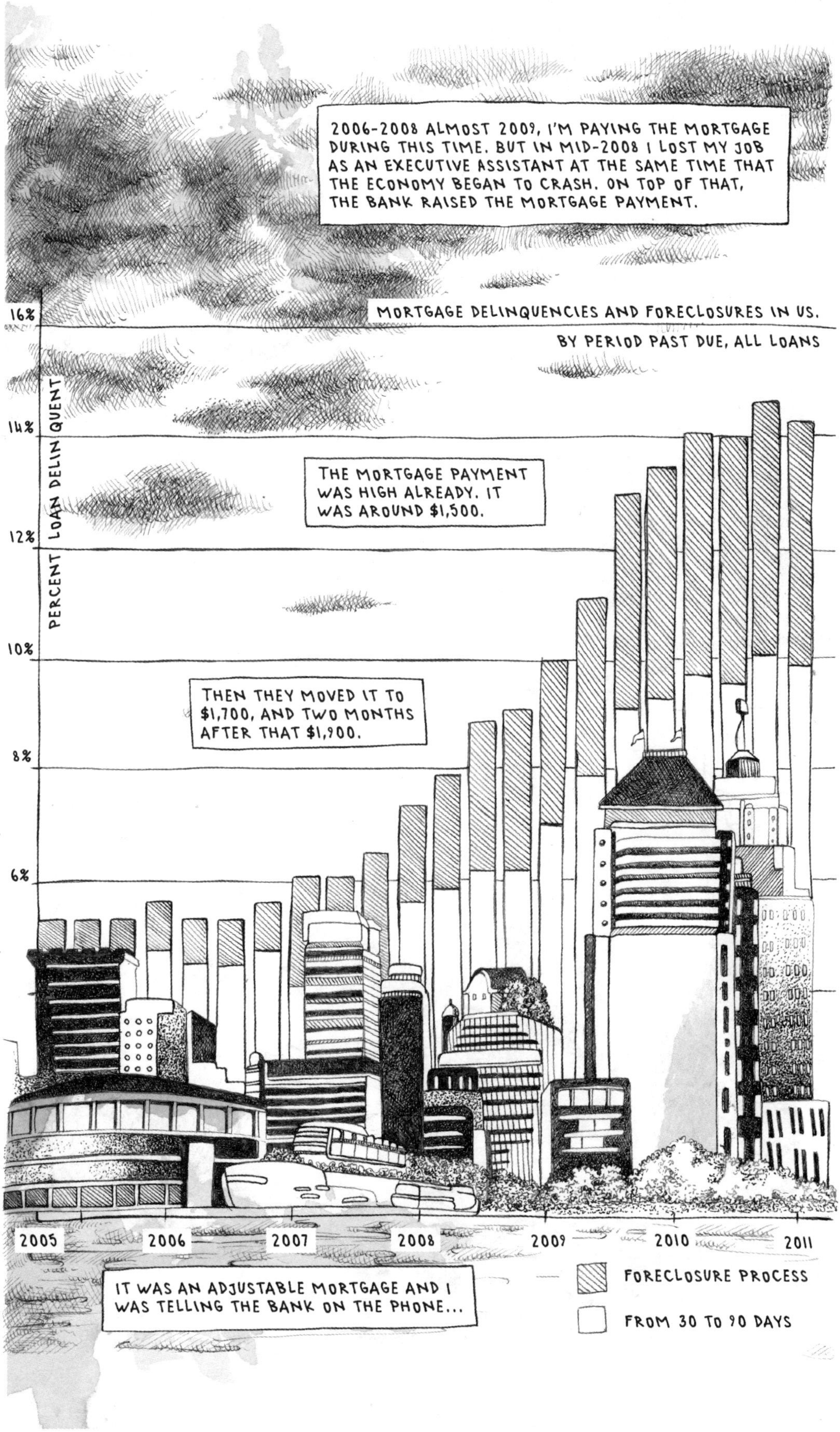
2006-2008 ALMOST 2009, I'M PAYING THE MORTGAGE DURING THIS TIME. BUT IN MID-2008 I LOST MY JOB AS AN EXECUTIVE ASSISTANT AT THE SAME TIME THAT THE ECONOMY BEGAN TO CRASH. ON TOP OF THAT, THE BANK RAISED THE MORTGAGE PAYMENT.
MORTGAGE DELINQUENCIES AND FORECLOSURES IN US.
BY PERIOD PAST DUE, ALL LOANS
PERCENT LOAN DELINQUENT
16%
14%
12%
10%
8%
6%
THE MORTGAGE PAYMENT WAS HIGH ALREADY. IT WAS AROUND $1,500.
THEN THEY MOVED IT TO $1,700, AND TWO MONTHS AFTER THAT $1,900.
2005
2006
2007
2008
2009
2010
2011
IT WAS AN ADJUSTABLE MORTGAGE AND I WAS TELLING THE BANK ON THE PHONE...
FORECLOSURE PROCESS
FROM 30 TO 90 DAYS

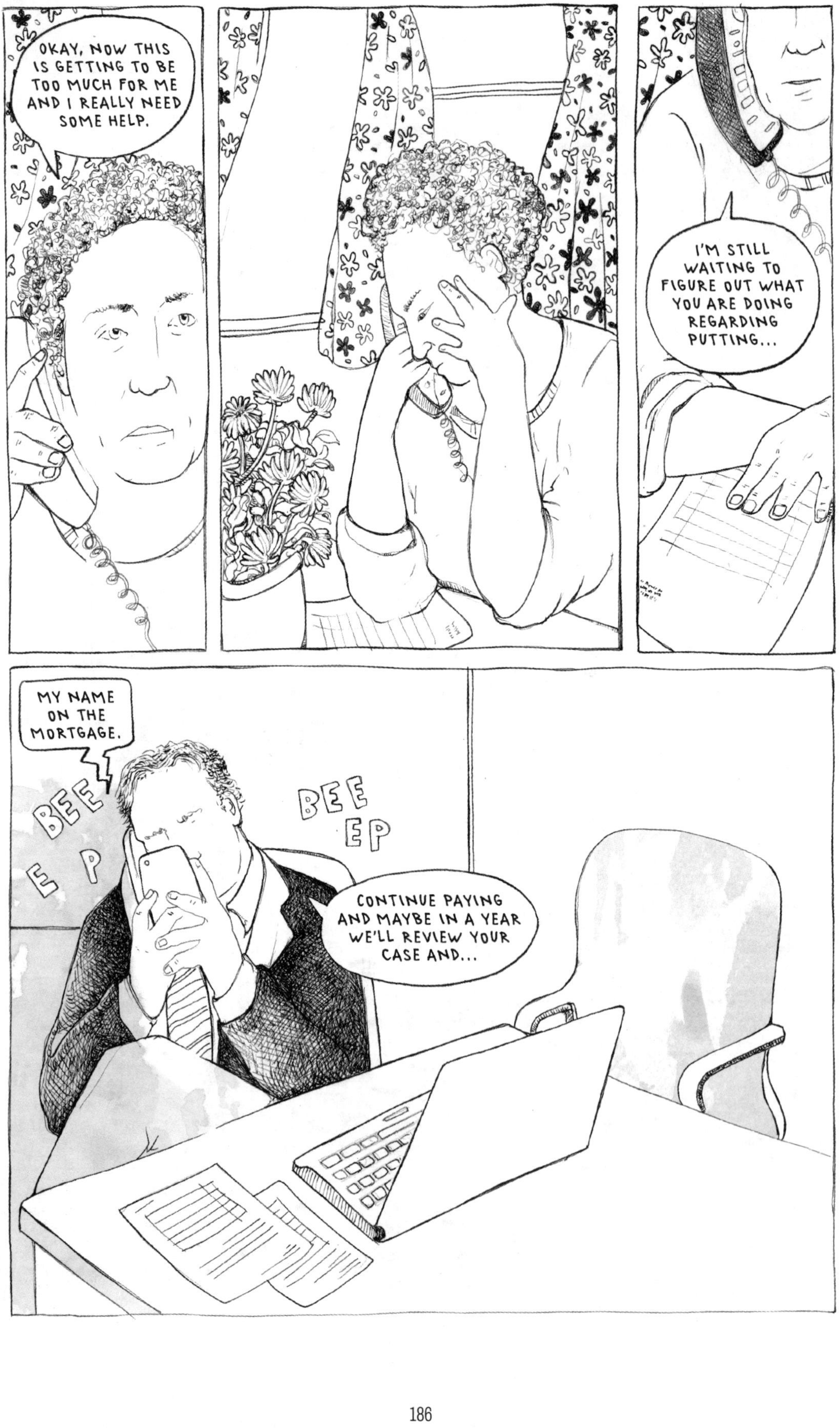
OKAY, NOW THIS IS GETTING TO BE TOO MUCH FOR ME AND I REALLY NEED SOME HELP.
I'M STILL WAITING TO FIGURE OUT WHAT YOU ARE DOING REGARDING PUTTING...
MY NAME ON THE MORTGAGE.
BEEEP
BEEEP
CONTINUE PAYING AND MAYBE IN A YEAR WE'LL REVIEW YOUR CASE AND...

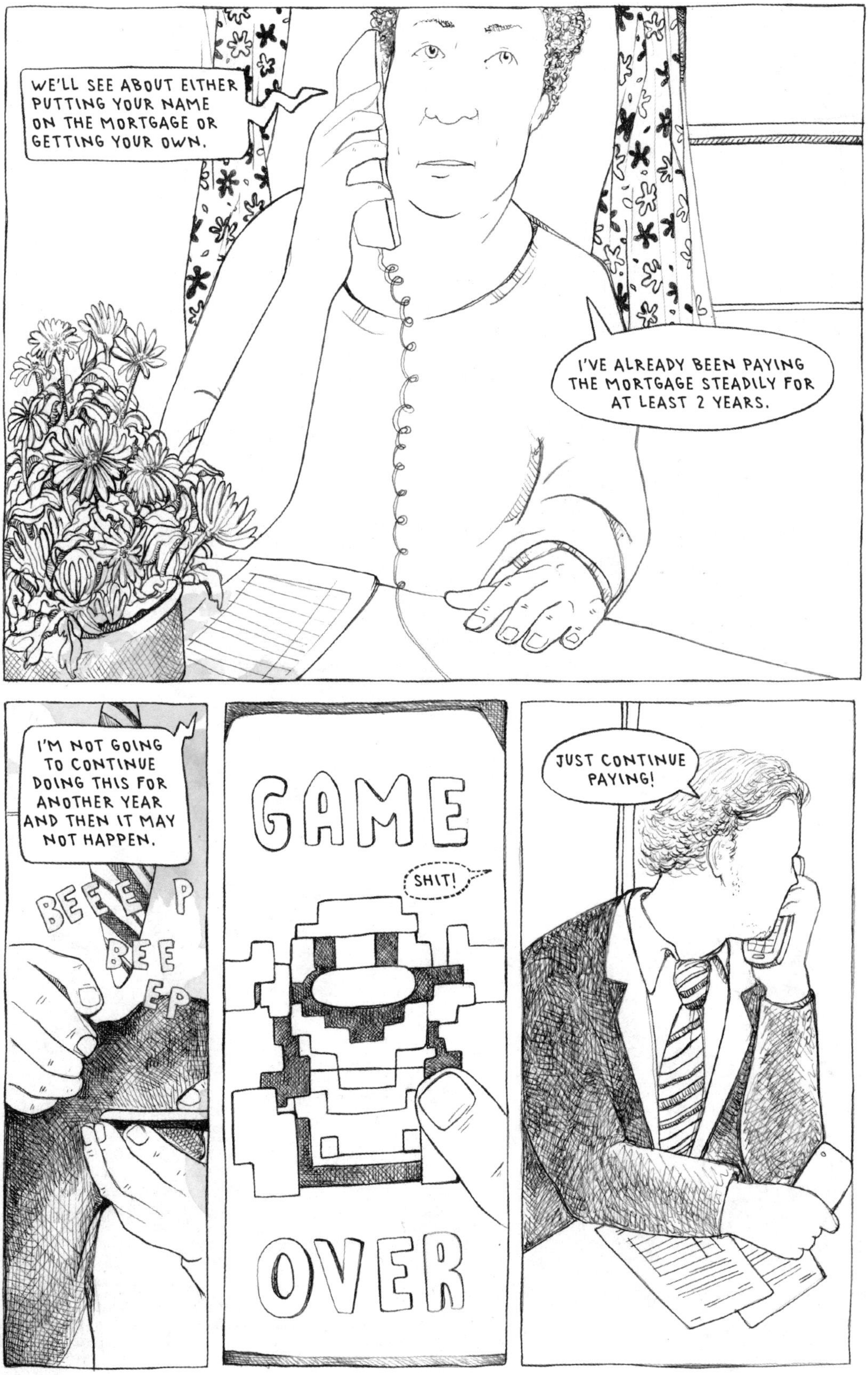
WE'LL SEE ABOUT EITHER PUTTING YOUR NAME ON THE MORTGAGE OR GETTING YOUR OWN.
I'VE ALREADY BEEN PAYING THE MORTGAGE STEADILY FOR AT LEAST 2 YEARS.
I'M NOT GOING TO CONTINUE DOING THIS FOR ANOTHER YEAR AND THEN IT MAY NOT HAPPEN.
BEEEP
BEEEP
GAME
SHIT!
OVER
JUST CONTINUE PAYING!

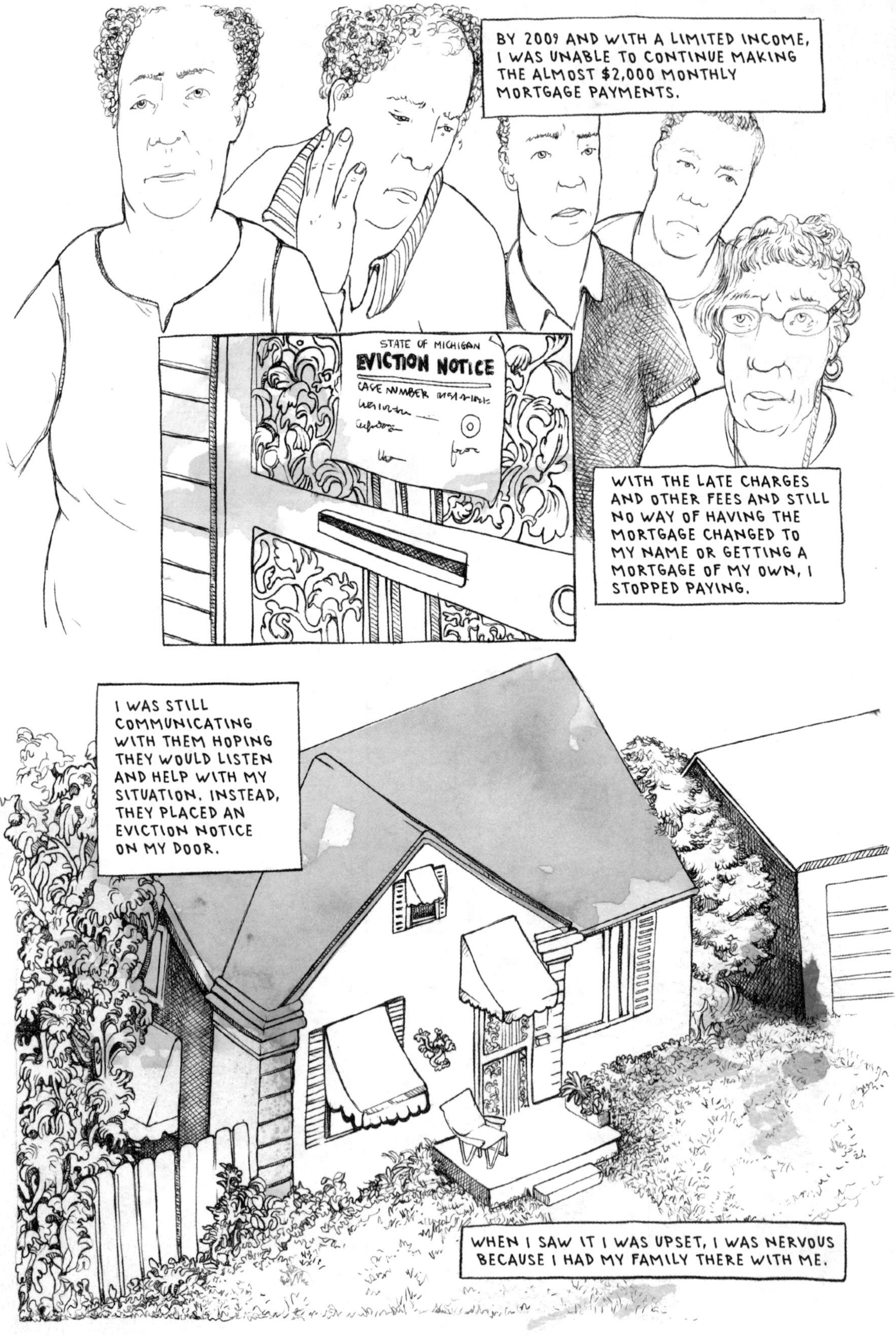
BY 2009 AND WITH A LIMITED INCOME, I WAS UNABLE TO CONTINUE MAKING THE ALMOST $2,000 MONTHLY MORTGAGE PAYMENTS.
STATE OF MICHIGAN
EVICTION NOTICE
CASE NUMBER
WITH THE LATE CHARGES AND OTHER FEES AND STILL NO WAY OF HAVING THE MORTGAGE CHANGED TO MY NAME OR GETTING A MORTGAGE OF MY OWN, I STOPPED PAYING.
I WAS STILL COMMUNICATING WITH THEM HOPING THEY WOULD LISTEN AND HELP WITH MY SITUATION. INSTEAD, THEY PLACED AN EVICTION NOTICE ON MY DOOR.
WHEN I SAW IT I WAS UPSET, I WAS NERVOUS BECAUSE I HAD MY FAMILY THERE WITH ME.

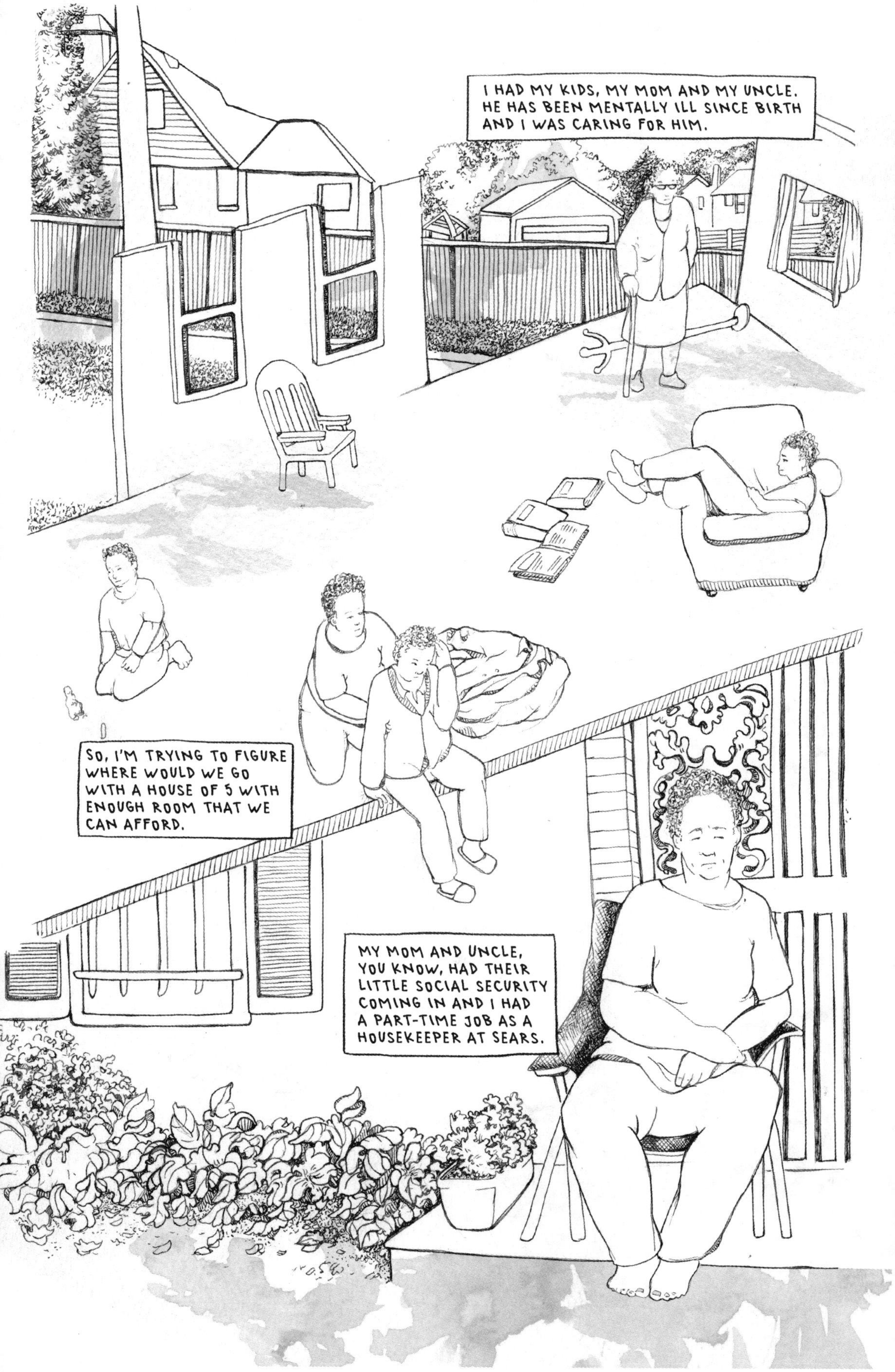
I HAD MY KIDS, MY MOM AND MY UNCLE. HE HAS BEEN MENTALLY ILL SINCE BIRTH AND I WAS CARING FOR HIM.
SO, I'M TRYING TO FIGURE WHERE WOULD WE GO WITH A HOUSE OF 5 WITH ENOUGH ROOM THAT WE CAN AFFORD.
MY MOM AND UNCLE, YOU KNOW, HAD THEIR LITTLE SOCIAL SECURITY COMING IN AND I HAD A PART-TIME JOB AS A HOUSEKEEPER AT SEARS.

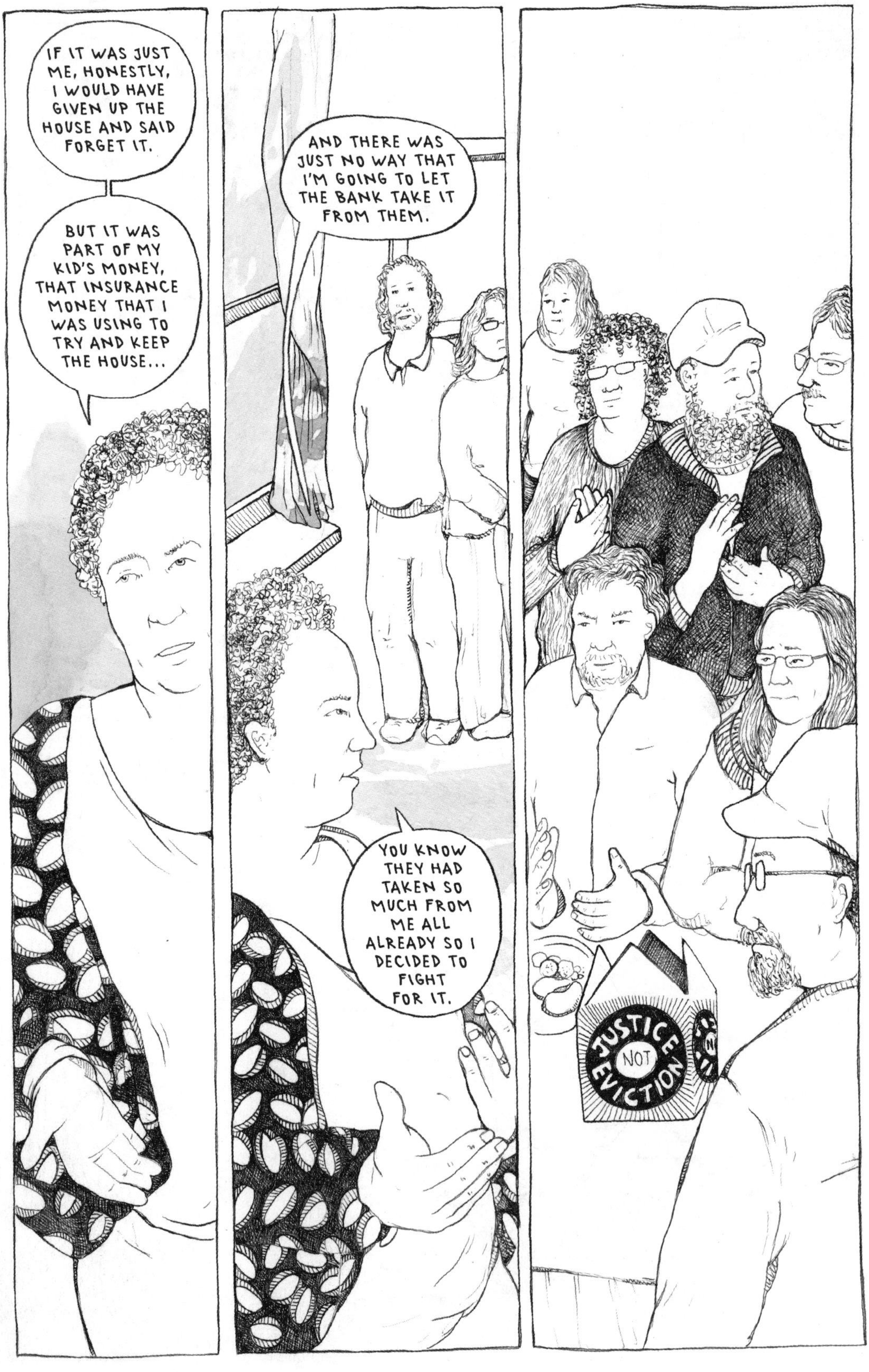
IF IT WAS JUST ME, HONESTLY, I WOULD HAVE GIVEN UP THE HOUSE AND SAID FORGET IT.
BUT IT WAS PART OF MY KID'S MONEY, THAT INSURANCE MONEY THAT I WAS USING TO TRY AND KEEP THE HOUSE...
AND THERE WAS JUST NO WAY THAT I'M GOING TO LET THE BANK TAKE IT FROM THEM.
YOU KNOW THEY HAD TAKEN SO MUCH FROM ME ALL ALREADY SO I DECIDED TO FIGHT FOR IT.
JUSTICE NOT EVICTION

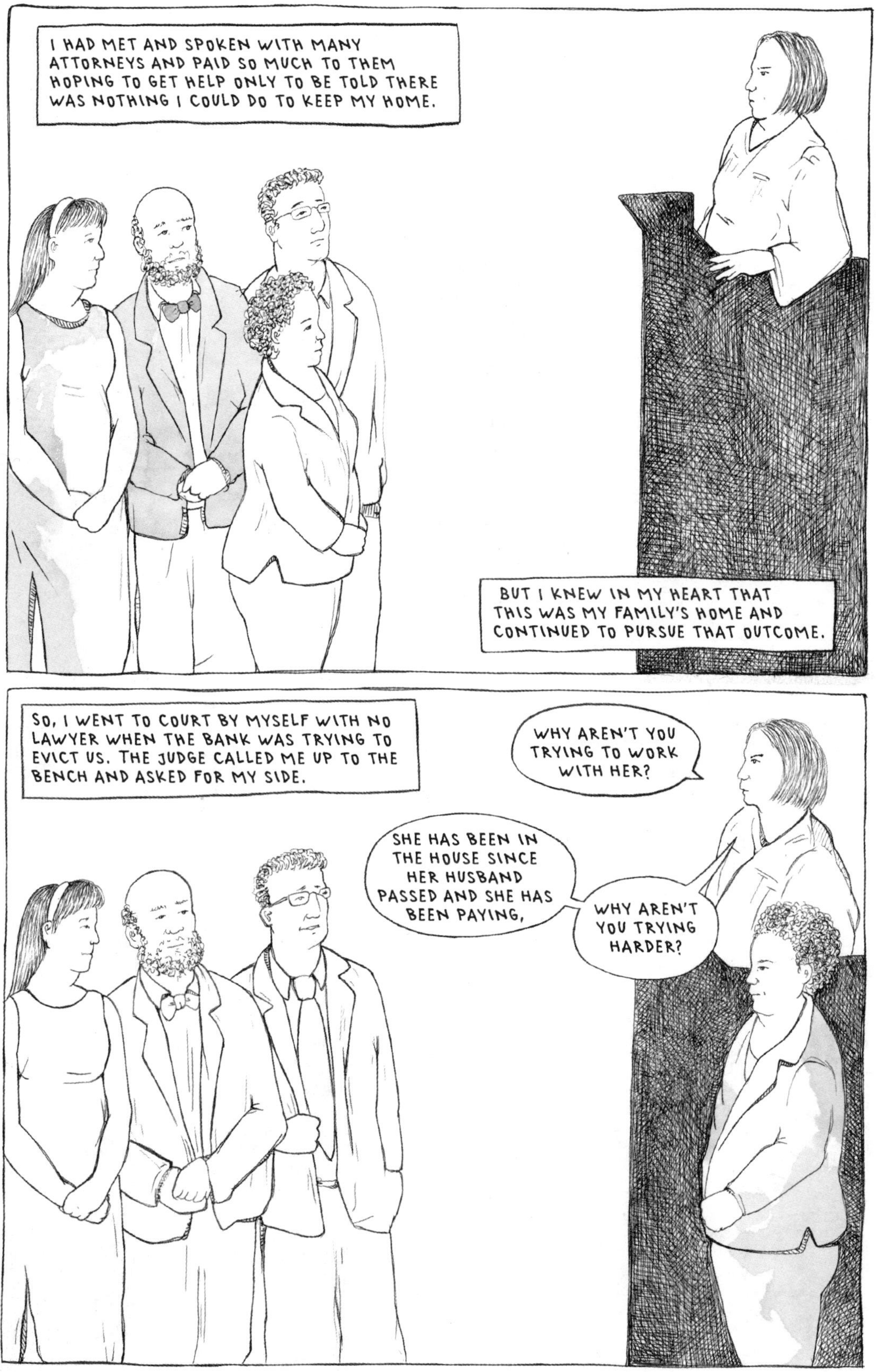
I HAD MET AND SPOKEN WITH MANY ATTORNEYS AND PAID SO MUCH TO THEM HOPING TO GET HELP ONLY TO BE TOLD THERE WAS NOTHING I COULD DO TO KEEP MY HOME.
BUT I KNEW IN MY HEART THAT THIS WAS MY FAMILY'S HOME AND CONTINUED TO PURSUE THAT OUTCOME.
SO, I WENT TO COURT BY MYSELF WITH NO LAWYER WHEN THE BANK WAS TRYING TO EVICT US. THE JUDGE CALLED ME UP TO THE BENCH AND ASKED FOR MY SIDE.
WHY AREN'T YOU TRYING TO WORK WITH HER?
SHE HAS BEEN IN THE HOUSE SINCE HER HUSBAND PASSED AND SHE HAS BEEN PAYING,
WHY AREN'T YOU TRYING HARDER?

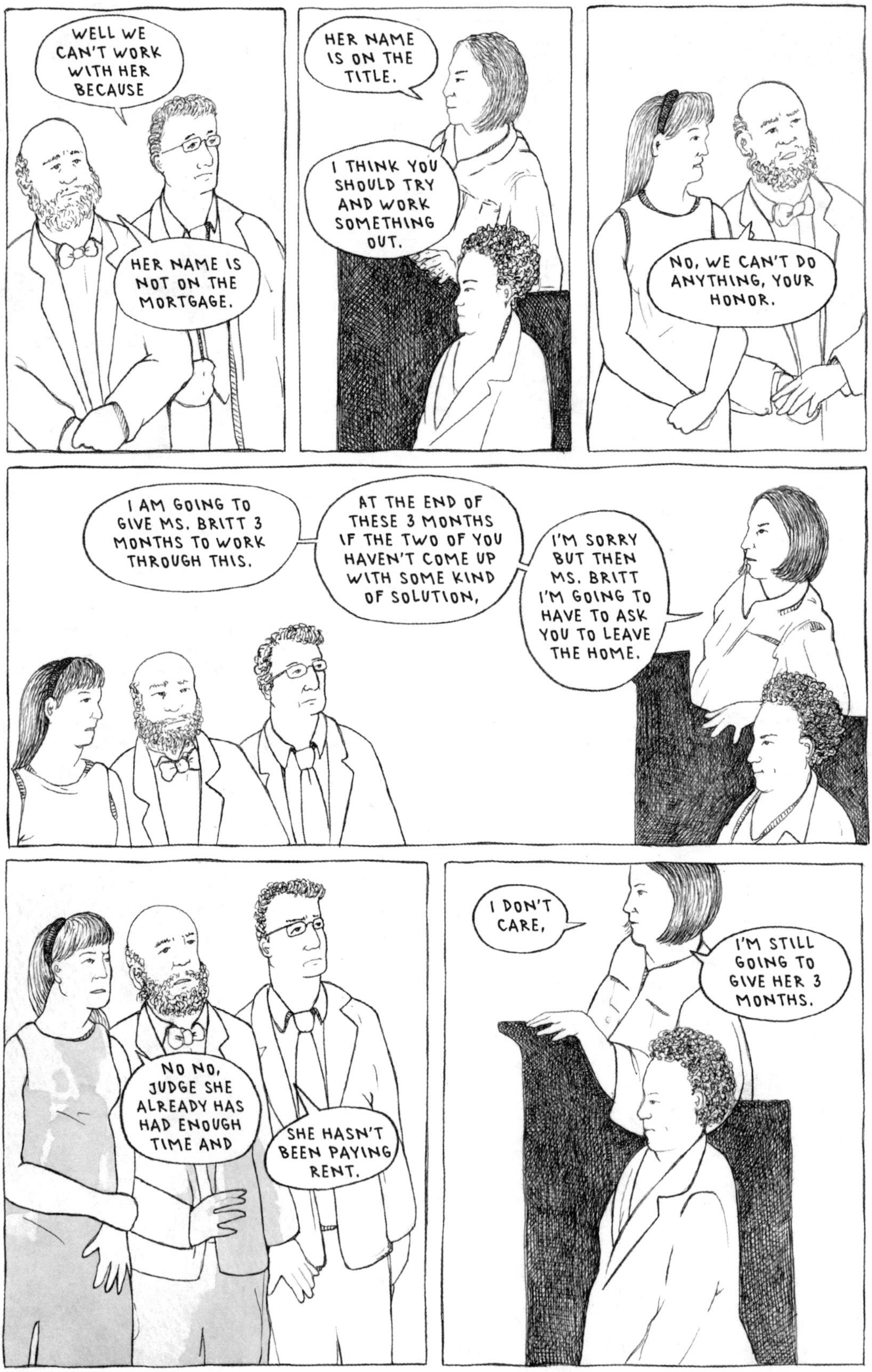
WELL WE CAN'T WORK WITH HER BECAUSE
HER NAME IS NOT ON THE MORTGAGE.
HER NAME IS ON THE TITLE.
I THINK YOU SHOULD TRY AND WORK SOMETHING OUT.
NO, WE CAN'T DO ANYTHING, YOUR HONOR.
I AM GOING TO GIVE MS. BRITT 3 MONTHS TO WORK THROUGH THIS.
AT THE END OF THESE 3 MONTHS IF THE TWO OF YOU HAVEN'T COME UP WITH SOME KIND OF SOLUTION,
I'M SORRY BUT THEN MS. BRITT I'M GOING TO HAVE TO ASK YOU TO LEAVE THE HOME.
NO NO, JUDGE SHE ALREADY HAS HAD ENOUGH TIME AND
SHE HASN'T BEEN PAYING RENT.
I DON'T CARE,
I'M STILL GOING TO GIVE HER 3 MONTHS.

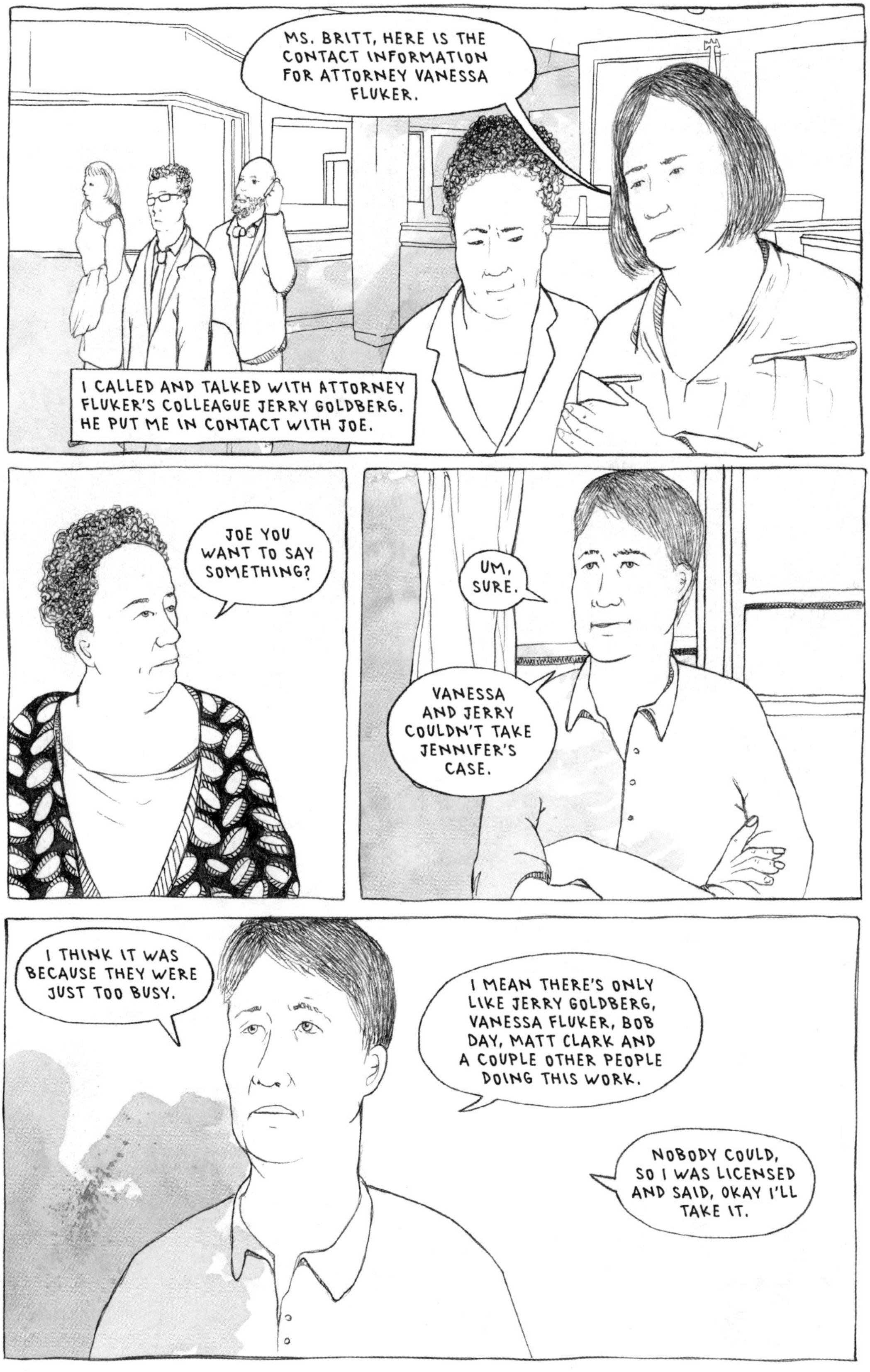
MS. BRITT, HERE IS THE CONTACT INFORMATION FOR ATTORNEY VANESSA FLUKER.
I CALLED AND TALKED WITH ATTORNEY FLUKER'S COLLEAGUE JERRY GOLDBERG. HE PUT ME IN CONTACT WITH JOE.
JOE YOU WANT TO SAY SOMETHING?
UM, SURE.
VANESSA AND JERRY COULDN'T TAKE JENNIFER'S CASE.
I THINK IT WAS BECAUSE THEY WERE JUST TOO BUSY.
I MEAN THERE'S ONLY LIKE JERRY GOLDBERG, VANESSA FLUKER, BOB DAY, MATT CLARK AND A COUPLE OTHER PEOPLE DOING THIS WORK.
NOBODY COULD, SO I WAS LICENSED AND SAID, OKAY I'LL TAKE IT.

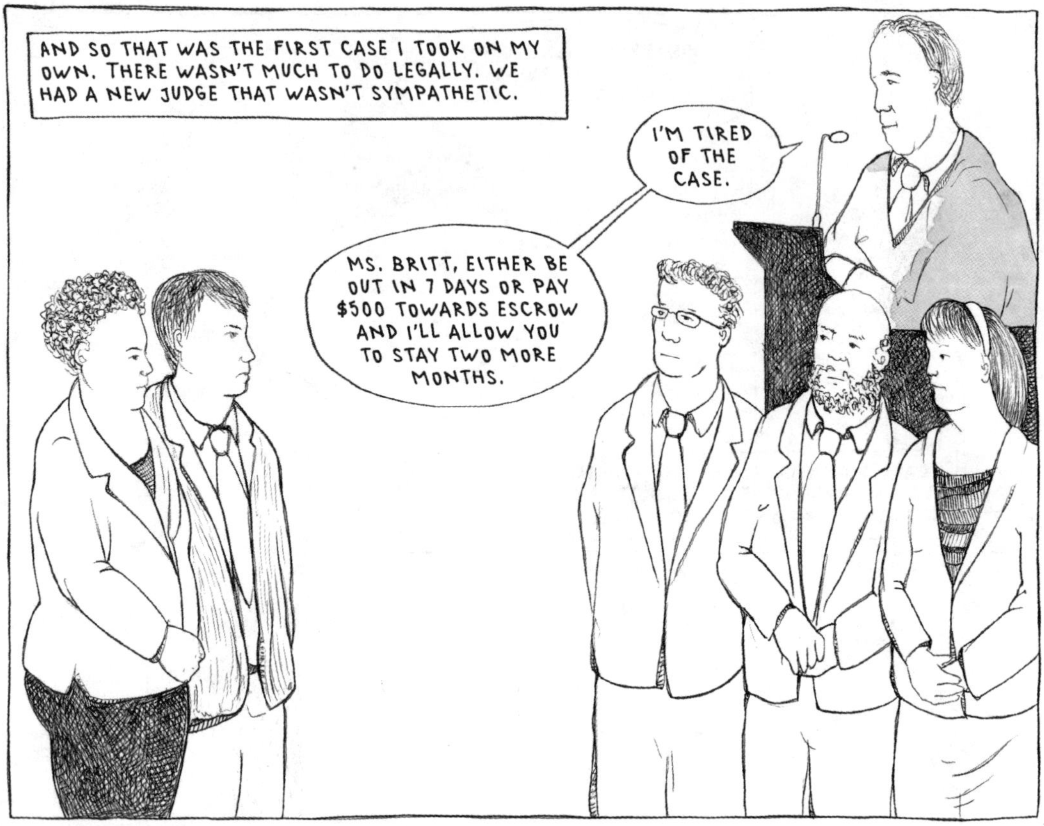
AND SO THAT WAS THE FIRST CASE I TOOK ON MY OWN. THERE WASN'T MUCH TO DO LEGALLY. WE HAD A NEW JUDGE THAT WASN'T SYMPATHETIC.
I'M TIRED OF THE CASE.
MS. BRITT, EITHER BE OUT IN 7 DAYS OR PAY $500 TOWARDS ESCROW AND I'LL ALLOW YOU TO STAY TWO MORE MONTHS.

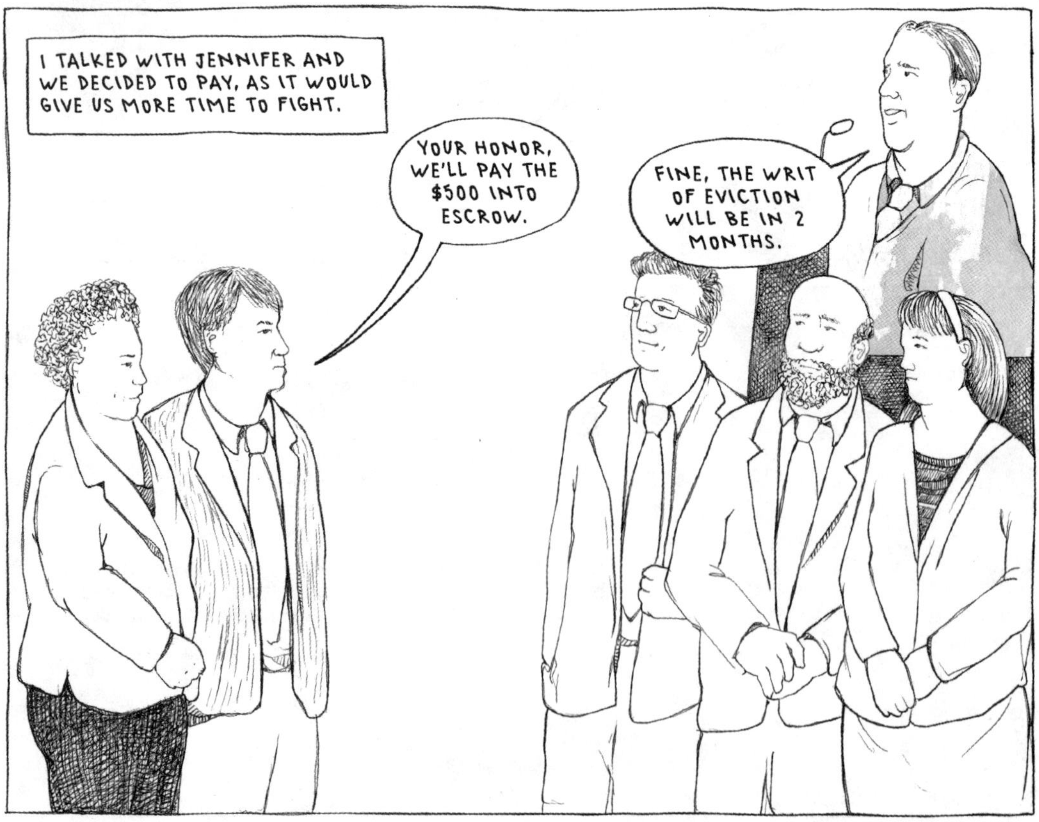
I TALKED WITH JENNIFER AND WE DECIDED TO PAY, AS IT WOULD GIVE US MORE TIME TO FIGHT.
YOUR HONOR, WE'LL PAY THE $500 INTO ESCROW.
FINE, THE WRIT OF EVICTION WILL BE IN 2 MONTHS.

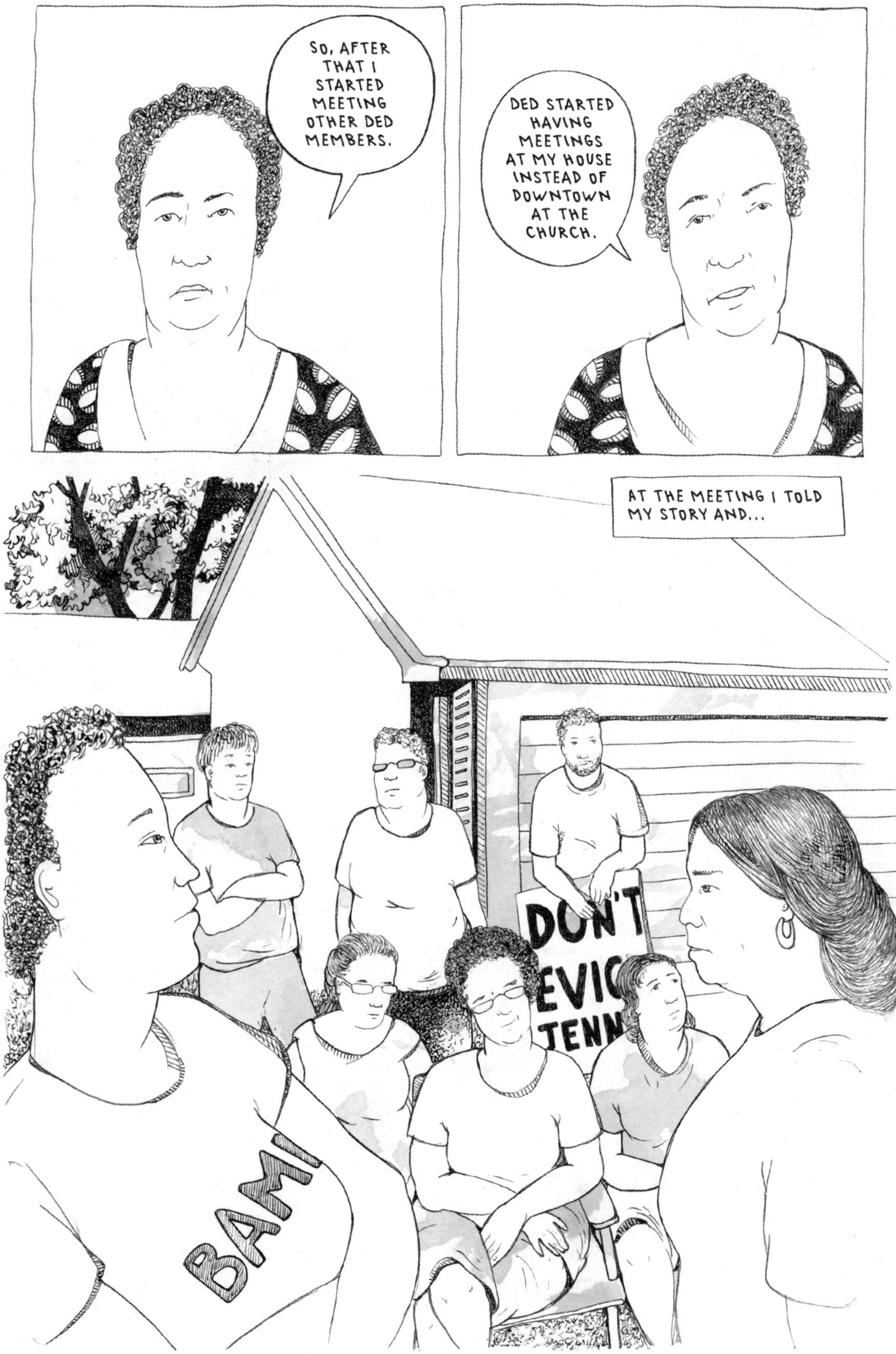
SO, AFTER THAT I STARTED MEETING OTHER DED MEMBERS.
DED STARTED HAVING MEETINGS AT MY HOUSE INSTEAD OF DOWNTOWN AT THE CHURCH.
AT THE MEETING I TOLD MY STORY AND...
DON'T EVIC TENN
BAM!

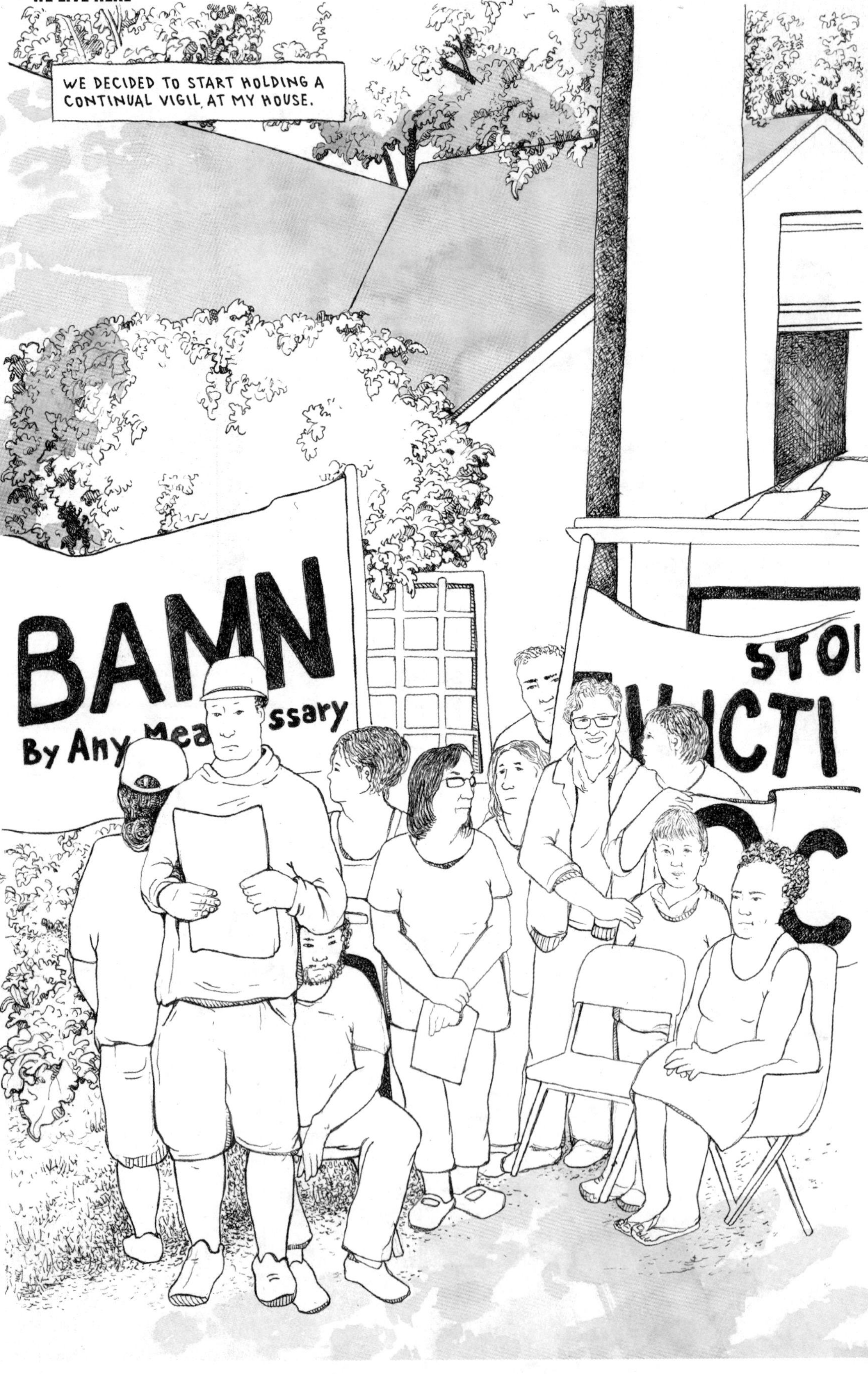
WE DECIDED TO START HOLDING A CONTINUAL VIGIL AT MY HOUSE.
BAMN
By Any Mea ssary
STO
ICTI

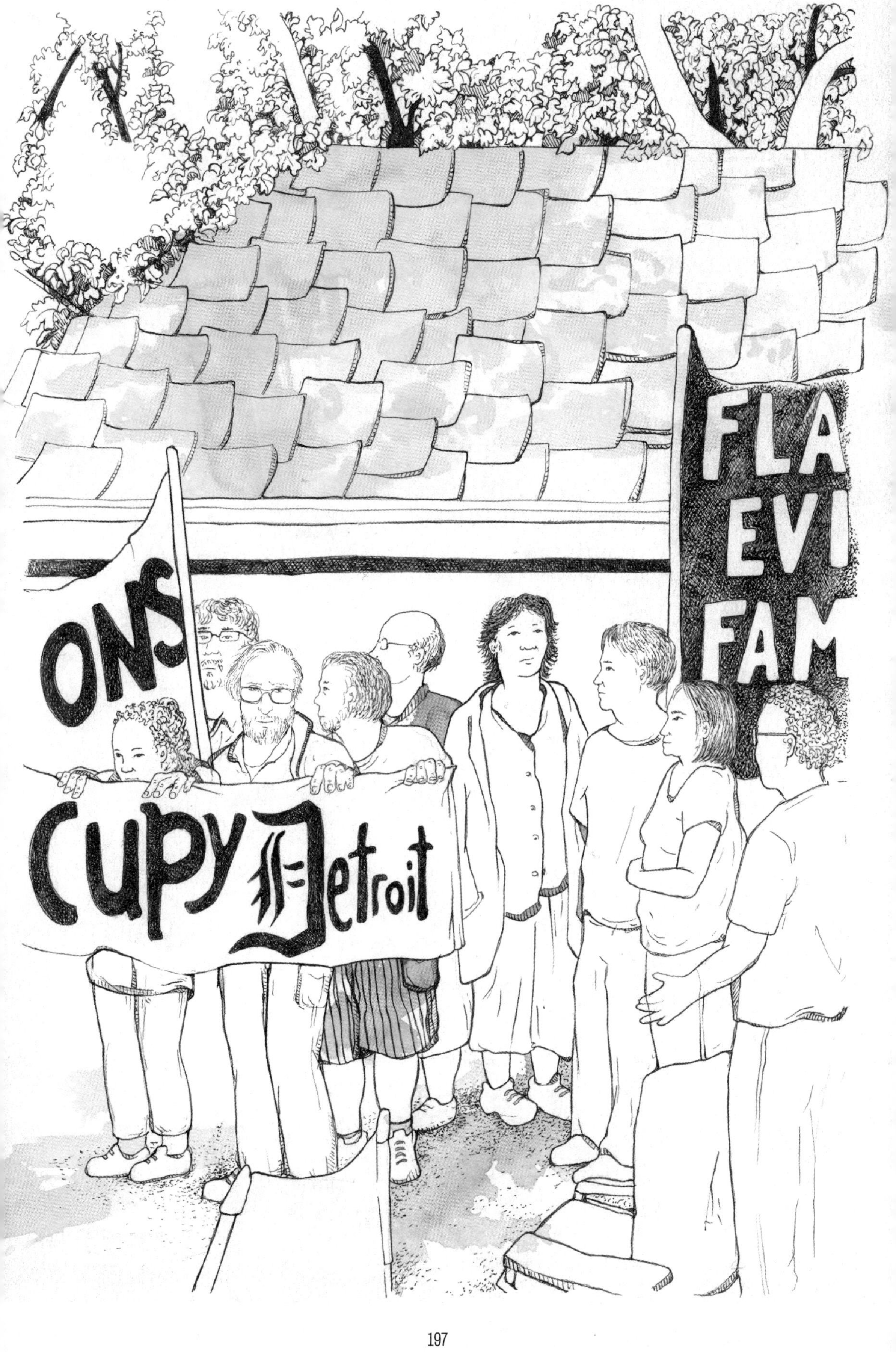
ONS
Cupy Detroit
FLA
EVI
FAM

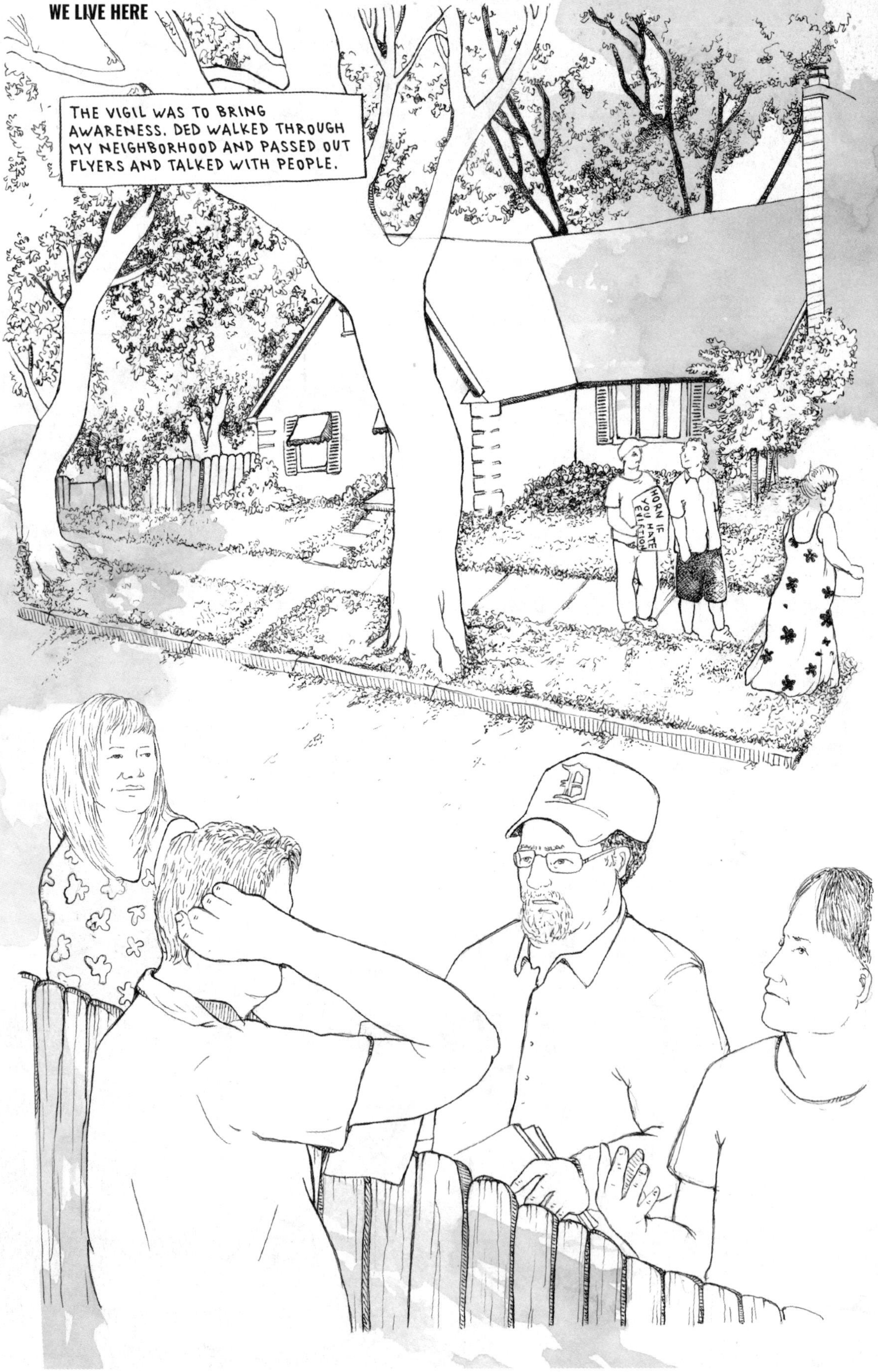
THE VIGIL WAS TO BRING AWARENESS. DED WALKED THROUGH MY NEIGHBORHOOD AND PASSED OUT FLYERS AND TALKED WITH PEOPLE.
HORN IF YOU HATE EVICTION

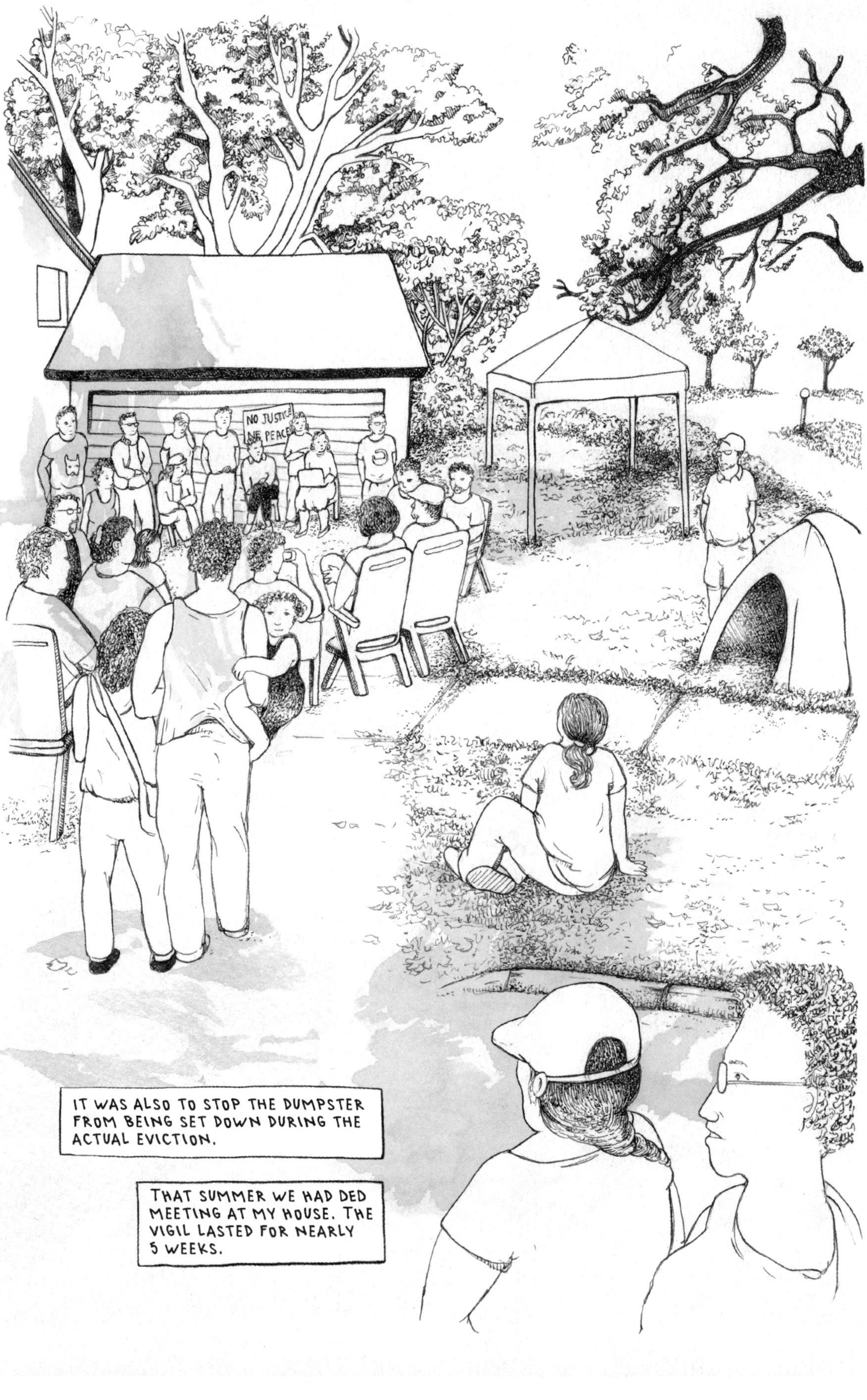
NO JUSTICE
PEACE
IT WAS ALSO TO STOP THE DUMPSTER FROM BEING SET DOWN DURING THE ACTUAL EVICTION.
THAT SUMMER WE HAD DED MEETING AT MY HOUSE. THE VIGIL LASTED FOR NEARLY 5 WEEKS.

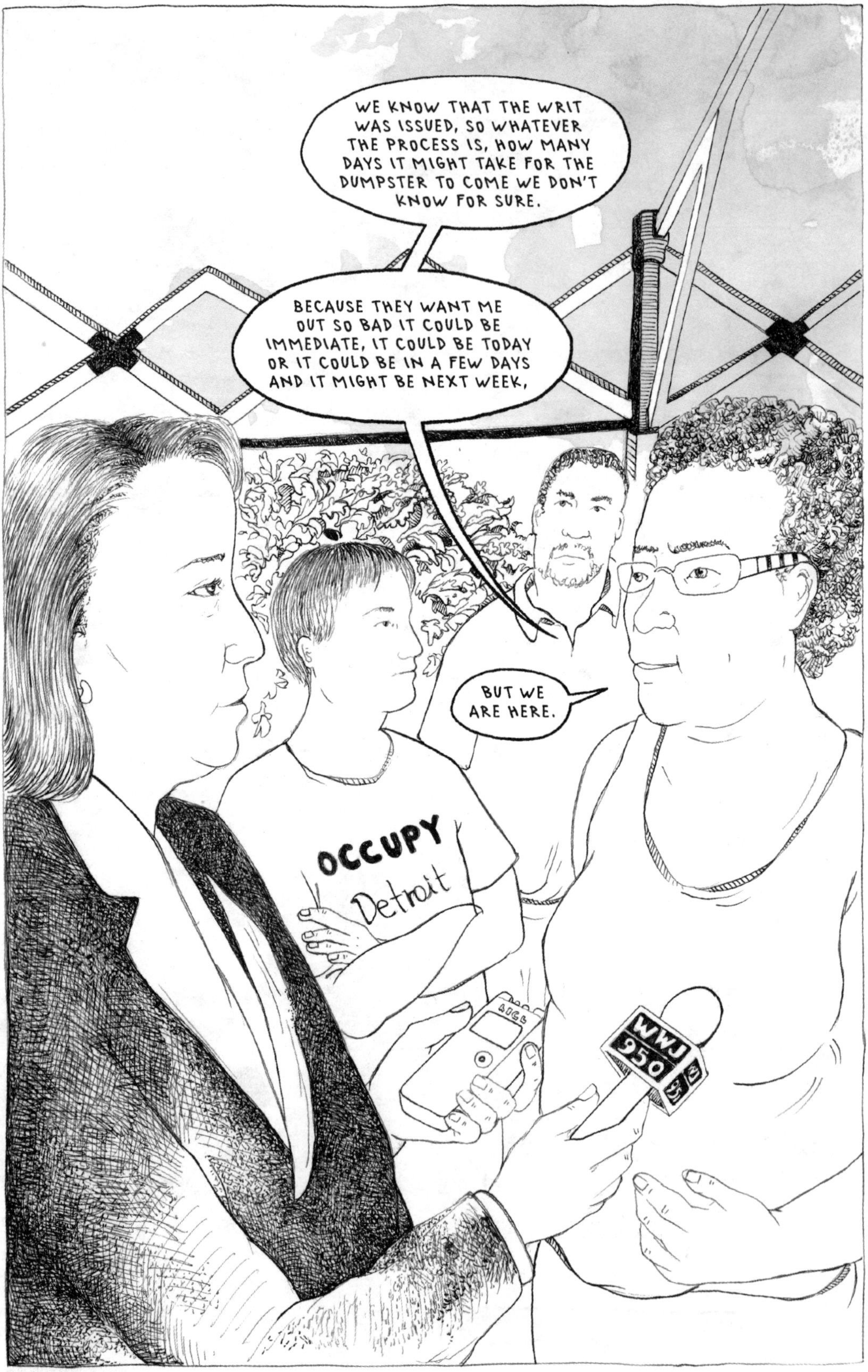
WE KNOW THAT THE WRIT WAS ISSUED, SO WHATEVER THE PROCESS IS, HOW MANY DAYS IT MIGHT TAKE FOR THE DUMPSTER TO COME WE DON'T KNOW FOR SURE.
BECAUSE THEY WANT ME OUT SO BAD IT COULD BE IMMEDIATE, IT COULD BE TODAY OR IT COULD BE IN A FEW DAYS AND IT MIGHT BE NEXT WEEK,
BUT WE ARE HERE.
OCCUPY
Detroit
WWJ
950

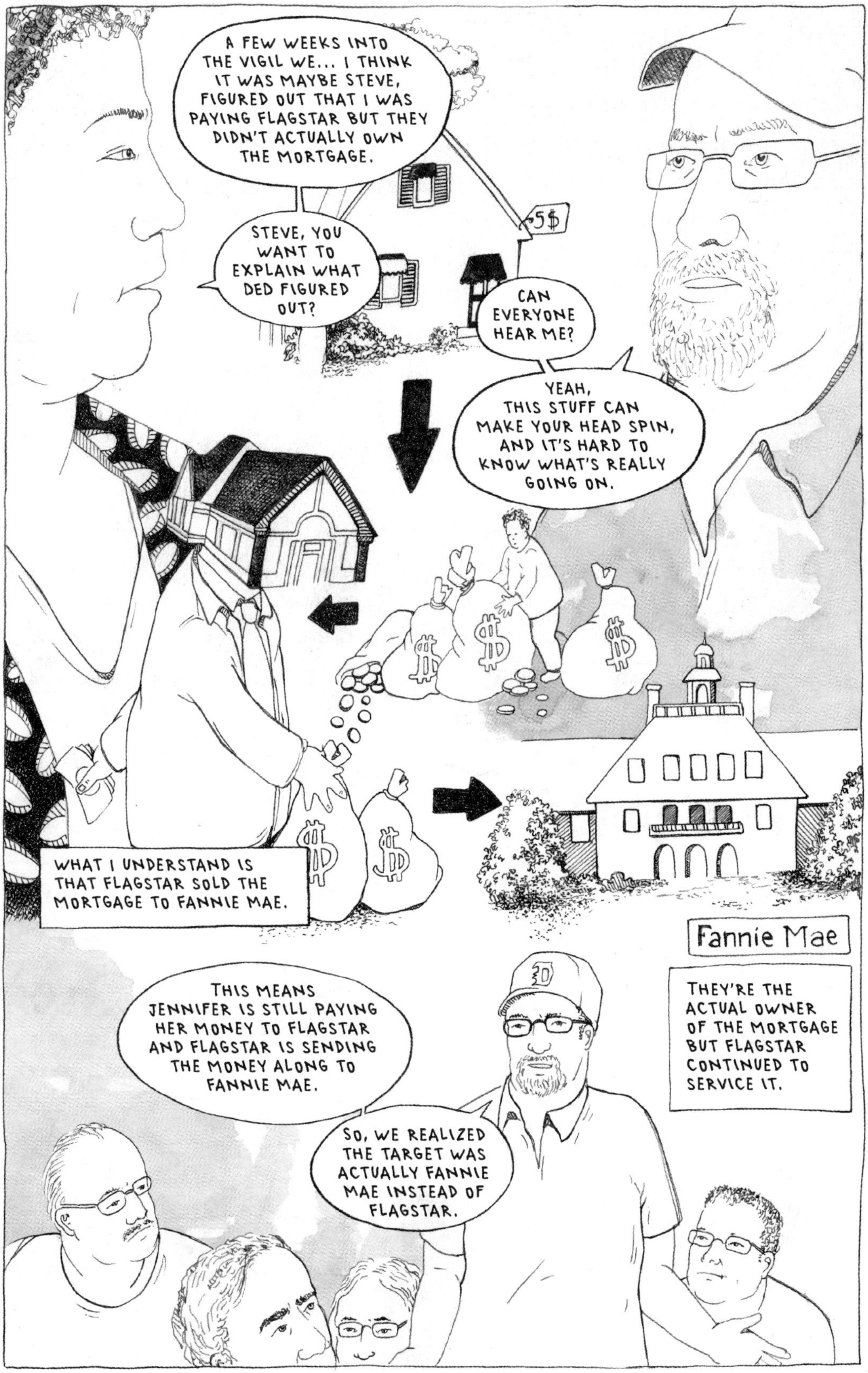
A FEW WEEKS INTO THE VIGIL WE... I THINK IT WAS MAYBE STEVE, FIGURED OUT THAT I WAS PAYING FLAGSTAR BUT THEY DIDN'T ACTUALLY OWN THE MORTGAGE.
STEVE, YOU WANT TO EXPLAIN WHAT DED FIGURED OUT?
5$
CAN EVERYONE HEAR ME?
YEAH, THIS STUFF CAN MAKE YOUR HEAD SPIN, AND IT'S HARD TO KNOW WHAT'S REALLY GOING ON.
WHAT I UNDERSTAND IS THAT FLAGSTAR SOLD THE MORTGAGE TO FANNIE MAE.
Fannie Mae
THEY'RE THE ACTUAL OWNER OF THE MORTGAGE BUT FLAGSTAR CONTINUED TO SERVICE IT.
THIS MEANS JENNIFER IS STILL PAYING HER MONEY TO FLAGSTAR AND FLAGSTAR IS SENDING THE MONEY ALONG TO FANNIE MAE.
SO, WE REALIZED THE TARGET WAS ACTUALLY FANNIE MAE INSTEAD OF FLAGSTAR.

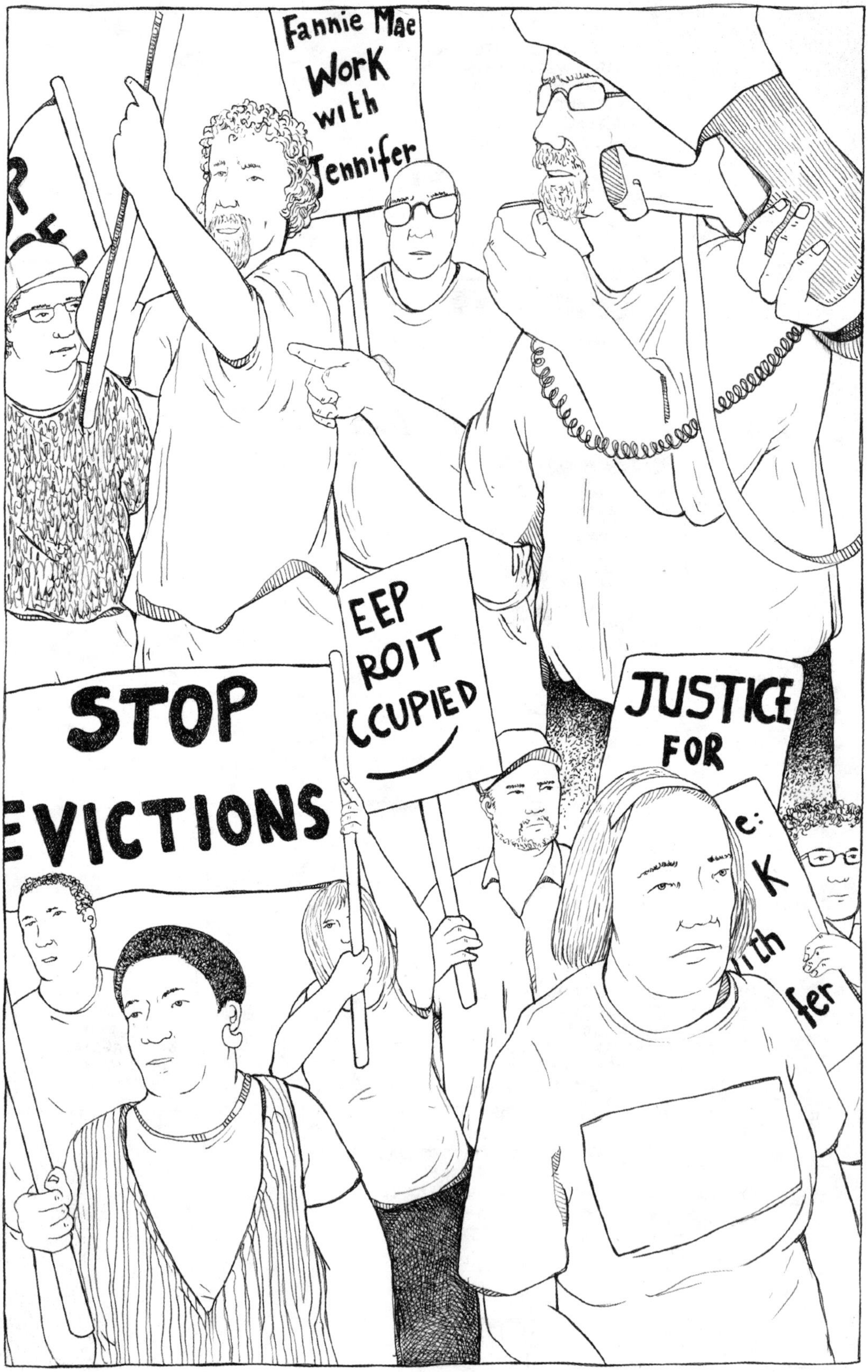
Fannie Mae Work with Jennifer
STOP
EVICTIONS
EEP
ROIT
CCUPIED
JUSTICE
FOR

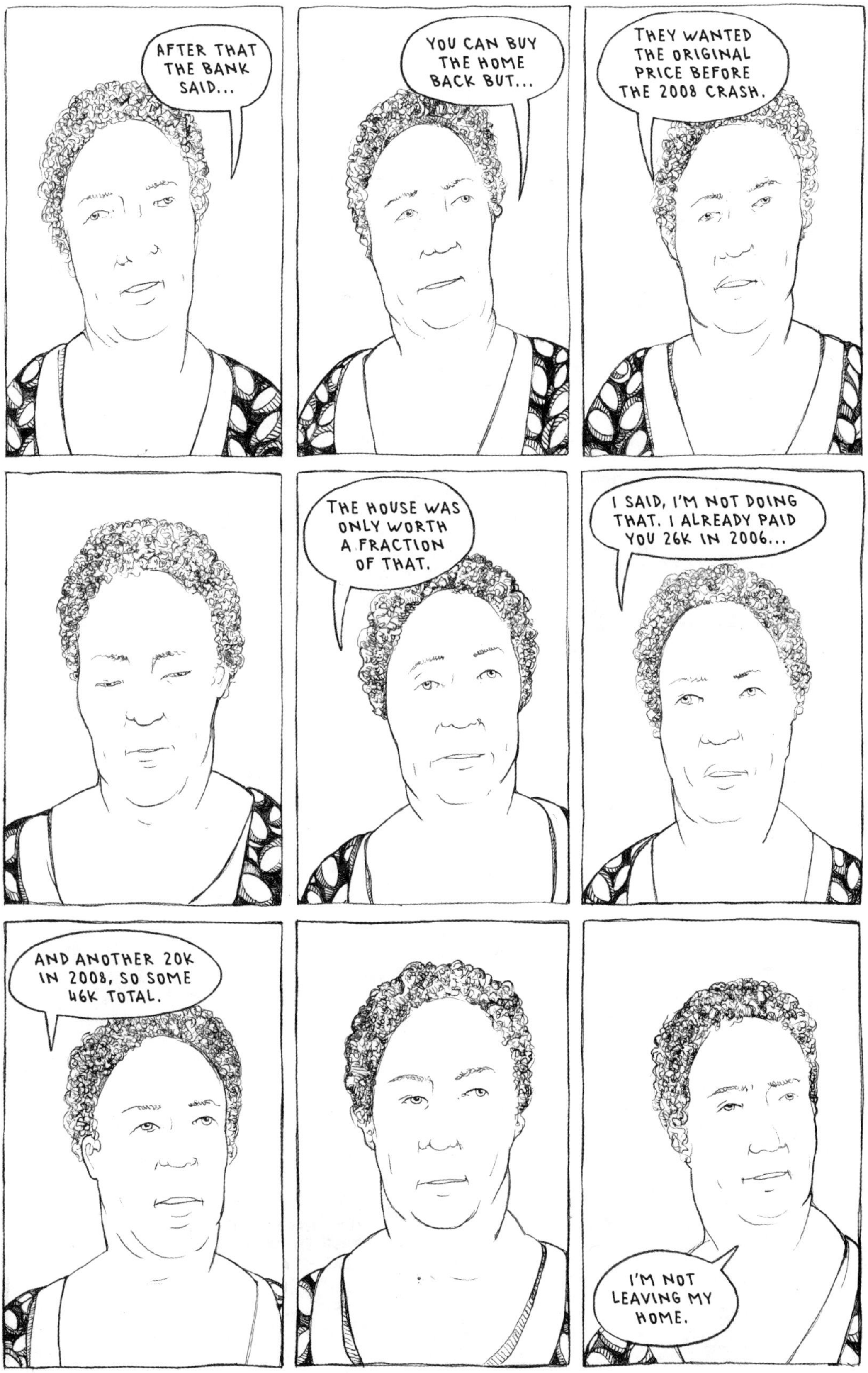
AFTER THAT THE BANK SAID...
YOU CAN BUY THE HOME BACK BUT...
THEY WANTED THE ORIGINAL PRICE BEFORE THE 2008 CRASH.
THE HOUSE WAS ONLY WORTH A FRACTION OF THAT.
I SAID, I'M NOT DOING THAT. I ALREADY PAID YOU 26K IN 2006...
AND ANOTHER 20K IN 2008, SO SOME 46K TOTAL.
I'M NOT LEAVING MY HOME.

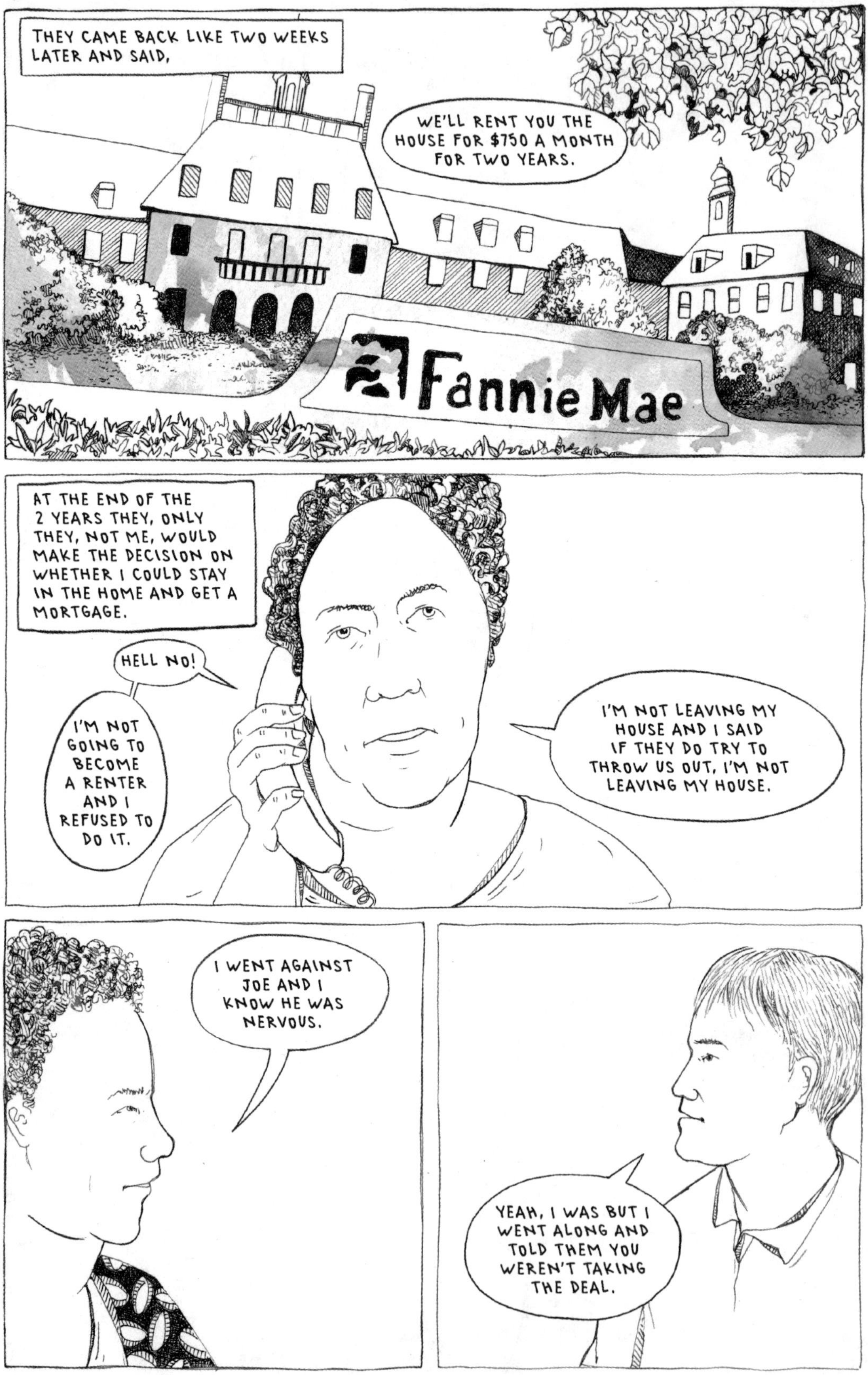
THEY CAME BACK LIKE TWO WEEKS LATER AND SAID,
WE'LL RENT YOU THE HOUSE FOR $750 A MONTH FOR TWO YEARS.
Fannie Mae
AT THE END OF THE 2 YEARS THEY, ONLY THEY, NOT ME, WOULD MAKE THE DECISION ON WHETHER I COULD STAY IN THE HOME AND GET A MORTGAGE.
HELL NO!
I'M NOT GOING TO BECOME A RENTER AND I REFUSED TO DO IT.
I'M NOT LEAVING MY HOUSE AND I SAID IF THEY DO TRY TO THROW US OUT, I'M NOT LEAVING MY HOUSE.
I WENT AGAINST JOE AND I KNOW HE WAS NERVOUS.
YEAH, I WAS BUT I WENT ALONG AND TOLD THEM YOU WEREN'T TAKING THE DEAL.

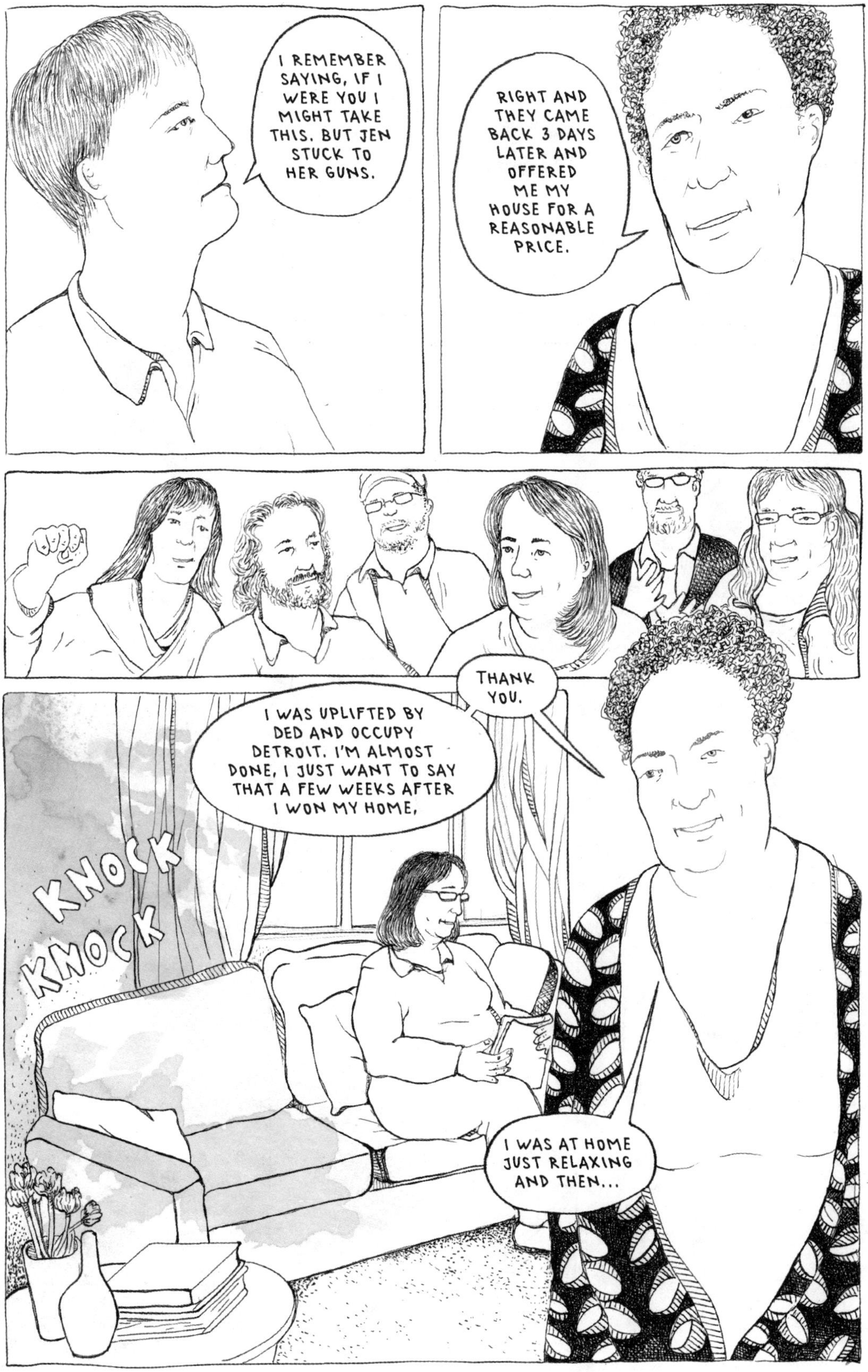
I REMEMBER SAYING, IF I WERE YOU I MIGHT TAKE THIS. BUT JEN STUCK TO HER GUNS.
RIGHT AND THEY CAME BACK 3 DAYS LATER AND OFFERED ME MY HOUSE FOR A REASONABLE PRICE.
THANK YOU.
I WAS UPLIFTED BY DED AND OCCUPY DETROIT. I'M ALMOST DONE, I JUST WANT TO SAY THAT A FEW WEEKS AFTER I WON MY HOME,
KNOCK KNOCK
I WAS AT HOME JUST RELAXING AND THEN...

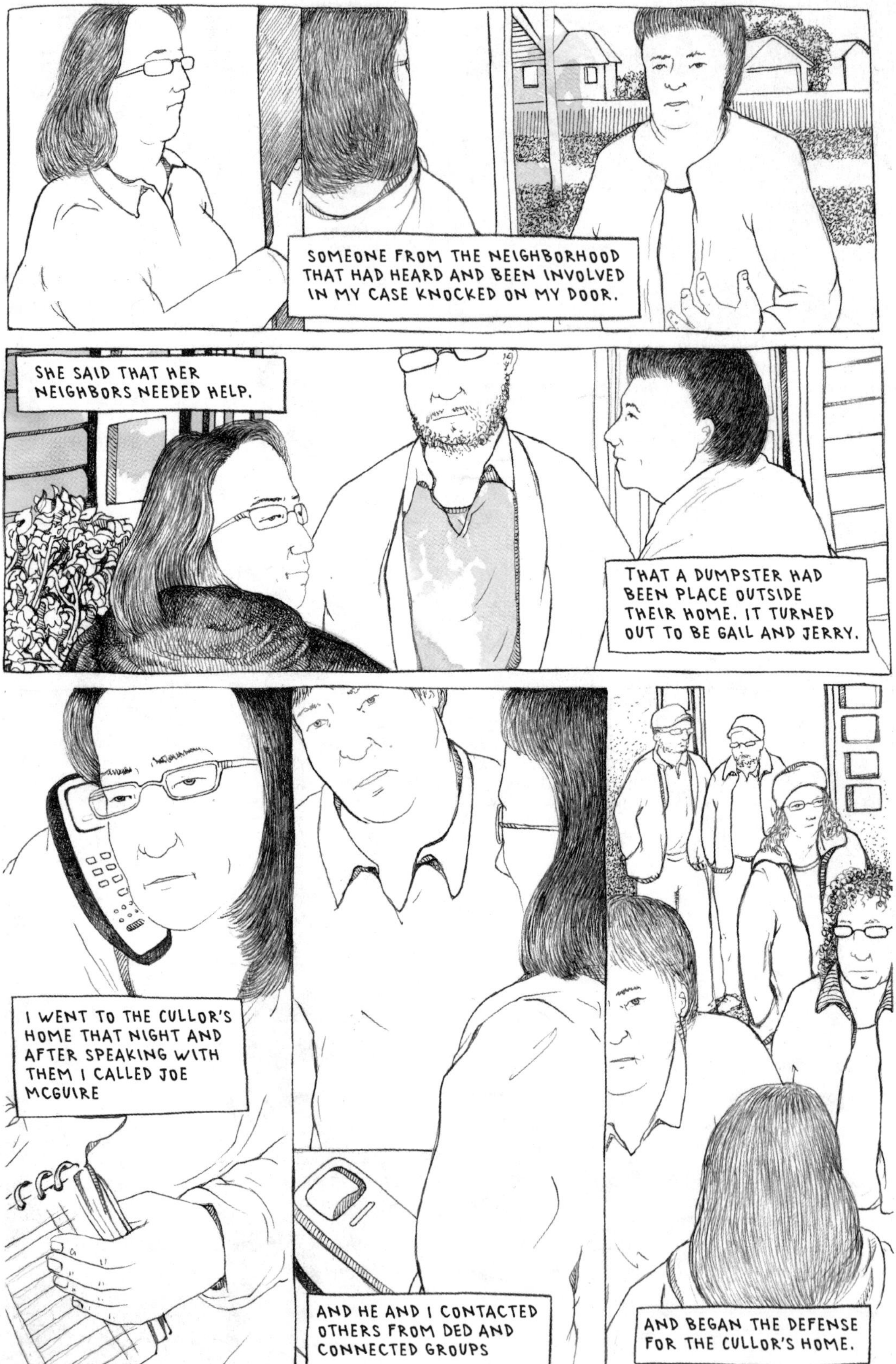
SOMEONE FROM THE NEIGHBORHOOD THAT HAD HEARD AND BEEN INVOLVED IN MY CASE KNOCKED ON MY DOOR.
SHE SAID THAT HER NEIGHBORS NEEDED HELP.
THAT A DUMPSTER HAD BEEN PLACE OUTSIDE THEIR HOME. IT TURNED OUT TO BE GAIL AND JERRY.
I WENT TO THE CULLOR'S HOME THAT NIGHT AND AFTER SPEAKING WITH THEM I CALLED JOE MCGUIRE
AND HE AND I CONTACTED OTHERS FROM DED AND CONNECTED GROUPS
AND BEGAN THE DEFENSE FOR THE CULLOR'S HOME.

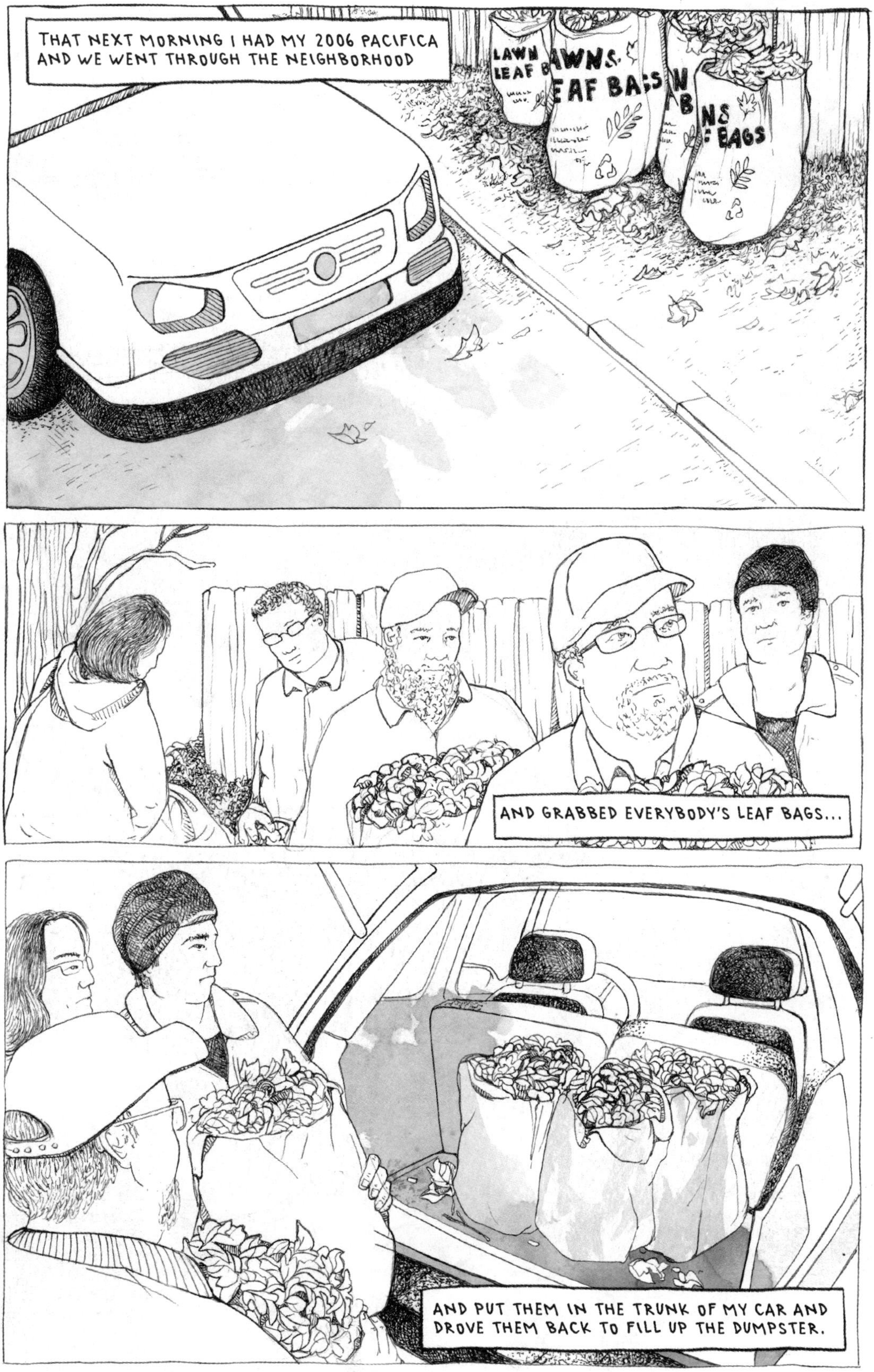
THAT NEXT MORNING I HAD MY 2006 PACIFICA AND WE WENT THROUGH THE NEIGHBORHOOD
LAWN LEAF B
AND GRABBED EVERYBODY'S LEAF BAGS...
AND PUT THEM IN THE TRUNK OF MY CAR AND DROVE THEM BACK TO FILL UP THE DUMPSTER.

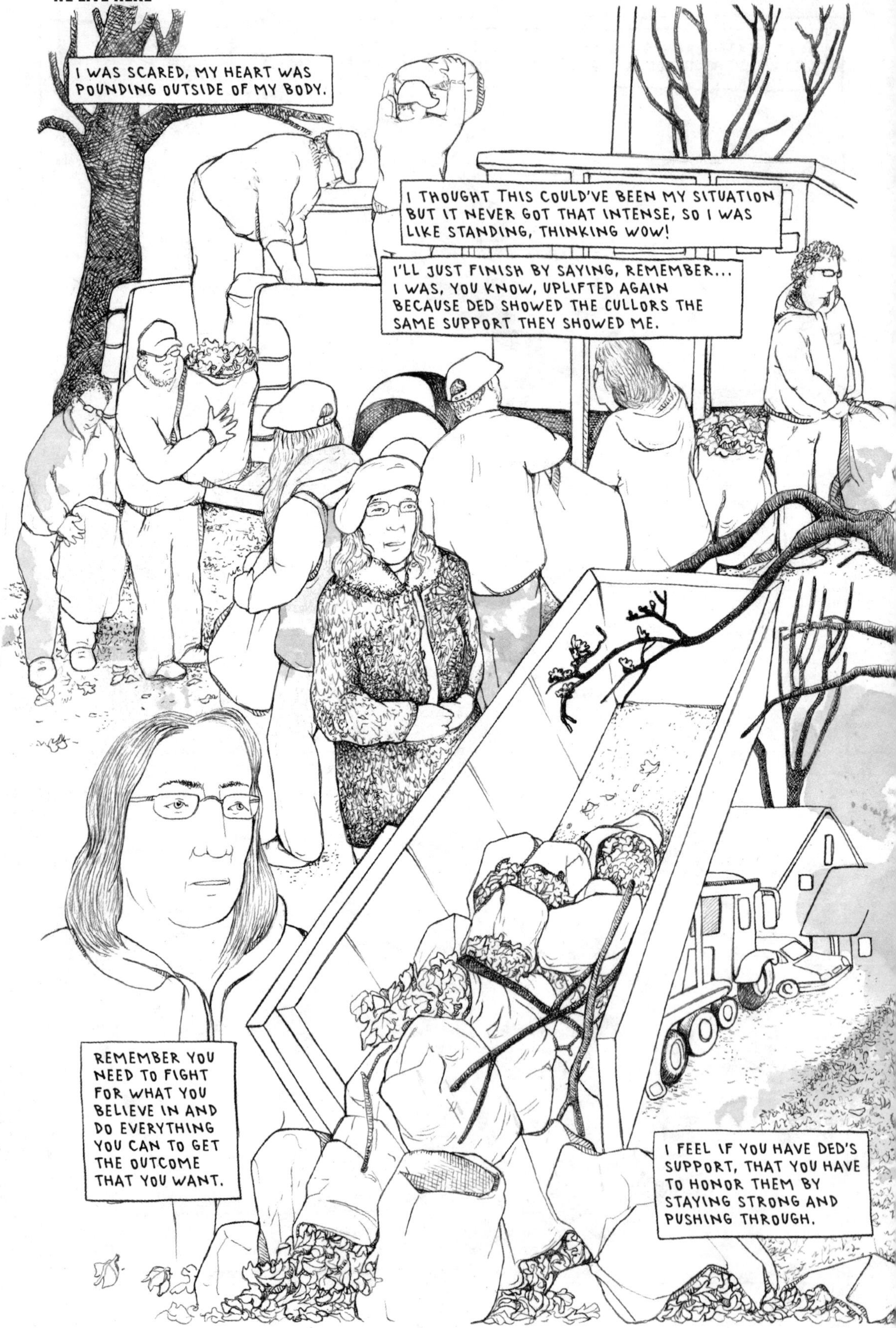
I WAS SCARED, MY HEART WAS POUNDING OUTSIDE OF MY BODY.
I THOUGHT THIS COULD'VE BEEN MY SITUATION BUT IT NEVER GOT THAT INTENSE, SO I WAS LIKE STANDING, THINKING WOW!
I'LL JUST FINISH BY SAYING, REMEMBER... I WAS, YOU KNOW, UPLIFTED AGAIN BECAUSE DED SHOWED THE CULLORS THE SAME SUPPORT THEY SHOWED ME.
REMEMBER YOU NEED TO FIGHT FOR WHAT YOU BELIEVE IN AND DO EVERYTHING YOU CAN TO GET THE OUTCOME THAT YOU WANT.
I FEEL IF YOU HAVE DED'S SUPPORT, THAT YOU HAVE TO HONOR THEM BY STAYING STRONG AND PUSHING THROUGH.

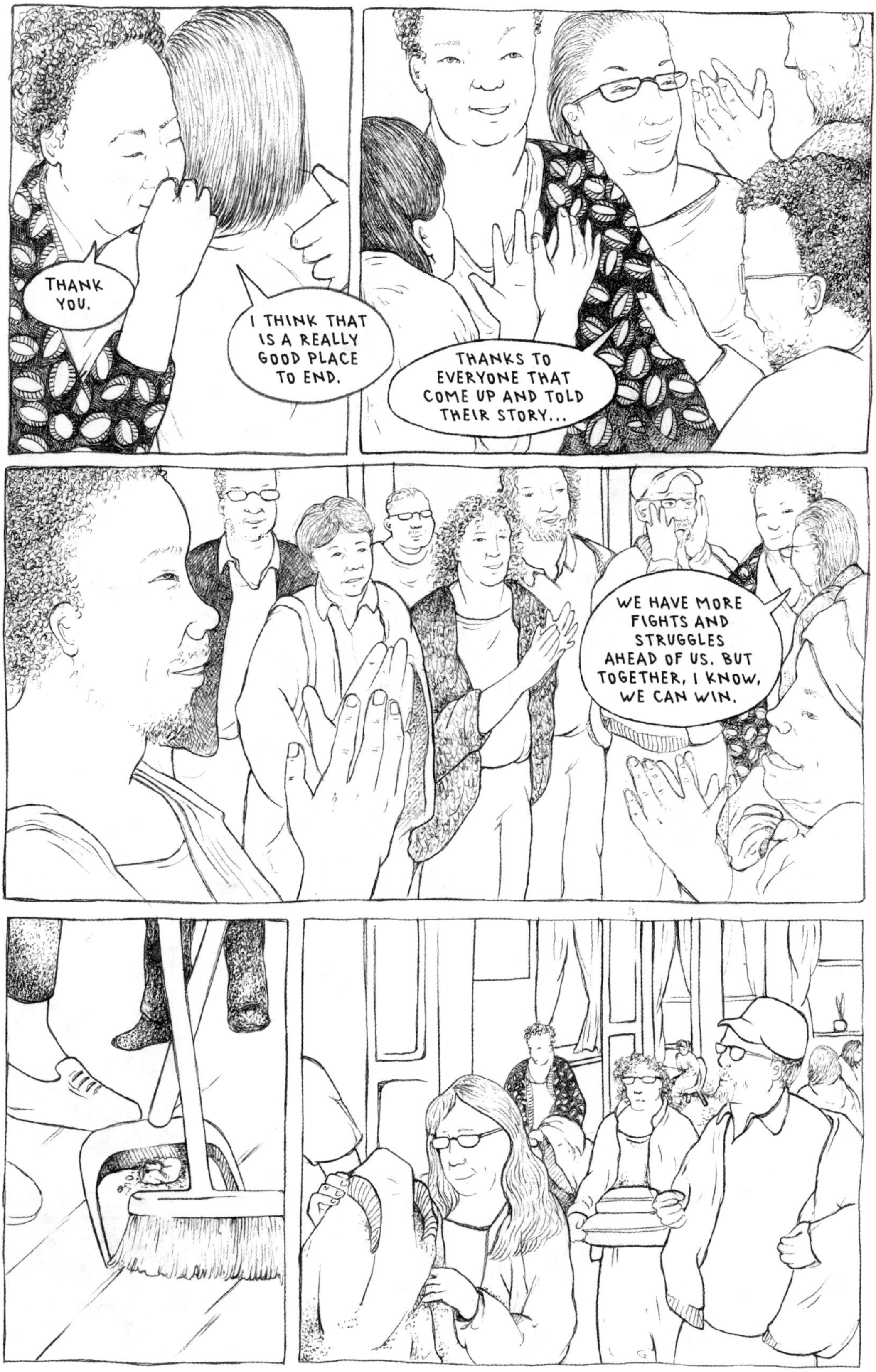
THANK YOU.
I THINK THAT IS A REALLY GOOD PLACE TO END.
THANKS TO EVERYONE THAT COME UP AND TOLD THEIR STORY...
WE HAVE MORE FIGHTS AND STRUGGLES AHEAD OF US. BUT TOGETHER, I KNOW, WE CAN WIN.

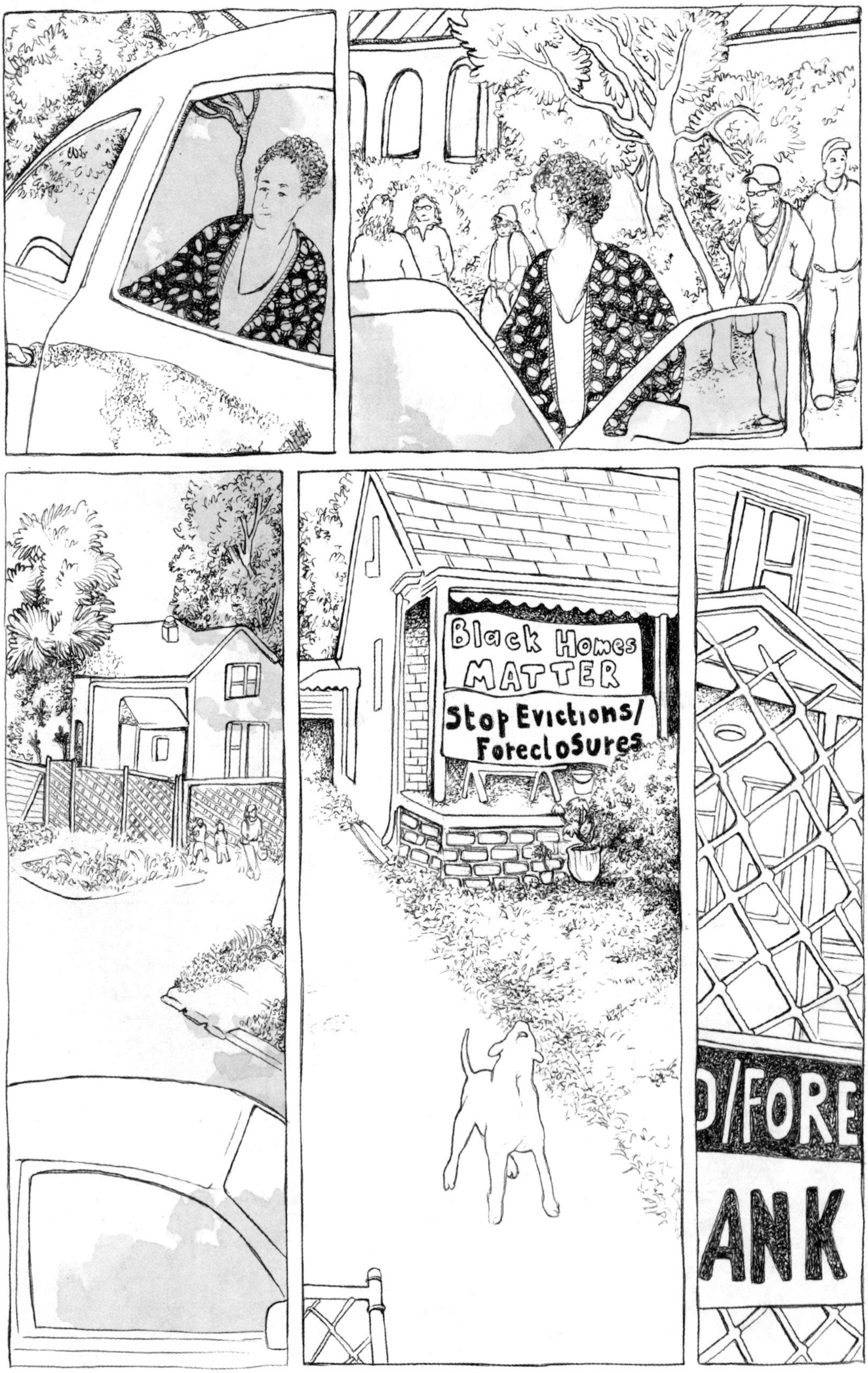
Black Homes MATTER
Stop Evictions/ Foreclosures
D/FORE
ANK

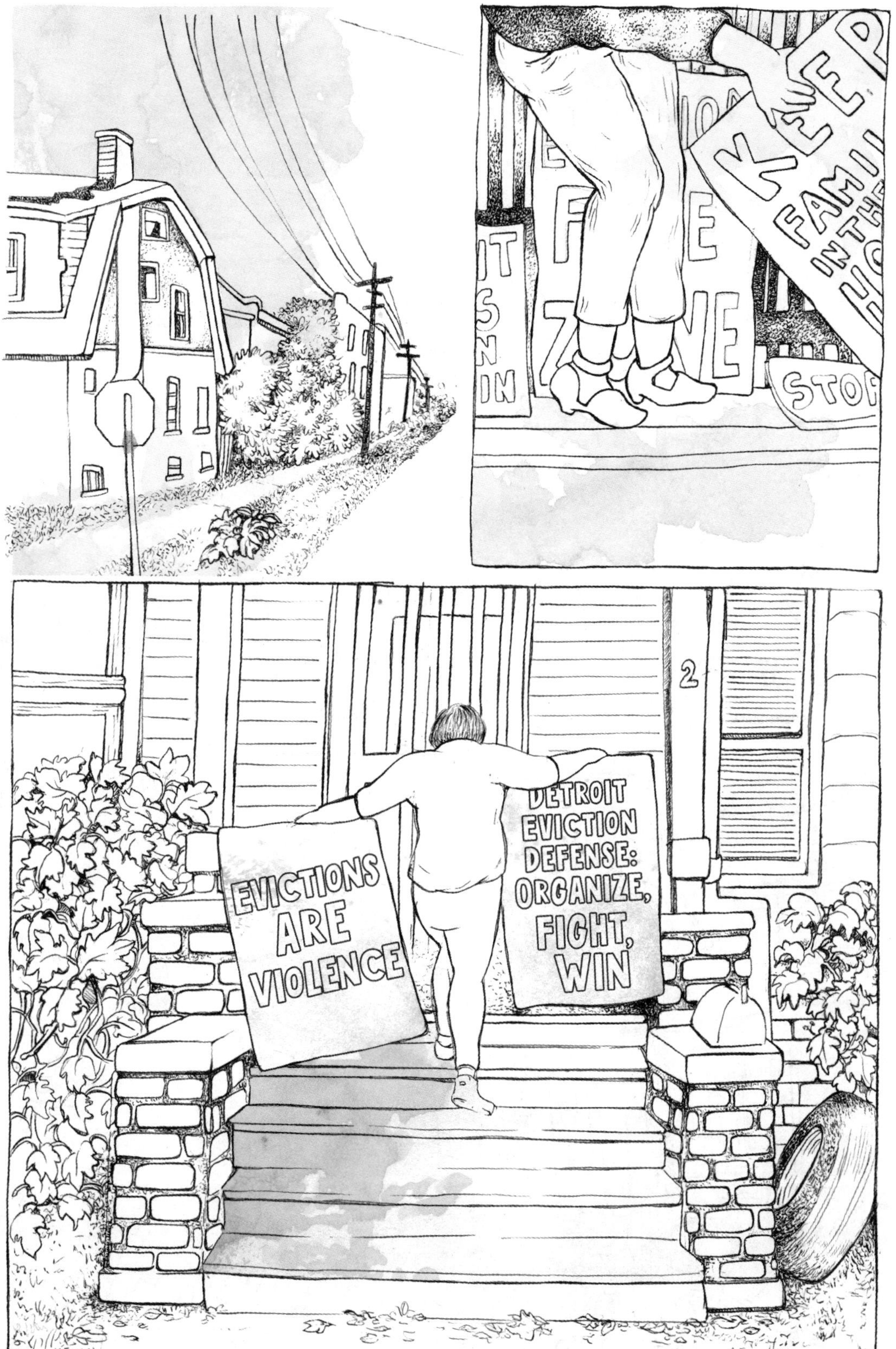
KEEP
EVICTIONS ARE VIOLENCE
DETROIT EVICTION DEFENSE: ORGANIZE, FIGHT, WIN
2

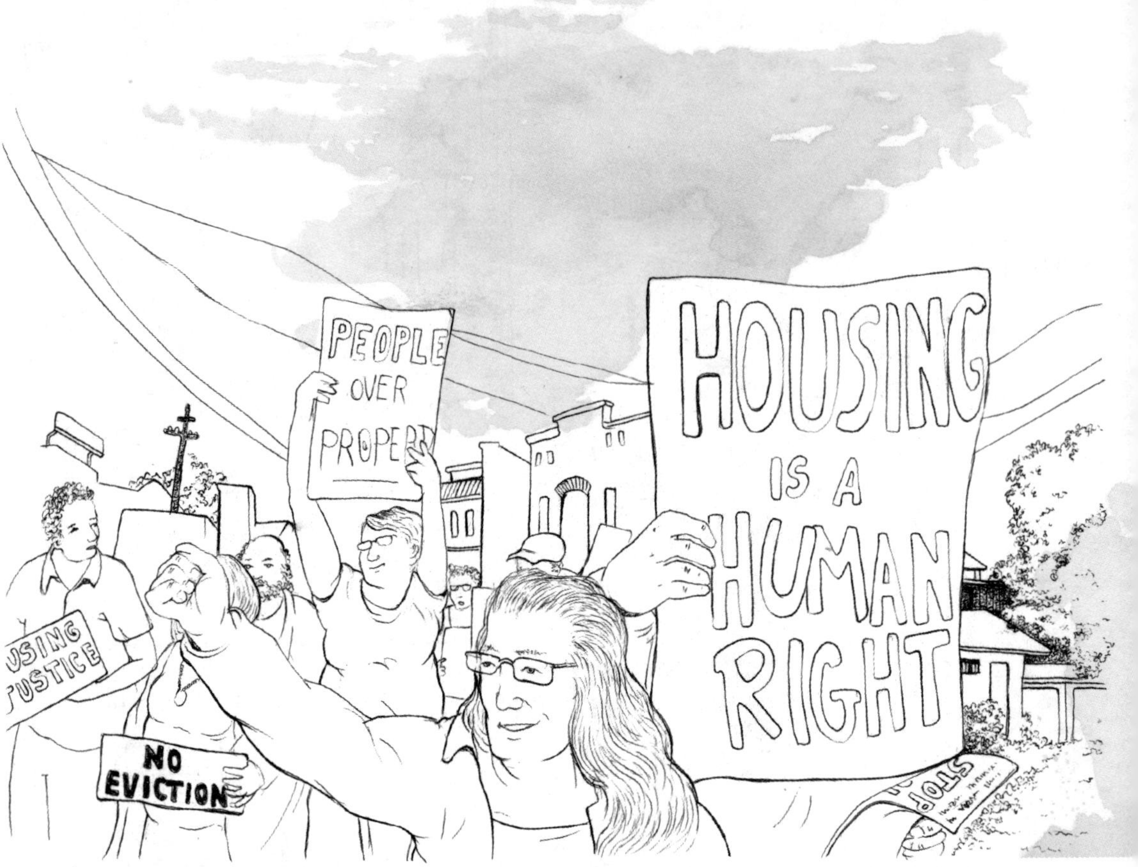
PEOPLE OVER PROPERT
HOUSING IS A HUMAN RIGHT
USING JUSTICE
NO EVICTION
STOP

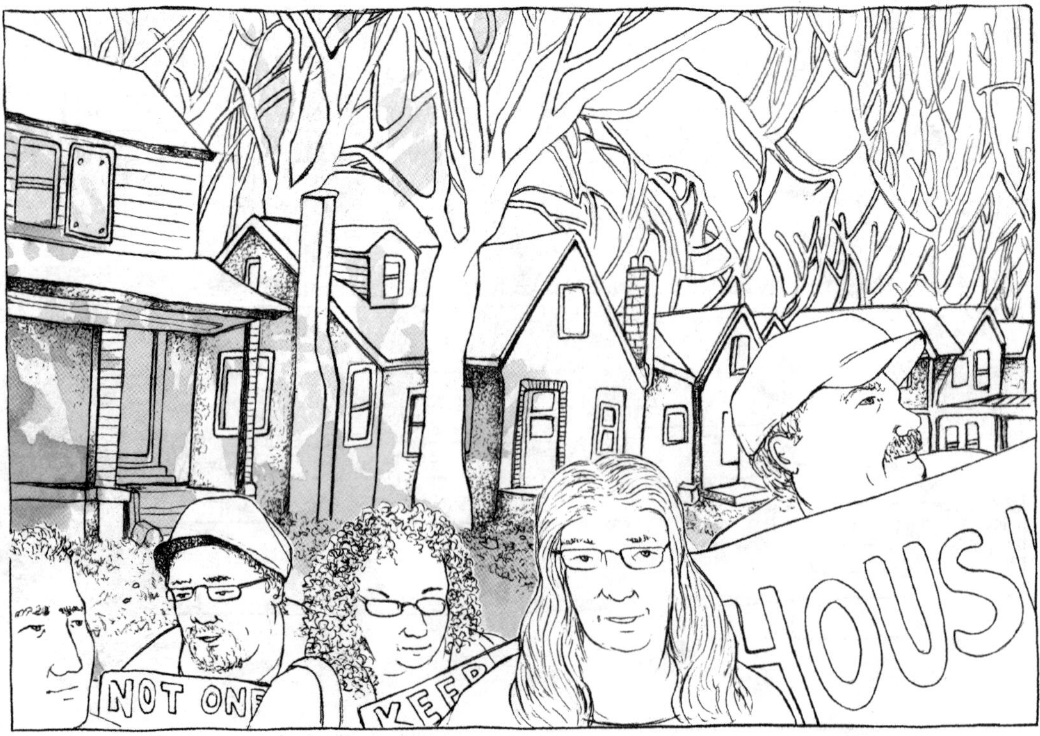
NOT ONE
KEEP
HOUS

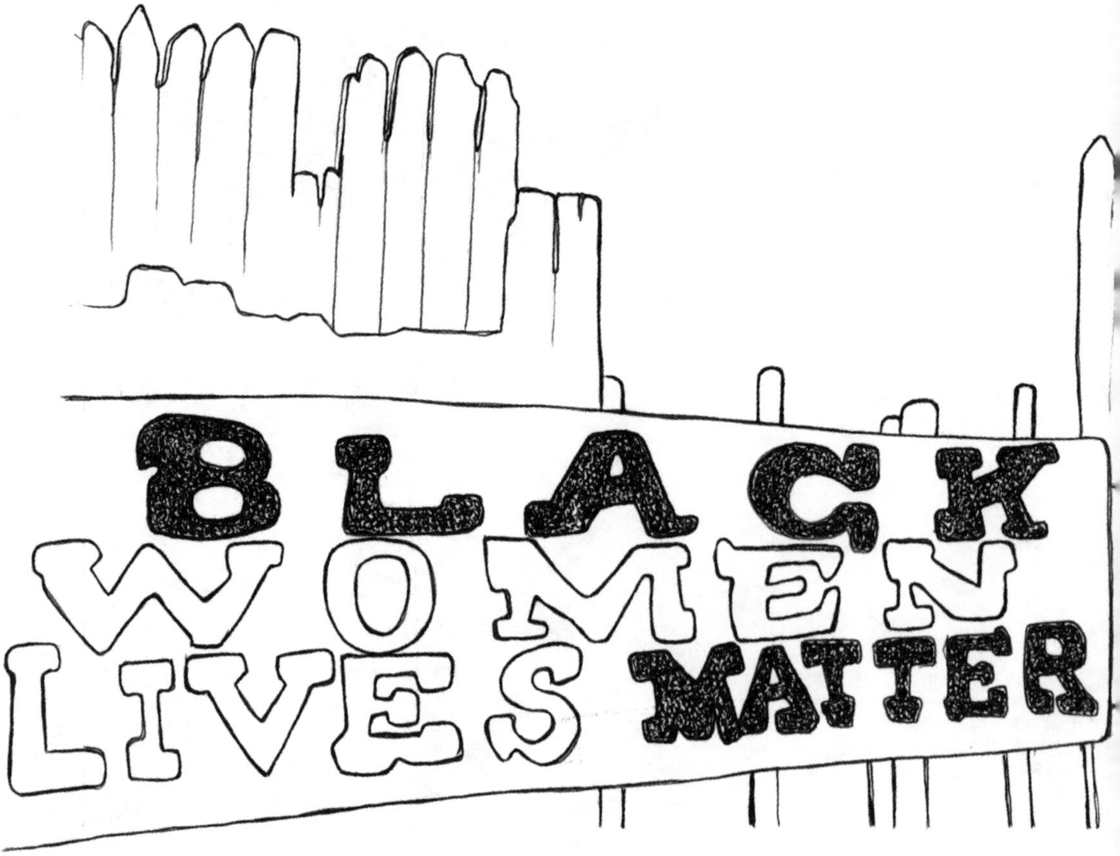
BLACK
WOMEN
LIVES MATTER

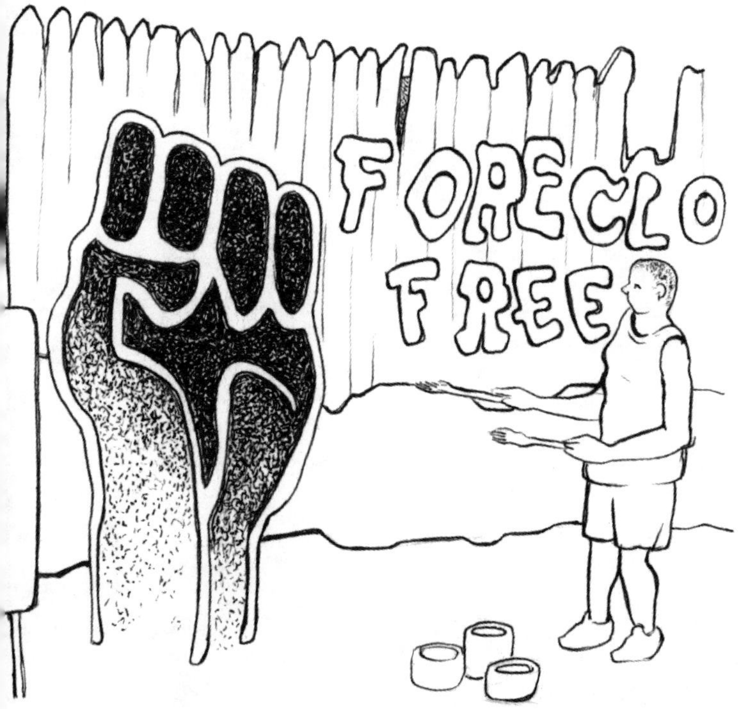
FORECLO
FREE

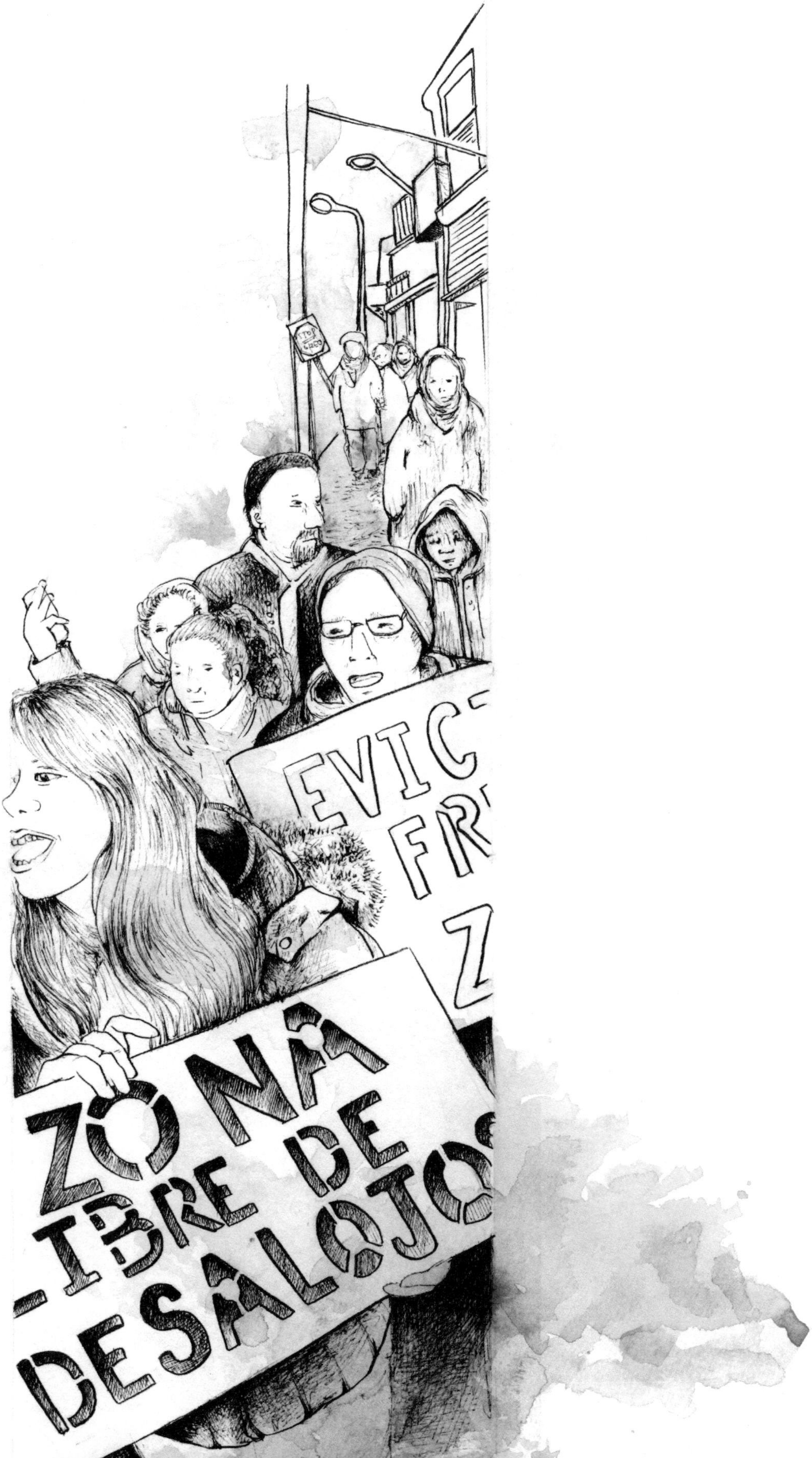
EVICT
FR
Z
ZONA
IBRE DE
DESALOJOS

NOTES FROM AN ANTI-RACIST RESEARCHER

JEFFREY WILSON

RACIAL CAPITALISM

Statistics that speak to housing dispossession in Detroit, while offering a stark reminder of the scope and scale of devastation, also obfuscate the ideas that animate the rebuilding of Detroit. Groups like DED are not only struggling against the material evictions of families but also a particular conception of the city's future. For instance, labeling mortgage and tax foreclosures as a "housing crisis," describing the situation as a kind of unique event or even a natural disaster like a "hurricane," seems to miss a fundamental point about housing in Detroit. What we are witnessing is a systematic attack against Black homeownership that began decades ago. What appears to be a crisis during the concentrated foreclosure periods of 2008 and 2015 should more appropriately be conceived of as a recalibration of racial capitalism, one that has been continually retooled to perpetuate value extraction from Black homes. The uncomfortable truth is that housing displacement, for many, to invoke Walter Benjamin, is "not the exception but the rule" (Benjamin, "Theses on the Philosophy of History").

While housing dispossession is an ongoing process, there is a particular set of ideas that have guided housing policy in Detroit since 2008. These are worth considering because Detroit often acts as a laboratory for experimenting with new techniques of neoliberal management. It is no coincidence that Kevyn Orr, the former emergency manager of the city between 2013–2014, went on to advise similar policies of austerity in Atlantic City, or that a well-known Detroit-based data company honed its skills in the city and has extended its network and tools for housing surveillance internationally. One critical vantage point for considering how racial capitalism works in a post-2008 Detroit is to reflect on the convergence of ideas of data experts, the business class, and government officials with respect to seeing urban space.

Technocrats and the managerial class of Detroit have continuously reiterated the need to visualize and collect various kinds of data on property in order to reestablish markets, firm up the tax bases, and raise property values. According to them, this narrative knowledge of real estate (property data and the very value of a house) was lost because of an "inept government." One set of tools for creating this post-2008 real estate taxonomy was a massive surveillance project that sought to collect data on every single parcel of property in the city and then map the information. This included everything from taking pictures of properties seasonally in order to create a sense of the property over time to centralizing a property's current tax status. To do so, a mobile application called "Blexting" (a neologism combining "blight" and "texting") was developed and takes as its central goal the surveying, mapping, categorizing, coding, and centralizing of information on all of Detroit's more than 380,000 properties (Force, 2014). After initial survey teams were sent to "microhoods," the Blexting platform was then expanded. Individuals can now contribute to the mapping and surveying of neighborhoods by simply downloading the application, taking pictures of properties, and answering questions. This type of data collection and mapping ultimately provides racial capital and the state with clear lines of sight over the entire urban landscape for speculation, investment, taxation, and blight removal.

The use of such tools is centered on a particular set of ideas about the city. Specifically, parcel level data is focused upon as a fundamental way of knowing the city and is assumed to be critical for it to be rebuilt. In doing so, the city itself is reduced to nothing but a collection of parcels that wait to be examined, sorted, and rendered intelligible. One data expert noted, if "you put on your X-Ray glasses and you can see a deeper level of how the world works, and how the government works, and how the economy works, really the world is made of parcels" (interview, 2016). This kind of colorblind statement, or cartographic positivism, underlines much of the discussion about rebuilding Detroit. It reflects a racist view of the city that ultimately erases people and history from place (Wilson, 2018).

Similar sentiments are echoed by Dan Gilbert, billionaire owner of Detroit-based Quicken Loans and cochair of the city's Blight Removal Task Force. He rhetorically asks about blight removal, "How can you prioritize [which

Afterwords

homes to demolish] if you have no visibility?" (*Detroit Free Press*, 2013). An
official from the City of Detroit I interviewed evoked militarized language
for visualizing properties. He noted the need to see property more clearly,
equating the bulldozing of blighted properties with dropping bombs, stating
that, if the city is sending a "Tomahawk missile" into a building, they'll need
clear information and visual data on the property (interview, 2018).

Why does this matter? Why does the convergence of the thoughts of
city officials, billionaires, and data experts matter in a graphic novel about
housing activism? First, these ideas have animated the rebuilding of Detroit
and have exposed people to speculative capital and state mechanisms of
dispossession. While the above are only anecdotal statements, a massive
amount of money has been mobilized to promote their conception of urban
space. And while this collection of actors moves to rebuild the city, they are
lauded, visible, and well-funded. The unseen and unspoken impact on people
losing their homes remains largely muted.

THE RESEARCH AND WHY STORIES MATTER

We Live Here emerged from my PhD research at the University of Arizona.
It is based on two years of ethnographic fieldwork. In many ways, this
book is a kind of visual scholarship or maybe a collection of illustrated
interviews. While my time organizing with DED significantly helped inform
my perspective, the interviews, which exceed hundreds of hours of recorded
material, are the foundation for this comic. During those years in Detroit, I
always intended for the interviews to be incorporated into a comic book. After
my dissertation was completed, it took me approximately a year to sift through
those visually rich interviews to then write the script for the comic and
imagine the design of the pages. To bring the book to life I then entered into a
collaboration with artist and coauthor Bambi Kramer, who has implemented
the storyboarding and designed the book to its final stage.

Why did I go through the extra work to create a comic from my PhD
research? From the beginning, I didn't want these interviews to gather
dust on a bookshelf as an expensively bound dissertation or have them
confined to academic journals. Too often stories of resistance and solidarity
collected during fieldwork are concealed behind journal paywalls or

cemented into inaccessible academic jargon. I felt the stories shared with me by homeowners in Detroit were too important to limit the scope of the audience. The graphic novel is a powerful medium to capture the nuances and complexities of place-based struggles while making them accessible as stories rather than as "analyses."

Beyond desiring a nonacademic audience, there are other ways that I felt these stories worked best in a visual narrative. DED activists taught me that stories of housing justice and solidarity are an essential tool for fighting against evictions. I don't mean this in abstract terms. While it is the case that these stories might be personally empowering for homeowners to share, it is also true that within movements for housing justice there is a real and material impact to these stories being heard and, in this case, seen.

It is not uncommon in the final stages of an anti-eviction campaign that the homeowner is required to sign a nondisclosure agreement. These agreements are often a condition for a final settlement by speculators or institutions like Fannie Mae and generally require that the homeowner cannot speak publicly about their case. Why would Bank of America or Fannie Mae insist on such terms? My suspicion is that they don't want it known publicly that people fought back against them. They certainly don't want the details of a victory by housing activists publicized. Silencing the homeowner controls the story of housing debt, eviction, and, importantly, resistance. One interviewee described how Fannie Mae offered to sell a house back to her at pre-2008 prices for $100k. The former homeowner said, "No way! I want it for 2016 market value," which was about $15k. For Fannie Mae to capitulate is dangerous, and letting it be known that they did so is revolutionary.

The role of large institutions is one part of the loss of housing in Detroit; housing speculators represent another. Typically, individual speculators work in the shadows and don't want the public to know the number of homes they own, how former owners were treated, or the various hustles they use to lure people into outrageous rental agreements, land contracts, or other nefarious scams. Speculators typically buy homes during the tax foreclosure auction held yearly by Wayne County. For example, 90 percent of all purchases between 2005–2015 during the tax auction were by investors buying in bulk.

The minimum bid during these auctions is $500 and the median winning bid is $1,300 (Akers & Seymour, 2019).

In one case, a speculator bought a home at a tax auction and then tried to sell the home back to the former owner for $45k, despite the mortgage having already been paid in full. When she refused, they then offered to rent her own home back to her at an inflated price of $950 a month; the median rent in Detroit at the time was around $700. In this particular case, the homeowner, a retired Chrysler worker, lost the home at a tax auction while she was recovering from cancer. She made every effort to pay the taxes but, as with many people that I interviewed, the county government "lost" or didn't "register" her payments and after three years the home was sold at tax auction. Desperate to stay in her home of thirty-three years, she went to the office of the speculator to sign a rental agreement only to find him insisting she sign a blank lease and that he would "fill in the details later." This particular speculator would also post signs on her front door in large red letters stating "SQUATTER." This caused her to not leave her home for extended periods of time for fear of eviction. After these behaviors were exposed publicly, the speculators finally agreed to sell the home back to her at what she saw as a fair price. However, they were adamant that DED remove all material related to the case from their website and forced her to sign a nondisclosure agreement.

These stories of housing activism matter because we often think of large financial institutions, local speculators, and the rules governing their practices as inflexible, immovable, or, worse, natural. The general assumption is "what they say goes." Basically, it is their game and our role is to play along. Yet the stories offered in this book fracture that view by showing that Fannie Mae and local real estate buyers did cave to former owners' demands, that organized communities can force moneyed interests back to the negotiating table, and that homes can be won back. Nondisclosure agreements are but one testament to the significance of telling stories. "The ultimate, hidden truth of the world," David Graeber writes, "is that it is something that we make, and could just as easily make differently" (Graeber, 2016). Sharing stories about housing justice help us to not only imagine the world but shape it differently.

In thinking about how to share these stories, I wanted to ensure that the comic embraced an anti-racist perspective. To be an anti-racist, as historian Ibram X. Kendi reminds us, "is a reflection of what a person is doing in each moment" (PBS, 2020). There is no middle ground or "not racist," meaning there is "no neutrality in the racism struggle" (Kendi, 2019). As historian Howard Zinn notes, neutrality is in fact a position. To engage with the world as an anti-racist is to make a series of choices. It's a movement towards an ideal, which ultimately is never settled, requiring "persistent self-awareness, constant self-criticism, and regular self-examination" (Kendi, 2019). For this comic to function as an anti-racist document, I felt that it was important to engage in a dialogue with those interviewed and to acknowledge the ways in which my background and perspective informed the comic.

At the time of this research, I was underwater on a home in a working-class neighborhood in Lansing, MI, which is about an hour west of Detroit. The home was a small bungalow a mile from a General Motors assembly plant, purchased in the pre-2008 world of predatory mortgage loans. The mortgage company approved me for this house despite my only income coming from a minimum wage bookseller's job. Getting the mortgage was a clear case of white privilege but it was also a function of a predatory lending machine targeting working class people. Like those in this book, I had a perspective on what it meant to be ensnared by the mortgage crisis with only a few changes in life circumstances and demographic differences separating my family from eviction.

And yet Lansing is not Detroit. Places and the context that forms them matter. Doing research in Detroit, I didn't want to go into the city to collect personal stories from mostly Black women about their housing struggles, which are at once deeply personal and also tied into the larger history of housing in Detroit, and then leave to write a book. My experience is that, since 2008, Detroit has been a hotspot for academics and journalists. It is a place overresearched and yet people are underconsulted. Key to making the book less extractivist was creating a dialogue with the people interviewed once an initial pencil sketch of the book was completed. During this time, I put the project on pause so that interviewees could see how their stories were represented in comic book form. Ultimately, I was attempting to follow the lead of the interviewees.

Marie's chapter is an example of how this worked. After receiving the initial sketches of her chapter, she thought it needed to present more of the history of Black Bottom, the predominantly Black neighborhood in which she grew up. This surprised me. I had assumed that the feedback generally would center on her personal foreclosure narrative, like maybe a sequence of events wasn't quite right or a person was added into a scene that wasn't actually there. But Marie, who is a housing activist and union member, saw her personal and family history as inseparable from the Black Bottom neighborhood, her family's journey from the South to Detroit, and the subsequent citywide urban renewal projects of the late '50s and '60s.

The entire neighborhood of Black Bottom, along with Marie's childhood home, was bulldozed to build a highway connecting the largely white suburbs to downtown Detroit. This was part of a larger national urban renewal strategy beginning in 1949 and continuing until approximately 1962. During this time, federal funds were allocated to cities under the Housing Act of 1949 for "slum clearance" and "blight removal" in order to facilitate "business development." These clearances disproportionately targeted Black and Brown neighborhoods. By 1985 Detroit had received nearly $13.5 billion for such projects (Crawford, 2019). As Marie pointed out in a follow-up interview, for a place like Black Bottom such practices destroyed thriving and well-established Black businesses, which included record stores, jazz and blues clubs, theaters, physician's offices, restaurants, multiple grocery stores, and drugstores. For her it wasn't simply a childhood house that was demolished; she wanted the reader to also know that those bulldozers buried a center of Black wealth and community.

I had deemphasized Black Bottom in Marie's chapter by only giving it two panels. Doing so shifted conceptions of housing injustice toward individual actions and away from racist policies and legacies of housing dispossession. For Marie there is a connection between the urban renewal policies that bulldozed her childhood home, the destruction of Black wealth in her former neighborhood, and the predatory mortgage market she found herself in as an adult. The process of dialogue helped me follow Marie's lead and more clearly situate the history of Black Bottom within her story. This moved the chapter away from my initial misstep to more clearly articulate an anti-racist ideal.

Nothing is perfect when representing another's story, but this example shows how steps can be taken to build solidarity and understanding.

Another aspect of enacting an anti-racist method was to actively participate with DED during my fieldwork. I was not a passive observer but tried to practice solidarity as a research method. I attended meetings, helped to write flyers and develop the website, participated in protests, and helped to organize fundraisers. During this time, I also wrote a few short comics to publicize some DED cases where I saw blatant acts of racism by housing officials during a tenant organizing campaign.

The maps below were compiled by Data Drive Detroit (D3) and help give a sense of the scope and scale of the mortgage and tax foreclosure crisis at the census track level in Detroit. Specifically outlined are the neighborhoods from which the stories in this book are drawn.

Each legend is meant to reflect the total number of foreclosures for the given indicator in the map. For example, if a legend has 226–431 on the tax foreclosure map, this means there were between 226 and 431 tax foreclosures in that census tract and so on for each map.

These maps reflect that, while the stories in *We Live Here* are specific to each family's situation, they are regrettably ordinary in the larger scope of housing dispossession in Detroit.

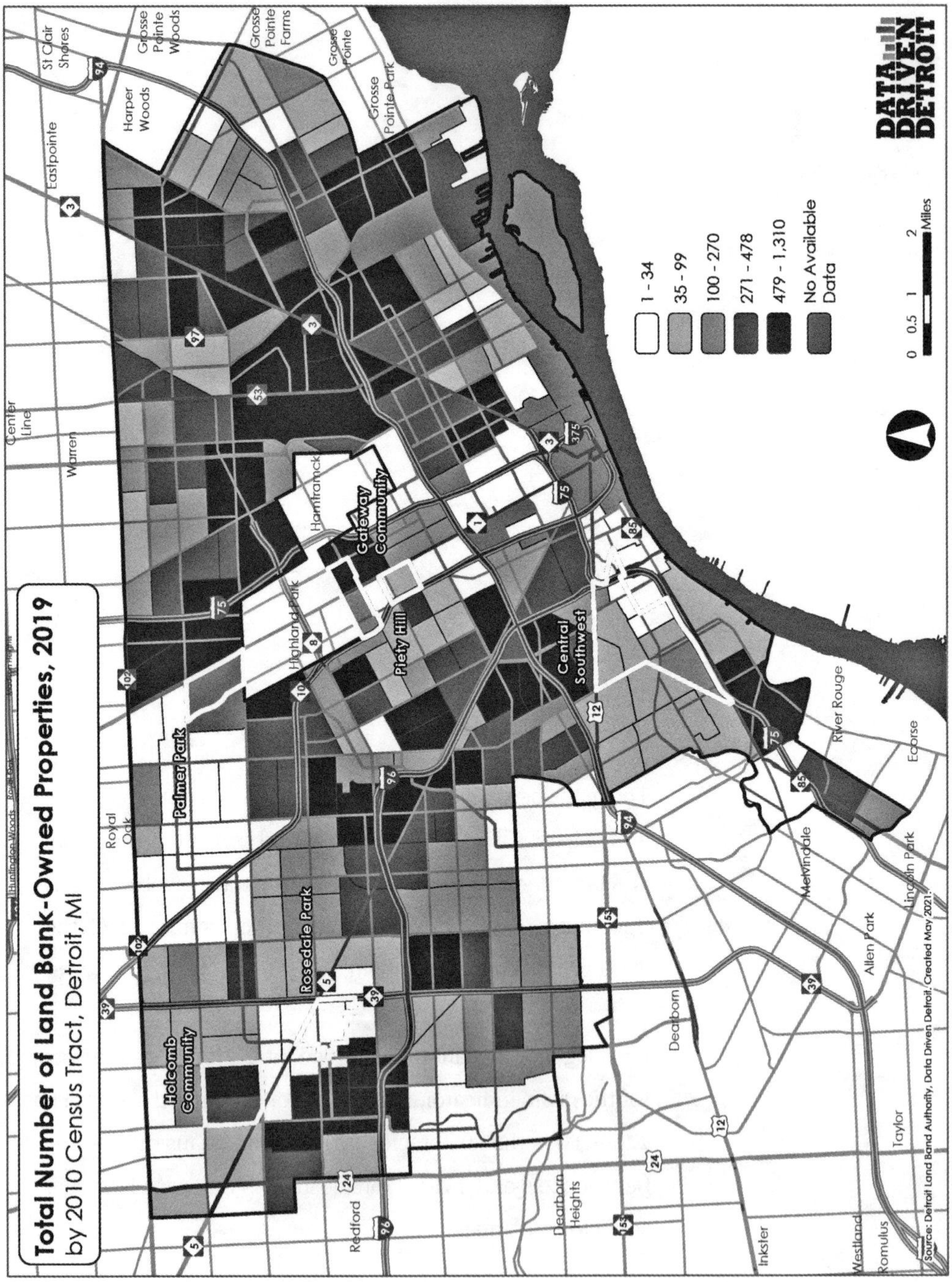
Total Number of Land Bank-Owned Properties, 2019
by 2010 Census Tract, Detroit, MI
1 - 34
35 - 99
100 - 270
271 - 478
479 - 1,310
No Available Data
0 0.5 1 2 Miles
DATA DRIVEN DETROIT
Holcomb Community
Rosedale Park
Palmer Park
Piety Hill
Gateway Community
Central Southwest
Highland Park
Hamtramck
Redford
Dearborn Heights
Dearborn
Inkster
Westland
Romulus
Taylor
Allen Park
Lincoln Park
Melvindale
Ecorse
River Rouge
Royal Oak
Warren
Center Line
Eastpointe
Harper Woods
St Clair Shores
Grosse Pointe Woods
Grosse Pointe Farms
Grosse Pointe
Grosse Pointe Park
Source: Detroit Land Band Authority, Data Driven Detroit. Created May 2021.

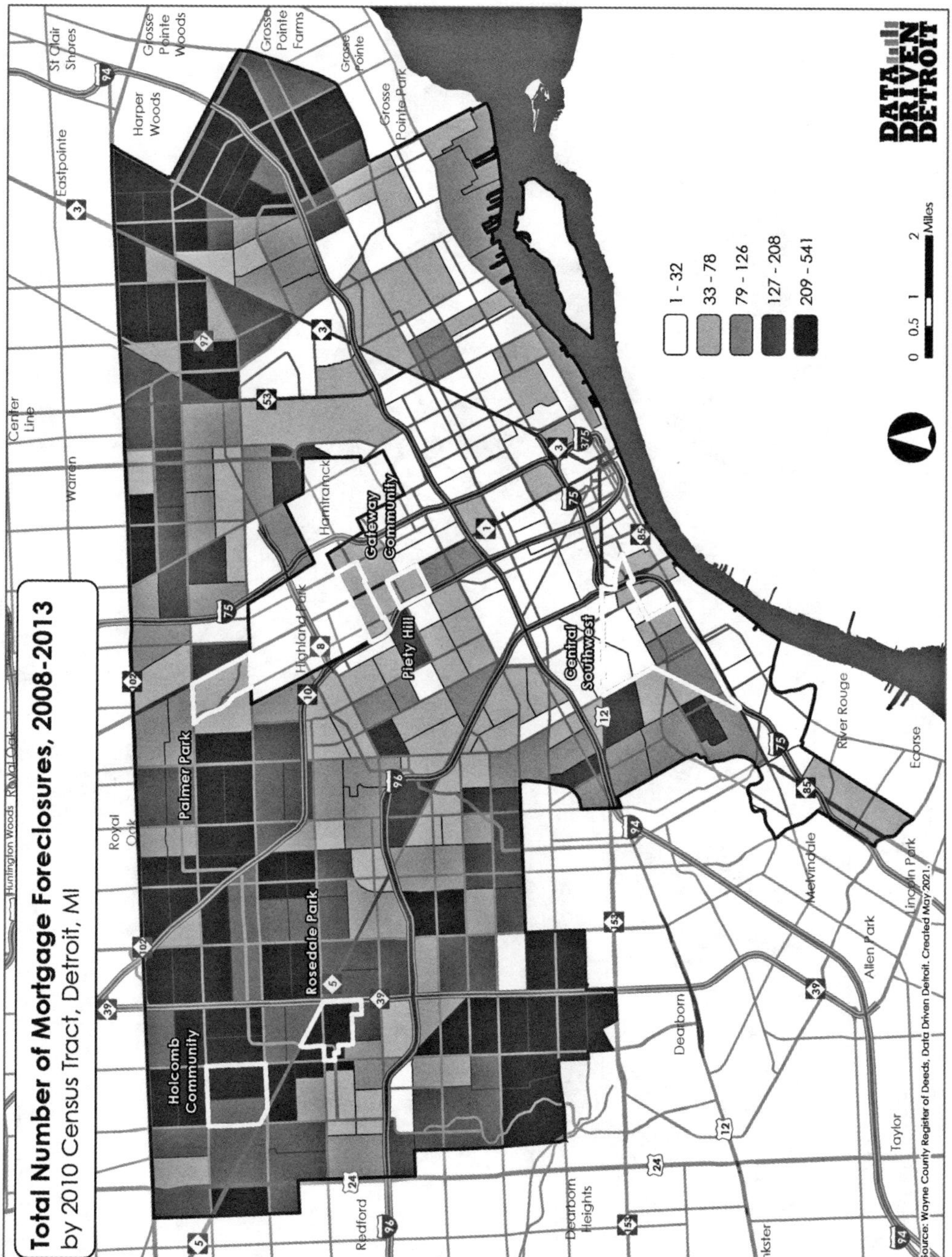
Total Number of Mortgage Foreclosures, 2008-2013
by 2010 Census Tract, Detroit, MI
Holcomb Community
Rosedale Park
Palmer Park
Highland Park
Piety Hill
Gateway Community
Hamtramck
Central Southwest
Warren
Center Line
Eastpointe
Harper Woods
St Clair Shores
Grosse Pointe Woods
Grosse Pointe Farms
Grosse Pointe
Grosse Pointe Park
Royal Oak
Huntington Woods
Redford
Dearborn Heights
Dearborn
Inkster
Taylor
Allen Park
Melvindale
Lincoln Park
Ecorse
River Rouge
1 - 32
33 - 78
79 - 126
127 - 208
209 - 541
0 0.5 1 2 Miles
DATA DRIVEN DETROIT
Source: Wayne County Register of Deeds, Data Driven Detroit. Created May 2021.

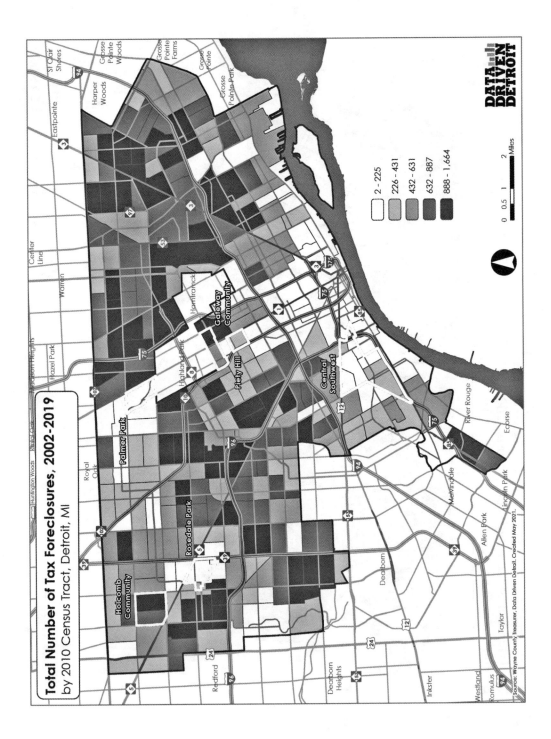

Total Number of Tax Foreclosures, 2002-2019
by 2010 Census Tract, Detroit, MI

2 - 225
226 - 431
432 - 631
632 - 887
888 - 1,664

0 0.5 1 2
Miles

Source: Wayne County Treasurer, Data Driven Detroit. Created May 2021.

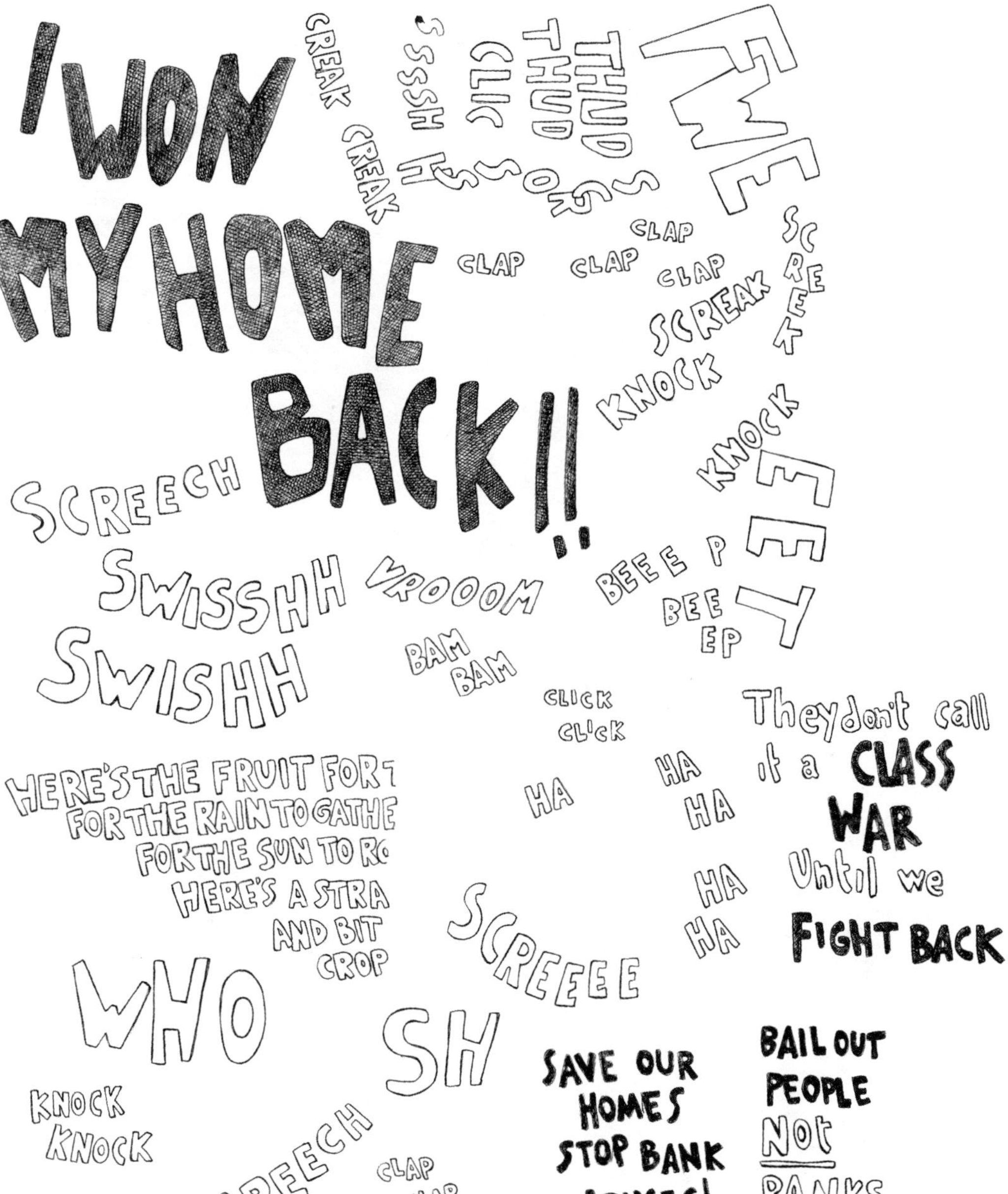

I WON MY HOME BACK!!
CREAK CREAK
SSSSH H
CLIC S
THUD THUD SOG
FWEE
CLAP
CLAP
CLAP
CLAP
SCREAK
SCREEK
KNOCK
KNOCK
EET
SCREECH
SWISSHH
VROOOM
BEEE P
BEE EP
SWISHH
BAM BAM
CLICK CLICK
They don't call it a CLASS WAR Until we FIGHT BACK
HA
HA
HA
HA
HA
HA
HERE'S THE FRUIT FOR T
FOR THE RAIN TO GATHE
FOR THE SUN TO RO
HERE'S A STRA
AND BIT
CROP
SCREEEEE
WHO
SH
SAVE OUR HOMES STOP BANK ABUSES!
BAIL OUT PEOPLE NOT BANKS
KNOCK KNOCK
SCREECH
CLAP CLAP

WORKS CITED

Louis Aguilar, "As Michigan's ban on property tax foreclosures expires, some in Detroit fear a new wave of people losing their homes," *Bridge Detroit*, July 2, 2020, https://www.bridgedetroit.com/as-michigans-ban-on-property-tax-foreclosures-expires-some-in-detroit-fear-a-new-wave-of-people-losing-their-homes/.

Joshua Akers & Eric Seymour, "The eviction machine: Neighborhood instability and blight in Detroit's neighborhoods," Poverty Solutions at the University of Michigan, July 2019, https://poverty.umich.edu/files/2019/08/Akers-et-al-Eviction-Machine-Revised-August-12.pdf.

Bernadette Atuahene, "Predatory Cities," *California Law Review* 108, no. 1 (February 2020): 107. https://scholarship.kentlaw.iit.edu/fac_schol/996.

"Bestselling Author Ibram X. Kendi: How to Be an Antiracist." *Amanpour & Company*, PBS, February 13, 2020. Video retrieved July 18, 2022, from https://www.pbs.org/wnet/amanpour-and-company/video/bestselling-author-ibram-kendi-how-to-be-an-antiracist/.

Amy Crawford, "Capturing Black Bottom, a Detroit Neighborhood Lost to Urban Renewal," *Bloomberg*, February 15, 2019, https://www.bloomberg.com/news/articles/2019-02-15/photos-detroit-s-black-bottom-before-urban-renewal.

Dan Denvir, "Race for Profit with Keeanga-Yamahtta Taylor," *The Dig*, Jacobin, February 28, 2020, https://thedigradio.com/podcast/race-for-profit-with-keeanga-yamahtta-taylor/.

Erin Einhorn & Aaron Mondry, "A 'fake landlord' home rental scam is destroying lives in Detroit," *NBCnews*, November 10, 2021, https://www.nbcnews.com/news/us-news/fake-landlord-home-rental-scam-detroit-rcna4941.

Detroit Blight Removal Task Force, Force, "Every Neighborhood Has a Future: Mike Duggan's Neighborhood Plan," *Dugan for Detroit*, 2014, https://assets1.cbsnewsstatic.com/i/cbslocal/wp-content/uploads/sites/15909782/2013/09/duggan-crime-reduction-plan.pdf.

Laura Gottesdiener, *A Dream Foreclosed: Black America and the Fight For a Place to Call Home* (Zuccotti Park Press, 2013).

David Graeber, *The Utopia of Rules: On Technology, Stupidity, and the Secret Joys of Bureaucracy* (Melville House, 2016).

Ibram X. Kendi, *How to Be an Antiracist* (One World, 2019).

Joel Kurth & Christine MacDonald, "Foreclosures fuel Detroit blight, cost city $500 million," *The Detroit News*, July 8, 2015, https://www.detroitnews.com/story/news/special-reports/2015/06/03/detroit-foreclosures-risky-mortgages-cost-taxpayers/27236605/.

Joel Kurth, Mike Wilkinson & Laura Herberg, "Sorry we foreclosed your home. But thanks for fixing our budget," *Bridge Michigan*, June 6, 2017, https://www.bridgemi.com/urban-affairs/sorry-we-foreclosed-your-home-thanks-fixing-our-budget.

Ryan Ruggiero, Josh Rivera & Patrick Cooney, "A Decent Home: The Status of Home Repair in Detroit," *Poverty Solutions*, University of Michigan, October 2020, https://poverty.umich.edu/files/2020/10/The-Status-of-Home-Repair-in-Detroit-October-2020.pdf.

Keeanga-Yamahtta Taylor, *Race for Profit: How Banks and the Real Estate Industry Undermined Black Homeownership*, University of North Carolina Press (April 2021).

Mike Wilkinson, "Whites get half of mortgages in Detroit, nation's largest majority black city," *Bridge Michigan*, June 13, 2019, https://www.bridgemi.com/urban-affairs/whites-get-half-mortgages-detroit-nations-largest-majority-black-city.

Jeffrey Wilson, "A Study of Tax Foreclosures, Evictions and Health in Detroit, Michigan," (doctoral diss., University of Arizona, 2018), http://hdl.handle.net/10150/631380.

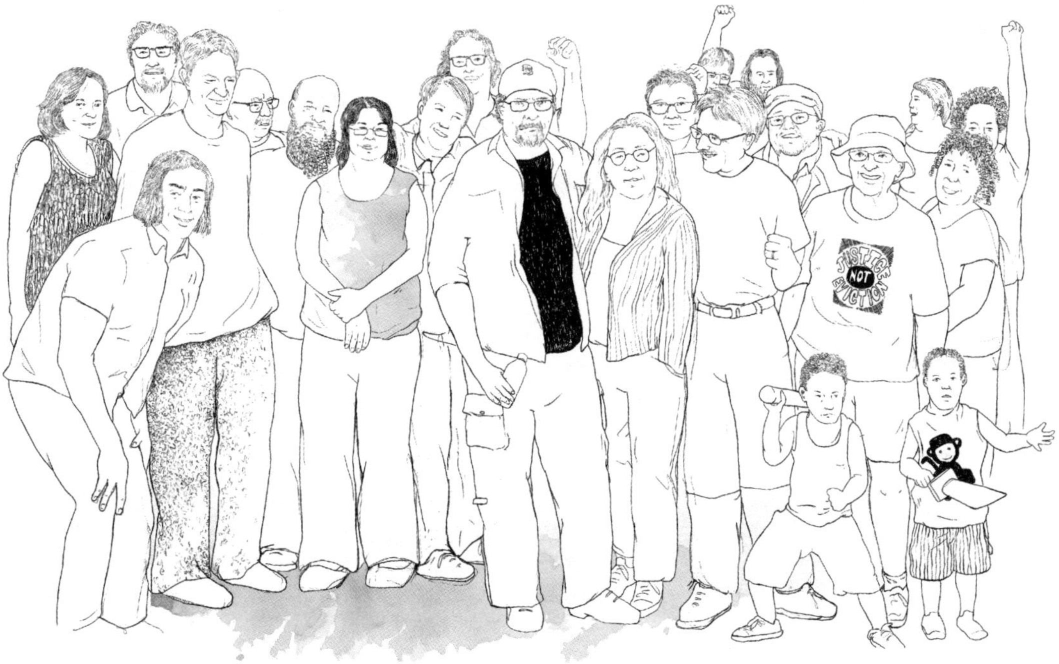
JUSTICE
NOT
EVICTION

WE LIVE HERE

AKNOWLEDGMENTS

JEFFREY WILSON:

I would like to thank everyone who helped make this book possible, starting with my daughter Miriam Eloise Wilson, don't forget it takes strength to be gentle and kind. Thank you to my partner Rachel Katonak, my undying love and respect. Much love and respect to my parents Diane and Fred Wilson. Thanks to everyone at Seven Stories Press, especially Dan Simon and Ruth Weiner, for believing in this project. Thanks to Roam Agency. Thank you to Róisín Davis for guiding this project in its early stages and Anthony Arnove for your continued openness and guidance with my various book projects. Special thanks to Conor Cash for comments on the introduction. Thanks to my dissertation committee Joshua Akers, Sallie Marston, Vincent Del Casino, and Liz Oglesby. This book is probably the dissertation I should've written. Thanks to Geoff Boyce for our early conversations about the city. Many thanks to Bambi Kramer for your collaboration and dedication to the work.

Deepest respect and admiration to all the people organizing with Detroit Eviction Defense. Thank you to David Mitchell, this project would not have been possible without you brother. Thank you to Steve Babson, Miriam Pikens, Ann Talley, Sandi Combs, Kenny Brinkley, Urealdene Henderson, Marie Sims, Jennifer Britt, Bertha Garrett, Michele Finley, Jerry and Gail Cullors, Barbara Campbell and her son Garrett, Matt Clark, Joe McGuire, Lish, Jim Dwight, Diana Feeley, Christian Ogilvy, and Mary Byrnes. Special thanks to Tim for the place to crash! And to Ben, Maggie, Maeryn, and Fiona for letting me take over a room in your apartment.

BAMBI KRAMER:

As a book doesn't come out just from or because of its authors, a deeply heartfelt thank you goes to my whole family, the human and nonhuman one, the biological family as much as my kin-group in its widest possible meaning. Particularly I want to say thank you to my son, Laszlo: your strong patience, deep empathy, and stubborn and loving desire to share are your greatest power, always take care of it. To Valerio Bindi, my partner in crime and always challenging soulmate: for your unwavering love and support, for lunches and dinners, for your priceless professionalism and competence, thank you. Because if doing a comic is not a land for women, it's even less for mothers. So to my Ninja Mothers Clan, who backed me hundreds of times while I was facing late pick up, busy afternoons and nights, exhausting chats sitting on the sidewalk: thank you. Thanks to Luca Raffaelli for his friendship and support.Thanks to Róisín Davis whose love and esteem lead me into this project, to Dan Simon and the whole Seven Stories Press team for believing in it. Thank you Jeffrey Wilson for sharing this project with me, for every time you trusted me, and for the times that you didn't, helping me to stay focused and grow up personally and professionally.

All my respect and gratitude to the people of Detroit Eviction Defense. Even though I didn't get to know you personally, being able to get in touch with your work and your stories was a rare and precious opportunity. I hope through this comic that I have been able to give something back to you, even minimally contributing to spreading the strength and inspiration you have given me.

WE LIVE HERE CROWDFUNDING

We'd like to acknowledge all the crowdfunding contributors.

Thank you for your support and understanding!

Special thank you to Camilia Zhang for your early guidance on the crowdfunding campaign. Thanks to Rob Macy for spinning some records as you do. Thanks to all those who helped spread the word about the campaign.

We'd like to especially recognize these crowdfunding contributors:

Michael Litos, Dillon Mahmoudi, Maria Serena Barreca, Joshua Akers, Craig Metcho, Amy Knight, Maria Plaxco, Pierluigi Sabbatini, Khalifa Kinshasa Mczeal, Beth Phillips, Uè Underground Eccetera Fest, Fortepressa, and all the Crack! Festival horde.